Global Justice Activism and Policy Reform in Europe

Routledge Advances in Sociology

For a complete list of titles in this series, please visit www.routledge.com

61 **Social Theory in Contemporary Asia**
Ann Brooks

62 **Foundations of Critical Media and Information Studies**
Christian Fuchs

63 **A Companion to Life Course Studies**
The social and historical context of the British birth cohort studies
Michael Wadsworth and John Bynner

64 **Understanding Russianness**
Risto Alapuro, Arto Mustajoki and Pekka Pesonen

65 **Understanding Religious Ritual**
Theoretical approaches and innovations
John Hoffmann

66 **Online Gaming in Context**
The social and cultural significance of online games
Garry Crawford, Victoria K. Gosling and Ben Light

67 **Contested Citizenship in East Asia**
Developmental politics, national unity, and globalization
Kyung-Sup Chang and Bryan S. Turner

68 **Agency without Actors?**
New Approaches to Collective Action
Edited by Jan-Hendrik Passoth, Birgit Peuker and Michael Schillmeier

69 **The Neighborhood in the Internet**
Design Research Projects in Community Informatics
John M. Carroll

70 **Managing Overflow in Affluent Societies**
Edited by Barbara Czarniawska and Orvar Löfgren

71 **Refugee Women**
Beyond Gender versus Culture
Leah Bassel

72 **Socioeconomic Outcomes of the Global Financial Crisis**
Theoretical Discussion and Empirical Case Studies
Edited by Ulrike Schuerkens

73 **Migration in the 21st Century**
Political Economy and Ethnography
Edited by Pauline Gardiner Barber and Winnie Lem

74 Ulrich Beck
An Introduction to the Theory of Second Modernity and the Risk Society
Mads P. Sørensen and Allan Christiansen

75 The International Recording Industries
Edited by Lee Marshall

76 Ethnographic Research in the Construction Industry
Edited by Sarah Pink, Dylan Tutt and Andrew Dainty

77 Routledge Companion to Contemporary Japanese Social Theory
From Individualization to Globalization in Japan Today
Edited by Anthony Elliott, Masataka Katagiri and Atsushi Sawai

78 Immigrant Adaptation in Multi-Ethnic Societies
Canada, Taiwan, and the United States
Edited by Eric Fong, Lan-Hung Nora Chiang and Nancy Denton

79 Cultural Capital, Identity, and Social Mobility
The Life Course of Working-Class University Graduates
Mick Matthys

80 Speaking for Animals
Animal Autobiographical Writing
Edited by Margo DeMello

81 Healthy Aging in Sociocultural Context
Edited by Andrew E. Scharlach and Kazumi Hoshino

82 Touring Poverty
Bianca Freire-Medeiros

83 Life Course Perspectives on Military Service
Edited by Janet M. Wilmoth and Andrew S. London

84 Innovation in Socio-Cultural Context
Edited by Frane Adam and Hans Westlund

85 Youth, Arts and Education
Reassembling Subjectivity through Affect
Anna Hickey-Moody

86 The Capitalist Personality
Face-to-Face Sociality and Economic Change in the Post-Communist World
Christopher S. Swader

87 The Culture of Enterprise in Neoliberalism
Specters of Entrepreneurship
Tomas Marttila

88 Islamophobia in the West
Measuring and Explaining Individual Attitudes
Marc Helbling

89 The Challenges of Being a Rural Gay Man
Coping with Stigma
Deborah Bray Preston and Anthony R. D'Augelli

90 Global Justice Activism and Policy Reform in Europe
Understanding When Change Happens
Edited by Peter Utting, Mario Pianta and Anne Ellersiek

United Nations Research Institute for Social Development

UNRISD was established in 1963 to create an independent, autonomous space within the United Nations system for policy-relevant research and dialogue on important social issues. The UNRISD mission is to generate knowledge and articulate policy alternatives on contemporary social development challenges and processes. Through its multidisciplinary research in collaboration with partners throughout the world, events and publications, the Institute works in support of policies and practices that reduce poverty and inequality, advance well-being and rights, and create more democratic and just societies.

Global Justice Activism and Policy Reform in Europe

Understanding When Change Happens

Edited by Peter Utting, Mario Pianta and Anne Ellersiek

NEW YORK LONDON

First published 2012
by Routledge
711 Third Avenue, New York, NY 10017

Simultaneously published in the UK
by Routledge
2 Park Square, Milton Park, Abingdon, Oxfordshire OX14 4RN

First issued in paperback 2014

Routledge is an imprint of the Taylor and Francis Group, an informa business

Library of Congress Cataloging-in-Publication Data

Global justice activism and policy reform in Europe : understanding when change happens / edited by Peter Utting, Mario Pianta, and Anne Ellersiek. — 1st ed.
p. cm. — (Routledge Advances in Sociology ; 90)
Includes bibliographical references and index.
1. Social movements—Political aspects—Europe. 2. Europe—Economic policy. 3. Social responsibility of business—Europe. 4. Social justice. 5. Social change. I. Utting, Peter. II. Pianta, Mario, 1956– III. Ellersiek, Annekathrin.
HM881.G5526 2012
303.48'4094—dc23
2012008991

ISBN 978-0-415-89913-0 (hbk)
ISBN 978-1-138-92056-9 (pbk)
ISBN 978-0-203-09788-5 (ebk)

Typeset in Sabon
by IBT Global.

Contents

Annexes

Figures

Tables

Acronyms and Abbreviations

AC!	Agir contre le Chômage
ACP	African Caribbean and Pacific Group
AFD	Agence Française du Développement
AFDI	Agriculteurs Français et Développement International
AGPB	Association Generale des Producteurs de Ble
AITEC	Association Internationale de Techniciens, Experts et Chercheurs
ALTER-EU	Alliance for Lobbying Transparency and Ethics Regulation at the EU
APGOOD	Parliamentary All-Party Group on Overseas Development
APO	Agricultural Professional Organization
ATDO	Aid, Trade and Development Organizations
Attac	Association pour la Taxation des Transactions pour l'Aide aux Citoyens
AU	African Union
BAT	British-American Tobacco
BINGO	Business-Interest Non-Governmental Organization
BIS	Bank for International Settlements
BP	British Petroleum
BVA	Brulé-Ville Associés
C2A	Commission Agriculture et Alimentation
CA	Administrative Council
CADTM	Committee for the Abolition of Third World Debt
CAF	Conseil de l'Agriculture Française
CAFOD	Catholic Agency for Overseas Development
CAP	Common Agricultural Policy
CBI	Confederation of Business and Industry
CCD	Commission for Cooperation and Development
CCFD	Catholic Committee against Hunger and for Development
CCFOM	Caisse Centrale de la France d'Outremer
CCPD	Centre de coopération policière et douanière franco-suisse
CEDETIM	Centre d'études et d'initiatives de solidarité international

CEI	Conferenza Episcopale Italiana
CERII	Chaire d'Ensegnement et de Researche Interethnique et Interculturels
CETIM	Centre Europe-Tiers Monde
CF	Collège des Fondateurs
CFDT	Confédération française démocratique du travail
CFS	Cooperative Financial Services
CFSI	Comité Français pour la Solidarité Internationale
CFTC	Confédération Française des Travailleurs Chrétiens
CGC	Confederation Generale des Cadres
CGT	Confédération Générale du Travail
CICID	Comité Interministeriel de la Coopération Internationale
CIDSE	Coopération Internationale pour le Développement et la Solidarité
CIMADE	Comité Inter-mouvements Auprès des Evacués
CIRAD	Centre de Coopération Internationale en Recherche Agronomique pour le Développement
CISL	Confederazione Italiana Sindacati Lavoratori
CL	Committees Locales
CNCCEF	Conseilleurs du Commerce Exterieur de la France
CND	Campaign for Nuclear Disarmament
CNJA	Centre National des Jeunes Agriculteurs
CNSTP	Confédération Nationale des Syndicats de Travailleurs Paysans
CORE	Corporate Responsibility Coalition
CRBM	Campagna per la Riforma della Banca Mondiale
CRID	Centre de Recherche et d'information pour le développement
CS	Scientific Council
CSA	Conseil, Sondage, Analyses
CSO	Civil Society Organization
CSR	Corporate Social Responsibility
CTM	Confederación de Trabajadores de México
CTT	Currency Transactions Tax
CUT	Central Única dos Trabalhadores
CVO	Civil Voluntary Organization
DAC	Development Assistance Committee
DAGRIS	Developpement Des Agro Industries Du Sud
DCI	Development Co-Operation Instrument
DEV	Directorate-General for Development
DFID	Department for International Development
DGCID	Direction Générale de la Coopération Internationale et Développement

DPEI/SDEPEO	Deputy Director of Evaluation, Forecasting, Research and Orientation
DTC	Department for Technical Cooperation
DTI	Department of Trade and Industry
ECB	European Central Bank
ECGD	Export Credits Guarantee Department
ECHO	Directorate-General for Humanitarian Aid
EDF	European Development Fund
EEC	European Economic Community
EITI	Extractive Industries Transparency Initiative
ENA	École Nationale d'Administration
ENGREF	École Nationale du Génie Rural, des Eaux et des Forêts
ENSAE	École Nationale de la Statistique et de l'Administration
EPA	Economic Partnership Agreement
ESF	European Social Forum
EU	European Union
EURODAD	European Debt and Development Network
FAO	Food and Agriculture Organization
FARM	Fondation pour l'Agriculture et la Ruralité dans le Monde
FDI	Foreign Direct Investment
FERT	Formation pour l'Epanouissement et le Renouveau de la Terre
FIDES	Fonds d'investissement
FNSEA	Fédération Nationale des Syndicats d'Exploitants Agricoles
FNSP	Fédération Nationale des Syndicats Paysans
FOCSIV	Federazione Organismi Cristiani Servizio Internazionale Volontario
FoE	Friends of the Earth
FOP	Fédération française des producteurs d'Oléagineux et Protéagineux
FSU	Federation Syndicale Solidaires
FTAA	Free Trade Agreement of the Americas
FTT	Financial Transaction Tax
GAS	Gruppi di Acquisto Solidale
GATS	General Agreement on Trade in Services
GATT	General Agreement on Tariffs and Trade
GCAP	Global Coalition Against Poverty
GFA	Global Financial Architecture
GJM	Global Justice Movement
GMO	Genetically Modified Organism
GNI	Gross National Income
GONGO	Government Organized NGO

GRET	Groupe de Recherche et d'Echange Technologique
HADO	Humanitarian, Aid and Development Organization
HCCI	Haut Conseil de la Coopération Internationale
HIPC	Heavily Indebted Poor Country
IASB	International Accounting Standards Board
ICC	International Criminal Court
ICFTU	International Confederation of Free Trade Unions
ICSID	International Council for the Settlement of Investment Disputes
IDOC	International Documentation and Communication Centre
IFA	International Framework Agreements
IFFIC	International Financial Facility for Humanization
IFG	International Forum on Globalization
IFI	International Financial Institution
IFOP	Institut Français d'Opinion Publique
IFRS	International Financial Reporting Standard
IIC	Inter-Institutional Committees
ILO	International Labour Organization
IMF	International Monetary Fund
INGO	International Non-Governmental Organization
INRA	Institut National de la Recherche Agronomique
IPC	Intellectual Property Committee
IPR	International Property Rights
IRAM	Institut de Recherche et d'Application des Méthodes de développement
ITUC	International Trade Union Confederation
IUF	International Food and Allied Workers' Association
J2000	Jubilee 2000 Coalition
JA	Jeunes Agriculteurs
JDC	Jubilee Debt Campaign
JITAP	Joint Integration Technical Assistance Programme
LCI	La Chaîne Info
LCR	Ligue Communiste Revolutionnaire
LDC	Least Developed Countries
MADPTM	Mouvement pour Abolition de la Dette du Tiers Monde
MAE	Ministère des Affaires Etrangères
MAI	Multilateral Agreement on Investment
MCNG	Mission de la Coopération Non-gouvernementale
MDC	Mouvement Des Citoyens
MDGs	Millennium Development Goals
MDRI	Multilateral Debt Relief Initiative
MNC	Multinational Corporation
MOD	Ministry of Overseas Development
MOMA	Mouvement pour une Organisation Mondiale de l'Agriculture

MP	Member of Parliament
MPH	Make Poverty History
MTS	Multilateral Trade Issues
NEF	New Economics Foundation
NGO	Non-Governmental Organization
NIGD	Network Institute of Global Democratisation
NOMA	Non-Agricultural Market Access
NSM	New Social Movement
OCT	Overseas Countries and Territories
ODA	Official Development Assistance/Overseas Development Administration
OECD	Organisation for Economic Cooperation and Development
OEEC	Organisation for European Economic Co-operation
OFR	Operating and Financial Review
ORIT	Inter-American Regional Organization of Workers
OSI	Organisations de Solidarité Internationale
OWINFS	Our World Is Not for Sale
Oxfam	Oxford Committee for Family Relief
PCF	Parti Communiste Français
PCLU	PAK Cigarette Labour Union
PGA	People's Global Action
PPP	Public–Private Partnerships
PRS	Poverty Reduction Strategy
PS	Parti Socialiste
PWYP	Publish What You Pay Campaign
RELEX	Directorate-General for External Relations
ROPPA	Reseau des Organizations Paysannes et de Producteurs de l'Afrique de l'Ouest
SAP	Structural Adjustment Programme
SAWTEE	South Asia Watch on Trade, Economics and Environment
SEATINI	Southern and Eastern African Trade Information and Negotiations Institute
S2B	Seattle to Brussels Network
SFP	Strategic Framework Partnership
SG	Steering Group
SIN	Sakhalin Island Network
SNES	Syndicat National de l'Enseignement Secondaires
SNESUP	Syndicat National de l'Enseignement Supérieur
SNUI	Syndicat National Unifié des Impôts
SNUIPP	Syndicat National Unifié des Instituteurs et Professeurs d'Ecole
SOFIPROTEOL	Société Financière de la Filière des Oléagineux et Protéagineux

SOLAGRAL	Solidarité Agro-Alimentaire
SPS	Single Payment Scheme
SUD	Solidaires Unitaires Democratiques
SUD-PTT	Solidaires Unitaires Démocratiques—Postes Télégrammes et Télécommunications
TJM	Trade Justice Movement
TNC	Transnational Corporation
TNS-Sofres	Taylor Nelson Sofres
TOES	The Other Economic Summit
TRIMS	Agreement on Trade Related Investment Measures
TRIPS	Agreement on Trade Related Aspects of Intellectual Property Rights
TUAC	Trade Union Advisory Committee
TUC	Trade Union Congress/ National Trade Union Confederation
TWN	Third World Network
UDF	Union pour la Démocratie Française
UGICT-CGT	Union Générale des Ingénieurs, Cadres et Techniciens
UN	United Nations
UNCAC	United Nations Convention against Corruption
UNEF	Union Nationale des Etudiants de France
UNRISD	United Nations Research Institute for Social Development
UNSA	Union Nationale des Syndicats Autonomes
WCL	World Confederation of Labour
WDM	World Development Movement
WEED	World Economy, Ecology and Development
WFTU	World Federation of Trade Unions
WHO	World Health Organization
WIPO	World Intellectual Property Organization
WSF	World Social Forum
WTO	World Trade Organization

Preface

Since the 1990s, European governments have come under increasing pressure to address not only issues of inequality and social exclusion within their national or regional borders, but also North–South inequality and persistent poverty in the Global South. Civil society activism in Europe has increasingly addressed global issues, such as aid and trade policy, international finance and taxation and the role of transnational corporations. Contestation and advocacy have challenged policies at different levels—those of national governments, of Europe as a whole and of international institutions such as the World Trade Organization (WTO) and G7/8 summits.

This book examines the evolving patterns of contestation and activism associated with global justice and North–South inequality and investigates their impact on policy and institutional reform. Why—and through which mechanisms—do civil society actors demand a change in policies? What conditions and contexts are conducive to policy influence? And how do powerful actors and institutions respond to activist demands and mobilizations? To answer these questions this volume focuses on four issue areas that have been prominent within global justice activism: debt relief, trade policy, international taxation and corporate accountability. The focus is on experiences in France, Italy and the United Kingdom, and on global mobilizations centred on the WTO. These are countries where not only is global justice activism particularly vibrant, but where variations in policy regimes and state-business-society relations yield important insights into the nature of the activism–policy nexus.

Most of the chapters emanate from research carried out during 2006–2008 by the United Nations Research Institute for Social Development (UNRISD) as part of a larger project on 'Inequality: Mechanism, Effects and Policies' (INEQ), funded by the European Commission's Sixth Framework Programme. As in the case of all UNRISD research, this work would not have been possible without core funding support, which, at the time, was provided by the governments of Denmark, Finland, Mexico, Norway, Sweden, Switzerland and the United Kingdom.

Numerous people at UNRISD provided support for this volume. We are particularly grateful to Daniela Barrier, who managed the UNRISD project.

Valuable editorial and research assistance was provided by Philip Arejola, Rebecca Varghese Buchholz, Ksenia Gerasimova, Chris Kip, Agnes de Mauroy, Rafaela Pannain, Samyukta Rajagopal, Kiah Smith, Hanna Sjolund, Anita Tombez and Natalie Tomlinson. We would also like to thank Kléber Ghimire who was one of the co-ordinators of the UNRISD project when it began in 2006, Maurizio Franzini, who co-ordinated the INEQ project and the other scholars who participated to the research consortium.

Anne Ellersiek, Mario Pianta and Peter Utting
Geneva and Rome, August 2011

Introduction

Understanding the Activism–Policy Nexus

Anne Ellersiek, Mario Pianta and Peter Utting

INTRODUCTION

On 15 October 2011, demonstrations in 950 cities in eighty countries protested against the social effects of the economic crisis that started with the financial collapse of 2008. The 'indignados' of Spain and Greece, the students of Chile and the numerous mobilizations inspired by the 'Occupy' movement opened up a new wave of protest against neoliberal policies of austerity and the injustice of the economic order. Periodic waves of activism spur increasing interest in the question of how civil society actors and social movements influence public policy. Such was the case in the 1970s with the emergence of so-called 'new social movements' (NSMs) and, more recently, with the rise of mobilizations centred on global justice issues (Giugni 2004). Such 'global justice activism'[1] (della Porta 2007) connotes the increasing connectedness of civil society and activism across borders and at multiple scales (local, national, regional and international), involving 'transnational activist networks' (Sikkink 2005). Issues such as third world debt, liberalization of trade and investment regimes and the need to regulate global finance and to make corporations accountable emerged in the mid-1990s as important areas of public concern, leading to waves of mobilizations broadly associated with the contestation of neoliberal globalization. Global justice activism came under the media and political spotlight and gained considerable public support. Protests, campaigning and lobbying, plus the fact that activists increasingly participated in knowledge networks or 'epistemic communities' that informed public policy, challenged governments and politicians, as well as policymakers in international organizations and global business, to listen and respond to their demands for change.

What were the outcomes of such efforts? Several events—starting with the decision to abandon the Multilateral Agreement on Investment (MAI) in October 1998 at the OECD, and 'the Battle for Seattle' at the WTO Ministerial Conference in 1999—showed that activists could prevent or slow down the introduction of 'neoliberal' policy reforms. But could activists also push through their 'progressive' agendas aiming at a more inclusive and sustainable pattern of development?

This volume addresses this question by focusing on four issue areas that are prominent within the justice movement: debt relief, trade justice, corporate accountability and international taxation. In relation to all these areas, activists have gone beyond the politics of rejection to demands for substantive policy reform. Such a transition inevitably intensifies the nature of the activist–policy nexus and formalizes the organization and co-ordination of advocacy organizations and networks (McCarthy and Zald 1987).

The chapters in this volume look at global justice activism at both the transnational and national levels, paying particular attention to civil society actions in three European countries—France, the United Kingdom and Italy. In these countries, social activism is not only vibrant on both the global and national stage, but multiple channels and institutional arrangements exist for potentially influencing policy processes. At the national level, various chapters examine the forms of mobilization and the nature of engagement with the policy process, as well as policy responses and outcomes. Strong variations emerge in the national experiences of activism in the three countries, and a wide range of outcomes are found, from success in changing national or business policies to failure to engage policymakers and public opinion. What factors explain such a diversity of activism trajectories? What national contexts and forms of mobilization are conducive to policy reform? And how do these factors influence each other and impact on outcomes? In short, how can activism make change happen?

CONCEPTS, APPROACHES AND ANALYTICAL GAPS

To understand the dynamics of what we call the 'activist–policy nexus', this volume draws on both theory and empirical evidence. The theoretical contributions, developed in Part 1, aim to identify conceptual elements that are key for understanding both 'success' and 'failure' as well as considerable variations in forms of mobilizations and outcomes that are identified in the case studies that make up Part II. Chapters 1 and 2 draw on neo-Gramscian and path-dependence theory to understand how elites reproduce control and how limits to change derive from historically constructed institutions. Chapters 3 and 4 refer to social movements and organization theory to highlight the possibilities for change associated with some of the relatively recent features of collective action associated with networking and transnational activism.

By referring to these different perspectives the volume aims to address weaknesses that characterize various perspectives used to analyse global justice activism, including gaps in analysis and the fragmentation of approaches and disciplines.

So-called 'realist' political studies have traditionally been concerned with how institutional politics (national and supranational) works and how state actors (and multilateral institutions) shape policies and address controversies. Less attention has been paid to the roles of other—non-state—actors, in particular NGOs and NGO networks. The drawbacks of such a realist approach to the study of policy change have long been highlighted. First, by putting too much weight on traditionally powerful actors, i.e. states, the role of civil society and activism is often disregarded or narrowly confined to its influence on (global) public opinion and to specific efforts for lobbying policymakers. Second, traditionally state-centred analyses neglect the capacities of non-state elite actors, such as business interests and powerful lobbies to repress, capture, co-opt and exert power (Escobar 1995; Wainwright and Kim 2008). Third, and apart from the actors involved, a 'realist' approach tends to confine change and the potential impact of activism to alterations in institutional arrangements and policies. Yet, although non-state actors and activists often do not hold the decision-making power and authority of states and supranational institutions (Wendt 1999), their role in initiating, designing and increasingly also implementing and monitoring change is undeniable (Arts 2000; Wolf 2005). Attempts at understanding change thus require nuanced analyses of the social and temporal dimensions of politics and transformation and an assessment of the impact of non-state actors at different stages and levels of these processes.

The burgeoning 'governance' literature, in contrast, has broadened attention to the roles of non-state actors, particularly in the context of globalization and economic liberalization. Utilizing policy-process and regime theories (see Okereke, Bulkeley and Schroeder 2009), scholars examine the multi-stakeholder governance systems that emerge at different levels, locally, nationally, regionally and transnationally, around certain issues, such as trade, development, finance, climate and human rights (see, for example, Arts, Noortmann and Reinalda 2001). Although activists and other non-state actors are recognized as ever more important initiators and drivers of change, critical perspectives on this development claim that their impact may be overrated (Yanacopulos 2005) because still, 'change ultimately happens *through* states' (Wendt 1999: 9). Furthermore, by emphasizing the primacy of consultation and social dialogue in processes of policy reform, aspects associated with unequal resources, conflicting interests and bargaining are often sidelined (Yanacopulos and Smith 2008).

Sociological literature, in particular social movement and organization theories, have focused on explaining the increasing involvement of all kinds of non-state actors, individual organizations, groups and networks in various policy areas and service spheres (Smith 2007; Tarrow 2005). This approach, however, tended to focus on the behaviour of specific sets of actors (such as NGOs) and lacked the theoretical and historical contextualization for understanding the relationships between forms of mobilization and policy change. In the case of civil society coalitions, often insufficient attention is directed to power relations between networked organizations and other aspects of internal governance.

The social movement literature builds upon a long and rich tradition of comparative research on mobilization in and across national policy contexts (della Porta and Diani 2006; Kriesi and Duyvendak 1995). From this literature emerged key analytical concepts of political opportunity structures, resource mobilization and framing that help to understand the activist–policy nexus and devise typologies of contexts and activist mobilizations. A stream of this literature has addressed the question of the outcomes of mobilizations. The early study of Gamson (1990) distinguished between the achievement of particular aims ('new advantages') and success in being recognized as a legitimate claimant ('acceptance'). Giugni, McAdam and Tilly (1999) distinguished between direct links from claims of mobilizations and effects and outcomes resulting from a combination of claims and outside events. Schumaker (1975) focused on the phases of the policy-making process when the effects of activism emerge, considering *access*, *agenda setting*, *policy*, *implementation of legislation* and *impact*, i.e. the specific consequences of a change in policy (for a broader discussion, see della Porta et al. 2010).

At the national level, the effects of mobilizations have generally been linked to political opportunities, the scale of resources available, forms of activism and access to policymakers. In a study of ecological, antinuclear and peace mobilizations in Europe, Giugni (2004) found that success was associated with the presence of favourable political opportunities, strong political alliances and the viability of claims (higher in domestic, low-profile issues; lower in foreign policy and high-profile issues).

With the rise of transnational movements addressing global issues (della Porta 2007), the contexts and conditions of success of activism have broadened. A less structured system of governance of global issues can be open to new forms of cross-border contestation, with novel opportunities for policy change. Authors della Porta et al. (2010) draw lessons from studies of twelve cases of transnational mobilizations at the European and global levels, on economic, social and disarmament issues. They find that success in policy change is associated to the presence of multilevel political opportunities, strong protest networks, global framing of issues and multiple forms of transnational activism.

The persistent role of national factors—such as domestic political opportunities and constraints—in shaping mobilizations and their possibilities of success has been emphasized in several studies. National factors are important even when the mobilizations address transnational issues (Giugni, Bandler and Eggert 2006; Goodwin and Jasper 2004; Smith 2004).[2]

This volume aims to overcome the theoretical and analytical limitations related to the disciplinary divides highlighted in the preceding and to build a stronger conceptual framework. Such a framework includes the relevance of national contexts, institutional path dependence and 'activist traditions'; hegemonic elite dominance by powerful business interests; and the dynamics within civil society, including power relations within networks and among different actors. To do so, it draws on diverse streams of literature, in particular, political economy, institutional and neo-Gramscian perspectives, as well as social movement and organization theory. Furthermore, it takes a comparative empirical perspective and examines differences in the context and nature of mobilizations, across activist experiences and national and transnational policy settings.

OVERVIEW OF CHAPTERS

Part I of the book, 'Actors, Institutions and Networks', draws on various literatures and theoretical perspectives to address the following questions:

- In a context where state-business-society relations and forms of governance are undergoing significant changes, what opportunities and constraints does this afford for counter-hegemonic struggles and reform initiatives?
- How do corporate elites attempt to retain the reins of control over processes of policy reform associated with justice activism?
- What role do history and institutional path dependence play in explaining opportunities and constraints for policy-oriented action, as well as variations in policy response by country?
- Can civil society strategies centred on networking at the national level overcome the limitations of atomized civil society organizations pursuing their own agenda?
- What is the nature of transnational mobilizations, and what role is played by cross-border networks in complementing national activism and in opening up contestation at the global level?

In the first chapter, 'Elite Business Power and Activist Responses', Peter Utting identifies the significant variations in traditional modes of domination, governance, regulation and policy-making that have occurred in contexts of globalization and liberalization. Such changes are reflected in terms and concepts that have entered the lexicon of scholarly studies: the 'competition' state; 'technocratic', 'multilayered' and 'good' governance; knowledge networks, epistemic communities and 'civic networks', where the latter, in particular, are seen as sources of 'counter-hegemony' to the unleashing of global market forces and neoliberal economic ideologies. The chapter examines how both elites and civil society actors are responding to these changes to gain influence and control. Particular attention is given to different forms of pressure and influence exerted by NGOs and trade unions that relate to the role of transnational corporations (TNCs) in development and issues of corporate social responsibility and accountability. The chapter also examines what powerful actors and institutions are doing to resist, accommodate, shape or, indeed, lead processes of policy and institutional reform, as well as how the strategies of activists and civil society organizations have evolved and adapted to changing patterns of governance and domination. The chapter ends with a reflection on the potential and limits of such strategies from the perspective of progressive policy reform.

Chapter 2, by Daniela Barrier, on 'National Policy Regimes: Implications for the Activism–Policy Nexus', is concerned with the effects of history and institutional path dependence on activism and policy reform. It draws from the case studies presented in Part II of this volume as well as historical institutionalism literature and other research conducted by the author to compare the development of the activism–policy nexus in the contexts of France and the UK. In particular, it examines how the nature of activism and state–civil society relations vary under differing policy regimes, social models and political narratives—differences which relate to notions of the UK 'spectator' state and the French 'interventionist' state. The chapter first briefly reviews the relevant variations in the nature of the French and UK state-business-society relations and colonial models. It then describes the evolution of social movements concerned with development issues since the beginning of the twentieth century in both countries. Finally, it examines variations in terms of resource mobilization, action repertoires, framing and political opportunities, arguing that the development activism–policy nexus in France and the UK is highly path dependent and remains closely linked with each national context, despite the recent rise of cross-border and transnational activism.

In Chapter 3, 'The Potential and Practice of Civic Networks', Jem Bendell and Anne Ellersiek examine the promises and practices of networks among activist groups as a key mechanism for advocacy for global justice. Four networks based in the UK are analysed in the light of the promises extracted from the literature with regard to the 'network effect' on mobilization. The authors show that network participants consciously seek to maximize the benefits of networks, and what this implies for the network participants' awareness of, and autonomy from, social structures; the effectiveness and legitimacy of the impacts of networks; and the implications for their effective management with regard to policy impact. The authors reflect on problems of network legitimacy and effectiveness and suggest the need for a shift from 'noble to global', whereby networks further align participant organizations' practices and agendas with network-related activities and goals, involve more groups and movements from the South and adopt an agenda more aligned with universal values and concerns than national issues and interests.

The emerging structures of global social movements and their impact on policy change are examined in Chapter 4, 'Global Social Movement Networks and the Politics of Change', by Raffaele Marchetti and Mario Pianta. The authors identify three key novelties of such networks. First, they organizationally constitute the backbone of a new political agency that it is openly global, thus different from traditional contentious agency at the national level; second, they show a degree of political maturation in the framing of issues from local and national protest to global proposals; and, finally, they develop a specific strategic-political skill in both challenging and implementing institutional policy-making at the state and international levels. Organizational structure, themes and strategy constitute the three elements characterizing the unique nature of transnational social networks as key elements for understanding global politics in general, and global contentious politics in particular. The chapter concludes with examples of how these global social movements have concretely affected transnational and national policies, illustrating the 'global activism–policy nexus' and its manifestations at different levels of governance.

Part II of the book, 'The Activism–Policy Nexus in Practice', examines concrete cases of mobilizations associated with debt relief or cancellation, trade justice, international taxation and corporate accountability at both global and national levels (see Table I.1)

Table I.1 Overview of Cases

		Debt Relief	*Trade Justice*	*Global Taxation*	*Corporate Accountability*
WTO Conferences	Cancún, Mexico: 10–14 September 2003		X		
	Doha, Qatar: 9–13 November 2001		X		
France	Ça suffit comme ça	X			
	Plate-forme Dette & Développement	X			
	Coalitions on trade justice	X	X		
	Attac		X	X	
UK	War on Want	X	X	X	
	Jubilee 2000	X	X		
	Trade Justice Movement (TJM)	X	X		
	Sakhalin Network				X
	The Corporate Responsibility (CORE) Coalition				X
	Publish What You Pay (PWYP)				X
Italy	Coalitions on trade justice		X		
	Sdebitarsi	X			

Chapter 5, 'Global Networks on Trade Policy: The Case of the WTO Conference in Cancún', by Federico Silva, investigates the emergence of transnational mobilizations on trade justice, and the opportunities and challenges they faced in the run-up to and during the WTO Ministerial Conferences, particularly Cancún. The focus of the chapter is the interaction between global networks and policymakers. Specific attention is devoted to the development of the policy decisions, to the networks' activities aimed at influencing these decisions and to the outcomes that emerged. The chapter identifies the relevant factors and causal mechanisms that have facilitated (Cancún) or impeded (Doha) policy impact. The analysis shows that in social movement strategies, success is determined both by internal factors pertaining to social movements and external factors; by the simultaneous presence of lobbying, protest and an epistemic-like community; and by key factors in the political opportunity structure such as trust and alliances. An additional important finding concerns the complexity of the interactions between the national and the transnational level, the presence of both 'boomerang effects' and of a 'return to the national' where a decisive role can be played by a few national delegations acting in alliance with global networks.

The remaining chapters are devoted to case studies of national mobilizations in the UK, France and Italy. Chapter 6, 'Advocacy for Corporate Accountability and Trade Justice: The Role of "Noble Networks" in the United Kingdom', by Jem Bendell and Anne Ellersiek, examines the policy impacts of the mobilizations of British coalitions over issues of trade justice and corporate accountability. The authors look at how different coalitions' interacted with policy-making institutions, noting their relatively moderate agenda, both in terms of the preferred means of collective action (advocacy and lobbying rather than protest) and the nature of their goals. In the case of trade, the analysis finds that activists have been highly permeable to the British government's views and proposals on trade policy. In the case of corporate accountability, the coalitions have adopted a legalistic approach to activism, targeting the legislation-making process as well as British commitments to international agreements and using legislation already in place to seek redress. Despite the significant degree of access to policymakers enjoyed by the coalitions, achievements related to even conservative policy reforms have been quite limited. The chapter reflects on needed reforms in NGO advocacy and mobilizing strategies, with a particular focus on the organization of activism in networks and the challenges of arriving at and effectively communicating joint agendas.

Reforming agricultural and trade policy in France is the topic of Chapter 7, by Benoit Daviron and Tancrède Voituriez. Investigating the demands and policy positions of key actors and organizations in relation to agricultural trade policy, they find a substantial convergence of 'radical' thinking among a diverse set of activist, professional and governmental actors and institutions. In order to understand this convergence and evaluate its impact on policy, the chapter analyses the resources and framings of four main civil society organizations active on the issue. The convergence in agendas is due to the emergence of a cohesive epistemic community, made possible by three main factors: the strong influence among intellectuals of the ideas and principles stated in the European Union's Common Agricultural Policy in the 1960s; the weight of agricultural specialists in activist and professional organizations; and the high levels of permeability between civil society organizations and government personnel. The coalition failed, however, to mobilize key workers' unions and larger movements such as Attac, as well as the wider public. The chapter proceeds to analyse the interactions of these organizations with policy-making circles, and in particular the ministries of agriculture and trade, finding that despite significant consensus among some key national-level actors and a large epistemic community, this had little policy influence at the EU level, where trade policy is largely determined.

In Chapter 8, 'Debt Relief and Trade Justice in Italy', Paolo Gerbaudo and Mario Pianta examine the different ways in which debt and trade issues have been framed in the political and social arenas in Italy and the role of solidarity groups, development NGOs, environmental and peace groups, trade unions and Catholic organizations. Although Italian activism is strongly rooted in domestic political cultures, it was able to link up from an early stage to transnational mobilizations—a key factor which shaped national actions. The chapter investigates mobilization capacities, forms of actions and interactions with policymakers. In the case of debt, a unified campaign, *Sdebitarsi*, reached an important policy success with the passing of legislation on debt relief. In the case of trade, several coalitions have been active with little success in affecting policies that were mainly decided at the European and WTO levels. Such campaigns, however, spurred the growth of fair trade experiences.

Chapter 9, 'Dropping the Debt? British Anti-debt Campaigns and International Development Policy', by Claire Saunders and Tasos Papadimitriou, shows that the issue of debt relief became political and passionate in Britain during the late 1990s. This period marked a break from the previously moderate lobbying actions of British civil society organizations concerned with development issues and brought the debt issue for the first time to the wider public debate as well as government forums. The chapter first presents the structural and ideological reasons for this increased interest on debt relief. Based on data gathered via questionnaires and interviews, it analyses the composition and resources of the two coalitions that best represent the anti–third world debt activism born in the UK in the mid-1990s: Jubilee 2000 and Make Poverty History. Despite the overall dominating presence of large development NGOs, it finds important variations with regards to resources, membership and framing between the two coalitions, with Jubilee 2000 enjoying larger membership of labour, environmental and missionary organizations, but marked by internal dissent, and Make

Poverty History being better resourced and closer, in agenda and actual relationships, to policy-making circuits. The study then analyses chronologically and in detail the effects of these variations on activists' interactions with relevant government institutions, as well as the differences in their policy impacts between those two coalitions.

The struggle for third world debt relief in France is the topic of Chapter 10, by Rodrigo Contreras, who first analyses the resources and framing aspects of the two main anti-debt coalitions in France—Ça suffit comme ça—created to prepare the world-wide Jubilee 2000 campaign, and Plateforme Dette & Développement, created to enlarge the existing coalition. It finds that overall, French anti-debt coalitions are poorly resourced and rely largely on the voluntary work of their members. There is, however, continuity of membership and framing. Demanding total debt cancellation, both coalitions were formed by Christian solidarity, anti-imperialist and development NGOs, as well as labour unions, and both linked debt to the French colonial heritage and to unequal power relations between North and South. The chapter analyses the coalitions' interactions with the Ministry of Finance, their main interlocutor in government. It finds that the wide membership base and the continuity of activists' agendas gained them credibility with the government and resulted in the institutionalization of periodic consultations. However, in a context of scarce resources and where the French government chose to promote its own pro-development initiative, the coalitions managed neither to make the issue of debt accessible to the wider public nor to obtain public government support for their demands.

Chapter 11 by James Brassett, 'Global Justice and/as Global Democracy: The UK Campaign for a Tobin Tax', focuses on the experience of War on Want, the main British organization that promoted an international currency transaction tax (CTT). The chapter examines the nature of the demands that emerged, noting that the UK campaign for a CTT falls within the moderate range of proposals related to such a tax, and that the framing of demands evolved over the course of the campaign. The ambitious original demands for a version of the Tobin Tax, which contained important democratizing and transformative dimensions, shifted towards a more strategic and straightforward 'tax for development' aimed at raising revenues to contribute towards the British government commitments to the Millennium Development Goals. This evolution took place as large development NGOs joined the CTT cause to form the 'Stamp Out Poverty' coalition which brought the CTT issue to the Make Poverty History Campaign. The chapter goes on to examine the policy impact of the CTT movement, in particular through the movement's interactions with the Treasury and the Department for International Development (DfID). Finding very limited impact, the analysis discusses the reasons for this in the light of a political and economic context in Britain with its strongly finance-oriented economy and a set of legal constraints on the political activities of charities. The coalition, however, had more impact at the EU level, forcing the European Central Bank to justify its position on taxing capital and contributing towards existing debates that place social redistribution on the agenda of European governance.

Chapter 12, 'Campaign or "Movement of Movements"? Attac France and the Currency Transaction Tax', by Edouard Morena, refers to political opportunity structures, resource mobilization and framing to study the trajectory and impacts of the French organization Attac and its interactions with policy-making circles. First, it analyses the political and economic contexts within which Attac was created, suggesting that its success and high-profile presence on both the French and international political scenes can be seen as the direct result of a convergence between its objectives and those of mainstream politics and public opinion over one triggering issue: globalization. Regarding the question of resource mobilization, the analysis reveals that Attac was set up by a coalition of like-minded organizations (trade unions, civic associations, NGOs, newspapers, academics and individual militants) that had grown aware of the proximities between their analyses with regards to neoliberal globalization and the crisis of mainstream politics, and had campaigned together during large national social mobilizations. This coming together of like-minded organizations provided incentives to all: unions widened their support network and legitimacy, and civic associations gained access to tangible and intangible resources. With regards to framing, the demands of Attac France evolved progressively from the Tobin Tax demand towards other forms of global taxation. This evolution in framing, it is argued, was partly related to changes in the political context: concerns at the level of public opinion and the legislature about unregulated financial markets had subsided, whereas the executive branch sought to regain international status and find innovative sources of funding for development in view of commitments for the Millennium Development Goals.

The concluding chapter, 'How Can Activism Make Change Happen?', by Mario Pianta, Anne Ellersiek and Peter Utting, distils the main findings in terms of variations in demands, proposals and policy and discursive impacts by issue area, type of mobilization and country. It identifies key elements related to institutional and historical context, power relations and political opportunities for understanding such variations, as well as 'internal' dimensions of activist organization and networks. Such dimensions relate to resource issues; representation and legitimacy; identity, cohesion and coherence; and the monitoring and sustainability of action. The chapter ends by reflecting on the implications of the findings for activism in the contemporary context of global crises.

NOTES

1. For the purpose of this volume, *activism* is defined as organized efforts to change (or resist change in) some major aspect of society (Ballantine & Roberts 2011: 548). *Justice activism* refers to mobilizations that centre on such societal aspects as equity, sustainability, rights and democracy.

2. This approach argues that 'the forms and dynamics [of activism] we see in the transnational arena resemble their national and local predecessors, even as they are adapted to fit a transnational political context' (Smith 2004: 320).

BIBLIOGRAPHY

Arts, B. (2000). 'Regimes, Non-State Actors and the State System: A 'Structurational' Regime Model', *European Journal of International Relations*, 6 (4): 513–542.

Arts, B., Noortmann, M., and Reinalda, B. (eds) (2001). *Non-State Actors in International Relations*, Aldershot: Ashgate.

Ballantine, J.H. & Roberts, K.A. (eds) (2011). *Our Social World: Introduction to Sociology*, Pine Forge Press: Thousand Oaks

della Porta, D. (ed) (2007). *The Global Justice Movements. A Cross-National and Transnational Perspective*, Boulder, CO: Paradigm.

della Porta, D., Alcalde, J., Parks, L., and Silva, F. (2010). *The Effects of Transnational Protest: Some Reflections on 12 Protest Campaigns and More.* Paper for the conference on Social Movement Outcomes, Geneva, 16–17 February.

della Porta, D., and Diani, M. (2006). *Social Movements*, Oxford: Blackwell.

Escobar, A. (1995). *Encountering Development: The Making and Unmaking of the Third-World*, Princeton, NJ: Princeton University Press.

Gamson W.A. (1990). *The Strategy of Social Protest*, Belmont, CA: Wadsworth Publishers.

Giugni, Marco. (2004). *Social Protest and Policy Change*, Lanham, MD: Rowan and Littlefield.

Giugni, Marco, Bandler, M., and Eggert, N. (2006). *The Global Justice Movement: How Far Does the Classic Social Movement Agenda Go in Explaining Transnational Contention?* Programme Paper No. 24, UNRISD, Geneva.

Giugni, Marco, McAdam, Doug, and Tilly, Charles. (1999). *How Social Movements Matter*, Minneapolis: University of Minnesota Press.

Goodwin, J., and Jasper, J.M. (2004). 'Caught in a Winding, Snarling Vine: The Structural Bias of Political Process Theory', *Sociological Forum*, 14 (1): 27–54.

Kriesi, H., and Duyvendak, J.W. (1995). 'National Cleavage Structures', in Hanspeter Kriesi et al. (eds), *The Politics of New Social Movements in Western Europe. A Comparative Analysis*, Minneapolis: University of Minnesota Press.

McCarthy, J. D. and Zald, M. N. (1987). 'Resource Mobilization and Social Movements: A Partial Theory', in S.M. Buechler and F.K. Cylke (eds) *Social Movements: Perspectives and Issues*, Mountain View, CA: Mayfield Publishing.

Okereke, C., Bulkeley, H., and Schroeder, H. (2009). 'Conceptualizing Climate Change Governance beyond the International Regime', *Global Environmental Politics*, 9:56–76.

Schumaker, P.D. (1975). 'Policy Responsiveness to Protest-Group Demands', *Journal of Politics*, 37 (2): 488–521.

Sikkink, K. (2005). 'Patterns of Dynamic Multi-Level Governance and Insider–Outsider Coalitions', in D. della Porta and S. Tarrow (eds), *Transnational Protest and Global Activism*, Lanham, MD: Rowan and Littlefield.

Smith, J. (2004). 'Transnational Processes and Movements', in D.A. Snow, S.A. Soule and H. Kriesi (eds), *The Blackwell Companion to Social Movements*, Oxford: Blackwell.

———. (2007). *Social Movements for Global Democracy. Themes in Global Social Change*, Baltimore, MD: Johns Hopkins University Press.

Tarrow, S. (2005). *The New Transnational Activism*, Cambridge: Cambridge University Press.

Wainwright, J. and Kim, S.K. (2008). 'Battles in Seattle Redux: Transnationalism and Urban Resistance to Neoliberalism', *Antipode*, 40 (4): 513–534.

Wendt, A.E. (1999). *Social Theory of International Politics*, Cambridge: Cambridge University Press.

Wolf, K.D. (2005). 'Private Actors and the Legitimacy of Governance Beyond the State: Conceptual Outlines and Empirical Explorations', in A. Benz & I. Papadopoulos (eds), *Governance and Democratic Legitimacy: Transnational, European, and Multi-Level-Issues*, London: Routledge.

Yanacopulos, Helen. (2005). 'The Strategies that Bind: NGO Coalitions and Their Influence', *Global Networks*, 5 (1): 93–110.

Yanacopulos, Helen, and Smith, Matt Baillie. (2008). 'The Ambivalent Cosmopolitanism of International NGOs', in A.J. Bebbington, S. Hickey and D.C. Mitlin (eds), *Can NGOs Make a Difference? The Challenge of Development Alternatives*, London: ZED Books.

Part I

Actors, Institutions and Networks

1 Elite Business Power and Activist Responses

Peter Utting

INTRODUCTION

For those who empathize with the struggles of activists for global justice, the analysis of when progressive institutional and policy change actually occurs can make for difficult reading.[1] Such change is hard to come by. Explanations of the limits of change often focus on the relatively weak power base and capacities of subaltern groups and civil society organizations or networks to mobilize resources, build coalitions, sustain collective action and access relevant policy processes (della Porta and Diani 2006; Tarrow 1994). Considerable attention is also paid to the capacity of elites to repress, capture and co-opt (Escobar 1995). But elites have at their disposal multiple ways of retaining and gaining control and influence. Furthermore, the rapidly changing nature of governance in contexts of contemporary globalization and liberalization has magnified the complexity of power and domination.

This chapter has two objectives. First, it seeks to examine the diverse ways in which powerful business actors and institutions, in particular transnational corporations, finance capital and business associations, assert and reassert control, legitimacy and 'hegemony' (Bøas and McNeill 2004). Second, it examines the implications of these developments for activism associated with global justice and policy change in issue areas that are the focus of this volume, namely, corporate accountability, international taxation and trade justice.

The chapter is structured as follows. The first section turns to some of the theoretical literature on state-business-society relations, power and governance for pointers about the implications of the changing dynamics of business power for activism and policy reform. The next three sections examine the instrumental, structural and discursive dimensions of business power (Fuchs 2005). A concluding section sums up some of the main observations and reflects on the implications for activist strategy.

PERSPECTIVES ON POWER AND GOVERNANCE

The nature of state-business-society relations has long been at the centre of debates within various disciplines. Crude interpretations which trace their lineage to ideal-typical Marxian and Weberian notions of the state as 'the executive committee of the bourgeoisie' or a rational arbiter of conflicting interests, respectively, have ceded ground to more nuanced and complex understandings. Similarly perspectives on global corporations have evolved. Hitherto seen by some as agents of imperialism (Radice 1975) and the conduit by which resources and surplus are drained from the Global South or 'periphery' to the 'centre' of the world system (Gunder Frank 1967), and by others as progressive agents of modernization and development (Rostow 1960); there is wider recognition today of 'varieties of capitalism', variations in firm preferences and policy regimes and the new political role of business.[2] Such aspects have significant implications for state-business-society relations.

Learning from Theory

Structuralist explanations of institutional and social change, as well as power resources theory, are useful in highlighting the ways in which structures and power relations shape the scope and substance of policy change. In contrast to some of the 'good governance' discourse and literature, examined in the following, such analysis is useful for understanding the limits to civil society advocacy and change given the nature of structural constraints and gross imbalances in power relations. They also point to the crucial link between progressive policy change and the reconfiguration of the balance of social forces through social mobilization, coalitions and alliances.

Such explanations, however, often mask the heterogeneous preferences and interests within 'the state', 'business' and 'civil society', as well as the complex relations between advocacy and contestation on the one hand and mainstream institutions on the other hand. As Tarrow and others have pointed out it is essential to understand the mechanisms and processes that bridge contentious and conventional politics and shape and constantly alter the dynamics of policy change (Tarrow 2006).

Key in this regard are variables associated with "political opportunity structure", i.e. the degree of openness or closure within conventional politics related to such aspects as splits with ruling elites, coalitions, allies, coercion and hegemony (della Porta and Diani 2006; Tarrow 2006).

Various analytical perspectives have emphasized the role of not only actors and agency, but, in particular, ideational factors (ideas, beliefs, values, identity and discourse) in processes of policy and institutional change. These include constructivist approaches, organizational theory and New Institutional Economics, as well as cultural political economy (Giddens 1984; Jessop and Sum 2006; Nye 2005; Ruggie 1982, 2003).

The Gramscian concept of hegemony is particularly useful for understanding how elites do not have to resort to coercion to gain control but can respond proactively and positively to societal concerns, accommodate oppositional demands and exercise moral, cultural and intellectual leadership. Much of the analysis following focuses on the capacity of elites to both shape and lead processes of reform by accommodating oppositional demands, as well as by framing agendas—a process that involves defining what constitutes legitimate issues for debate and action and what remains 'unreasonable' and off-limits. In a similar vein, welfare state literature and French regulation theory explain how business elites are driven not only by immediate economic interests or pressures associated with profit maximization and competitiveness, but also the need to ensure longer-term stability and legitimacy via class compromises and social pacts (Esping-Andersen 1990; Jessop and Sum 2006). Such perspectives point to the potential for activist agendas to resonate and interact with the mainstream and incorporate certain business interests in coalitions for change.

Patterns of elite maintenance are continually evolving. During the post–Second World War era, Keynesianism, social democracy and welfare state consolidation took place, particularly in Western Europe, against the backdrop of the strengthening of neo-corporatist institutions, new social pacts and so-called Fordist compromises that facilitated collaboration among state, business and civil society actors. Citizens often identified with elite discourses proclaiming the virtues of the emerging consumer society and the promise of full employment. Civil society pressures were ever present, notably through a well-organized labour movement, but the nature of those pressures and the way they were exerted changed as trade union organizations transitioned from being 'challengers' to polity members and exacted certain compromises and reforms through their links to mainstream political parties (Tilly 1978).

Changing Modes of Governance

One of the most pronounced institutional developments associated with contemporary globalization and liberalization relates to changing modes of governance, with new, different or multiple actors playing a significant role in regulation and policy-making. Developmental welfare states, neo-corporatist (tripartite) arrangements, hierarchical decision-making and 'command and control' state regulation have in some policy and regulatory areas ceded ground to 'competition' states that aim to facilitate market-led growth and private sector development, pluralistic consultative processes involving a variety of non-state actors and private regulation where regulatory authority is delegated to non-state actors or multi-stakeholder institutions (Rittberger and Nettesheim 2008). As Cutler, Haufler and Porter (1999: 4) explain, not only are firms and business associations assuming a more prominent role in rule-making and standard-setting, this role and the cooperation it implies among firms and other non-state actors is both given legitimacy by governments or legitimacy is acquired through other factors such as expertise.

Given the multiple contexts, interests and logics that underpin such developments it is difficult a priori to say what they imply for progressive policy change. Indeed, different literatures draw sharply differing conclusions in this regard.

Governance theory is concerned with the emergence and crafting of institutional arrangements that can address both the limitations of the state and traditional structures of authority and legitimacy in contexts of globalization and liberalization, and associated negative (social, environmental, human rights, developmental) externalities. A key feature of such arrangements is collaborative forums and networks in which public and private actors 'mesh . . . more effectively in a way that would be regarded as legitimate by attentive publics' (Keohane 2002: 16). According to Beck, under contemporary globalization 'there is one rule that applies equally to all the different groups of players and their strategies in the meta-power game: no single actor—neither capital nor advocatory movements nor states—can achieve their goals . . . on their own. They are all dependent on forming coalitions if they want to see their goals realized. This leads to a dynamic of integration through which the boundaries between "pro" and "contra" become blurred and interwoven . . . ' (2005: 288).

From the perspective of elites, 'multiplayered' or collaborative governance serves multiple functions: it provides a means to enhance legitimacy, and deal with increasing risk, complexity and transaction costs—solutions to problems are best found through co-ordination, collaboration and networking involving multiple actors (Beck 2005; Mattli and Woods 2009). Elites need to build constituencies and form coalitions. Such interaction both builds the power base needed for policy and institutional change and legitimizes the process.

Elite participation in consultative and other dimensions of policy processes and networks is also an important means of 'capture'. This relates not only to the capture of state institutions or state-led policy processes, but also of civil society. Normative dimensions of 'good governance' associated with participation, dialogue, transparency and accountability have facilitated and formalized the interaction of policymakers and civil society organizations. The proliferation of so-called BINGOs—business-interest non-governmental organizations—and their proactive participation in policy processes is indicative of the capacity of business elites to adapt to and colonize new spaces for influence that have emerged in the context of the changing patterns of governance. Such participation and influence is aided and abetted by the tendency of mainstream policy institutions to be highly selective in whom they invite to the table, as well as their reluctance to distinguish between BINGOs and public-interest NGOs (United Nations General Assembly 2004). In practice such distinctions are often difficult to establish given the tendency for many NGOs to develop commercial activities or, indeed, legally constitute themselves as companies. This does not mean that such entities necessarily share similar interests to business corporations, but it often does mean that professional, financial and sociocultural ties between NGOs and business or governments are strengthened, with the result that NGO discourse, demands and tactics lose their radical edge and become somewhat sanitized (Heap 2000).

The notion of good governance also emphasizes the importance of 'evidence-based' research and policy, and it discursively frowns upon policy agendas overtly driven by ideology (read particular ideologies). In contexts of heightened risk and complexity under globalization, policymakers crucially need to access knowledge from diverse sources. This is also one of the basic premises of stakeholder theory, which promoted a new approach to business management and provided much of the intellectual underpinning of the contemporary corporate social responsibility movement that gathered momentum in the 1980s (Freeman 1984).

Furthermore, the technical nature of certain bodies of knowledge increases the influence of so-called 'experts' in the policy process. Various development agencies now project themselves as 'knowledge agencies' (Utting 2006). Policy change is said to result increasingly from 'communities of shared knowledge and not simply domestic or transnational interest groups' (Haas 1989: 377). These 'epistemic communities' involve the formation of networks that link policymakers, professionals, scientists and activists. According to this analysis, specialized knowledge and experts have come to play a more significant role in modern-day policy-making in various fields. This suggests that some aspects of policy-making have become more technocratic in the sense that policy reforms are decided increasingly by individuals, institutions or networks deemed to be repositories of specialist knowledge, whereas some traditional institutions such as parliamentary bodies have been side-lined (UNRISD 2000).

Such developments and arrangements yield a complex set of opportunities and constraints for activists seeking to influence the policy process. It opens up spaces for NGOs and other civil society actors to have their voices heard and to acquire a seat in policy forums. As governments and international organizations buy into the new governance agenda, some civil society organizations find themselves positively affected in terms of both resource mobilization and political opportunities, i.e. the two key attributes identified within social movements theory as key for policy influence. Even when restricted to consultation and information exchange, contemporary collaborative governance constitutes a qualitatively different scenario to the 'closed' spaces of government that previously characterized policy-making (Cornwall 2004: 5). The density of multi-stakeholder and inter-sectoral linkages represents a qualitative shift in the nature of policy making that yields important spaces for civil society activists.

But as Brock and Cornwall point out, the participatory substance of collaborative institutions and the transformative potential of top-down 'invited spaces' can vary considerably. Often they contrast with institutional arrangements associated with 'popular' or 'conquered spaces' where contestation, bargaining and social pressures are more overt (Brock, Cornwall and Gaventa 2001; Cornwall 2004). Path dependency in terms of institutional conservativeness and hierarchical relations, co-option and cosmetic or ritualized participation can all stifle change. As Cornwall observes, viewed in isolation, it is tempting to focus on the transformative potential of collaborative institutions. In practice they are embedded in varied cultural, institutional and political contexts that heavily condition the dynamics and scope of change (Cornwall 2004: 9).

De Sousa Santos and Rodríguez-Garavito (2005) point to the failure of governance theory to grapple adequately with the question of power. Concerned with the need to promote an alternative or counter-hegemonic globalization, they write: 'the kind of political action envisaged by the governance approach is a far cry from [this]. Given its conception of power and its focus on problem solving, the governance approach tends to bracket deep power asymmetries among actors . . . and to view the public sphere as a rather depoliticized arena of collaboration among generic 'stakeholders' (2005: 8). They go on to point out that governance theory lacks a theory of political agency suited to the task of deep reform or restructuring institutions (2005: 8): 'By default or by design, those doing the [institutional] imagining are the elites or members of the middle-class with the economic and cultural capital to count as 'stakeholders''(2005: 9).

Others are concerned about the moral turn associated with governance theory and strategizing, in particular that associated with writings on cosmopolitan democracy (Held 1995). Mouffe (2005) notes the problematic tendency to assume that antagonism and conflict can fade into the past and be supplanted by consensual processes based on 'transparent communication among rational participants'. The struggle in the 'post-political era' is no longer between 'left and right', but between 'right and wrong'. As played out in practice, this approach can be exclusionary because it can only accommodate fairly like-minded actors and perspectives. Those proposing very different alternatives often find themselves dismissed as naïve, passé or ideological, and are not invited to the table. Others may be invited but remain marginal in consultative and policy-making processes, often serving to legitimize the multi-stakeholder process. They may have 'voice' but are in no real sense 'players' (Utting and Zammit 2006: 42).

BUSINESS POWER

Another vantage point to understand the potential and limits of justice activism and associated policy change is to examine not only the changing nature of policy processes associated with new forms of governance, but also how elites attempt to secure control through different dimensions of business power. The following sections analyse three such dimensions related to instrumental, structural and discursive power, and consider their implications for activism and policy change.

Instrumental Power

Instrumental power refers to the capacity of interest groups to exert influence through interpersonal relations, inter-institutional collaboration and participation in consultative and decision-making processes. Such power can be exercised through both formal and informal channels, and can be both direct and indirect, as well as legal and illegal or extra-legal.

Leaving aside bribery, obvious mechanisms through which to exercise such power typically involve lobbying policymakers and political campaign contributions. But there are many more (Slob and Weyzig 2010). These include, for example, so-called revolving doors, constituency building and participation in knowledge networks, stakeholder dialogues or epistemic communities.

Whereas in the past the rise of both representative democracy centred on electoral competition and neo-corporatist governance favoured alliance-building and organic links between some sectors of civil society, notably labour organizations and political parties, contemporary governance often favours the individualized participation of particular business, professional and public-interest organizations. Business actors have proven extremely adept at exercising such instrumental power.

The resources that activists can mobilize to push a particular cause or agenda often pale in comparison with those of elite business interests. This is apparent not only in relation to financial resources, but also human capital or skill sets that enhance the capacity of different actors to shape policy processes and outcomes, and social capital, i.e. social relations and networks they can draw on to connect professionally, socially and culturally with policymakers.

The instrumental power of business is particularly relevant for understanding the potential and limits of activism associated with trade justice and corporate accountability. This emerges in the discussion of specific that follows on lobbying and changing patters of governance involving both multiple actors or stakeholders and levels of policy-making.

Lobbying

Lobbying associated with trade policy has been well documented at the level of the WTO where big business interests were influential in processes leading to the agreements on investment (TRIMS) and intellectual property (TRIPS) (Sell 2003), as well as in subsequent negotiations on the General Agreement on Trade in Services (GATT) (Vander Stichele, Bizzarri and Plank 2006). In an effort to strengthen international protection for intellectual property, twelve corporate executives of U.S.-based TNCs formed the Intellectual Property Committee (IPC) in 1986, which effectively formed a triad coalition involving U.S., European and Japanese business interests that lobbied their respective governments to ensure that most of their demands were incorporated in the 1994 TRIPS agreement.

As Sell explains: 'What is new in this case is that industry identified a trade problem, devised a solution, and reduced it to a concrete proposal that it then advanced to governments' (2003: 96). They employed both direct and indirect means and had powerful members with close ties to government. Such strategy and tactics left transnational global justice activism looking relatively impotent. But once the TRIPS agreement was in place, it soon generated significant opposition. Activism gathered force in the late 1990s when, in the context of the global AIDS pandemic, transnational activist networks, certain developing country governments and their generic drugs firms, as well as public opinion, rallied against IPCs that were seen as putting the profits of 'big pharma' before the public policy interests of developing countries (Sell 2003: 25).

The instrumental power of business interests also plays a crucial role in shaping bilateral trade agreements (Bull 2010; Carrión 2009). This is brought out clearly in the case of trade agreements negotiated between Central American countries and the United States in 2003–2004 and, at the time of writing, with the European Union. Not only are smaller developing countries at a considerable negotiating disadvantage vis-à-vis the powerful countries, but civil society groups interested in influencing the negotiations tend to find themselves overwhelmed by certain business actors that can mobilize considerable technical and other resources. In a context where the stakes are loaded against them, civil society organizations and networks often split into two camps on the issue of free trade and investment agreements, with some groups trying to reform from within and others mobilizing on the outside to try and block the negotiations. In contrast, dominant business interests involved in both multilateral and bilateral negotiations have often been able to form fairly cohesive coalitions through business associations and other forums.

Civil society networks have proven to be more adept at throwing a spanner in the works of international negotiations for new agreements than fundamentally shaping their content. This occurred, for example, at the hemispheric level, in relation to the Free Trade Agreement of the Americas (FTAA), and at the global level in connection with the Multilateral Agreement on Investment (MAI), which was negotiated at the Paris-based OECD during 1995–1998. In these cases, the civil society networks involved achieved their immediate objectives. Proactive and well-organized mobilizations were, however, only one part of the reason for 'success'. Particularly important was the implicit or explicit alliance with powerful states—notably in these cases, Brazil (FTAA) and France (MAI), which for their own political, economic or cultural reasons were reluctant to proceed with the negotiations.[3]

Lobbying is also an important issue for the corporate accountability movement. This is apparent in two respects. The first relates to the seemingly contradictory situation where large corporations and business associations may engage fairly proactively with the corporate social responsibility

(CSR) agenda, i.e. voluntary initiatives that purportedly aim to improve the social, environmental and human rights performance of companies, whilst simultaneously lobbying for public policies and regulations that can have perverse social, environmental and human rights implications (Slob and Weyzig 2010). These relate, for example, to the deregulation or flexibilization of labour markets; regulations restricting the organization of, and contestation by, trade unions; strict patent protection in the field of health products; subsidies for environmentally harmful production systems; and efforts to oppose climate change regulation.

Second, organized business interests often lobby to ensure that 'hard' regulation centred on law, mandatory regulations and strengthening institutions for redress plays second fiddle to 'soft' regulation based on corporate self-regulation or voluntary initiatives. Numerous efforts to promote a harder regulatory environment for TNCs operating in developing countries have resulted in a diluted compromise due to the active lobbying of both corporate interests and certain states or ministries therein. As the following examples indicate, international business regulation is replete with such compromises:

- In a context where the non-aligned movement in the 1970s was calling for a new international economic order and controls on TNCs, the voluntary OECD Guidelines for Multinational Enterprises and the eventual collapse of the initiative to establish a UN code of conduct for TNCs emerged.
- The initiative (from 1999 to 2003) to draft the 'Norms on the responsibilities of TNCs and other business enterprises with regard to human rights', which focused on hardening international law, was rejected politically and replaced with a process that placed greater emphasis on voluntary initiatives and state compliance with existing law.[4]
- Efforts by the Publish What You Pay (PWYP) campaign to get governments to oblige corporations in the extractive industries to report their payments to foreign governments resulted in a set of voluntary guidelines and procedures associated with the Extractive Industries Transparency Initiative (EITI) that was launched in 2003.

The issue of 'responsible lobbying' has slowly begun to appear on the CSR agenda (MacGillivray et al. 2005; SustainAbility and WWF-UK 2005), but few corporations disclose their public policy positions (Slob and Weyzig 2010). They may disclose their political donations but, as Slob and Weyzig point out, compared to other mechanisms such as direct lobbying, constituency building for a particular position and collective action through business associations, this is one of the least important lobbying channels.

The rise in the instrumental power of business is not simply a function of enhanced resources that are mobilized and allocated for the purpose of influencing policy processes. It also reflects the ways in which organized business interests have adapted to and shaped changing modes of governance. Contemporary governance is said to be multiplayered and multilayered.

Multiplayered Governance

Institutional developments associated with the engagement of multiple actors or 'stakeholders' in consultative and decision-making processes have created and expanded spaces for dialogue and interactions among individuals and organizations associated with business, civil society, the state and international agencies. Bilateral and regional trade negotiations involve a far broader range of actors (Mejido Costoya, Utting and Carrión 2010; Shadlen 2008). Similarly, the corporate social responsibility movement has been propelled to a large extent by the interplay of corporations and NGOs interacting through stakeholder dialogues and a variety of multistakeholder initiatives (Reed, Utting and Mukherjee-Reed 2012; Utting 2002).

The question of expert knowledge in both discourse and practice has major implications for NGOs engaged in advocacy. NGOs are investing far more time, energy and resources in knowledge generation and dissemination and in accessing epistemic communities. Certain NGOs and networks examined in this volume have excelled in this role, both in generating knowledge—as occurred, for example, in relation to international taxation in France (Chapter 12) and CSR in the UK (Chapter 6)—and in terms of participating in consultative processes and policy dialogues, as occurred with trade policy in France (Chapter 7) and debt relief in the UK (Chapter 9).

The knowledge question is also a key factor that explains variations in the activism–policy nexus in France and the UK. UK NGOs constitute a rich source of knowledge on diverse development issues, which often feeds into epistemic communities. Furthermore, in the knowledge-based policy environment, so-called single-issue NGOs run the risk of being dismissed or marginalized in mainstream circles for seemingly not being able to grasp the bigger picture, as occurred, for example, in the case of the Sakhalin Island Network and its attempts to reform the policy of the Export Credits Guarantee Department (ECGD) in the United Kingdom (Bendell and Ellersiek 2009).

Multilayered Governance

'Multilayered governance' refers to the broadening of the locus of decision-making with not only the national level but also the local, regional and international levels appearing as prominent arenas for interaction and decision-making related to corporate and public policy. This situation raises crucial challenges for activists. It calls for 'transnational activist networks' (Keck and Sikkink 1998) or 'multi-scalar' activism (van Alstine 2010). As Peter Evans (2008) explains, both social movements and democratic governance must operate on a scale commensurate with the system they are trying to change, in particular the global scope of production and exchange.

The strengthening of transnational activist networks is potentially an important development in this respect, both in the sense of enabling local struggles to gain leverage through their national and international connections and visibility and allowing activists to exercise instrumental power in multiple institutional arenas. In practice, as the analysis of trade justice reform in France shows (see Chapter 7, this volume), activism is still often focused on the national level in contexts where decision-making power has shifted to the supranational level, be it regional (such as the EU), or international (such as the WTO).

A major challenge associated with multilayered governance relates to the capacity of elites to 'forum hop'—to periodically move policy processes from one scale or institutional setting to another. Again, this is particularly apparent in relation to trade policy. In a context where some Southern governments and advocacy networks mobilized against the WTO TRIPS agreement in general and global pharmaceutical companies in particular, so-called IP maximalists who wish to see the TRIPS agreement as a floor and not a ceiling have attempted to ensure not only that its provisions are enforced, but also that IP standards ratcheted up, through other institutions such as international legal enforcement agencies, the World Intellectual Property Organization (WIPO) and bilateral and regional trade agreements (Drahos 2007; Sell 2008). In their assessment of the potential and limits of the Trade Justice Network in the United Kingdom, Bendell and Ellersiek (see Chapter 6, this volume), observe that campaigning focused more on UK and WTO trade policy and institutions and did not adjust sufficiently rapidly to the emergence of bilateral and regional trade agreements and the key role of the EU in such negotiations.

Structural Power

The structural power of capital has increased markedly under globalization, particularly through FDI, the expansion of global value chains and 'capital's new country-hopping mobility' (Beck 2005: 6). As examined in the following chapter, technocratic or political opposition to activist demands and proposals relates not only to aspects of institutional culture and dynamics associated with path dependency, but also the responsiveness of certain state institutions to the interests of capital or big business.

Structural Marxism (notably, Nicos Poulantzas) and a 'business as capital' strand of political economy have long pointed out that national states are constrained in their policy choices by the need to avoid 'exit' and to cater to the long-term interests of a capitalist class that requires systemic and societal cohesion and equilibrium.[5]

This means that in addition to instrumental power to influence the policy process or 'agency', business also possesses significant structural power.

Structural power plays a crucial role in shaping the worldviews, priorities and preferences of policymakers who must judge the validity of activist demands and weigh up the merits of different lobbying positions and formal submissions to the policy process by non-state actors and organizations.

The structural power of capital not only conditions the perspectives of policymakers related to such aspects as national competitiveness, private sector development, FDI and so forth, but it can also constrain policy space and disempower the state. According to Beck, this is achieved through two basic strategies: the neoliberalization of the state through, for example, the privatization of state services and reductions in state spending (and taxation) and 'decoupling' law and authority from the state through private and supranational regulation (Beck 2005: 118–119).

Through these processes the nature of the state has been transformed. We are said to live in the era of the intermediary (Kaul 2006), regulatory (Braithwaite 2005; Levi-Faur and Jordana 2005) or competition (Cerny 2000) state. Accordingly, states are less concerned with owning and controlling important areas of production and exchange and more interested in facilitating private sector development through securing property rights, privatization of public services and state-owned enterprises, public–private partnerships, the flexibilization of labour markets and other forms of 'freeing up' markets. Such a regime, however, requires not only certain types of deregulation, but new or different regulatory institutions and approaches (Braithwaite and Drahos 2000).

In this changing regulatory environment, there has been a shift from so-called 'command and control' regulation to modes of regulation that are more business friendly. Of particular importance is the burgeoning arena of private regulation, where companies, business associations and some civil society organizations play an increasingly important role in setting standards, and overseeing the implementation of voluntary initiatives associated with CSR (Cutler, Haufler and Porter 1999; Reed, Utting and Mukherjee-Reed 2012; Rittberger and Nettesheim 2008).

We also see the emergence of the so-called 'audit society' (Power 1997), characterized by the proliferation of monitoring and verifications procedures related to financial, environmental, social, quality and other dimensions of management and organizational performance. As Power (1997: 10) points out: 'By virtue of pushing control further into organizations, relying on the cognitive and economic resources of self-control, markets for internal and external auditing have been created to satisfy the need to connect internal organizational arrangements to public ideals'.

Activism in the UK associated with corporate accountability (see Chapter 9, this volume) comprises a sector of the NGO community that has focused their attention on such forms of engagement with large corporations. As noted earlier, this has important implications for the nature of business–civil society relations and the nature of activist demands and strategies. Here it is also important to distinguish between different phases of the regulatory process. Research on private labour regulation—the involvement of both companies and civil society organizations in setting labour standards and overseeing implementation—reveals that activists often play a key role in initiating the process but in subsequent stages of institutionalization, business-interest NGOs play a prominent role with the effect that civil or private business regulation becomes fragmented among organizations with quite different perspectives and levels of 'regulatory stringency' (Fransen 2009).

At the same time, certain features of contemporary capitalism and neoliberalism are being locked-in via what has been called 'New Constitutionalism' (Gill 1995); the building and consolidation of a legal and regulatory apparatus at national, regional and global levels that facilitates financialization, privatization, FDI, export orientation and 'free trade', and secures the rights of corporations and investors in these fields.

Particularly relevant are the establishment or strengthening of certain institutions at the supranational level—such as the WTO TRIPS agreement and the World Bank's International Council for the Settlement of Investment Disputes (ICSID), which in effect, constitute a trump card that can be used by corporate elites to overrule progressive reforms and regulations at the national level. A key vehicle of New Constitutionalism has been the proliferation of international investment agreements, in particular Bilateral and Regional Investment Treaties, which aim to create an enabling environment for foreign direct investment and reinforce the role of transnational dispute settlement bodies. Contemporary free trade agreements go well beyond conventional issues of market access. They promote so-called 'deep integration' (Mejido Costoya, Utting and Carrión 2010; Sánchez-Ancochea and Shadlen 2008; Woll and Artigas 2007) through which countries must enshrine in law a range of norms and regulations that not only strengthen the rights of investors, but also shift processes of arbitration from national to global institutions such as the World Bank. Such developments clearly impose limits on policy reform associated, for example, with trade justice and corporate accountability.

In relation to the TRIPS agreement discussed earlier, the instrumental power of business meshed in a synergistic way with structural dimensions of power. Not only did decision-making move to the WTO, but as Susan Sell explains: 'changes in the structure of global capitalism animated competitiveness concerns among American policy makers. The private sector IP activists employed both direct and indirect power to ensure their desired outcomes. However, their efficacy must be viewed in a broader context in so far as they crafted their advocacy to respond to competitiveness concerns that preoccupied U.S. government officials' (2003: 28).

Under economic globalization and liberalization, structural power has also altered the relative weight of different ministries in shaping government policy, with ministries of finance, trade and industry often having greater voice. This raises important issues for global justice activism, which can often find allies within the so-called spending ministries dealing, for example, with social affairs or overseas development assistance but finds access to the economics ministries far more difficult. The analysis of the limitations of trade justice activism in France (Chapter 7, this volume) shows that despite having formed a relatively broad-based coalition of actors and institutions, which included the Ministry of Agriculture, key state institutions such as the ministries of trade and finance did not lend their weight to reform efforts.

Structural power has induced deregulatory competition among states in relation to trade, investment and labour markets, notably in developing and transitional economies. The perceived or real threats of 'capital flight' and 'capital strikes' (such as withholding investment from a country), coupled with the belief that FDI is key for development, often shape the policy preferences of politicians and technocrats, and heavily constrain the scope for the types of progressive policy reforms that activists demand (Farnsworth 2010). For example, structural power appears as a determinant of elite resistance to Tobin tax activism in the United Kingdom (see Chapter 11, this volume). In a context where the UK financial services industry had grown phenomenally since the 1980s, government officials were reluctant to engage with any such reform proposals that might rock the boat in the City of London and upset the sacred cow of the British economy.

Structural change has globalized the presence of capital and corporations. FDI and value chains mean that corporations are increasingly visible at global, regional, national, subnational and local levels. As Evans (2008) observes, the challenge for contemporary activism is to organize and mobilize on a scale commensurate with economic systems and institutions of governance that require change. Hence, as emphasized in Chapters 4 and 5 in this volume, the importance of transnational activist networks that span multiple scales (Keck and Sikkink 1998).

Mobilization at the transnational level and the consolidation of transnational activist networks that connect the global and local scales not only potentially strengthen contestation in key international and national decision-making arenas, but also can give disadvantaged groups leverage in local struggles (Evans 2008). The struggles of indigenous peoples affected by mining and oil extraction are particularly relevant in this regard.[6]

Transnational activism can also have structural implications when it serves to embed social rights and standards in legal or standards-based institutions. Ongoing contestation centred on corporate practices and the growing international 'corporate accountability movement' have gradually resulted in the ratcheting-up of standards and procedures that aim to promote CSR (Utting 2005, 2008). There are now many instances where standards designed under voluntary initiatives are internalized in national law and international soft law. Referring to Latin America, Saguier (2012) argues that grass-roots mobilizations and institutionalized complaints procedures associated with the Permanent Peoples' Tribunal, which hears cases involving human rights abuses, are also shaping the international regulatory framework for human rights and corporate accountability.

A key point here is not simply that activism is connecting at multiple scales, but that it is adapting to changes in governance systems which have seen the national stage lose some ground to local, regional and international levels. Adaptation is also apparent in relation to the emergence of a broader portfolio of actions. The earlier discussion of the need for law, public policy, voluntary initiatives and naming and shaming and other sorts of contestation suggests that activism must engage with multiple institutional and political arenas and adopt multiple strategies and tactics.

Discursive Power

Powerful actors and institutions in the field of development have responded to societal concerns and pressures by adapting their discourse, often taking on the language of their critics. The language of international financial institutions and bilateral agencies is imbued with 'buzzwords' and feel-good terms that connote a sense of commitment, action and solidarity that is in tune with both reformist and radical agendas of change (Cornwall and Brock 2006). Increasingly, corporations and business associations are cultivating the discourse of corporate social responsibility and corporate citizenship, and identifying themselves discursively with 'inclusive', 'sustainable' and 'rights-based' development. The increasing discursive power of business has major implications for activism and policy change.

Related to the issue of discursive power is the increasing reliance on 'soft power', through which elites attempt to rule through attraction rather than coercion (Nye 2004). This bears some similarity to Gramsci's concept of hegemony noted earlier. Values, norms, vision and discourse are crucial in this regard. So too are civil society organizations and 'organic intellectuals' through which hegemony is secured.

The new development discourse opens up certain spaces and opportunities for activists to promote reform but also limits the scope for policy change. Regarding the former, elites nationally and internationally often identify with a normative agenda that emphasizes values associated with business ethics and democracy. Neoliberalism is about the promotion of not only market-led development that is unfettered by collective institutions, but also particular institutions that can act as a substitute or tame them, for example, corporate self-regulation and private standards-based initiatives, as well as representative democracy and freedom of the press. Such institutional arrangements open up numerous spaces for civil society actors to organize and mobilize, contest injustices and collaborate with elite interests in reformist projects. In relation to CSR not only do numerous NGOs work with large corporations to improve their social, environmental and human rights performance, but there is also the tendency for voluntary CSR initiatives to be ratcheted up through time, gaining more substance or sometimes evolving into international soft law. The examples of the OECD Guidelines for Multinational Enterprises and sectoral initiatives such as the Forest Stewardship Council and the Ethical Trading Initiative are pertinent in this regard (Reed et al 2012).

The adoption of the language of empowerment, human rights and sustainability by powerful actors and institutions may, of course, mask attempts to co-opt. But it may also reflect advances at the level of discursive struggle. As Sen observes in relation to the changing gender discourse of the World Bank and other agencies, it is important to recognize the capacity of institutions to adopt the language of those seeking change and to hollow out the meaning of progressive terms. But 'if knowledge is power, then changing the terrain of discourse is the first but very important step [in the struggle for change]. It makes it possible to fight the opposition on the ground of one's choosing' (Sen 2006: 39).

Discursive power can be effective in deflating opposition and social and regulatory pressures. It may ultimately have the effect of legitimizing an approach to development that is more ameliorative than transformative, placating opposition and challenges to power structures and ensuring that business regulation involves voluntary as opposed to legalistic approaches (Cornwall and Brock 2006; Guttal 2006; Utting 2006).

Discursive power constrains transformative change in two important respects. First, by 'talking the talk', elites can convey a sense of progressive change when in practice any change remains largely cosmetic. In other words, there is often a large disconnect between discourse and practice, in the sense that little is done to change corporate practices, policies and power relations that underpin maldevelopment and global injustice. Such situations are legion in the field of CSR, reflected in the term 'greenwash'—which appeared as a new entry in the *Concise Oxford Dictionary* in the late 1990s—meaning 'disinformation disseminated by an organization so as to present an environmentally responsible public image'. Corporations often expend far more effort in talking about their environmental or social credentials than in actually improving their performance. Many large corporations developed codes of conduct that remain at the level of very general principles, and they issued sustainability reports that were short on hard data by which to measure concrete changes in corporate social and environmental performance.

Non-compliance with basic reporting procedures forced the world's largest CSR initiative, the United Nations Global Compact, to delist many of the companies that had formally agreed to adhere to the Compact's ten principles. These companies were gaining reputational mileage through their association with the initiative but were not disclosing progress towards realizing the principles. The cosmetic dimensions of discursive power are particularly apparent during early phases of CSR, as occurred in the UK in the 1990s (Murphy and Bendell 2002) and more recently in France (Capron 2009).

Second, through discursive power elites have the ability to frame agendas and 'common sense', to determine what are legitimate issues of contention and negotiation, and what remains as 'blind spots' and off-limits (Ocampo 2006). Elites may respond to subaltern concerns and demands, but in a way that sets limits on the scope for policy change. They attempt to mould or 'frame' issues in ways that are compatible with their worldview and institutional mandates and cultures (Bøas and McNeill 2004). This means that certain issues and principles are not up for discussion. In the mainstream CSR agenda, for example, it is legitimate to focus on improvements in environmental management systems, eco-efficiency, occupational health and safety and company–community relations. Far less attention, if any, is paid to issues such as executive pay, corporate taxation levels, tax avoidance, lobbying practices, subcontracting beyond first-tier suppliers, consumption patterns and absolute levels of use of non-renewable resources and pollutants. Similarly, in the field of development policy associated with poverty reduction, attention is often focused on expanding social policy, channelling aid to depressed areas, market access and integrating small producers in value chains, whilst the macro-economic policy framework and processes that characterize neoliberalism, i.e. export-orientation, foreign direct investment (FDI), financialization and fiscal discipline largely remain off-limits.[7]

IMPLICATIONS FOR GLOBAL JUSTICE ACTIVISM

The analysis in this chapter suggests that any assessment of civil society influence on policy must consider key aspects of 'structures of political opportunities' that concern (a) what powerful actors and institutions are doing to resist, accommodate, shape or, indeed, lead processes of policy and institutional reform; and (b) how effectively civil society actors are engaging with rapidly evolving modes of governance.

Through the lens of the structural, instrumental and discursive dimensions of power, it is clear that business elites have a broad portfolio of means by which to influence both policy processes and the nature of the activist–policy nexus. The preceding analysis reveals a complex mix of constraints and opportunities for activists and advocacy associated with the different dimensions of business power and changes in the dynamics of policy-making and regulation.

As regards constraints, we have seen how the structural power of finance capital stifled consideration of the Tobin tax in UK policy circles. Instrumental power, associated, for example, with lobbying, providing technical knowledge, revolving doors and forum-hopping has seen business interests assume prominent roles in processes associated with the negotiation of free trade, investment and intellectual property agreements. Civil society advocacy has been more effective in throwing an occasional spanner in the works to delay or stop such policy processes, or to work on the outside promoting, for example, 'fair trade' alternatives, rather than effectively negotiating the content of such agreements.

Discursive power was seen to be a key factor in shaping a business-friendly CSR agenda that often does more to legitimize big business than fundamentally improve social, environmental and human rights performance of large corporations. Civil society campaigns and other social pressures have been instrumental in the fields of private regulation related to environmental, labour and human rights issues, notably in framing agendas and actually designing standards.

In relation to the hegemonic dimension of power, we have also seen how elite interests may support policy and institutional change associated with activist demands. In the field of corporate accountability, however, it is clear that discursive shifts often run well ahead of concrete changes in corporate practices, 'soft' regulation sometimes crowds out 'hard' regulation, and convenient blind spots mean that sensitive issues remain off-limits. Furthermore, business interests have proven extremely adept at controlling processes associated with implementation and enforcement of new standards.

Partnerships and coalitions between some sectors of business and NGOs can have a divide and rule effect. Big business interests are versed in the art of not only state capture, but also, increasingly, civil society capture. This is achieved through setting up business-oriented NGOs and engaging proactively with civil society organizations through stakeholder dialogues, partnerships and consultancies. The increasing proximity of companies to NGOs can have the effect of distancing these 'collaborative' NGOs ideologically and strategically from social movements and other public-interest NGOs, including trade unions.

As regards opportunities for reform, numerous possibilities have been identified. Structural power has certain limits and can generate potential allies for progressive institutional change. As seen earlier in the cases of trade liberalization and intellectual property rights, pro-business change eventually led to a backlash and acted as a catalyst for social mobilization. Structural changes associated with the organization of economic activity under globalization and liberalization have heightened risk, complexity and transaction costs, and they cultivated a constituency of business interests that stand to gain from certain standard-based initiatives related to labour, environment and human rights. Such contexts can be conducive to building coalitions involving business and civil society organizations.

Changes in governance and policy-making associated with dialogue, consultation, knowledge networks and epistemic communities have clearly opened up spaces for accessing policymakers and senior management—through both formal and informal channels. Hegemony, like co-optation, is a two-way street. It implies limits on the scope for progressive policy change but also creates spaces for activists and advocacy to influence agendas and reform processes. Indeed, hegemony implies the possibility of counter-hegemonic struggle through which subaltern groups mobilize in favour of alternative agendas of change.

This complexity cautions against broad generalizations and romanticized assessments of the potential for transformative change associated with global justice activism. Furthermore, changing contexts and patterns of power and governance pose fundamental challenges for activists in terms of the need for multi-scalar activism and broad-based coalitions, strengthening links between NGOs and both social movements and progressive political parties. Such developments also suggest the need for different and varied forms of mobilization and interaction both within civil society itself and with elite and mainstream policy institutions, depending on issue area and institutional context. Each episode of activism and intended policy reform may involve quite different dynamics and policy impacts. Indeed, this would seem to be confirmed by the varied outcomes, noted in Chapter 13 of this volume, related to the issue areas considered in this volume.

The preceding analysis confirms what scholarship on social movements has often observed (della Porta and Diani 2006: 232); namely, that civil society global justice advocacy has often had more success in framing public and policy agendas than in actually transforming policy, if policy is understood as a purposeful course of action. Such possibilities suggest that as much, if not more, effort should be put into awareness-raising about the root causes of global injustice, blind spots within mainstream development and CSR agendas and alternative policy approaches and meanings of development, than efforts to tweak public or corporate policy. As others have pointed out, this suggests that advocacy NGOs should attach a high priority to critical thinking and the search for alternatives, and connect far more strategically and organically with social movements (Bebbington, Hickey and Mitlin 2008).

In contexts where the scope for progressive institutional and policy change is highly constrained, there would seem to be a premium on veto power; that is, blocking certain types of policy and legislative reform. The chronic imbalances in power relations and weak accountability structures noted earlier also point to the crucial role of civil society organizations and networks in scrutinizing the powerful through a variety of watch-dog activities, complaints procedures and critical research.

The rise of both the 'good governance' agenda and the service delivery orientation of NGOs have propagated the notion that activists should do less criticizing, be less confrontational and more pragmatic and cooperative. The preceding analysis suggests, however, that such forms of 'collaborative governance' need to be assessed critically. On the one hand, stakeholder dialogue, social learning, partnerships and other forms of collaboration can facilitate the task of moving activist competencies beyond agenda-setting and advancing with respect to other aspects of policy change, such as getting an issue into policy and law, or getting policy and law actually implemented (Schumaker 1975). On the other hand, skewed power relations, the question of who gets invited to the table and the rules of the game within such arrangements are often loaded against transformative change. Such political and institutional dimensions also run the risk of crowding out various forms of contentious politics, regulation, bargaining and negotiation that remain essential in the struggle for global justice.

NOTES

1. The terms *progressive* and *transformative* are used in this chapter to refer to changes in the policies of both states and corporations that favour subaltern groups, through practices associated with social and environmental protection, redistribution and the extension or realization of rights.
2. See, for example, Esping-Andersen (1990); Hall and Soskice (2001); Huber (2002); Scherer and Palazzo (2011).
3. For relevant analysis related to the FTAA, see Mejido Costoya, Utting and Carrión (2010); Newell and Tussie (2006); Saguier (2007). For an analysis of the MAI, see Picciotto and Mayne (1999).
4. This process culminated with the adoption by the UN Human Rights Council in 2011 of the 'Protect, Respect and Remedy Framework' for business and human rights.
5. See, for example, Hirschman (1978); Maxfield and Schneider (1997); Poulantzas (1973); van den Berg and Janoski (2005).
6. See, for example, Murphy and Bendell (2002); Rodríguez-Garavito and Arenas (2005).
7. In the aftermath of the global financial crisis there are some signs of a revival of Keynesian approaches that have challenged another pillar of neoliberal orthodoxy, namely, the rolling back of the state and constraints on 'policy and fiscal space'. There are considerable doubts, however, whether this is anything more than a short-term corrective measure (Jessop 2009).

BIBLIOGRAPHY

Bebbington, Anthony J., Hickey, Samuel, and Mitlin, Diana C. (eds) (2008). *Can NGOs Make a Difference? The Challenge of Development Alternatives*, London: Zed Books.

Beck, Ulrich. (2005). *Power in the Global Age: A New Global Political Economy*, Malden, MA: Blackwell Publishing.

Bendell, Jem, and Ellersiek, Anne. (2009). *Noble Networks? Advocacy for Global Justice and the 'Network Effect'*. Programme on Civil Society and Social Movements, Paper No. 31, UNRISD, Geneva.

Bøas, Morten, and McNeill, Desmond. (2004). *Global Institutions and Development: Framing the World?* London: Routledge.

Braithwaite, John. (2005). *Neoliberalism or Regulatory Capitalism*. Occasional Paper No. 5, Regulatory Institutions Network, Australian National University, Canberra.

Braithwaite, John, and Drahos, Peter. (2000). *Global Business Regulation*, Cambridge: Cambridge University Press.

Brock, Karen, Cornwall, Andrea, and Gaventa, John. (2001). *Power, Knowledge and Political Spaces in the Framing of Poverty Policy*. IDS Working Paper No. 143, Institute of Development Studies, Brighton.

Bull, Benedicte. (2010). 'Business Participation in Free Trade Negotiations in Chile: Impacts on Environmental and Labour Regulation', in J.C. Marques and P. Utting (eds), *Business, Politics and Public Policy: Implications for Inclusive Development*, Basingstoke: Palgrave Macmillan/UNRISD.

Capron, Micheal. (2009). *De la Franceafrique à la Responsabilité Sociale des Entreprises: Les Dynamiques Entre les Firmes, l'Etat et les Mouvements Sociaux en France.* Programme on Markets, Business and Regulation, Paper No. 6, UNRISD, Geneva.

Carrión, Gloria. (2009). *Trade, Regionalism and the Politics of Policy Making in Nicaragua.* Programme on Markets, Business and Regulation, Paper No. 5, UNRISD, Geneva.

Cerny, Phil. (2000). 'Political Globalization and the Competition State', in R. Stubbs and G. Underhill (eds), *Political Economy of the Changing Global Order*, Oxford: Oxford University Press.

Cornwall, Andrea. (2004). 'New Democratic Spaces? The Politics and Dynamics of Institutionalised Participation', *IDS Bulletin*, 35 (2): 1–10.

Cornwall, Andrea, and Brock, Karen. (2006). 'The New Buzzwords', in P. Utting (ed), *Reclaiming Development Agendas: Knowledge, Power and International Policy Making*, Basingstoke: UNRISD/Palgrave Macmillan.

Cutler, Claire, Haufler, V., and Porter, Tony. (eds) (1999) *Private Authority and International Affairs*, Albany: State University of New York.

della Porta, Donatella, and Mario Diani. (2006). *Social Movements: An Introduction*, 2nd ed., Oxford: Blackwell Publishing.

de Sousa Santos, Bonaventura, and Rodríguez-Garavito, Cesar A. (2005). 'Law, Politics, and the Subaltern in Counter-Hegemonic Globalization', in Bonaventura de Sousa Santos and Cesar A. Rodríguez-Garavito (eds), *Law and Globalization from Below: Towards a Cosmopolitan Legality*, Cambridge: Cambridge University Press.

Drahos, Peter. (2007). 'Four Lessons for Developing Countries from the Trade Negotiations over Access to Medicines', *Liverpool Law Review*, 28:11–39.

Escobar, Arturo. (1995). *Encountering Development: The Making and Unmaking of the Third-World*, Princeton, NJ: Princeton University Press.

Esping-Andersen, Gosta. (1990). *Three Worlds of Welfare Capitalism*, Cambridge: Polity Press.

Evans, Peter. (2008) 'Is an Alternative Globalization Possible?', *Politics & Society*, 36 (2): 271–305.

Farnsworth, Kevin. (2010). 'Business Power, Social Policy Preferences and Development', in J.C. Marques and P. Utting (eds), *Business, Politics and Public Policy*, Basingstoke: Palgrave Macmillan/UNRISD.

Fransen, Luc. (2009). *Minding Their Own Business? Firms and Activists in the Making of Private Labour Regulation*, PhD thesis, University of Amsterdam.

Freeman, Edward R. (1984). *Strategic Management: A Stakeholder Approach*, Boston: Pitman.

Fuchs, Doris A. (2005). *Understanding Business Power in Global Governance*, Krakow: Nomos.

Giddens, Anthony. (1984). *The Constitution of Society: Outline of the Theory of Structuration*, Cambridge: Polity Press.

Gill, Stephen. (1995). 'Globalization, Market Civilization, and Disciplinary Neoliberalism', *Millennium: Journal of International Studies*, 24 (3): 399–423.

———. (2003) *Power and Resistance in the New World Order*, New York: Palgrave Macmillan.

Gunder, Frank A. (1967). *Capitalism and Underdevelopment in Latin America: Historical Studies of Chile and Brazil*, New York: Monthly Review Press.

Guttal, Shalmali. (2006). 'Challenging the Knowledge Business', in P. Utting (ed), *Reclaiming Development Agendas: Knowledge, Power and International Policy Making*, Basingstoke: Palgrave Macmillan/UNRISD.

Haas, Peter M. . (1989). 'Do Regimes Matter? Epistemic Communities and Mediterranean Pollution Control', *International Organization*, 43 (3): 377–403.

Hall, Peter A., and Soskice, David. (eds) (2001). *Varieties of Capitalism: The Institutional Foundations of Comparative Advantage*, Oxford: Oxford University Press.

Heap, Simon. (2000). *NGOs Engaging with Business: A World of Difference and a Difference to the World*, Oxford: INTRAC.

Held, David. (1995). *Democracy and the Global Order: From the Modern State to Cosmopolitan Governance*, Stanford, CA: Polity Press and Stanford University Press.

Hirschman, Albert. (1978). 'Exit, Voice and the State', *World Politics*, 31 (1): 191–199.

Huber, Evelyne. (ed) (2002). *Models of Capitalism: Lessons for Latin America*, University Park: Pennsylvania State University Press.

Jessop, Bob. (2009). *Narratives of Crisis and Crisis Response: Perspectives from North and South.* Paper presented at the UNRISD Conference on Social and Political Dimensions of the Global Crisis: Implications for Developing Countries, Geneva: UNRISD, 12–13 November.

Jessop, Bob, and Sum, Ngai-Lim. (2006). *Beyond the Regulation Approach: Putting Capitalist Economies in Their Place*, Cheltenham: Edward Elgar.

Kaul, Inge. (2006). 'Blending External and Domestic Policy Demands: The Rise of the Intermediary State', in I. Kaul and P. Conceição (eds), *The New Public Finance: Responding to Global Challenges*, Oxford: Oxford University Press.

Keck, Margaret, and Sikkink, Kathryn. (1998). *Activists beyond Borders*, Ithaca, NY: Cornell University Press.

Keohane, Robert. (2002). *Power and Governance in a Partially Globalized World*, London: Routledge.

Levi-Faur, David, and Jordana, Jacint. (2005). 'Regulatory Capitalism: Policy Irritants and Convergent Divergence', *Annals of the American Academy of Political and Social Science* 598: 191–197.

MacGillivray, A., P. Raynard and S. Zadek. (2005). *Towards Responsible Lobbying: Leadership and Public Policy*, London: AccountAbility.

Mattli, Walter, and N. Woods, Ngaire. (2009). *The Politics of Global Regulation*, Princeton, NJ: Princeton University Press.

Maxfield, Sylvia, and Schneider, Ben Ross. (eds) (1997). *Business and the State in Developing Countries*, Ithaca, NY: Cornell University Press.

Mejido Costoya, Manuel, Utting, Peter, and Carrión, Gloria. (2010). *The Changing Coordinates of Trade and Power in Latin America.* Programme on Markets, Business and Regulation, Paper No.7, UNRISD, Geneva.

Mouffe, Chantal. (2005). *On the Political: Thinking in Action*, Abingdon: Routledge.

Murphy, David F., and Bendell, Jem. (2002). 'New Partnerships for Sustainable Development', in P. Utting (ed), *The Greening of Business in Developing Countries*, London: Zed Books.

Newell, Peter, and Tussie, Diana. (2006). *Civil Society Participation in Trade Policy-Making in Latin America: Reflections and Lessons.* IDS Working Paper No. 267, Institute of Development Studies, Brighton.

Nye, Joseph Samuel. (2004). 'Soft Power and American Foreign Policy', *Political Science Quarterly*, 1 (19): 255–270.

———. (2005). *Soft Power: The Means to Success in World Politics*, New York: Public Affairs.

Ocampo, Jose Antonio. (2006). 'Foreword: Some Reflections on the Links between Social Knowledge and Policy', in P. Utting (ed), *Reclaiming Development Agendas: Knowledge, Power and International Policy Making*, Basingstoke: Palgrave Macmillan/UNRISD.

Picciotto, Sol, and Mayne, Ruth. (1999). *Regulating International Business: Beyond Liberalization*, Basingstoke: Macmillan Press.

Poulantzas, Nicos. (1973). *Classes in Contemporary Capitalism*, New York: New Left Books.

Power, Michael. (1997). *The Audit Society: Rituals of Verification*, Oxford: Oxford University Press.

Radice, Hugo. (ed) (1975). *International Firms and Modern Imperialism*, Harmondsworth: Penguin Books.

Reed, Darryl, Utting, Peter and Ananya Mukherjee-Reed (eds) (2012). *Business Regulation and Non-State Actors: Whose Standards? Whose Development?*, London: Routledge.

Rodríguez-Garavito, Cesar A., and Arenas Luis Carlos. (2005). 'Indigenous Rights, Transnational Activism, and Legal Mobilization: The Struggle of the U'wa People in Colombia', in C.A. Rodríguez-Garavito and B. Santos (eds), *Law and Globalization from Below: Toward a Cosmopolitan Legality*, Cambridge: Cambridge University Press.

Rittberger, Volker, and Nettesheim, Martin. (2008). *Authority in the Global Political Economy*, Basingstoke: Palgrave Macmillan.

Rostow, Walt Whitman. (1960). *The Stages of Economic Growth: A Non-Communist Manifesto*, Cambridge: Cambridge University Press.

Ruggie, John Gerard. (1982). 'International Regimes, Transactions, and Change: Embedded Liberalism in the Postwar Economic Order', *International Organization*, 36 (2): 379–415.

———. (2003). 'Taking Embedded Liberalism Global: The Corporate Connection', in D. Held and M. Koenig-Archibugi (eds), *Taming Globalization: Frontiers of Governance*, Cambridge: Polity Press.

Saguier, Marcelo. (2007). 'The Hemispheric Social Alliance and the Free Trade Area of the Americas Process: The Challenges and Opportunities of Transnational Coalitions against Neo-Liberalism', *Globalizations*, 4 (2): 669–689.

———. (2012). 'Peoples' tribunals in Latin America', in D. Reed, P. Utting and A. Mukherjee-Reed (eds), *Business Regulation and Non-State Actors: Whose Standards? Whose Development?*, London: Routledge.

Sánchez-Ancochea, Diego, and Shadlen, Ken. (2008). *Responding to Globalization: The Political Economy of Hemispheric Integration in the Americas*, Basingstoke: Palgrave Macmillan.

Scherer, Andreas, and Palazzo, Guido G. (2011). 'The New Political Role of Business in a Globalized World: A Review of a New Perspective on CSR and its Implications for the Firm, Governance, and Democracy', *Journal of Management Studies*, 48 (4): 899–931.

Schumaker, Paul D. (1975). 'Policy Responsiveness to Protest-Group Demands', *Journal of Politics*, 37 (2): 488–521.

Sell, Susan K. (2003). *Private Power, Public Law: The Globalization of Intellectual Property Rights*, Cambridge: Cambridge University Press.

———. (2008). *The Global IP upward Ratchet, Anti-Counterfeiting and Piracy Enforcement Efforts: The State of Play.* IQsensato Occasional Paper, No. 1, The Open Society Institute, Geneva.

Sen, Gita. (2006.) 'The Quest for Gender Equality', in Peter Utting (ed), *Reclaiming Development Agendas: Knowledge, Power and International Policy Making*, Basingstoke: Palgrave Macmillan.

Shadlen, Kenneth C. (2008). 'Globalization, Power and Economic Integration: The Political Economy of Regional and Bilateral Trade Agreements in the Americas', *Journal of Development Studies*, 44 (1): 1–20.

Slob, Bart, and Weyzig, Francis. (2010). 'Corporate Lobbying and Corporate Social Responsibility: Aligning Contradictory Agendas', in J.C. Marques and Peter Utting (eds), *Business, Politics and Public Policy: Implications for Inclusive Development*, Basingstoke: Palgrave Macmillan/UNRISD.

SustainAbility and WWW-UK. (2005). *Influencing Power: Reviewing the Conduct and Content of Corporate Lobbying*, London: SustainAbility/WWF-UK.

Tarrow, Sidney. (1994). *Power in Movement: Collective Action, Social Movements and Politics*, Cambridge: Cambridge University Press.

———. (2006). 'Confessions of a Recovering Structuralist', *European Political Science*, 5 (7): 7–20.

Tilly, Charles. (1978). *From Mobilization to Revolution*, Reading, MA: Addison-Wesley.

United Nations General Assembly. (2004). *We the Peoples: Civil Society, the United Nations and Global Governance*. Report of the Panel of Eminent Persons United Nations-Civil Society Relations, A/58/817. New York: United Nations.

United Nations Research Institute for Social Development. (2000). *Visible Hands: Taking Responsibility for Social Development*, Geneva: UNRISD.

Utting, Peter. (2002). 'Regulating Business via Multistakeholder Initiatives', in NGLS/UNRISD (ed), *Voluntary Approaches to Corporate Responsibility: Readings and a Resource Guide*, Geneva: NGLS/UNRISD.

———. (2005). *Rethinking Business Regulation from Self-Regulation to Social Control*, Geneva: UNRISD.

———. (ed) (2006) *Reclaiming Development Agendas: Knowledge, Power and International Policy Making*, Basingstoke: UNRISD/Palgrave Macmillan.

———. (2008). 'The Struggle for Corporate Accountability', *Development and Change*, 39 (6): 959–975.

Utting, Peter, and Zammit, A. (2006). *Beyond Pragmatism: Appraising UN-Business Partnerships*, Geneva: UNRISD.

Van Alstine, James. (2010). 'Spaces of Contestation: The Governance of Industry's Environmental Performance in Durban, South Africa', in J.C. Marques and P. Utting (eds), *Corporate Social Responsibility and Regulatory Governance*, Basingstoke: Palgrave Macmillan/UNRISD.

Van den Berg, Axel, and Thomas Janoski. (2005). 'Conflict Theories in Political Sociology', in Thomas Janoski, Robert Alford, Alexander Hicks, and Mildred Schwartz (eds), *The Handbook of Political Sociology: States, Civil Societies, and Globalization*, Cambridge: Cambridge University Press.

Vander Stichele, Myriam, Bizzarri, Kim, and Plank, Leonard. (2006). *Corporate Power over EU Trade Policy: Good for Business, Bad for the World*, Brussels: Seattle to Brussels Network.

Woll, Cornelia, and Artigas, Alvaro. (2007). 'When Trade Liberalization Turns into Regulatory Reform: The Impact on Business-government Relations in International Trade Politics', *Regulation & Governance*, 1 (2): 121–138.

2 National Policy Regimes
Implications for the Activism–Policy Nexus

Daniela Barrier

INTRODUCTION

Contemporary social movements mobilizing on issues of global justice have been described by various authors as Global Justice Movements (GJMs). These movements are seen to share certain characteristics such as their transnational scope, multiple affiliations, global identity and concerns and a common interpretation of global social injustice which identifies neoliberalism as the common 'enemy'.[1] But far from being a transnational, homogenous movement, GJMs originate from a variety of activist traditions and affiliations, and are inserted in specific national contexts which result in variations of agendas, repertoires of actions and ability to influence policy-making.

Whereas these differing national contexts are recognized in social movement theory as having an effect on activism, 'context' has remained a concept open to interpretation. Authors often fail to disaggregate and differentiate the roles of state institutions and social actors, as well as how processes of policy making and social pacts vary in different countries. Limited attention has also been paid to understanding the implications of history and path dependence[2] for activism and policy influence. In 1986, Kitschelt contributed to the debate with a groundbreaking comparative study where he analysed and compared different political systems according to their degree of receptiveness and openness to the demands of social movements, falling short, however, in explaining how institutions have an impact on activism. In 1989, Tarrow redefined the concept of political opportunities structure to include as variables the degree of openness of a given political system, elite interests and government administration to social movements, and the degree of stability of political alliances. Ten years later, Giugni (1996) took a step further towards analysing the nexus between activism and institutions when he identified the mirror effect between the structures of movement organizations and those of the state, up against whom these movements stood.

In the same year however, Gamson and Meyer (1996) argued that the concept of political opportunity structure was in danger of becoming a sponge that absorbed virtually all aspects of the environment of social movements—political institutions and culture, all sorts of crises, political alliances, changes in government policy, etc. In *Regimes and Repertoires*, Charles Tilly (2006), a historian and sociologist, acknowledged the need to look at the bigger picture from a historical perspective, rather than continuing to focus on actor-centred research. In this seminal work, he looks into how political regimes affect the means by which people protest—their repertoires of contention. In order to do that, Tilly overlaps two maps, one of regimes and one of repertoires, in which the definition of regimes remains highly political and includes two main points: variations in governmental capacity and degree of democracy. The analysis of how government institutions actually affect activism, however, remains marginal. In their comparative study, Joachim and Locher (2009) take a step further into investigating why, how and to what degree institutions shape, determine, influence or limit the agency of non-governmental organizations (NGOs). They find that the patterns of engagement in the United Nations (UN) and the European Union (EU) are more alike than different due to the fact that both regulate and constrain access to their institutions in a similar way, concluding that further research towards how 'agency is affected by structure' is needed.

This chapter is concerned with investigating further how historically built government institutions affect activism and policy reforms. Examining the case of France and the United Kingdom (UK), the analysis draws on historical institutionalism and, in particular, the welfare regime approach[3] as well as other literature concerned with the role of ideas and discourse in shaping institutions and legitimating policy change.[4] By focusing on class relations, interest articulation and class conflicts, the welfare regime literature provides a framework, complementary to social movement theory, for better understanding the relationship between government institutions and activism over time. The chapter considers how social movements and, in particular, development NGOs and trade unions, interact with development policy institutions from the colonial past to the present day.[5]

First I identify key differences in each country at the broader level of policy regimes. The next section looks in more detail into the evolution of development institutions in the UK and France, as well as each country's position within the EU's development and cooperation programme. The final section of the chapter describes the evolution of resources, agendas and policy influence of social movement organizations in both countries.

VARIATIONS IN WELFARE REGIMES

Britain and France are two countries with very similar background conditions. Neighbouring European countries with a parallel colonial past, they have similar-size economies, similar weight and ambitions in the international arena and a similar set of core institutions. In 2005 both spent about eleven billion dollars in Overseas Development Assistance (ODA) (including debt relief) and committed to allocate 0.7 per cent of their respective GNIs in ODA before 2015. Over the past decades, both countries have undergone significant economic reforms, associated with monetarist macro-economic policies, deregulation, privatization, labour market flexibility, tightening social spending and subscribing to a number of EU directives favouring economic liberalization. Such changes are seen to be reactions to accelerating processes of global economic integration. Yet, the pace and extent to which both countries have adopted these changes vary widely, as do the political narratives adopted to justify such reforms. In France, as opposed to the UK, globalization and market liberalization are seen by the majority of citizens more as a threat than an opportunity,[6] and the anti-globalization agenda is not only defended by civil society organizations (Fougier 2002a), but claimed by both right- and left-wing parties.[7] Equally diverse are the role and voice of civil society actors in each country's governance structure, and their respective stands regarding development issues.

Esping-Andersen (1990) provides a framework capable of explaining such differences. He describes Britain as a *liberal* or *spectator* state and France as a *dirigiste* or *interventionist* state. Whereas in Britain the state largely limits its role to arbitrating among economic actors and leaves the administration of the rules to self-governing bodies, in France it is more involved in economic activities through planning, industrial policy and state-owned enterprises. At the level of social pacts, the UK is described as a voluntaristic country in which the state is relatively absent from direct intervention in negotiations, privileging voluntary collective bargaining as a method of labour regulation. In France, trade unions are fragmented, highly ideological and only loosely connected to political parties. The main tripartite bodies through which employer and trade union confederations can hope to influence government policy-making are described as purely consultative.[8] Furthermore, the ability to secure cooperation within a highly unequal state–civil society partnership is seen to derive from the existence of a ruling elite with connections and high mobility between the private and public sectors, partly due to education in the French elite academic institutions, the *grandes écoles*. In the UK, the relationship among civil society, business and government has traditionally favoured governance practices involving dialogue amongst these groups. Some constitute a well-established 'policy community', enjoying insider status in policy-making and carrying out certain tasks and services, thus saving governments the expense of providing them (Jordan and Richardson 1987). These complex subtleties of state-business-civil society configurations in France and the UK, as well as the role played by history in influencing them, constitute the focus of this study for understanding the contemporary development of the policy–activism nexus.

These diverging political narratives and institutional legacies influence each country's contemporary relations with the Global South, as manifested through development aid, debt relief, international taxation, trade, finance and the role of transnational corporations (TNCs). In relation to corporate social responsibility (CSR), for example, quite different approaches have been adopted in France and the UK, with NGOs and NGO–business partnerships, promoting voluntary CSR initiatives, being far more common in the UK (see Chapters 3 and 6, this volume). In France, both government and unions have been more active, promoting alternative approaches which have involved both legal reporting requirements and more traditional collective bargaining (Beaujolin and Capron 2005).

Differences in approach are also apparent with regard to the issue of international taxation. The demands of Attac (Association for the Taxation of Financial Transactions and Aid to Citizens) have had more echoes in France than in the UK (see Chapters 11 and 12, this volume), partly because the concept of promoting international redistribution through the tax system resonates with French universalism and the interventionist model.[9]

The French government has actively supported the publicly run International Solidarity Levy on Airline Tickets designed to finance health and immunization programmes in developing countries via UNITAID, a public drug purchasing facility. This contrasts with the existing British IFFIC (International Finance Facility for Immunisation Company), which is a UK-registered charity that uses long-term pledges from donor governments to mobilize funds for the Global Alliance for Vaccines and Immunization (GAVI), a public–private partnership, by selling 'vaccine bonds' on the capital markets. At the level of international liberalization of finance, policy and political reactions in France and the UK have also varied significantly. Whereas France was the first country to pull out of the Organisation for Economic Co-operation and Development's (OECD) Multilateral Agreement on Investment (MAI) in 1998, partly in response to pressure from civil society groups (as well as from businesses and both the executive and legislative branches),[10] in the UK, the financial services industry and related elites have tremendous economic, political and discursive clout and favour deregulation (see Strange 1986).

Differences in the agendas of British and French civil society organizations are also visible in areas such as development aid and international trade policies. Large British NGOs, partly financed by the state, focus on pressuring for more aid and improved use of aid. With far lower levels of state financing, French civil society organizations (CSOs) tend to pressure for the channelling of a larger share of development aid via CSOs. When it comes to trade policies, and in particular agriculture, a wide consensus exists around the *mythe d'une exception agricole*, a protectionist approach faithful to historical protectionist trade relations with former colonies and the notion of policy space for developing countries (see Chapter 7, this volume). In the UK, on the other hand, where the importance of agriculture to the economy has seen a long-term decline since the nineteenth century, the state has pursued an agricultural trade liberalization agenda—favouring market access and lower subsidies—supported by proactive development NGOs whose position is seen to be aligned with that of developing countries dependent on agricultural exports.

DEVELOPMENT INSTITUTIONS AND POLICY

In historical institutionalism, institutions are seen to be at the origin of distinct political opportunity structures (Pierson 2000) as they influence the ability of non-state actors to mobilize members, structure collective bargaining and influence the legislative process within which they operate. In *dirigiste* France, for instance, a recent reform gave yet more weight to the Foreign Ministry, placing cooperation at the heart of state diplomacy (Delaye 2003). In contrast, in the UK, the Labour government of Tony Blair elevated the development portfolio to a highly influential and outspoken ministry, Department for International Development (DFID), permeable to the ideas of specialists and established NGOs. These distinct institutional trajectories have also reflected the policy choices related to either country's support of the European Commission's development programmes. Furthermore, these distinct contemporary institutional design and policy choices originate from the distinct colonial administration models chosen by Britain and France. Different colonial models would lead to different approaches with regards to decolonization, and subsequently, to different development institutions and policies.

British and French Colonial and Decolonization Models[11]

Born as the science of colonial administration concerned with the methods of governance by colonial administrators, 'development' was taught in France and the UK in the early 1900s to an audience of candidates for posts in the colonial administration. France and the UK were associated with two distinct colonial administration models: the French 'assimilation' model, closely associated with a centralized ruling structure and with universal values, and the British 'indirect ruling' model, which was a legitimacy-based system closer to individualistic values (Crowder 1964). Although these models began to be questioned by scholars in both countries during the 1960s,[12] and did not always correspond to the reality on the ground, they resonated with the respective cultural view of the world held by the English and the French public. On the one hand, the indirect rule concept (associated with 'divide and rule') reflected the individualist and liberal beliefs of the British people. It also reflected the more 'advanced' stage of British capitalism, which was influenced early on by the laissez-faire economic liberalism of Adam Smith and featured the construction of an 'informal empire' underpinned by free trade. On the other hand, the assimilation model is associated with

Cartesianism and the Universalist values of eighteenth-century France, as well as with an economic model based on a strong military-politico-financial alliance, and sustained by a *mission civilisatrice*, which is at the origins of the contemporary politics of *francophonie.*

In the UK, a public debate soon arose regarding the contradictions between economic interests and the actual needs of recipient countries (Hayter 1966). In France, on the other hand, national economic interests were perceived by the public and policy makers as both parallel and integral to the promotion of French culture and values (Hayter 1966). In other words, French aid—or French transfers of financial resources (because 'aid' to developing countries was not a concept in France before the 1960s)—was not designed to achieve the recipient's self-sufficiency, but rather their integration with France. As a result of these opposing views, British governments tended to disengage and promote trade, whereas French governments increased expenditures in their overseas territories considerably.

The relationship between the state and business in French and British colonies also varied. Both governments helped business in the early days of colonization by granting monopolies, or by publicly financing private investments abroad via export credit agencies. British businesses, of which the most prominent example remains the East India Company, were granted ruling responsibilities. In the French case, however, the task of policy-making remained in the hands of the French state throughout despite strong—and some argue opaque—connections between the state and the business world.[13] Such relations have implications for policy and corporate behaviour even today. In their study of the politics of corporate social responsibility (CSR) in the oil industry, Utting and Ives suggest that the contemporary uneven trajectory of CSR amongst the biggest oil multinationals is partly explained by the 'historical legacies that shape corporate policy and practice' (Utting and Ives 2006: 25).

Before the 1930s, French and British colonies were not encouraged to look to the metropolitan government for financial aid, and there were no programmes for colonial development. France's Governor General of French Indochina Albert Sarraut (1912–1919), who was later prime minister, became a well-known advocate for a national policy to promote social and economic development in the colonies. His initiative, however, took two decades to be adopted. In the UK, assistance to the colonies increased after 1929, driven less by altruism and more by the need to reduce unemployment in the UK by promoting commerce with, or industry in, the UK, in the context of the financial crash of that same year.

The First Development Institutions

With the breakup of the British and French empires after WWII and the economic, political and social crisis that followed within most ex-colonies, assistance to the former colonies became an issue discussed at international forums. At the same time, Cold War imperatives reinforced the political and ideological determinants of North–South relations. In 1961, in an attempt to adapt its institutions to this 'new reality of development', the British Conservative government established the Department for Technical Cooperation (DTC). Many staff (and consequently the ideas and the expertise) from the Colonial Office were transferred to the DTC. Throughout the 1960s and 1970s successive governments often changed the lead institution with responsibility for ODA, in name, in terms of its political weight and administrative capacity and in the level of intimacy with British business interests (with more or less emphasis on tied aid). Whereas Labour governments would generally attempt to strengthen the institution's role and independence (from the Foreign Office), Conservative governments tended to downsize. A significant shift from project-tied aid was proposed by Labour in the mid-1970s. More bilateral aid was to go to the poorest countries. The important role of multilateral organizations was also given greater recognition. Labour, however, could not prevent aid from being driven by business objectives. Under pressure from the business community and the Department of Trade and Industry, the government approved the 1977 Aid and Trade Provision, which linked aid to non-concessionary export credits, and both to the procurement of British goods and services.

Whereas in the UK the orientation of development institutions and policy has largely swung between left and right agendas, in France an autonomous and permanent development policy transcended the traditional political cleavages (Martin 1995) in accordance with a 'Gaullist-socialist consensus'. This policy was inherited from colonial years and maintained throughout the Fifth Republic.[14] In the 1960s, policy under Charles de Gaulle centralized French cooperation within one institution and extended French aid beyond the Franc Zone, arguing that this system was no longer beneficial for France.[15] The 1975 Lomé Conference, under Giscard d'Estaing, is another turning point. France announced new cooperation priorities, shifting from purely bilateral aid to more multilateral aid, and re-evaluating the privileged relations it held with former colonies. Thus began a delicate balancing act of attempting to increase the self-sufficiency of the former colonial states without destroying their attachment to France and French values.

Contemporary Development Institutions and Policy Preferences

As during the decolonization period, the institutional standing and the priorities of British development policy continued to fluctuate widely in subsequent decades, largely reflecting the ideology of the party in power. Two major turning points stand out. First, with the victory of the Conservative Party and Margaret Thatcher in 1979, aid was more explicitly linked with industrial and commercial interests (Bose and Burnell 1991). The new development policy was interpreted as an invitation to subsidize exports and to use aid for short-term political gain (Vereker 2002). Second, with Tony

Blair's New Labour coming to power in 1997, international development was converted into a fashionable matter (Hewitt 2001). Whereas during the 1980s nearly half of British aid was allocated to goods and services originating from the UK, this figure generally declined in the 1990s, accounting for only 15 per cent of bilateral aid by 1996. The pressure to break the link between aid and commercial considerations was further increased in 1994, by the High Court ruling in the Pergau Dam affair, which had exposed the links between large-scale aid and British arms sales to Malaysia. The ruling established that there was no legal basis for the government to use development funds primarily for commercial purposes.

For decades, a fairly constant feature of British aid institutions and policy had been that the overseas department concerned itself largely with aid and was not allowed to assume broader responsibilities for shaping Britain's relations with developing countries. Furthermore, foreign assistance had been driven by Cold War considerations, during which strategic and security interests had affected the government's choice of which country to support and how, as well as by the need to support the UK's balance of payments by linking aid and exports. By the mid-1990s these pressures had eased, rendering the New Labour's 'foreign policy with an ethical dimension' proposal audible and acceptable (Mitchell 1991).

After decades of institutional weaknesses and volatility, 'development' became a core government priority. Clare Short, Tony Blair's Secretary of State for International Development, not only became a member of the Cabinet, but also a member of several interdepartmental Ministerial committees dealing with issues such as the environment, drug abuse, gender, health and export credits including arms sales (Barder 2005). The newly formed Department for International Development (DFID), independent from the Foreign Office, opened its doors to a wide range of external actors including NGOs, academic institutes and representatives of the diasporas in Britain. There was a substantial increase in ODA funding destined to the Joint Funding Scheme, which co-funded development projects with British civil society organizations. If the sums were modest in the 1980s, they increased in the 1990s to account for just over 10 per cent of total bilateral assistance in 2005.[16] But, as Hewitt (2001) argues, perhaps Claire Short's biggest success over the first four years of Labour government (1997–2001) was to make international development a fashionable subject.

As Chancellor of the Exchequer, Gordon Brown chose to use aid and development policies to make his mark internationally, championing debt relief through his 'heavily indebted poor countries' initiative, proposing an international finance facility to help poor countries raise capital, and supporting the G8 initiative in 2005 to double aid to Africa. Some argue that the renewed interest of Labour for the development cause came as a 'desperate attempt to salvage something of its foreign policy after Iraq' (Quarmby 2005:1) in the face of high public discontent. Between 2002 and 2005, UK ODA more than doubled from five to eleven billion dollars.[17]

In France, the government did not enjoy the same success in turning its development policy into a fashionable topic. According to a public opinion poll[18] commissioned by the Agence Française du Développement (AFD) and published in July 2006, citizens over sixty-five were by far the ones most concerned about the role France has to play in international development and humanitarian aid. Moreover, half of the population believed (as the British did in the 1970s and 1980s), that foreign aid should not affect the levels of aid given to the poorest at home. Despite the efforts of the government to reform development policy and institutions, 41 per cent of the French public still saw public aid as inefficient, and 45 per cent believed more transparency was needed in the aid allocation process.

In 1998, after several failed reform attempts and under the 'co-habitation' government of socialist prime minister, Lionel Jospin, and centre-right president, Jacques Chirac, a major reform of the North–South cooperation institutions and policies took place. It was influenced by the international development agenda, and notably, by the OECD-DAC Peer Review recommendations. The official priority was to tackle the lack of policy and institutional coherence, efficiency and co-ordination of the French aid system. In order to do that at the institutional level, a Comité Interministeriel de la Coopération Internationale (CICID) was created, presided by the prime minister. At the same time (and taking a step in the opposite direction to the British New Labour reform with the creation of DFID), the former Ministère de la Coopération was merged with the Foreign Ministry (Ministère des Affaires Etrangères [MAE]), and a Direction Générale de la Coopération Internationale et Développement (DGCID) was created within the MAE, responsible for long-term strategy and policy-making. The existing AFD was strengthened for executing projects on the ground. Another major aim was to promote cooperation among the public institutions and non-governmental ones such as labour unions, local governments, NGOs, firms, universities, associations, etc. For that, a Mission de la Coopération Non-gouvernementale (MCNG) was created within the DGCID, in charge of co-financing projects with civil society. Also, a 'Club des OSI' (Organisations de Solidarité Internationale) was established within the AFD. Finally, the creation of the Haut Conseil de la Coopération Internationale (HCCI), dependent on the prime minister and chaired by representatives of the government as well as civil society, was meant to facilitate and institutionalize dialogue between the two.

The reform, however, fell far short of achieving its objectives, primarily due to the configuration of power within the state and the inability of the actors involved in conceiving the reform to change existing balances of power (Bianco 2003). The institutional changes reflected the power struggles inherent in the 'co-habitation'. Although the DGCID, under the mandate of the socialist prime minister and his Minister of Foreign Affairs Hubert Vedrine, was conceived to counter-balance the influence of the 'Elysée'—the presidential office—in defining development politics, it lacked financial and human resources. The AFD assumed the de facto role of defining political strategies. At the same time, the CICID was gradually hollowed out, particularly during President Chirac's second term. In 1998 DGCID-MAE announced that French development policy was to give priority to decentralization and empowerment of civil society, granting a nearly 50 per cent increase in ODA allocation to core support to national NGOs and other private bodies the following year. By 2003 however, NGOs received only 1 per cent of total ODA, one of the lowest allocations of all OECD countries (OECD Development Assistance Committee 2004: 33).

With the election of President Nicolas Sarkozy in May 2007, a newly created and controversial 'Ministère de l'immigration, de l'intégration, de l'identité nationale, et du codéveloppement'[19] shared with the Foreign Affairs Ministry the role of determining France's development policy. By directly 'linking development and cooperation with migration policies',[20] the concept of co-development was aimed at involving the immigrants settled in France in the development of their country of origin. This may be interpreted as a sign that North–South relations and national identity continue to be two highly integrated matters in France.

France and the UK in the EU: Institutions and Policy Preferences

Variations in French and UK aid policy are also apparent within the development cooperation structures of the European Union. Providing over U.S.$10 billion in aid in 2006, the European Community with its twenty-seven member states accounts for more than one-half of all official development assistance recorded by the OECD's DAC. Although the global financial crisis of 2008 and subsequent austerity measures have affected levels of aid spending, in 2005, member states committed to increase ODA to 0.51 per cent of GNI by 2010 (0.17 per cent for the new member countries) and to 0.7 per cent of GNI by 2015 (0.33 per cent for new member countries).

A 2006 reform consolidated some thirty-five financial instruments (both ODA and non-ODA funds) into a more manageable set of ten instruments. The largest flows are found in the European Development Fund (EDF) and the Development Cooperation Instrument (DCI). Together they represent the majority of all EC's ODA. They are however, conceived and managed differently. EDF is a multi-annual programme managed by the Directorate-General for Development (DEV) and funded by voluntary contributions from member states outside the community's budget. It provides support essentially to the seventy-seven African Caribbean and Pacific (ACP) countries, of which forty-three were former British colonies and twenty were former French colonies. DCI is managed by the Directorate-General for External Relations (RELEX). It is financed directly from the community's annual budget and supports development programmes mainly in Asia and Latin America.

In 2005, France and the UK contributed, respectively, 1,811 and 1,180 million U.S. dollars to the EC's development programme. But whereas

France gave 781 million dollars out of its total contributions to EDF, the UK's contribution to EDF was 194 million dollars, the rest of it going to the annual EC budget. These variations in contributions reflect the development priorities of each country. On the one hand, France remains committed to the development of the poorest ACP countries and former colonies, whereas the UK increasingly favours trade interests in Asia and Latin America.

According to the European Community 2007 DAC Peer Review, the EC's current development policy is the result of an evolving mosaic ranging from assistance to the former colonies of member states to the stabilization of the European 'neighbourhood'. The implementation of a European consensus for development, the report says, will require DEV and RELEX to work more closely together and to challenge their historically separate responsibilities. As the EC seeks to move its development programme beyond the lingering influences of history, a key question is whether it will call on member states to stop viewing development cooperation as an instrument of foreign policy.

ACTIVISM AND SOCIAL PACTS IN FRANCE AND THE UK

In this section, I examine the structure, agenda and advocacy capabilities of British and French civil society organizations since colonial days, and consider the extent to which they have been influenced by the historical and institutional legacies examined previously in this chapter. I will focus on civil society networks active on issues such as CSR, trade, aid, debt relief, ODA and international taxation. In addition to NGOs, particular attention will be paid to the role of trade unions, firstly because they are an important part of the welfare regime analyses; and secondly because there has been a rapprochement between NGOs and trade unions in recent years, which has affected the resources, agendas and advocacy capabilities of both sets of civil society actors.

Trade Unions

The labour movements born before WWII in the British and French colonies were highly influenced by the trade union culture of their respective colonial masters (Giacometti 1957). Thus, in keeping with the British indirect rule approach, most existing workers' unions in British Africa were independent from the UK ones, whereas in French Africa they were affiliated to the different union confederations headquartered in France, as a result of the assimilation model. At the ideological level, whereas the question of racism (and consequently of human rights) was a central issue of labour struggle in the British colonies, the question of imperialism (and consequently of anti-imperialism or anti-globalization) was central in the French case.[21]

With the end of WWII and the advent of neo-corporatism, French and British trade unions became 'social partners' and legitimate actors both in domestic policy-making and some of the then emerging international organizations.[22] As a result, trade unions engaging in transnational activities often did so to further the interests of their home government, as participants in the 'new statecraft' (Josselin 2001). All throughout the Cold War, the world's political divide shaped the international activities of labour organizations, notably through the fight for adherents and prestige between the Soviet-led World Federation of Trade Unions (WFTU), of which the French CGT (Confédération Générale du Travail) was a member until 1994; and the anti-communist International Confederation of Free Trade Unions (ICFTU),[23] of which the British TUC was a member.[24]

At the end of the 1960s, with decolonization and the growing influence of transnational corporations (TNCs) on industrial relations, increasing levels of foreign direct investment (FDI) became a major concern for trade unions. International labour union organizations responded by international solidarity initiatives that could be labelled as 'TNC containment' (see Cox 1971, cited in Josselin 2001; also Gallin 2006). Their main objective was to create an international collective bargaining situation by co-ordinating action against TNCs in the various countries in which they operated, in order to prevent fragmentation when bargaining with a multi-plant corporation.[25] But international solidarity in the shape of TNC containment produced mixed results. International trade union confederations began then to promote and conclude private agreements—or International Framework Agreements (IFAs)—with multinational enterprises.[26] The first IFA was signed in 1988 between the International Union of Food and Allied Workers' Association (IUF) and the French multinational BSN (renamed Danone in 1994), the French CFDT (Confédération française démocratique du travail) playing an active role as intermediate in the negotiations (Gallin 2006). Overall, whereas British unions have preferred to assist social movements in their partnerships with individual firms to formulate codes of conduct (at the time of writing no British TNCs had signed an IFA), French unions prefer to support agreements signed between global union federations and TNCs,[27] claiming corporations are likely to use civil society partnerships in order to justify exiting from more traditional forms of social dialogue involving unions and the state.

As we have seen, in France, trade unions are inserted in a tradition of independent unionism with more or less explicit sympathy to different left-wing political groups, resulting in the creation of a highly fragmented unions system with weak worker representation and weak bargaining power.[28] British labour unions, despite a significant loss of power and influence over government and employers as a result of the Thatcher policies, have kept strong links with the Labour Party since the end of WWII, uniting around one single national Trade Union Confederation (TUC). Despite these distinct characteristics, trade union density is in decline in both countries,[29] as the result of increasing economic globalization and labour market flexibilization.

Some argue, however, that the acceleration of globalization has had a positive impact on the ability of trade unions to mobilize their members and to co-ordinate action transnationally through new alliances with non-governmental organizations. Some unionists favour a shift to 'social unionism', in which trade unions act as vehicles for a broad social mobilization around the world (DeMartino 1999, cited in Josselin 2001). Labour movement NGOs such as SOLIDAR have been created with the priority of assisting the trade union movement in dealing with challenges of globalization. But perhaps the most relevant illustration of social unionism is the creation of the International Trade Union Confederation (ITUC) in November 2006. The largest trade union confederation ever founded, ITUC positioned itself to tackle not only issues of decent work, but also poverty, equality and the effects of globalization more generally.

Closer to 'outsider' groups than their British counterparts, French trade unions have had more influence over, and been influenced by, civil society organizations and networks concerned with global justice issues. And although relations between the more traditional French labour unions and such networks remain ambiguous, new critical unions have repositioned themselves, linking local workers' struggles with the anti-globalization and anti-neoliberal agenda, and framing labour issues in terms of global justice. The support of French unions from different political groups for the creation of Attac (Association pour la Taxation des Transactions pour l'Aide aux Citoyens)[30] is symbolic of a different approach to development and North–South inequality; as is the creation of Solidaires, Unitaires, Démocratiques (SUD), a union defining itself as antiliberal and active in campaigns associated with global justice.[31]

In the UK, mostly due to the close links between unions and the Labour Party, the involvement of trade unions in international solidarity activities remains largely inspired by the mainstream development agenda. Centralized labour unions close to the Labour Party also remain dependent on state funding for their development activities. In July 2006, TUC and the DFID signed a Strategic Framework Partnership (SFP), renewing the existing Strategic Grant Agreement. The SFP has three main objectives: to increase awareness and understanding of development among trade union members in the UK; to build a closer engagement of the TUC, a number of affiliated unions and DFID with unions in the South; and to enhance cooperation between TUC, affiliates and DFID on the international development agenda.[32]

Development NGOs and Networks

Charities and missionary groups were present in the French and British colonies of Africa. They have been described as providers of low-cost private welfare, as pacifiers of social unrest and as bearers of civilization through Christian indoctrination (Manji and O'Coill 2002). More often than not, they were perceived as extensions of the colonial rulers' authority. In the first half of the twentieth century, a new type of charity emerged whose main concerns were the effects of wars and humanitarian relief, mostly within Europe. Save the Children was created in 1919 in London, as relief to victims of the Russian Civil War; Oxfam (Oxford Committee for Family Relief, founded in 1942), and the French CIMADE (Comité Inter-mouvements Auprès des Evacués, founded in 1939) were created to provide aid to victims of WWII.

After the Marshall Plan and with the wave of decolonization in the 1960s, these humanitarian organizations partly shifted their approach 'from the humanitarian business to the business of development' (Black 1992: 194), and thus redirected their efforts towards long term poverty relief and the development of former colonies. In France, Le Secours Catholique engaged in poverty relief in the former French colonies, and Emmaüs extended its action internationally with the creation of a 'Research and Action Institute on Global Hunger' (Institut de recherche et d'action sur la misère du monde). In the UK, Oxfam, Save the Children and Christian Aid were highly supportive of the first UN Decade of Development.[33] They also supported the Freedom from Hunger Campaign of the UN Food and Agriculture Organization (FAO).[34] As they engaged with development activities, these civil society organizations began to receive a higher share of public financing and moved gradually closer to government policy-making circles, in particular in the UK. At the same time, a new line of anti-colonial and human rights movements emerged. In the UK, Amnesty International was created in 1961. In France, the 'Centre d'études anti-impérialistes' was founded in 1966 by left-wing government employees. The 1960s and 1970s also saw the birth of a new breed of social movements (so-called New Social Movements) concerned with post-materialistic issues external to the workplace such as feminism, the environment, the homeless and world peace. The intertwining of experiences, agendas and resources from these different movements are at the origins of contemporary GJMs in both countries. In France, early examples of these bridges include the creation of CRID (Centre de Recherche et d'information pour le développement) by Catholic movements and small farmer unions, and the 'Centre d'études et d'initiatives de solidarité international' (CEDETIM), composed of movements both from Marxist and from Christian solidarity backgrounds. In the UK, Greenpeace and Shelter have borrowed lobbying techniques from more traditional development charities, adding innovative, media-oriented tactics of public protest to the repertoire of action.

A founding moment for the French GJM was the 1989 anti–third world debt campaign *Ça suffat comme si*, which coincided with the celebration of the bicentennial of the French Revolution as well as a G7 Summit in Paris. For the first time, it brought together movements from traditions such as

Trotskyists, communists and anti-colonialists, alongside the most progressive fractions of the Catholic Church. The campaign was also innovative as it linked the problem of third world debt with a wider discourse on the economic interdependence at a global level, holding the international financial organizations responsible for grievances in the South. In order to do that, it inaugurated the formula of the counter-summit (Agrikoliansky 2003).

In Britain as in France, the debt relief movement incarnated by the Jubilee Network was also an important reference to contemporary North–South activism and marks a relative break from the previously moderate political work of British development NGOs (see Chapter 9, this volume). At the origins of the Jubilee Network, the World Development Movement (WDM) was established by former Oxfam, Christian Aid and War on Want personalities, and backed by religious organizations and trade unions, as a limited company in order to bypass the political straitjacket of charity laws. But despite successes such as the 1985 'Manifesto for World Development', which called on members of Parliament to demand improvement on trade and food debts, the WDM was unable to mobilize activists and the public as much as it had hoped during the 1980s, and remained an 'outsider' actor in the British development context.

At the same time, main British development NGOs including Oxfam and Christian Aid, backed by human rights and health-related organizations, launched a campaign coalition called the Trade Justice Movement (TJM), aimed at changing what they considered to be unjust rules and institutions governing international trade. The TJM was formed as a result of inter-organizational discussions about how best to influence the UK government's stance during and after the Doha round of trade negotiations. As a result of the dominance of large ATDOs, the Jubilee Network saw the TJM as essentially undemocratic. Thus emerged one of the most distinct characteristics of the British global justice movement: the cleavages within the movement itself between insider and outsider groups to the policy-making and grant-allocating spheres (Rootes and Saunders 2007). The Make Poverty History coalition of over 450 organizations was an attempt to unite conflicting interests around the wide-encompassing causes of trade justice, drop the debt and more and better aid. Its pinnacle was a 225,000-strong protest march in Edinburgh that coincided with the G8 Summit at nearby Gleneagles in 2005. Despite its ability to retain public attention and celebrity support,[35] the coalition's agenda was seen to have been dominated by big development NGOs and co-opted by the Labour Party.

Due to charity law constraints preventing British movements from being overtly political (Black 1992), they share a long history of moderate forms of political action and lobbying, and enjoy considerably higher access to government decision-making and funding than their French counterparts. Today, the British global justice movement is a loose group of networks dominated by the long-established development NGOs. Organized around specific, highly visible campaign coalitions, their preferred repertoires of action are lobbying and advocacy (Rootes and Saunders 2007), and their agendas and demands focus social justice in the South mainly through trade justice related issues.

The French global justice movement, on the other hand, is seen as originating from three main concerns, namely, North–South inequality (Agrikoliansky 2003), the relegitimization of the state as the central instrument for social transformation and for the defence of French values (Fougier 2001) and cuts in the welfare state (Sommier and Combès 2007). These concerns are synthesized under a common frame of 'politics against global markets' or 'alter-globalization' (Ancelovici 2002). Compared to the British, the French movement is poorly funded and relies more on street protest (Sommier and Combès 2007).

Trade Unions and Development NGOs: A Rapprochement

Social movements are often considered to be different from neo-corporatist organizations such as trade unions: they are mainly pluralistic, loose networks with little formalized access to decision-makers (Lipsky 1965). In Tilly's (1978) words, movements are challengers, and neo-corporatist actors are polity members. But as many point out, in recent decades, and under intensifying processes of globalization and change in power relations and governance, the state has been challenged. As it began to downsize its commitments towards social justice under both left and right governments, it paved the way for the emergence of issue-oriented NGO networks and for trade unions to re-evaluate their international solidarity strategies, as seen in the preceding. NGO organizations and networks have become better structured at both national and supranational levels, acquiring substantial material resources and public support. As they develop into interest groups, a *rapprochement* between NGO networks and trade unions is taking place (della Porta 2006).

In the last decade, both in France and the UK, NGOs have often come together with trade unions. In France, numerous civil society organizations have joined unions in the streets to strike against pension reform, privatization of public services and the flexibilization of work relations (Contrat Première Embouche). During this period, new social actors emerged: notably new critical trade unions (SUD and FSU) and organizations for the defence of social rights (*mouvements des sans*—DAL, Droits devants! and AC!), that would, for the most part, influence the civil society networks in France concerned with global justice issues. The French CFDT (Confédération Française Démocratique du Travail), for instance, is a member of the coalition 'Plus d'Excuses' mobilizing for the achievement of the Millennium Development Goals (MDGs). Via its development NGO Institut Belleville, CFDT is also a member of Plateforme Dette-Développement, uniting social movements concerned with the third world debt, and a participant of the

Forum Citoyen pour la Responsabilité Sociale des Entreprises. In addition, it leads an international programme to fight union rights violations in cooperation with Amnesty International and has acted jointly with the Clean Clothes Campaign group (L'Ethique sur l'Etiquette in France).[36] Equally, the CGT (Confédération Générale du Travail) supported the Journée Mondiale Lutte Contre la Misère alongside more than fifty other civil society organizations and networks. The union is also a member of Plate-forme Dette et Développement.

In the UK, unions have increasingly gone beyond workplace issues to support other civil society causes such as fair trade, debt relief, CSR, the environment, peace or gender equality in the Global South. Furthermore, Royal Mail and London Underground strikes were supported not only by trade unions, but also by 'outsider' movements. In the UK, however, unified trade unions have not directly influenced global justice networks as much as large 'insider' development NGOs have.

CONCLUSION

This chapter has called attention to the need to better understand how state institutions and historical path dependence affect activism and policy change. It has sought to demonstrate the relevance of applying the welfare regime framework to not only studying institutions and policy preferences, but also activists' resources, repertoires and agendas (see Table 2.1). This analysis suggests that the nature of the activist–policy nexus in France and the UK reflects historically built social pacts, institutions and political narratives. It has identified three key sets of linkages.

First, concrete links between colonial and contemporary development-related institutions and policy. In the UK, for example, the voluntary model of consultation has shaped recent institutional reforms associated with ODA. Such reforms not only reflect long-term power struggles between the Foreign Office and DFID, but also demands from development NGOs and British public opinion. So whereas in the UK development policy made the centre stage of political debate, in *dirigiste* France, where low levels of consultation with social actors is the rule of the game, development policy remains a highly conflictual and impermeable affair, institutionally linked with issues of national identity, particularly since the election of Nicolas Sarkozy.

Second, concrete links between the institutional and policy regimes and activists' opportunities. Illustrative here are the calls of the French global justice movement for more state intervention rather than less; their agendas being associated not only with France's fragmented and ideologically charged labour unions, but also with Republicanism and *dirigisme*, supported over time by both right- and left-wing governments.

Table 2.1 French and UK Development Activism–Policy Nexus

	COLONIAL REGIME	
	FRANCE	*UK*
Values	Universalism and 'civilization mission'	Individualism
Administration	Assimilation	Indirect rule (divide and rule)
International Economic Strategy	National security	International finance
Labour	Pro-communist, centralized unions	Anti-communist, decentralized unions
Civil Society	Christian and anti-imperialist influence	Christian and human rights influence
Industry and Finance	Strong military-politico-financial alliance; protectionist Franc Zone	Business and industry; weak and open Sterling Zone
National Politics and Development Policy	Policy Continuity	Left–right policy cleavage
Decolonization	Engagement and investment	Disengagement and promotion of trade
	CONTEMPORARY POLICY–ACTIVISM NEXUS	
Development State Institutions	Ministry of Foreign Affairs and Ministry of Migration, Integration, National Identity and Co-development; low consultation with non-state actors; focus on French language, culture and identity	Ministry of Development (DFID); high consultation with non-state actors; focus on trade
Preferred EU Development Programme	EDF (focus on ACP countries)	Core annual budget (focus on Asia and Latin America)
Labour Unions	Weak and fragmented, strong links with Global Justice Movement	Centralized, organic links with the Labour Party, weak links with Global Justice Movement
Global Justice Movement	Origins in national social justice movements; protest action and transnational networking; alter-globalization; international taxation	Origins in trade and development charities; lobbying and advocacy at national level; corporate social responsibility and trade justice

In the UK, the focus on trade and development, and to some extent on human rights, reflects that country's perspective on decolonization. Another example is that of the 'more and better aid' agenda. Given the dominant role of the state in defining aid and trade policy, the policy influence of civil society organizations has been relatively limited, despite lobbying and large activist campaigns, particularly in the UK. The activism–policy nexus confronts highly stubborn institutional path dependencies. In the case of aid policy, civil society organizations tend to either opt out (the case of France) or be co-opted (the case of the UK), according to the characteristics of the social model in place (low and high consultation, respectively).

This leads to a third set of linkages, namely, between social pact models, on the one hand, and activists' resources, framing, agendas and repertoires, including the degree of cooperation between NGOs and trade unions. Illustrative here is the strong convergence in France of labour unions and global justice NGOs and grass-roots organizations. The low-consultation social model forces outsider groups of differing types to unite and adopt protest as their main form of influence. In the UK, on the other hand, where the government is more permeable to social consultation, large NGOs, which have long enjoyed insider status in the government have lead the global justice movement. There is relatively limited involvement with trade unions, and lobbying and advocacy are the preferred means of influence. Not surprisingly, French trade and development movements make use of their transnational networks more often than their British counterparts (Marchetti and Pianta 2007), as a means of by-passing national governments. Equally illustrative is the campaign for the cancellation of Third World debt, which has been an important cornerstone for North–South inequality activism in both countries. In this case, historically determined divisions within the British global justice movement have weakened actors defending a more 'radical' agenda which is closer to the demands or activists in the South. Policy concessions may be gained by NGO networks but they may do little for North–South equality. In France, on the other hand, the anti-debt movement has largely stood closer to the agenda of movements in the Global South, but has had very little impact on policy and politics.

Overall, the approach of development NGOs in the UK to trade justice and CSR largely resonates with the country's international economic strategy and historical institutional preferences, as does that of France's global justice movement in relation to the issue of international taxation. But if linkages between colonial trajectories, institutional path dependence, national social pacts and contemporary activism appear as strong variables in this chapter, the analysis has also identified spaces where historical legacies count less than other variables in shaping the activism–policy nexus. These include, for example, public opinion and transnational activism. Future research should take all of these variables into account.

NOTES

1. Among others, see Giugni, Bandler and Eggert (2007), and Marchetti and Pianta in this volume.
2. In historical institutionalist scholarship, *path dependence* refers to the dynamics of self-reinforcing processes in a political system. Once established, these patterns of political life—patterns of political mobilization, patterns of policy processes—will often generate self-reinforcing dynamics difficult to change. Recent literature on path dependence further argues that by bringing context and history back in, this approach can reinvigorate the analysis of power relations by showing 'how inequalities of power, perhaps modest initially, are reinforced and can become deeply embedded in organisations, institutions, and dominant modes of political understanding' (Pierson and Skocpol 2002: 701) .
3. Within the field of historical institutionalism, the welfare regime approach, which highlights the role of institutions and social pacts, provides a general framework for comparing the two countries. Its most influential work, namely, *Three Worlds of Welfare Capitalism*, by Esping-Andersen (1990), examines variations in welfare provision among advanced industrial societies. Aggregate data on indicators that measure decommodification—the extent to which individuals are less dependent on markets for their well-being—stratification and mix of state-market provision on pensions show that countries tend to cluster into three regimes: liberal (the case of the UK), conservative (the case of France) and social democratic. In the francophone literature this approach is associated with 'French regulation theory', which accounts for the variability of forms of capitalism in space and time (see Amable 2003; Boyer 1990).
4. On the role of discourse and ideas see, for instance, Haas (1992) and Hall (1993). On comparing France and the UK, see Schmidt (2002); on the influence of ideas and discourse on development policies, see Utting (2006).
5. The analysis draws on data produced for the case studies presented in Part II of this volume as well as other research conducted by the author for the United Nations Research Institute for Social Development (UNRISD) under the European Union Sixth Framework Programme, Priority 7, INEQ Project.
6. A survey by the polling group Globescan (cited by the *Economist*, 26 October 2006, print edition), 'Reforming the Unreformable', showed that 71 per cent of Americans thought free market economy was the best system available, as did 66 per cent of the British and 65 per cent of the Germans. For France, the figure was 36 per cent.
7. The centre-right president of France, Jacques Chirac, was the only head of state present at the G7 Summit in 2002 (a presidential election year in France) to extend sympathetic words to World Social Forum participants. Whereas at the same occasion British Prime Minister Tony Blair thought of alter-globalization activists as a 'travelling circus', President Chirac declared that 'these protests gather an important amount of people and deserve our thought and attention (. . .) France is the country which is closest to the concerns of these NGOs [who want] to master and regulate globalization' (BBC News 2001). Also significant was the presence of José Bové, an 'anti-globalization' candidate in France's 2007 presidential election campaign.
8. These are the Economic and Social Forum and the Planning Commissions.
9. A Tobin Tax amendment to the French financial law (loi de finances 2002), was approved by the French Legislative Assembly in November 2001, following an initiative by an Attac committee within the National Assembly. The

amendment adopted, however, remains symbolic, as it will only be effective once, and if, all of the European Union countries adopt a similar law.

10. For more on the role of France in the negotiations of the MIA, see Fougier (2002b); Henderson (1999); Kobrin (1998).
11. The analysis in this section focuses on the colonial relations of both countries with the African continent, and on the colonial period from the 1900s to the 1950s and 1960s.
12. See Crowder (1964) and Deschamps (1963), both cited in Dimier (1998).
13. Malpractices, related to state–business relations, continued to exist in the colonies after decolonization, particularly in Africa, in what has become known by the French public as *La Françafrique*
14. From 1958 to the present day.
15. See Comité pour l'Histoire Economique et Financière de la France (1998).
16. Total bilateral British assistance in 2005 amounted to 2,504 million pounds, of which 261 million were channelled through civil society organizations (DFID 2007).
17. OECD database.
18. The poll was undertaken by Institut Français d'Opinion Publique (IFOP).
19. This name was changed in April 2008 to Ministère de l'immigration, de l'intégration, de l'identité nationale, et du développement solidaire.
20. See Délégation de l'Assembléée Nationale pour L'Union Européenne (2006).
21. Interview with Dan Gallin of the Global Labour Institute and former General Secretary of the International Federation of Food, Agriculture, Hotel and Catering, and Tobacco Workers' Unions (IUF), conducted on 1 March 2007, Geneva, Switzerland.
22. For instance, the Organisation for European Economic Co-operation (OEEC) gave them consultative status, which later became the Trade Unions Advisory Committee (TUAC) of the OECD (Josselin 2001).
23. In 2006, the ICFTU merged with the World Confederation of Labour (WCL) to form the International Trade Union Confederation (ITUC).
24. In Latin America for instance, the ICFTU backed the Inter-American Regional Organization of Workers (ORIT), whereas the French backed the creation of Central Única dos Trabalhadores (CUT) in Brazil.
25. One of the earliest solidarity actions from an international union took place in 1963, when the International Food and Allied Workers' Association (IUF) defended the PAK Cigarette Labour Union (PCLU), which represented workers at the Pakistan subsidiary of British-American Tobacco (BAT).
26. Over fifty IFAs have been signed up to today by five different Trade Union Confederations (TUCs). In the absence of an international legal framework, IFAs are entirely voluntary. Most IFAs include the respecting of the ILO Conventions.
27. Besides Danone, French TNCs such as Rhodia, Electricité de France, Renault, Carrefour and Accor have signed IFAs.
28. Today, seven main confederations exist: Confédération Générale du Travail (CGT, founded in 1895, communist); Confédération Française Démocratique du Travail (CFDT, founded in 1919, Christian-Democratic); Force Ouvrière (FO, dissidents from the CGT, founded in 1948, communist/radical); Confédération Française de Travailleurs Chrétiens (CFTC, dissidents from CFDT when this union abolished its Christian roots, founded in 1964); Confédération Générale des Cadres (CGC, sole occupational confederation, founded in 1944, conservative); Solidaires, Unitaires, Démocratiques (SUD, founded in 1988, anti-liberalism); and Union Nationale des Syndicats Autonomes (UNSA, founded in 1992, reformist, socialist, pro-corporatist). Trade union density in France amounts to 8 per cent, the lowest in all of the OECD countries. The highest membership rates are in the public sector.

29. In the UK over the past two decades, union membership fell by 5.5 million and density dropped from more than half to less than one-third of the workforce. Data from the 2004 Workplace Employee Relations Survey show that collective bargaining coverage halved from around 70 per cent to 37 per cent in the same period (European Industrial Relations Observatory 2007).
30. The following unions were founding members of Attac: CFDT—Fédération Banques; CGT—Fédération Finances; Confédération Paysanne; FSU (Fédération Syndicale Solidaires); SNES (Syndicat National de l'Enseignement Secondaire); SNESUP (Syndicat National de l'Enseignemen Supérieur); SNUI (Syndicat National Unifié des Impôts—from the Direction Générale des Impôts or Tax Division of the Finance Ministry); SNUIPP (Syndicat National Unifié des Instituteurs et Professeurs d'Ecole); SUD-PTT; UNEF (Union Nationale des Etudiants de France); and UGICT-CGT (Union Générale des Ingénieurs, Cadres et Techniciens).
31. SUD was a member of the organizing committee of the Genoa Social Forum.
32. See www.tuc.org.uk/international (accessed 2 March 2007).
33. The first UN Development Decade was launched by the UN General Assembly in December 1961, and called on all member states to intensify their efforts to mobilize support for measures required to accelerate progress toward self-sustaining economic growth and social advancement in the developing countries.
34. The 1963 'Freedom from Hunger Campaign' was the FAO's main contribution to the United Nations First Development Decade. A Special Assembly on 'Man's Right to Freedom from Hunger' was convened and attended by twenty-nine world-renowned personalities, including several Nobel Prize winners.
35. Bob Geldof became the spokesperson of the campaign, which staged a 'Live8 concert' including music stars such as Madonna.
36. The mobilization was organized to help workers from a Bangladeshi textile factory that collapsed in April 2005 killing sixty-four and leaving five thousand with no jobs. Carrefour was one of the factory's clients. Previous to the accident, Carrefour had established a social responsibility chart and adopted a form of social audit associating unions such as the CFDT and the International Federation for Human Rights.

BIBLIOGRAPHY

Agrikoliansky, Eric. (2003). *De l'anticolonialisme à l'altermondialisme: généalogie(s) d'un nouveau cadre de l'action collective.* Paper presented at the Conference Les mobilisations altermondialistes, CERI, Paris, 3–5 December.

Agrikoliansky, Eric, Fillieule, Olivier, and Mayer, Nonna. (2005). *L'Altermondialisme en France. La longue histoire d'une nouvelle cause*, Paris: Flammarion.

Amable, Bruno. (2003). *The Diversity of Modern Capitalism*, Oxford: Oxford University Press.

Ancelovici, Marcos. (2002). 'Organising against Globalisation: The Case of ATTAC in France', *Politics and Society*, 30 (3): 427–463.

Barder, Owen. (2005). *Reforming Development Assistance: Lessons from the UK Experience.* Centre for Global Development Working Paper No. 70. www.cgdev.org/files/4371_file_WP_70.pdf (accessed 5 December 2006).

BBC News online, 16 June 2001. 'Blair: Anarchists will not stop us'. http://news.bbc.co.uk/2/hi/uk_news/politics/1392004.stm (accessed 5 December 2007).

Beaujolin, François, and Capron, Michel. (2005). 'The Characteristics of CSR in France', in André Habisch, Jan Jonker, Martina Wegner and René Schmidpeter (eds), *Corporate Social Responsibility across Europe*, Berlin: Springer.

Bianco, Jean-Louis. (2003). 'La dernière réforme de la coopération française', in Haut Conseil de la Coopération Internationale (ed), *Coopérer au XXI siècle. Pourquoi ? Comment ? Questions sans Préjugés*, Paris: Editions Khartala.

Black, Maggie. (1992). *Oxfam: The First 50 Years*, Oxford: Oxfam.

Bose, Anuradha, and Burnell, Peter. (1991). *Britain's Overseas Aid since 1979. Between Idealism and Self-Interest*, Manchester: Manchester University Press.

Boyer, Robert. (1990), *The Regulation School: A Critical Introduction*, New York: Columbia University Press.

Capron, Michel. (2009), *De la Françafrique à la responsabilité sociale des entreprises: Les dynamiques entre les firmes, l'Etat et les mouvements sociaux en France.* Programme on Markets, Business and Regulation, Paper No. 6, UNRISD, Geneva.

Cox, Robert W. (1971.'Labor and Transnational Relations'. *International Organisation*, 25 (3): 554–584.

Crowder, Michael. (1964). 'Indirect Rule: French and British Style', *Africa—Journal of the International African Institute*, 34 (3): 197–205.

Delaye, Bruno. (2003). 'La Coopération dans la politique extérieure de la France', in Haut Conseil de la Coopération Internationale (ed), *Coopérer au XXI siècle. Pourquoi ? Comment ? Questions sans Préjugés*, Paris: Editions Khartala.

Délégation de l'Assembléée Nationale pour L'Union Européenne. (2006). *Rapport d'information sur la Négociation des Accords de Partenariat Economique avec les Pays d'Afrique, des Caraibes et du Pacifique.* Rapport No. 3251, 5 July. http://www.ambafrance-us.org/news/statmnts/2006/Immigration_girardin_article_echos041206.asp (accessed 5 December 2007).

della Porta, Donnatella. (2006). 'From Corporatist Unions to Protest Unions? On the (Difficult) Relations between Organized Labour and New Social Movements', in Colin Crouch and Wolfgang Streeck (eds), *The Diversity of Democracy. Corporatism, Social Order and Political Conflict*, Cheltenham: Edward Elgar.

DeMartino, G.F. . (1999). *'Global Economy, Global Justice'*, London, Routledge.

Deschamps, Hubert. (1963). 'Et Maintenant Lord Lugard?' *Africa*, 33 (4): 294–305.

DFID. (2007). *Statistics on International Development.* http://www.dfid.gov.uk/aboutdfid/statistics.asp (accessed 26 March 2007).

Dimier, Véronique. (1998). *Le Discours Idéologique de la Méthode Coloniale chez les Français et les Britaniques de l'entre-deux guerres à la décolonisation, 1920–1960.* Document No. 58–59, Centre d'Etudes d'Afrique Noire, Institut d'Etudes Politiques de Bordeaux.

Esping-Andersen, G. (1990). *The Three Worlds of Welfare Capitalism*, Princeton, NJ: Princeton University Press.

Fougier, Eddy. (2001). 'Perceptions de la mondialisation en France et aux Etats-Unis', *Politique Etrangère*, 66 (3): 569–585.

———. (2002a). 'La Contestation de la mondialisation: une nouvelle exception française?' *Les Notes de l'IFRI* 46 (October): 1–6.

———. (2002b). 'Le Mouvement de Contestation de la Mondialisation', in *Annuaire français des relations internationales*, vol. 3, Brussels: Bruylant.

Gallin, Dan. (2006). *International Framework Agreements: A Reassessment, International Institute for Labour Studies.* Paper presented at the Workshop on 'Cross-Border Social Dialogue and Agreements: An Emerging Global Industrial Relations Framework?' ILO, Geneva, 15–16 December.

Gamson, W.A., and Meyer, D.S. (1996). 'Framing Political Opportunity', in D. McAdam, J. McCarthy and M. Zald (eds), *Comparative Perspectives on Social Movements*, Cambridge: Cambridge University Press.

Giacometti, André. (1957). 'The Labour Movement in Tropical Africa—II', *New International Review*, 23 (1).

Giugni, Marco. (1996). 'Federalismo e movimenti sociali', *Rivista Italiana di Scienza Politica*, 26 (1): 147–170.

Giugni, Marco, Bandler, Marko, and Eggert, Nina. (2007). *The Global Justice Movement: How Far Does the Classic Social Movement Agenda Go in Explaining Transnational Contention?* Programme on Civil Society and Social Movements, Paper No. 24, UNRISD, Geneva.

Haas, Peter. (ed) (1992). 'Knowledge, Power, and International Policy Co-Ordination', *International Organisation*, 46 (1): 1–35.

Hall, Peter A. (1993). 'Policy Paradigms, Social Learning and the State. The Case of Economic Policymaking in Britain', *Comparative Politics*, 25 (3): 275–296.

Hayter, Theresa. (1966). *French Aid*, London: Overseas Development Institute.

Henderson, David. (1999). *The MAI Affair. A Story and its Lessons*, London: Royal Institute of International Affairs.

Hewitt, Adrian. (2001). 'Beyond Poverty? The New UK Policy on International Development and Globalisation', *Third World Quarterly*, 22 (2): 291–296.

Joachim, Jutta, and Locher, Brigit. (2009). *Transnational Activism in the UN and the EU. A Comparative Study*, London: Routledge.

Jordan, Grant, and Richardson, Jeremy. (1987). *British Politics and the Policy Process—An Arena Approach*, London: Allen and Unwin.

Josselin, Daphne. (2001). 'Back to the Frontline? Trade Unions in a Global Age', in Daphne Josselin and William Wallace (eds), *Non-State Actors in World Politics*, New York: Palgrave.

Kitschelt, Herbert. (1986). 'Political Opportunities Structure and Political Protest: Anti-Nuclear Movements in Four Democracies', *British Journal of Political Science*, 16 (1): 57–85.

Kobrin, Stephen. (1998). 'Globalization at Work: The MAI and the Clash of Globalizations', *Foreign Policy*, 112:97–109.

Lipsky, Michael. (1965). *Protest and City Politics*, Chicago: Rand McNally and Co.

Manji, Fiorze, and Carl O'Coill. (2002). 'The Missionary Position: NGOs and Development in Africa', *International Affairs*, 78 (3): 567–583.

Marchetti, Raffaele, and Mario Pianta. (2007). 'Global Justice Movements. The Transnational Dimension', in D. della Porta (ed), *The Global Justice Movements. A Cross-National and Transnational Perspective*, Boulder, CO: Paradigm.

Martin, Guy. (1995). 'Francophone Africa in the Context of Franco-American Relations', in John W. Harbeson and Donald Rothchild (eds), *Africa in World Politics: Post–Cold War Challenges*, Boulder, CO: Westview Press.

Mitchell, John. (1991). 'Public Campaigning on Overseas Aid in the 1980's', in Anuradha Bose and Peter Burnell (eds), *Britain's Overseas Aid since 1979: Between Idealism and Self-Interest*, Manchester: Manchester University Press.

OECD Development Assistance Committee. (2004). *DAC Peer Review*, Paris: OECD.

Pierson, Paul. (2000). 'Three Worlds of Welfare State Research', *Comparative Political Studies*, 33 (6–7): 791–821.

Pierson, Paul, and Skocpol, Theda. (2007). 'Historical Institutionalism in Contemporary Political Science', in Ira Katznelson and Helen Milner (eds), *Political Science: State of the Discipline*, New York: Norton.

Quarmby, Katharine. (2005). 'Why Oxfam Is Failing Africa', *New Statesman*, 30 May.

Rootes, Christopher, and Saunders, Claire. (2007). 'The Global Justice Movement in Great Britain,' in Donatella della Porta (ed), *The Global Justice Movement. Cross-National and Transnational Perspectives*, Boulder, CO: Paradigm.
Schmidt, Vivien. (2002). 'The Politics of Economic Adjustment in France and Britain: Does discourse matter?' *Journal of European Public Policy*, 9 (6): 247–264.
Sommier, Isabelle, and Combès, Hélène. (2007). 'The Global Justice Movement in France,' in Donatella della Porta (ed), *The Global Justice Movement. Cross-National and Transnational Perspectives*, Boulder, CO: Paradigm.
Strange, Susan. (1986). *Casino Capitalism*, Oxford: Basil Blackwell.
Tarrow, Sidney. (1989). *Democracy and Disorder: Protest and Politics in Italy 1965–1975*, Oxford: Clarendon Press.
Tilly, Charles. (1978). *From Mobilization to Revolution*, Reading, MA: Addison-Wesley.
———. (2006). *Regimes and Repertoires*, Chicago: University of Chicago Press.
Utting, Peter. (ed) (2006). *Reclaiming Development Agendas. Knowledge, Power and International Policy Making*, Geneva: UNRISD and Palgrave Macmillan.
Utting, Peter, and Ives, Kate. (2006). 'The Politics of Corporate Responsibility and the Oil Industry', *STAIR*, 2 (1): 11–34.
Vereker, John. (2002). 'Blazing the Trail: Eight Years of Change in Handling International Development', *Development Policy Review*, 20 (2): 133–140.

3 The Potential and Practice of Civic Networks[1]

Jem Bendell and Anne Ellersiek

INTRODUCTION

The rise of advocacy non-governmental organizations (NGOs) in recent decades has seen this sector of civil society emerge as a key player in processes of policy reform. Yet individual NGOs engaged in advocacy are often small and weak relative to the powerful institutions they seek to reform. To address this situation, great store has been placed in the role of networking. The burgeoning literature on networks identifies numerous promises associated with resource mobilization and political opportunities involving, for example, stronger linkages among individuals and organizations, solidarity, improved information and resource flows, enlarged bases of support, enhanced legitimacy, a broader portfolio of tactics and greater policy impact.[2] This chapter assesses the potential of 'civic networks' by contrasting the promises identified in literature with observations from network activists (and those they attempt to influence) about actual performance.

We employ the term 'civic networks' (here and in Chapter 6) as a hybrid term that merges elements related to the concepts of social networks and civil society. A social network describes a social structure made of nodes (which are generally individuals or organizations) that are tied by one or more types of interdependency, exchange or interest, such as values or visions, finance, knowledge or friendship (Carrington, Scott and Wasserman 2005). Baldessari and Diani (2007: 736) describe networks as 'web[s] of collaborative ties and overlapping memberships between participatory organizations, formally independent of the state, acting on behalf of special, collective, and public interests'. Such networks are civic in the sense that they pursue normative goals, in contrast to non-normative definitions of civil society that refers to any form of association.

Scholars propose several reasons for the popularity of networks among NGOs. Smith (2005) sees networking as a response to the shift in authority, from the national to the international or global level, which increasingly constrains the policy choices groups can take advantage of in a national context. NGOs have also had to deal with the growing interdependence of issues by widening their organizational mandates. The broader and constantly more complex issues require new and different political strategies (Nelson 2002) which not only impact on the way NGOs approach their political environments, but also the way they organize themselves: in networks. Established NGOs also need to relate to the counter-globalization (or 'global justice') movement, 'whose political approaches differ sharply' (Nelson 2002: 378). A lack of capacity in less established groups—some of whom identify with counter-globalization—to effectively channel their claims and resources into the decisive policy context can result in a gap between NGO 'professionalism and populist protest' (Nelson 2002: 362), which some suggest is addressed through networks (Risse, Ropp and Sikkink 1999).

Most of the research on networks is *about* networks and their work in different policy contexts. Few studies examine the networks themselves and analyse this engagement from the perspective of the participants. This chapter reflects upon the network-related promises raised in the literature from the perspective of practitioners in networks and those who have been affected by them. The two sections that follow contrast the potential, or promises, put forward in the literature with the perceptions of participants in the networks studied, and the government officials and business representatives engaged by them. The first adopts an 'inside' perspective. It presents the results of interviews and a survey conducted with network participants, which shed light on aspects internal to networks, such as resource mobilization, identity and learning and network co-ordination and governance. Referring to the external environment, the second section takes an outside perspective. It discusses how working in a network changes activists' perception of their political environment and how the network is perceived externally, including how far perceptions of network members are reflected in the perceptions of important actors in their political environment, such as the civil servants and business representatives they engage with. A concluding section suggests the need for a strategic shift in approach and for networks to develop a 'movement mentality' in order to reduce the gap between promise and practice.

The empirical data for the assessment of network effects derive from four civil advocacy networks working in the United Kingdom (UK) in the area of economic policy with implications for international development. They include the Trade Justice Network, which promotes a fairer international trading system for developing countries; the Sakhalin Island Network, which aims to improve the conduct of oil companies and encourage financial institutions and export credit agencies that support investment projects to adopt ethical principles; the Publish What You Pay (PWYP) campaign, which promotes transparency in financial dealings of companies in the extractive industries; and the Corporate Responsibility (CORE) Coalition, which promotes various legal and other mechanisms to enhance corporate accountability. The data for each case were collected by means of document analysis and a combination of interviews, as well as a survey including respondents from all four networks and representatives of their counterparts in the policy process.[3]

Table 3.1 Network Promises (Internal)

Promises	*Source*
Networks bring additional strength for collective action through the exchange and pooling of resources (financial, knowledge, expertise, etc.)	Resource mobilization theory Keck and Sikkink (1998)
Networks facilitate knowledge exchange, learning and the generation of new and creative solutions among participants	Dumoulin (2002); Hibbert and Huxham (2007)
Networks enable groups to mobilize and bundle their resources strategically	Keck (1998)
Networks help to build a shared collective identity among participants beyond conventional movement sectors	Keck and Sikkink (1998) Diani (2003)
Networks help to bridge the gap between Northern and Southern groups	Crossley (2003) Jordan and van Tuijl (2000)
Networks help to decentralize existing relations among NGOs	Skjelsbaek (1971); Smith (2005)

INSIDE NETWORKS

Some of the promises of networks frequently mentioned in the literature about the internal, or inter-organizational, agenda of networks relate to: increased access to information, expertise and financial resources; higher efficiency through multiplier effects, which increase the reach and impact available to member organizations; solidarity and support; enhanced visibility of issues and underrepresented groups; risk mitigation; reduced isolation and increased credibility. An overview of the promises made in the literature is provided in Table 3.1.

Resource Mobilization in Networks

One area of focus for social movement scholars is how activists organize, with the term 'mobilization structures' used to describe the various means, 'informal as well as formal, through which people mobilize and engage in collective action' (McAdam, McCarthy and Zald 2005: 3). From this perspective, two general arguments for networks are mentioned in the literature (see Arquilla and Ronfeldt 2001): first, networks facilitate exchange (Borgatti and Foster 2003) that makes them advantageous compared to hierarchical, competitive and conflictive forms of organizing (Gray 2003). Whether accurate or not, implicit in many peoples' understandings of a network is that they provide network participants with an equal opportunity to share and receive resources, in particular knowledge and information. Second, through this increase in the flow of information between actors, networks are seen as changing the nature of resources relevant for political change (Fuchs 2005). Drawing on Arquilla and Ronfeldt's observation that in political processes today, 'more than ever before, conflicts revolve around "knowledge" and the use of "soft power"' (2001: 218), Gorgura (2003) proposes that networks not only channel these resources more effectively than traditional forms of organizing (for example, hierarchical), but also generate new knowledge and resources by connecting and rewiring ever new actors in collaborative, compared to competitive, environments. Therefore, networks build new grounds for resource mobilization (Diani 2001).

In the case of the networks examined for this study, the pooling of resources was the key motivation for organizations to join a network—apart from related reasons, such as facilitating interorganizational learning and the exchange of experiences among members. Knowledge sharing and exchange, and the joint creation of new knowledge, occurred along a dimension similar to the spectrum of knowledge sharing in networks suggested by Hibbert and Huxham (2007). On the one hand, the exchange of information as material for campaigns, especially targeted toward the media, was the primary mode of sharing; thus members used the network as a broad knowledge pool. On the other hand—although this was rare—knowledge sharing was described by the exchange of experiences and opening up of 'institutional boxes', as one interviewee put it. In this sense, knowledge and information are not only brought to the network and exchanged, but also newly created due to the changing perspectives of network participants. Participants argued that the network benefit for their organizations derived from the fact that:

> You have got different organizations with different strengths . . . [Some] may have more of a think tank or journalistic style . . . By working together I think we have been much more effective.[4]

> Different people have different connections, and get quite good intelligence of what's going on. In terms of being able to do media work it was critical to have pictures being sent as quickly as possible, to make it a new story, a live issue. It was good to be able to mix our approaches, and sometimes different groups led on different things.

However, two limitations to this network benefit became clear from the data. The first is limited capacities or willingness of organizations to contribute to shared campaigns, and in particular to the long-term development of capacities of the network itself, in terms of its co-ordinating function. Another limitation relates to the fact that loosely coupled networks require co-ordination in order to develop such long-term visions and shared network identities (Crossley 2003).

Limited capacities resulted in a narrow set of network activities—mainly campaign support—which seldom went beyond more punctual joint actions. Although the statements in the survey emphasized the importance of strong support and the willingness of members to substantially contribute to the networks, the interviews gave a more hesitant image of membership and resource contribution. In the survey almost half of the respondents (48 per cent) stated their work in the network was a major activity requiring contact with other members about once a week on average, and more than half of the respondents were granted a budget as well as a mandate for their work for the network for the upcoming year. Eighty-eight per cent confirmed that it was of crucial importance to their organization that the network lasts. In the interviews, however, resource scarcity was seen as a major obstacle to effective network operations. As commonly noted in the literature, resource scarcity is an obstacle to network formation and maintenance (Provan and Kenis 2008).

However, the case studies revealed issues of resource scarcity even within networks of relatively resource-rich organizations. The issue is not a lack of resources per se, as often reported by social movement scholars (Kriesi 1998), but rather the alignment of widely divergent strategies and the tensions between established organizational approaches and activities associated with networking and collective action. In particular, large organizations with a strong campaigning background in other fields, such as environment and human rights, reported on the limited allocation of resources to the network in contrast to the resources of their own organizations.

Hardy, Lawrence and Phillips (2006) describe this tension as inherent to collaborative processes when network participants are being caught between two stools: being representative of their own organizational interests and being part of a network and attached to a collective issue. The inherent struggle that derives from this situation is described by one participant who co-ordinated the involvement of one of the larger NGOs:

> The issue is when we do work in alliances, there's obviously a desire, which we would share, which is to get the brand of the alliance, the network, out there. At [name of the organization], we were, along with other organizations, wanting to get PWYP's identity out through the media. And we would happily do that, but we would also have a need to get our own brand out there as well, because that's part of our job—so the internal tensions that were created were that sometimes we were saying to our media colleagues 'can you do both these things?', and sometimes they would understandably come back to us and say, 'look, which is the more important?'

Even stronger tensions were observed when discrepancies exist between the strategies and values of the single organization and the overall strategy and campaigning approach of the network. The terms that best describe this internal conflict in the cases studied were those between so-called inside versus outside approaches (Schepers 2006) toward campaigning and policy change. Due to the nature of the networks, which are often used for campaigns with less focus on permanent policy work, established organizations often perceived difficulties in bringing in their competitive advantage, for example, of having the political capital that can be decisive for their mainly inside-oriented strategies. According to a member of an established group: 'The big tension [in the network] has been between our model, and a model that's been all "outsider"—the view is taken that change is only achieved from pressure from outside, and the insider track is dubious, or questionable.'

Representing the opposite side of this strategic spectrum, others—often strongly campaign-focused groups—add another important resource to the network: large supporter bases. These groups are public-oriented, especially in their interaction with the media. Network members, hence, are diverse and have unique resources that allow them to participate in a network and also define their potential role to play. Integrating those different approaches, however, is extremely difficult and often members struggle to switch between the organizational and the network roles:

> They [members of the network] may not always work as in a network formation—they spend much more time and energy meeting with [civil servants] wearing their own organizational hat . . . It can sometimes be limiting to operate as a network, because it may be better to use your own channels and reflect your own organization's perspective or expertise than stick to a collective voice.

However, concerted efforts on behalf of the network are key to a network's success in policy change processes, but this often requires a strategic balancing act:

> You need to channel your resources effectively and influence decision makers taking different angles: through direct lobbying and contacts that reach them personally, but you also need to build strong pressure from the grassroots and have a visible, more activist-oriented strand of your campaign. That's extremely difficult to co-ordinate sometimes but I think only both—those two together—create the climate for change.

Learning and Identity in Networks

Scholars propose that networks offer more for the development of knowledge resources than just facilitating information exchange; participants in a network can learn together about pursuing collective efforts, hence creating new knowledge (Hibbert and Huxham 2007).

However, this kind of value creation through learning in networks first of all requires a common objective or goal (Purdue 2007) in order to prevent participants from 'selfishly acquir[ing] knowledge exclusively for the participant's own organisation' (Hibbert and Huxham 2007: 124), which would run the risk of the resources of some partners being exploited by dominant parties and free riders. The definition of a mutual goal can prove difficult for civic networks.

The study found that civic networks focused on identifying goals that reflected the common objectives of participant organizations and sought to cherry-pick specific objectives, such as providing inputs to a particular policy consultation. The networks' activities were not explicitly concerned with developing a common understanding of deeper economic policy issues or unifying a grass-roots movement (Diani 2003). By not exploring the different perspectives on the systemic challenges of, for example, corporations, international trade and global capitalism, formal opportunities for learning about causes, solutions and strategies are limited within the networks. However, it also means that coalitions can be maintained at a more superficial level of agreement, and thus specific objectives can be pursued in the short term and the deeper issues addressed more informally by network participants.

Hence, rather than addressing challenges to processes of shared goal development based on different ideological grounds, participants put forward difficulties in aligning their different operational approaches. Related to these more concrete challenges, working in networks was generally seen as encouraging and motivating, especially for experts who normally work in relative isolation on issues of economic justice within their own organization. It requires a strategic balancing act:

> When you work on specific policies, you are struggling with this often alone. If there are others—counterpoints or colleagues in other organizations that you can come together and meet with regularly, it does form a sort of basis for encouragement, shared enthusiasm for what you are doing, as well as a reaffirmation of purpose.

Learning is often mentioned as contributing to the development of a shared identity and equal opportunities in networks (Bonner Daekwan and Cavusgil 2005). However, networks can also waste this potential when members 'exclude or side-line the consideration of learning: either implicitly, because the collaborative agenda is focused elsewhere; or explicitly, because it is regarded as unimportant' (Hibbert and Huxham 2007: 124).

The potential for learning was far from realized by the networks studied. Learning was generally seen as a side issue. In no case was learning found to be proactively initiated, fostered or formalized. Some respondents noted, however, that it did occur through general interaction. Indeed, this learning by doing mode was described as forcing members to 'think outside of their institutional box', representing a challenge especially to the majority of the established inside groups (Schepers 2006), getting them 'out of their comfort zone in the NGO community', as one respondent explained. Interviewees reported on cases where established inside-oriented groups joined campaigns that put forward messages to the public and the media that were not in line with 'the traditional message they [the established groups] would give to policymakers and corporations'.

Similarly, grass-roots-oriented groups may be urged by established groups to adapt their approach to the *joint* message the network wants to communicate in the policy process (Rosenblatt 2004). Such interactions can lead to compromises that may enable the realization of cultural commonalities and development of a shared identity within the networks, or—if not shared—create intellectual and strategic incoherence among parties (Bennett 2003).

Learning, then, results from the tensions that arise by combining the needs of different groups. The literature on networks proposes that learning in networks happens horizontally, developing cohesion out of fragmented and divided groups, and vertically, connecting less powerful (often local) groups to powerful groups, authorities, agencies and other groups relevant in the policy area (Purdue 2007).

Besides the learning opportunities between inside and outside groups, contestation between Northern and Southern groups is frequently mentioned in the literature as leading to special tensions but also as offering new identity-building potential in networks (Crossley 2003). Although networks were mainly preoccupied with targeting national policies, we expected that the transnational implications of those policies (see Marchetti and Pianta, Chapter 4, in this volume) would lead to a stronger direct involvement of Southern groups through networks.

However, with the exception of one network, this was not the case. Although almost all networks show links to Southern groups, and some report the issues they work on in the North as interesting for Southern groups as well, Northern–Southern correspondence remains mainly, as the respondents put it, on the level of Northern NGOs 'bringing [Southern] case studies forward' in order to get 'convincing material to back up' their claims and to 'maintain that legitimacy of representing a local view'. Except for this role of Southern NGOs as sources of 'credibility and advocacy' for Northern NGOs, only PWYP emphasized mutual exchange as essential to the network and highlighted the need for more active membership of Southern NGOs, advancing learning processes between Northern and Southern groups and herewith ownership and control of network' outcomes also for Southern groups.

Learning requires managing psychological dynamics, trust, defensiveness and conflict (Purdue 2007) and an openness and flexibility to reframe issues (Gray 2003). Reflection through network processes can offer a way to tackle differences step by step between members. A trusting network culture is thus required if network members do not want to settle for a half-hearted commitment to their cause. Learning in networks, related to identity building, thus goes beyond processes acquiring information and technical skills from other network members, to undergoing an internal change, creating new knowledge and developing greater reflexivity (Purdue 2007). Essential for this kind of knowledge sharing is an understanding of various dynamics specific to each network that does not derive from a one-size-fits-all approach but through processes of evaluation.

Evaluation mechanisms, however, barely existed among the four networks examined. In three of the cases, our inquiry was said to be the first external evaluation of the network. Because learning seems a side effect of the process rather than being systematically initiated and evaluated, this appears to constrain learning effects in networks. Many of the network members complained about a lack of reflection and analysis on how the network works: 'there hasn't been a great deal of creative learning' and 'it [the network] has been very much operationally focused and not reflective into what has worked and what hasn't.'

A shared identity and self-understanding of a network as being part of something bigger—features associated with a social movement (Diani 2001)—builds an important part of activism in networks compared to the efforts of a single organization. One factor facilitating strategic formation in a movement is its density or the linkages it shows between participants (Diani 2001). Yet, only a few respondents actually perceived their organization as part of a movement that goes beyond their direct partners: 'I really don't think of [the network] as a bigger movement or so. I think it is a quite narrow group of NGOs and getting involved in a network is a pragmatic matter to get more of our message out. That's about it.'

Although some of the networks possess an internationally oriented action plan and are members of global policy issue–oriented networks, co-ordination mechanisms among national groups were merely described as advisory boards, composed of national and regional representatives that keep an eye on national policy developments and the interventions of single groups and networks. Co-ordination efforts, in the sense of a transnational movement, thus remain on a more advisory level with informal exchange but no formalized co-ordinating structures or mutual strategic adjustments between networks. Therefore, strategy evolves and strategic commonalities emerge *en route* rather than being proactively identified and addressed by national or issue networks.

Civic Network Co-ordination and Governance

Questions about network governance and co-ordination are of crucial importance to enable processes of resource alignment, and learning and development in networks. It is an area of research, however, that gained attention in the literature only recently (Provan and Kenis 2008). Mostly, we found networks contrasted with markets and hierarchies, as a form of interorganizational co-ordination (Entwistle et al. 2007). The most prominent proposition in this literature is that networks are more decentralized, flexible and, as some argue, more democratic (Fuchs 2005) than traditional hierarchies. Yet, the way inter-organizational relations and processes are governed 'inside networks' has received only scant attention to date (Provan and Kenis 2008).

The diversity of organizations involved in civic networks represents, from a network governance and management perspective, a set of significant loosely arranged modules which can be rearranged to adjust to new challenges externally as well as internally (Rosenblatt 2004). This form of organizing comes close to what, in network research, is often labelled 'bounded autonomy' (Kickert, Klijn and Koppenjan 1997: 266): although the network benefits from the combination of different strengths, single identities are kept, and the identity of the network does not confound the goals and principles of individual participants (Diani 2001). Decisive in this respect is not only the strength of bounding ties, in the sense of developing solidarity among network members (Adler and Kwon 2002), but also the co-ordination and governance of networks as a whole (Provan and Kenis 2008) in order to take advantage of the different sources of potential value to collective action. Developing such structures in civic networks seems to require open discussion and negotiation, as well as learning and trust, among members about what kind of resource control and what level of formalization are acceptable to them (Diani 2003).

Scholars in the field of public service networks point to an array of steering and control mechanisms, formal and informal in nature, that enables network governance. They include outcome control (for example, goal setting and evaluation, performance monitoring and rewarding); behavioural control (such as planning, procedures, rules, norms and regulation); and social control and institutions (for example, boundary-setting processes through member selection, and trust building or peer evaluation).

Those mechanisms were only rarely found among the networks under study, which, in general, showed only low levels of formalization and co-ordination. For instance, reporting structures and evaluation, as discussed for network learning and identity, rarely happened through organized initiatives. Similarly, membership was loosely managed, in most cases not even requiring a letter of engagement, and only 25 per cent of the respondents said their network required a membership fee. All networks, however, had a board, and often sub-themes and groups were co-ordinated by these boards. Yet, these groups, from the perspective of the overall network, were very much fragmented. They showed high levels of independence, which means they were established for each campaign separately, and planned and implemented their actions independently. Although all networks showed basic structures of co-ordination, in terms of boards or steering committees and subunits, such as task forces that built the operational level of network operations, three challenges were frequently mentioned in the interviews: formalization, durability and interconnectedness.

A common concern put forward by the participants referred to the stability of the networks' own co-ordination and governance structures beyond punctual campaigning. These comprehensive and enduring structures were seen as essentially allowing members to work on cross-cutting issues—such as economic policies—increasingly extracting their 'systemic nature'. This was often mentioned as a request to build up a durable knowledge and resource base, which benefits all members' engagement in these issues in the long run while keeping their own individual organizational mandates.

Contrary to these concerns, a different organizing and co-ordinating paradigm was identified through the survey data on the actual network level itself that seems to oppose these intentions toward durable structures. A strong tendency toward punctual collaboration and campaigning was the major organizing principle among the networks under study. In particular, campaigning NGOs were described as strongly action- and outward-oriented, hence, hardly any attention, in terms of time and resources, was allocated to ongoing in-depth research and investigation. Although 88 per cent of the respondents said it was important for their organizations that the network lasts, some voiced their concern about a lack of investment of resources into continuous 'background policy work' that gives the network's claims credibility: 'I'm worried that they [future campaigns] won't have the bite they had in the past because they won't have that solid research background.'

Some future steps in the direction of more permanent structures for network co-ordination and governance, however, were proposed, often along with an expected growth of the network. An important issue for this process of organizational integration was the establishment of the network as a separate entity, mainly in terms of a formalization of membership of the board and decision-making structures, but also through membership fees, administrative reporting functions and annual reports. Besides recognizing this necessity of building mechanisms that help steer the network, however, several respondents emphasized the importance of 'keep[ing] the ground free of administrative pressures', and continuing to build 'specific alliances around certain areas'. Further, it was questioned by the respondents how far permanent structures in terms of steering committees also allow for continuous policy work. In order to build a strong core that develops substantial knowledge and resources upon which thematic groups and the steering committees can draw, resources are needed. Yet, resource scarcity was mentioned as the major obstacle to the development of a working core.

Building stronger linkages among network members as well as between networks was mentioned as a future challenge to effective network management in order to further tackle systemic issues of economic policy and contestation. At the time of the study, however, those linkages were rarely found. One criterion that facilitates such linkages across networks was identified through the parallel membership of leading organizations in two or more of the networks studied. Those linkages reveal the rather elite membership structure of these networks. So-called board interlocks among networks (Diani 2003) were most strongly found between two of the networks (CORE and PWYP) but were generally typical of the nature of network interconnectedness. Further, one network showed linkages to another European-wide coalition.

Although networks may allow organizations to address different issues by employing different approaches of activism at the same time, this study also found that lead organizations tend to have a fairly dominant influence on the strategic development of these civic networks. The question then remains how far learning can bridge and how far other organizations, besides those leading ones, in particular Southern groups,[5] can be integrated through such governance structures. Governance processes in networks were found to consider all participants through consensus-based decision–making; however, more systemic power hierarchies seem to leverage high levels of control and influence to a core group of organizations which appear to hold positions on the board of almost all networks.

OUTSIDE NETWORKS

Civic advocacy in networks involves learning political strategies and adopting strategic postures toward powerful governments and international organizations. NGOs that seek to influence public policy through networks employ diverse methods that conform to the dominant model of NGO advocacy strategies but also display significant differences.

Traditionally, political opportunities for activism are determined by the structures of institutional politics. These structures, on the one hand, define the level of responsiveness to activists' claims and, on the other hand, the level of repression of activism in a political system. Drawing on the works of political process theorists (McAdam 1982; Tarrow 1989, 1994), scholars, mainly European, have compared numerous national political settings and their influence on activism.[6] Since then scholars have been redefining the concept due to the transnational activities of networks and the increasingly dynamic relations to other actors than national governments (see, for instance, Chapter 4, this volume).

Although scholars find that national policy settings influence transnational activism in contemporary networks (Giugni, Bandler and Eggert 2007), activism is no longer seen as simply a matter of repressed groups fighting the state (Goodwin, Jasper and Polletta 2001). Instead, scholars situate activism in a dynamic relational field in which (Goodwin, Jasper and Polletta 2001) interests of allies and opponents, together with the openness of the public to change, and the existence of supporting groups and elites (Joppke 1993), all influence the emergence, activity and outcomes of contentious politics (Goldstone 2004). The literature on networks highlights numerous ways in which this mode of organizing activism transforms political opportunity structures in ways conducive to policy influence and change. These promises are summarized in Table 3.2.

Table 3.2 Network Promises (External)

Promises	*Source*
Networks strengthen the institutional flexibility of groups by addressing different institutional actors and levels (for example 'venue shopping', or 'boomerang pattern')	Baumgartner and Jones (1991, 1993); Keck and Sikkink (1998)
Networks show a more sophisticated awareness of the political opportunity structures within which they operate	Tarrow (1994)
Networks allow to directly and strategically explore political opportunities and address policy issues	Keck and Sikkink (1998)
Networks strengthen the visibility of activism and the impression of a collective approach of different groups in the policy process	Diani (2003)
Networks strengthen the political legitimacy of groups	Hudson (2001)
Networks bring new issues to the agenda of policy processes	Keck and Sikkink (1998)
Networks transform the terms and nature of policy debates	Keck and Sikkink (1998)
Networks increase the impact of activist groups on policy outcomes	Keck and Sikkink (1998)

Here we consider how far organizing activism in networks has changed the perceptions of network members about their role in the policy process, and the ways they have explored their environment for opportunities to pursue their claims.

Network Perspectives on Political Opportunities

The key set of promises identified in the literature and displayed in Table 3.2 relates to an increase in the awareness of political opportunities in networks, compared to a single organization's efforts, through a changed self-perception of members as part of a network. This network effect can be confirmed for the cases studied: for instance, 44 per cent of the respondents perceive the network to better demonstrate the 'interconnectedness of social and environmental challenges', and 51 per cent claim a larger supporter base: 'It makes us more effective than we would be individually; it gives us the opportunity to have platforms to be heard, or to organize events jointly, shared lobbying platforms . . . it opens up a number of ways in which we can maximize our input on the issue, in ways that we might not be able to if we were just working on an issue on our own.'

In a similar vein, 52 per cent of the network participants perceived the network as more legitimate and 76 per cent as more powerful, compared to the efforts of their individual organizations. As one participant remarked, 'Yes, I think you can extrapolate this to all issues. None of these [policy processes] are easy to change—I mean, to really show an impact—as an individual organization. But when you have a coalition then it does look much more solid, and people think "Wow, there are all these organizations working together with this message, there must be something serious going on".'

But how does this strong image substantially affect the opportunities explored by networks in comparison to traditional organizational strategies? One part of this expected change addresses shifting perceptions of what is possible, based on the means offered by the existing structure and brought to the network through the different institutional lenses of members. Although objective conditions of the political environment in which a network is embedded (Diani 2003) build the basis for the dynamics of contestation, these have to be interpreted by the network as opportunities or threats before they become reason enough for action. Therefore, activism is enabled not only by the effect these conditions have on power relations, but also their effect on the networks' interpretation of them (McAdam, McCarthy and Zald 2005). Hence, in a network the same event or intervention can be interpreted by some as an opportunity and by others as a threat, and an exchange of views may change them. This exchange of perceptions and possible change of perceptions through networks can create new opportunities and open up potential for intervention beyond those of single efforts, or as one NGO respondent put it:

> When NGOs work on their own they work within a fixed political framework of what matters to them, what falls into their responsibility and first, what they think is possible to change. Take, for instance, [organization XY]—they have the lens of international human rights law. There is no responsibility in international human rights law on companies, no legal responsibility. That's why they see all issues through the lens of the nation-state and that's why exchange is so important. It's all interwoven.

Such perspectives then have to pay close attention to the cultural traditions, ideological principles, institutional memories and political taboos that create and limit the single organization's perception of political opportunities (Diani 2003). However, the dominance and control of established groups over the probably less risk-aversive perceptions of political opportunities of other groups can lead networks to jeopardize this added network benefit. As one respondent stated:

> If you appear as a network you are expected to put forward a straight message. Without giving them all the list of side issues that popped up

> in our discussion but aren't useful to get our message through. You have to compromise. So if your organization thinks that is important and a great opportunity to push it through but others are more hesitant then it can be a disadvantage in that way.

However, looking at networks 'from the other side of the desk', as one civil servant put it, this network effect was less recognized. Although three out of seven civil servants generally perceived networks as more powerful than single NGOs in the interviews, not one of them reported a changed perception of an NGO because it was part of a network. Often, civil servants did not even know the composition of the networks. Therefore, they did not differentiate between whether their departments were approached by an NGO or a network's representative:

> We don't find that NGO networks specifically target us. Sometimes it's an individual NGO, sometimes it's a network of NGOs. We gratefully receive the comments from anybody. So there isn't anything specific about networks that makes them more or less attractive to us.
>
> They don't communicate with us on behalf of the [network]; they communicate with us and sometimes we see that they've copied those communications to everybody else. So we don't really differentiate between network and an individual NGO.

> It's difficult to say, because I don't know—nobody has formally told me—who actually is in the TJM [Trade Justice Movement].

In the eyes of the civil servants, the major obstacles encountered by networks in the policy process were the networks' lack of credibility, deep knowledge and reliable sources of information and knowledge about the policy process, as well as their overly confrontational approach. Often more credibility was ascribed to a single organization; some civil servants remarked that the co-ordination of information and its reliability were the major problems of networks, and often single organizations were seen as much more reliable. Moreover, the dominance of only a few leading organizations in the network, and their linkages and personal relations to civil servants, continued to represent the strongest impression of civil servant–NGO contacts and exchanges. During the interviews, the same NGO representatives were mentioned by the civil servants several times, regardless of their affiliation to one of the networks. One business representative saw one of the leading organizations, rather than the network as a whole, as the 'lobbying counterpart in the United Kingdom'. Similar to the board interlocks among the leading NGOs in the four networks, the interviews with external recipients revealed a more elite structure of NGOs in these civic networks.

Keck and Sikkink (1998) further argue that multiple organizational angles enable networks to grasp opportunities on different levels and with different actors, targets and allies in the policy process. Networks, in this respect, are not simply exposed to a political environment of opportunities and constraints offered. Instead, activists themselves can create opportunities by expanding the political sphere that is applicable to them, by creating ties to other actors and structures, national political systems, the international political system and international civic society and market systems (McAdam, McCarthy and Zald 2005).

Creating new ties, as mentioned in the literature, was found to be rather limited in the cases studied. Despite the small circle of well-known UK NGOs, only one network involved other sectors, such as government bodies and business representatives, but none in a governance capacity. Other networks were purely civic. For the future, their focus was in involving more NGOs in the network, such as those working on different issues (33 per cent), Southern NGOs (45 per cent), faith-based groups (41 per cent) and trade unions (45 per cent). A stronger involvement of business was less desirable (4.2 per cent) and governments not at all. Some benefit was seen in future involvement of multilateral institutions, such as the United Nations (8.2 per cent) and of media organizations (22 per cent).

The reason for this approach toward cross-sector involvement in the networks seems to be a critical view toward business influence on policy process. Eighty-six per cent of the respondents saw risks in the involvement of businesses in the work of the networks, and 98 per cent generally saw the involvement of businesses in policy processes as problematic. Although 48 per cent of the respondents said businesses lobbied on fairly similar issues as those advocated by the network, only 8 per cent perceived businesses' lobbying as sometimes in line with the network's aims, and 44 per cent saw no similarities in their lobbying goals. With government representatives, compared to business, the boundaries were more blurred. Twenty-five per cent of the respondents knew at least one person in their network who previously worked for the UK government, and 48 per cent were in contact, through the network, with civil servants who had previously worked for a NGO. The cases do not give much of an indication of the networks exploring new political opportunities through the generation of new ties to non-traditional partners. The reasons for this are many, as further involvement of either business or government would pose challenges to the ability of the networks to campaign. However, the potential of networks to connect diverse groups with different power means that this could be reconsidered, and is discussed later under strategic challenges.

Network Perspectives on Policy Change Processes

Another claim put forward by the literature proposes that networks enable more coherent and direct policy contestation as compared to single efforts, allowing members to put much more weight into their claims and strategies than through single efforts (Keck and Sikkink 1998). On the one hand, these promises point toward a more differentiated and strategic perception of the policy process through a network perspective. On the other hand, a more strategic and coherent application of strategies through networks compared to single unco-ordinated efforts is proposed.

McAdam, McCarthy and Zald (2005), drawing on Ross (1977), argue that errors in the attribution of cause, and therefore fault, are more likely when groups work on their own rather than in larger groups. Single groups frequently see grievances, concerns or dissatisfaction with how a policy process develops or with its outcomes, as a function of their own deficiencies rather than a feature of the surrounding system. Only system attributions and thus critiques, they argue, afford the necessary rationale for a network's activity (McAdam, McCarthy and Zald 2005), or as one of the respondents put it: 'collecting different opinions and experiences around an issue, we want to give the overall picture and clarify once and for all that company law and accountability is not a concern of a few niche NGOs but a widely shared system critique.'

Through networks it is proposed that activists are able to proactively scan the political landscape in order to develop systemic rather than individual critiques and thus establish a background of rationality for their claims, for example, pointing toward differences in policy settings and transfer solutions from one policy setting to another through analogous interpretation and framing. This recognition of parallels was a change in perceptions that occurred in the case studies:

> It became clear that this was going to be a big issue; it wasn't just isolated to the UK. It was an important one in many different countries. And there was a whole wave of corporate responsibility movements, NGO coalitions and campaigns on these developmental and CSR [corporate social responsibility] projects addressing all kind of institutional levels. So then it became clear that we here in the UK weren't the only ones busy with this stuff.

However, the question we had then was whether the shared critique and joint claims put forward by the network indeed appeared to be more systemic and fundamentally challenging than single efforts. Network participants believed this was the case, frequently reporting to better see 'the big picture' and develop a more comprehensive understanding of how policy change works.

The majority considered that policy processes are typified by decision-makers mediating between competing interests in society and that pressures come from within different governmental departments as well as from external stakeholders. Also important in the NGOs' assessment of how to interact with policymakers is their analysis of how other NGOs and groups influence those processes, as well as directly consulting civil servants.

The objectives of the network campaigns were equally determined by external factors, such as the government's policy focus and agenda, and ongoing efforts to change which offered a political window, as well as internal factors, such as the most commonly defined advocacy topics among members and a priori analyses of network founder organizations of the deepest challenges—its raison d'être. A more deliberate approach toward intervention in the policy process through networks was not obvious in the case studies. These more proactive strategies were partly realized through public campaigns and external pressures, which once again highlights the importance of both internal and external strategies of civic networks (Dalton, Recchia and Rohrschneider 2003). More frequently, however, we got the impression that the network enabled members to see more chances—political windows—but those were offered by the process and not proactively pushed for and opened up by the networks themselves. As one civil servant said: 'What TJM was aiming at and what they have got so far from us—they have got some things—are the bits which were always in relatively easy reach.'

So, are groups that organize in a network really more powerful in their interventions than single groups, or do all the negotiations in the network pre-emptively filter the more radical ideas in order to present the approach more coherently, thereby reducing the power of the advocates of more radical positions? The impression from the cases studied was mixed. A respondent describes it more negatively:

> Working through a coalition can make it easier for government to put you in a box. So, effectively, they'll get all the critics in one room at the same time and dress it up as a consultation, but actually what it means is that all of us lot have to engage with each other and not bring out our full agendas, which are what I think much more straightforward points than what comes out of the negotiations in the group. Those are often so full of compromises that it becomes difficult to see your message in there. And for them it is quite convenient. I mean they can just bat off questions that come from one group in one session, without having to feel the pressure of having to meet with a lot of different stakeholders and have to respond to them and justify their approach again and again.

Others see networks as an increased pressure on governance that also enable organizations that have fewer resources to engage in extensive long-term campaigning and policy-process advocacy and lobbying. Many of the respondents were prepared to accept a loss of direct expression of their positions, in return for the network benefit of long-term lobbying, credibility and resource flows:

> Many organizations just do need enhanced credibility. There are a lot of fairly radical NGOs that might find it hard for their voices to be heard in government, but they have a lot to say that's very legitimate. Becoming part of the broader, more mainstream, group together with less

> radical groups as well, church groups and unions, gives them a voice and a backing that they wouldn't have otherwise with government and others. I think for plenty, there is actually enormously enhanced credibility. Obviously there are costs that come with it, which are that you can't just push your line.

The literature suggests that cohesion among network participants leads to more effective interventions in the policy process and enhances the impact of NGO claims on decision-making (Sikkink 1993). What emerged from the participant surveys was the impression of a network's power and impact, compared to those of single organizations. However, the civil servants interviewed said that networks were easier to handle, compared to single efforts by several individual organizations. A lack of cohesion was also perceived as weakening the penetrating power of network claims because campaigners could not seem to agree when, how and whom to approach among the respective governmental departments and civil servants. The common perception of networks by civil servants was far from the impression of 'one voice, one claim':

> By no means do we only ever get one request for one thing. So the network will exist, but it's not formalized, and it's not infallible. We do get duplication, among those people that [the civil servant] will meet. And we might get requests from some of them, for effectively the same thing. So we don't see it as one voice—I think it is much more a loose, less formal network.

In conclusion, the self-perception of member organizations changed because they were part of a network. They perceived themselves as more powerful and benefited from the different perspectives and resources brought together. Only to a limited extent was this confirmed by their environment. Civil servants perceived networks as easy to handle because they felt that by talking to network representatives they could achieve at one time what used to take them numerous consultations.

Additionally, it is often argued that networks give leeway to members to follow up different strategies and allow for more radical approaches toward the policy process. However, civil servants do not really see the whole network, but rather continue to talk to the same people from the same leading organizations. The question therefore remains: how far are these organizations are really able and willing to push through the network approach, even though this is contrary to their own organizational goals and tactics?

Do networks enhance legitimacy, as claimed by the literature reviewed earlier? Michael Edwards (2003: 1) reminds us that 'those who speak out do not need to be formally representative of a constituency'. A group or person's voice can be valued simply for their relevant expertise and experience, or the degree to which they are affected by the issue concerned, or even their moral authority (Van Rooy 2004; Bendell 2006). For the civic networks discussed in this chapter, their accountability, expertise and experience are central to their legitimacy as policy advocates. These different factors appeared to be confused by many involved in the networks and policy processes. Some of the networks did not actively seek to develop these grounds for their legitimacy, whether through greater Southern NGO engagement, methodologically sound research or a more systematic gathering and sharing of relevant experiences. The reason for this appears to be the limited resources available, both to the network and to the participants for their network-related activities.

CONCLUDING REMARKS: TOWARD A MOVEMENT MENTALITY

With the rise of networks, NGOs have had to 'relearn—even to "unlearn"'—previously gained political lessons (Nelson 2002: 378). The political and institutional factors that require this political retooling include both the political environment and the internal restructuring (Rosenblatt 2004) among groups in and through networks. The contrast between the promise and practice outlined in this chapter, and explored further in Chapter 9 (this volume), suggests that this process of relearning is far from finished. Indeed, the analysis suggests than civic networks need to engage in a strategic shift in approach. A key aspect in this regard involves cultivating a movement mentality whereby networks and their constituent organizations focus more explicitly on both the root causes of injustice and processes of structural change, as well as craft a common identity and cultivate closer relations with subaltern groups affected by economic injustice. Regarding themselves as, and promoting understanding of, a global corporate accountability movement, could help increase their policy legitimacy and effectiveness (Bendell 2004).

Sixty per cent of NGO survey respondents do not have a documented, overarching analysis of social change and how to affect it, either at the organizational or departmental level. The majority of the respondents have not had independent evaluation of their advocacy work. This lack of clarity on strategy and absence of thorough processes of evaluation and learning mean that core questions about assumptions, values and politics are not explored. On the positive side, this allows the participants in networks to work together with differing perspectives, rather than spending scarce time and resources trying to negotiate on first principles. However, this also means that opportunities for greater cohesion and advocating a coherent agenda are lost. Instead, the unity of participants emerges through reacting to public policy processes, particularly in opposing policies. Similar to the global justice movement, where the phrase 'one no and many yeses' is prevalent, this approach means that the types of 'yeses' are not often agreed upon and campaigning remains largely reactive.

Currently the networks do not seek to educate their members or shape a common identity. The lack of a cohering approach means that a civic network's advocacy can appear like a laundry list of issues and demands that reflect a compromise between participants. To elaborate a more coherent agenda would require greater investment in participants learning about the common determinants of the problems the different NGOs campaign on. Although this can be time-consuming, given that identity shaping is key to both networks and social movements, a more deliberate effort on this could prove effective. One benefit is that it could enable the network and its participants to better consider complex challenges, such as their relations with the private and financial sector.

Another aspect of the strategic shift is to evolve the way participants think of themselves and the network in relation to society and social movements. Currently many of the NGO participants have an organization-centric and charity mentality to their work. By organization-centric, we mean that they focus primarily on how their interactions in the network and beyond can meet the needs of their organization. That may be understandable and inevitable, but it means that the full benefits of networks and participation in social movements is limited. This is particularly so in terms of role differentiation and co-ordination within networks to enable insider strategies involving collaboration with elites, and outsider strategies involving confrontation with them, to synergize rather than undermine each other. To achieve such differentiations and co-ordination requires NGO participants in networks to see the networks as a whole and how they can play a needed role within it.

The term *charity mentality* means that NGOs approach issues in a way that asks people to help others through an appeal to their morality. This may sound both reasonable and positive, but it presents a number of limitations. First, it means that the process of asking and the process of giving are seen to have value in their own right, for those doing the asking and giving, and this can sustain arrangements whether they are successful or not, as they provide an emotional benefit for the donor and the charity worker. Second, it ensures that the work agendas are shaped to a degree by the forms of awareness and interest of donors. Third, it creates a sense of otherness between the needy and those who help them. Fourth, it limits the view of how social change occurs, and how much, to that which can be funded by voluntary giving.

One result of this approach is the view many NGO participants express about the difficulty of persuading donors to invest in their work on economic justice, and that they need such money to 'raise awareness' and 'campaign'. However, the idea that issues of economic injustice are being experienced by people every day, all over the world, should guide us into exploring how such people are currently seeking to rectify that situation and the tools that are—or are not—at their disposal. This, in turn, could inform interventions that would service their needs in solidarity with them without relying on persuading large donors or powerful institutions to act out of moral concern. Projects that might evolve out of such an approach could include, for example, the creation of new mechanisms for legal support, or systems for channelling the experiences of intended beneficiaries into the risk assessments of financial institutions.

Another aspect of this strategic shift toward a movement mentality is that network conveners and participants could not only better recognize the limits of what they could achieve themselves through the network, but also ensure that they address those limitations by relating effectively to other processes in the movement. A key limitation found in the research was the networks' relationship to business and finance. The importance of business interests in shaping policy outcomes was widely recognized, and the majority of civic network participants were aware of some companies or businesspeople who were proactive in the 'corporate responsibility movement' (Bendell et al. 2009) and who shared the analysis and some of the policy recommendations of the network. Most NGO respondents, however, considered that such engagements would present difficult issues for the network, including concerns about co-optation, as well as undermining the trust certain constituencies had in the network.

Another limitation on networks is how 'radical' their member NGOs could be seen to be by donors, NGO boards, media or government regulators. The strategic implication is that the civic networks could facilitate more informal interactions between members and more grass-roots campaigners who are not network members, so that activities could be better co-ordinated when appropriate. With a movement mentality, such fluid collaborations with individuals in a variety of sectors may be more easily envisaged and organized.

The challenge facing all network conveners and participants in being more strategic with planning and evaluation is that of resources. Work on economic inequality and justice is marginal to most UK NGOs. This is reflected in the limited profile economic justice issues have in budget allocations and the communications of many of the NGO participants in the networks studied. The marginal nature of these issues to the mainstream NGOs means that the NGOs' own projects and campaigns on economic justice issues are conservative in agenda, tone and profile. Those working on economic justice are often marginal to mainstream strategy, policy, budgetary and staffing decisions in their organizations. The people working on economic justice issues in such NGOs have been connecting through civic networks as a means of coping with a comparative lack of organizational commitment and backing for such issues. It could be said the civic networks are coping mechanisms by activists working in co-opted or conservative organizations. There are some exceptions; for example, Friends of the Earth (FoE) decided to make corporate campaigns a focus during the early years of the twenty-first century. However, even that level of commitment is subject to the vagaries of institutional interests of an NGO. In the case of FoE, in 2007 it decided to downscale its corporate work and focus more on clearly environmental issues, given the rise in environmental awareness in the wake of growing climate concerns. Without secure and substantial financial and institutional backing, opportunities are missed and problems arise for the networks. For instance, they are not engaged with either beneficiaries or grass-roots activists as much as they might be, or should be, to be legitimate, informed and effective. Nor are the conveners or participants able to afford necessary processes of strategic planning, evaluation and project experimentation.

Civic networks and their participants will not be able to be more effective on economic justice issues without tackling the root cause of the resource scarcity they face. Therefore, the strategic shift toward more network excellence must include looking at how to influence the NGO participants' own organizational development so they might engage more fully in economic justice issues, social movements and civic networks. The challenge is to work through networks to help transform the organizations that form the networks, so they might all better enable social change. A key barrier to overcome will be the NGOs' concern for brand and resource protection, which can stifle innovation in projects and messaging.

NOTES

1. This chapter is drawn from Bendell and Ellersiek (2009).
2. See, for example, Carpenter (2007); Chiriboga (2001); DeNardo (1986); Donnelly (2002); Edwards (2003); Fabig and Boele (1999); Fox and Brown (1998); Giugni (1998); Hudson (2001); Jordan and van Tuijl (2000); Keck and Sikkink (1998); Schepers (2006); Smith (1997, 2005).
3. The data generated for this chapter and Chapter 6 are of four types. First, one of the author's participation in public meetings (TJM), conferences (PWYP), committee meetings (CORE), and liaison with network leaders (SIN and CORE) in 2006, helped to identify topics to follow up on in the following year. Second, an extensive document analysis was conducted in parallel, including online materials from the networks, official policy documents and printed information made available by network members and co-ordinators. Third, an online questionnaire was circulated to civic network participants, with the help of network co-ordinators, who were also asked to complete the survey. The network co-ordinators circulated the survey to British organizations that were active participants in their networks, totalling about eighty organizations. Thirty-one respondents completed the survey. Another survey was sent to fifteen civil servants who were identified by the networks as people they had engaged with. Nine completed the questionnaire. Finally, twenty-two in-depth interviews were conducted with civic network participants and co-ordinators and government civil servants, including a minimum of one co-ordinator and civil servant for each network and three NGO network participants. Additional information was gleaned from re-reading of the interview transcripts by our interviewees, follow-up correspondence with NGO participants and the media (for example, newspapers).
4. Quoted text is taken from the interviews.

5. This differentiation of Southern NGOs versus Northern NGOs is taken from the literature (Schepers 2006: 285).
6. See, for example, Kitschelt (1985); Kriesi (1998); Kriesi et al. (1995).

BIBLIOGRAPHY

Adler, Paul, and Kwon, Seok-Woo. (2002). 'Social Capital: Prospects for a New Concept', *Academy of Management Review*, 27 (1): 17–40.

Arquilla, John, and Ronfeldt, David. (eds) (2001). *Networks and Netwars: The Future of Terror, Crime, and Militancy*, Santa Monica, CA: RAND Corporation. http://www.rand.org/publications/MR/MR1382 (accessed July 2008).

Baldessari, Delia, and Diani, Mario. (2007). 'The Integrative Power of Civic Networks', *American Journal of Sociology*, 113 (3): 735–780.

Baumgartner, Frank R., and Jones, Bryan D. (1991). 'Agenda Dynamics and Policy Subsystems', *Journal of Politics*, 53 (4): 1044–1074.

———. (1993). *Agendas and Instability in American Politics*, Chicago: University of Chicago Press.

Bendell, Jem. (2004). *Barricades and Boardrooms: A Contemporary History of the Corporate Accountability Movement*. Programme on Technology, Business and Society, Paper No. 13, UNRISD, Geneva.

———. (2006). *Debating NGO Accountability, Development Dossier*, Geneva: UN-NGLS.

Bendell, Jem, and Ellersiek, Anne. (2009). *Noble Networks? Advocacy for Global Justice and the 'Network Effect'*. Programme on Civil Society and Social Movements, Paper No. 31, UNRISD, Geneva.

Bendell, Jem, Visser, Wayne, Peck, Jules, Cohen, Jonathan, Moon, Jeremy, Young, Mark, Bendell, Mark, Kearins, Kate, Concannon, Tim, Shah, Shilpa, Ives, Kate, Abrahams, Desirée, Gibbons, Paul, Shah, Rupesh, and Manoochehri, John. (2009). *The Corporate Responsibility Movement*, Sheffield: Greenleaf Publishing.

Bennett, Lance W. (2003). 'New Media Power: The Internet and Global Activism', in N. Couldry and J. Curran (eds), *Contesting Media Power: Alternative Media in a Networked World*, Lanham, MD: Rowman and Littlefield.

Bonner, Joseph M., Daekwan, Kim, and Cavusgil, S. Tamer (2005). 'Self-Perceived Strategic Network Identity and Its Effects on Market Performance in Alliance Relationships', *Journal of Business Research*, 58 (10): 1371–1380.

Borgatti, Stephen P., and Foster, Pacey C. (2003). 'The Network Paradigm in Organisational Research: A Review and Typology', *Journal of Management*, 29 (6): 991–1013.

Carpenter, R. Charli. (2007). 'Setting the Advocacy Agenda: Theorizing Issue Emergence and Non-Emergence in Transnational Advocacy Networks', *International Studies Quarterly*, 51 (1): 99–120.

Carrington, Peter J., Scott, John, and Wasserman, Stanley. (2005). *Models and Methods in Social Network Analysis*, New York: Cambridge University Press.

Chiriboga, Manuel. (2001). 'Constructing a Southern Constituency for Global Advocacy: The Experience of Latin American NGOs and the World Bank', in M. Edwards and J. Gaventa (eds), *Global Citizen Action*, Boulder, CO: Lynne Rienner Publishers.

Crossley, Nick. (2003). 'Even Newer Social Movements? Anti-Corporate Protests, Capitalist Crises and the Remoralization of Society', *Organization*, 10 (2): 287–305.

Dalton, Russell, Recchia, Steve, and Rohrschneider, Robert. (2003). 'The Environmental Movement and the Modes of Political Action', *Comparative Political Studies*, 30 (7): 743–771.

DeNardo, James. (1986). 'Power in Numbers: The Political Strategy of Protest and Rebellion', *Contemporary Sociology*, 15 (3): 463–465.

Diani, Mario. (2001). 'Social Movement Networks: Virtual and Real', in F. Webster (ed), *Culture and Politics in the Information Age: A New Politics?* London: Routledge.

———. (2003). 'Introduction: Social Movements, Contentious Actions, and Social Networks: From Metaphor to Substance?', in M. Diani and D. McAdam (eds), *Social Movements and Networks: Relational Approaches to Collective Action*, Oxford: Oxford University Press.

Donnelly, Elizabeth A. (2002). 'Transnational Advocacy Networks: The Case of Third World Debt and Structural Adjustment', in S. Khagram, J. Riker and K. Sikkink (eds), *Restructuring World Politics: Transnational Social Movements, Networks and Norms*, Minneapolis: University of Minnesota Press.

Dumoulin, David. (2002). *México-Washington-México-Lacanja Chansayab: Quels Rôles pour les ONGE dans la Légitimation des Savoirs Locaux sur la Biodiversité?* Paper presented at the seminar on NGOs, Indigenous Peoples and Local Knowledge: Politics of Power in the Biodiversity Domain, UNESCO, Paris, 27–28 May.

Edwards, Michael. (2003). *NGO Legitimacy—Voice or Vote?* Bond: http://www.globalpolicy.org/ngos/credib/2003/0202rep.htm (accessed July 2008).

Entwistle, Tom, Bristow, Gillian, Hines, Frances, Donaldson, Sophie, and Martin, Steve. (2007). 'The Dysfunctions of Markets, Hierarchies and Networks in the Meta-governance of Partnership', *Urban Studies* 44 (1): 63–79.

Fabig, Heike, and Boele, Richard. (1999) 'The Changing Nature of NGO Activity in a Globalising World', *IDS Bulletin*, 30 (3): 58–65.

Fox, Jonathan, and Brown, L. David. (1998). *The Struggle for Accountability: The World Bank, NGOs, and Grassroots Movements*, Cambridge, MA: MIT Press.

Fuchs, Doris. (2005). 'Commanding Heights? The Strength and Fragility of Business Power in Global Politics', *Millennium: Journal of International Studies*, 33 (3): 771–801.

Giugni, Marco G. (1998). 'Was It Worth the Effort? The Outcomes and Consequences of Social Movements', *Annual Review Sociology*, 98:371–393.

Giugni, Marco, Bandler, Marko, and Eggert, Nina. (2007). *The Global Justice Movement: How Far Does the Classic Social Movement Agenda Go in Explaining Transnational Contention?* Programme on Civil Society and Social Movements, Paper No. 24, UNRISD, Geneva.

Goldstone, Jack A. (2004). 'More Social Movements or Fewer? Beyond Political Opportunity Structures to Relational Fields', *Theory and Society*, 33 (34): 333–365.

Goodwin, Jeff, Jasper, James M., and Polletta, Francesca. (eds) (2001). *Passionate Politics: Emotions and Social Movements*, Chicago: University of Chicago Press.

Gorgura, Heather E. (2003). *The Net Repertoire: Global Activist Networks and Open Publishing.* University of Washington, Center for Communication and Civil Engagement: http://depts.washington.edu/ccce/assets/documents/heather-gorgura/netrep.pdf (accessed July 2008).

Gray, Barbara. (2003). 'Strong Opposition: Frame-based Resistance to Collaboration', *Journal of Community and Applied Psychology*, 14 (3): 166–176.

Hardy, Cynthia, Lawrence, Tom, and Phillips, Nelson. (2006). 'Swimming with Sharks: Creating Strategic Change through Multisector Collaboration', *International Journal of Strategic Change Management*, 1 (1/2): 96–112.

Hibbert, Paul, and Huxham, Chris. (2007). 'Collaboration, Knowledge and Learning: Integrating Perspectives', in T. Gössling, L. Oerlemans and R. Jansen (eds),

Inside Networks: A Process View on Multi-Organisational Partnerships, Alliances and Networks, Cheltenham: Edward Elgar Publishing.

Hudson, Alan. (2001). 'NGOs and Transnational Advocacy Networks: From Legitimacy to Political Responsibility', *Global Networks*, 1 (4): 331–352.

Joppke, Christian. (1993). *Mobilizing against Nuclear Energy: A Comparison of Germany and the United States*, Berkeley: University of California Press.

Jordan, Lisa, and van Tuijl, Peter. (2000). 'Political Responsibility in Transnational NGO Advocacy', *World Development*, 28 (12): 2051–2065.

Keck, Margaret. (1998). 'Planafloro in Rondonia: The Limits of Leverage', in J. Fox and L.D. Brown (eds), *The Struggle for Accountability: The World Bank, NGOs, and Grassroots Movements*, Cambridge, MA: MIT Press.

Keck, Margaret, and Sikkink, Kathryn. (1998). *Activists beyond Borders: Advocacy Networks in International Politics*, Ithaca, NY: Cornell University Press.

Kickert, Walter J.M., Klijn, Erik-Hans, and Koppenjan, Joop F.M. (eds) (1997). *Managing Complex Networks: Strategies for the Public Sector*, London: Sage.

Kitschelt, Herbert. (1985). 'New Social Movements in West Germany and the United States', *Political Power and Social Theory*, 5:273–324.

Kriesi, Hanspeter. (1998). 'The Interdependence of Structure and Action: Some Reflections on the State of the Art', in B. Klandermans, H.P. Kriesi and S. Tarrow (eds), *International Social Movement Research*, vol. 1, *From Structure to Action: Comparing Social Movement Research across Cultures*, Greenwich, CT: JAI Press.

Kriesi, Hanspeter, Koopmans, Ruud, Duyvendak, Jan Wilhem, and Giugni, Marco. (1995). *New Social Movements in Western Europe: A Comparative Analysis*, London: UCL Press.

McAdam, Doug. (1982). *Political Process and the Development of Black Insurgency, 1930–1970*, Chicago: University of Chicago Press.

McAdam, Doug, McCarthy, John D., and Zald, Mayer N. (2005). 'Introduction: Opportunities, Mobilizing Structures, and Framing Processes—Toward a Synthetic, Comparative Perspective on Social Movements', in D. McAdam, J.D. McCarthy and M. Zald (eds), *Comparative Perspectives on Social Movements*, Cambridge: Cambridge University Press.

Nelson, Paul J. (2002). *Human Rights, Economic and Social Policy, and International Politics: A New Model.* Paper presented at the Annual Meeting of the International Studies Association, New Orleans, 23–27 March.

Provan, Keith, and Kenis, Patrick J. (2008). 'Modes of Network Governance: Structure, Management, and Effectiveness', *Journal of Public Administration Research and Theory Advance Access*, 18 (2): 229–252.

Purdue, Derrick. (2007). 'A Learning Network Approach to Community Empowerment', in T. Gössling, L. Oerlemans and R. Jansen (eds), *Inside Networks: A Process View on Multi-Organisational Partnerships, Alliances and Networks*, Cheltenham: Edgar Elgar.

Risse, Tomas, Ropp, Stephen, and Sikkink, Kathryn. (eds) (1999). *The Power of Human Rights: International Norms and Domestic Change*, Cambridge: Cambridge University Press.

Rosenblatt, Gideon. (2004). *Movement as Network: Connecting People and Organisations in the Environmental Movement*, ONE/Northwest, Manchester. http://www.onw.org, www.onenw.org/toolkit/movementasnetwork-final-1–0.pdf (accessed July 2008).

Ross, Lee. (1977). 'The Intuitive Psychologist and His Shortcomings: Distortions in the Attribution Process', *Advances in Experimental Social Psychology*, 10:173–220.

Schepers, Donald H. (2006). 'The Impact of NGO Network Conflict on the Corporate Social Responsibility Strategies of Multinational Corporations', *Business and Society*, 45 (3): 282–299.

Sikkink, Kathryn. (1993). 'Human Rights, Principled Issue-Networks, and Sovereignty in Latin America', *International Organization*, 47 (3): 411–441.

Skjelsbaek, Kjell. (1971). 'The Growth of International Nongovernmental Organization in the Twentieth Century', *International Organization*, 25 (3): 113–133.

Smith, Jackie. (1997). *Transnational Social Movements and Global Politics: Solidarity beyond the State*, Syracuse, NY: Syracuse University Press.

———. (2005). 'Globalization and Transnational Social Movement Organisation', in G.F. Davis, D. McAdams, W.R. Scott and M.N. Zald (eds), *Social Movements and Organization Theory*, Cambridge: Cambridge University Press.

Tarrow, Sidney. (1989). *Democracy and Disorder*, Oxford: Clarendon Press.

———. (1994). *Power in Movement*, Cambridge: Cambridge University Press.

Van Rooy, Alison. (2004). *The Global Legitimacy Game: Civil Society, Globalization and Protest*, Basingstoke: Palgrave Macmillan.

4 Global Social Movement Networks and the Politics of Change

Raffaele Marchetti and Mario Pianta

SOCIAL MOVEMENTS IN A GLOBAL CONTEXT[1]

Political mobilizations on global issues have often been interpreted by extending in various directions the model of national social movements to a context of transnational actions (della Porta, Kriesi and Rucht 1999; Smith and Wiest 2005; Tarrow 2001). Whereas there is no shortage of empirical cases that fall into the pattern of a limited internationalization of domestic activism, we argue that this approach is unable to capture the fundamental novelty of the global mobilizations on global issues of the last two decades. Such novelty can only be understood if studied from a truly transnational perspective rather than as an extension of domestic political logic (Coleman and Wayland 2006; Pianta, Marchetti and Zola 2009).

In this regard, three directions for the study of transnational mobilization can be identified. A first group of studies in this transnational direction investigated the evolution of specific nationally (or locally) based campaigns that involved some cross-border dimensions, in terms of access to (or provision of) knowledge, resources, support, legitimation or political alliances with activist organizations (and sometimes also institutions) of other countries.[2] A second line of investigation has addressed mobilizations concerning international institutions as such. Here, social movements engage in conflict over the decisions, policies and behaviour of international institutions, whereas the role of single national governments loses importance. Transnational activism is of major importance in these cases, usually with a crucial co-ordinating role played by large networks of movements or organizations in many countries.[3] A third line of more specific investigations has addressed the rise of the Global Justice Movement (GJM). The specificity of such mobilizations is their focus on *global issues*, although they include a wide spectrum of actions ranging from nationally (or locally) rooted ones to the campaigns on supranational institutions.[4] In order to grasp the transnational component of social movements and civil society at large, it is crucial to focus on those specific processes and social actors that best express this transnational or, indeed, global-scale shift.

Within the broader spectrum of global social movements, transnational networks arguably offer the best instance of this new way of conceptualizing and implementing political relationships at the transnational level. Transnational networks can be considered as a novel expression of transnational politics for at least three main reasons. First, they constitute the organizational backbone of a new political agency that is openly global, thus different from traditional contentious agency at the national level. Second, they show a degree of political maturation of political issues and themes from local and national protest to global proposal. Crucial for this is the envisaging of new identities, awareness of global responsibilities, tolerance of diversity and capacity to building large alliances. Finally, they develop a set of strategies aiming at policy change in complex multilevel systems of governance, with a capacity to address both national and international institutions and policy processes. Innovative strategies and repertoires of action make parallel use of both radical protest and more moderate lobbying of authorities (see Silva's chapter in this volume); such strategies also tend to evolve rapidly, with immediate diffusion of successful models and shifts of the scale of activism. These three elements (organizational structure, themes and strategy) characterize the unique nature of transnational social networks as key elements for understanding global politics, in general, and global contentious politics, in particular. Hence, this chapter outlines the concepts needed to understand transnational networks in global social movements and their impact, providing a comprehensive overview of the main characteristics of transnational networks.[5]

From a transnational perspective, global activism of the last two decades has to be understood in the context of the evolving relationships between the spheres of politics, economy and society, resulting from the increasing international integration that has emerged since the 1980s (Florini 2000; Mittelman 2000; Pianta 2001b, 2001a). At the global level, the sphere of politics is structured by the interstate system, where national states and international institutions exercise their power. Whereas at the national level the political relationships between state and citizens have been defined by constitutions, law and democratic processes, at the global level no universally coercive power of law has yet emerged, and no democratic processes of participation and deliberation have developed for the world citizens. Disregarding the global democratic deficit, political powers have developed new rules for economic and social activities that remain both inefficient and illegitimate within the new context of globalization (Held and McGrew 2002; Marchetti 2008). The sphere of the economy is structured, according to the neoliberal global strategy, by the operation of firms and markets, which are driven by the search for profits. This generates a tendency to turn into commodities an increasingly wide array of activities previously provided and regulated by states and society, from knowledge to education and health, from public services to global public goods such as water and environmental protection. The resulting privatization, deregulation and liberalization, which have characterized the model of neoliberal globalization since the 1980s, have asserted the power of markets and large industrial and financial firms over decisions made in the political sphere and over social behaviours. The recent financial crises have not structurally altered such long-term trend.

Distinct from the spheres of politics and economics, a global sphere of social activities has also emerged. Here, we understand *global civil society* as the sphere of cross-border relationships and activities carried out by collective actors—social movements, networks and civil society organizations—operating independently from states and markets. Actors in the emerging global civil society have formulated a number of demands vis-à-vis the political and economic spheres that include: (a) demands for global democracy, human rights and peace to the political system; (b) demands for global economic justice to the economic system; and (c) demands for global social justice and environmental sustainability to both systems. Conversely, both the political and the economic systems have put pressure on global civil society to adhere to their own values and norms.

Since the 1980s, a growing activism has addressed global issues, defended fundamental rights and advocated change in a transnational perspective (Pianta 2005; Pianta and Marchetti 2007). At the national level, modern definitions of civil society have emphasized its autonomy from both the state and the economy looking at it as the contested terrain where counter-hegemonic projects are developed. In the last decades, however, the demands and activities of civil society moved beyond the domestic interaction, challenging political and economic power across and above national borders. Civil society activism has come to increasingly define itself on the basis of values and identities that transcend national loyalties and to act on global issues across boundaries. A growing field of activism with a transnational organizational structure, identity and scale of operation has thus emerged.

Within global civil society, however, highly heterogeneous actors operate. Among these, *global social movements* are key actors of protest at the global level. They can be identified as cross-border, sustained, collective social mobilizations on global issues; based on permanent and/or occasional organizations, networks and campaigns with a transnational co-ordination; moving from shared values and identities; challenging and protesting economic or political power; and campaigning for change in global issues. They share a global frame of the problems, have a global scope of action and may target supranational or national objectives. The analysis in the rest of the chapter will focus on the transnational networks associated with global social movements that have challenged the dominant model of relationships between global politics, economy and society, developing counter-hegemonic ideas and actions against neoliberal globalization. The characteristics of transnational networks, in both their internal and external dimensions, will be examined in order to identify their dynamics and policy impact. Internal aspects concern the organizational structure, the values and identities and the themes of the networks. External aspects concern the strategic attitude of networks; global political opportunities, the politics of change and the actions of transnational networks will be examined, leading to an assessment of their role and relevance.

THE RISE OF TRANSNATIONAL NETWORKS

Within global social movements, transnational networks are crucial political actors. In this context, a *transnational network* can be defined as a permanent co-ordination among different civil society organizations (and sometimes individuals, such as experts), located in several countries, based on a shared frame for one specific global issue, developing both protest and proposal in the form of joint campaigns and social mobilizations against common targets at the national or supranational level.[6] Transnational networks play a major role in terms of aggregation of social forces and development of common identities. Although embedded in global social movements, they provide political innovation in terms of conceptualization, organizational forms, communication, political skills and concrete projects to the broad archipelago of activism. Despite being subject, as much as any other social and political organization, to internal social competition which generates at times negative outcomes (Bob 2005; Silliman and King 1999), transnational networks can nonetheless be interpreted as positive tools for opening up opportunities for effective social struggles. In this regard, networks are structures created through political agency that alter the political scene in which social movements play.

In the last two decades, cross-border networks of civil society organizations have been the most typical actor promoting political and economic change on global issues. Typical examples of transnational networks active on global justice issues include Our World Is Not for Sale (OWINFS), which has a global reach on trade issues (Silva 2008; see Chapter 5, this volume); Via Campesina, with a global, South-based perspective on agricultural issues (Edelman 2003; McKeon 2009); Attac, as a global network of national associations addressing finance and economic policy (Kolb 2005; see Chapters 11 and 12, this volume); Jubilee 2000 and Jubilee South as global networks on debt issues (Donnelly 2002; see Chapters 6, 7 and 8, this volume); the various women networks active on human rights issues (Bunch 2001; Moghadam 2004); and People's Global Action (PGA), an informal network of grass-roots activists (Juris 2008). The International Committee that organizes the World Social Forum (WSF) can also be considered as a global network engaged in making the largest gathering of global social movements possible every year (de Sousa Santos 2006; Teivainen 2006; Waterman 2004).

Similar transnational networks have emerged in the fields of human rights—such as the campaign for creating the International Criminal Court

(Glasius 2005)—in human security and disarmament—from land mines to small arms (Alcalde 2009; Faulkner 2007)—in environmental issues (Seyfang 2003) and many other global themes.

Transnational networks are usually characterized by their advocacy function toward the promotion of normative change in politics (Keck and Sikkink 1998; Risse-Kappen 1995) that they pursue through the use of transnational campaigns. Many of these campaigns have had some success in influencing policy on global issues. Major examples are the efforts for the establishment of the International Criminal Court (ICC) (1995), which led to the approval of the Rome statute in 1998 (Glasius 2005); the Jubilee campaign on third world debt (1996), which induced creditor governments and the International Monetary Fund (IMF) to take some steps toward debt relief for highly indebted poor countries (Donnelly 2002); and the international campaigns to ban landmines (1992), which led to the intergovernmental conference in Ottawa were the Mine Ban Treaty (1997) was signed (Faulkner 2007). Beyond campaigns, however, transnational networks may also carry out alternative practices—such as solidarity actions or fair trade—that are largely separated from the spheres of global politics and the global economy.

In global political contestation, transnational networks play a twofold critical role: inside and outside global civil society. On the one hand, they can be considered as the backbone of social movements engaged in the political struggle for global justice for they provide essential connecting spaces for the growth of activism at all levels (Katz and Anheier 2006; Smith 2002). On the other hand, they are significant actors in international politics and global governance for they promote transnational campaigns on specific issues and more generally global contentious politics that may lead to policy change on specific issues (Armstrong, Farrell and Maiguashca 2003; Gills 2000; Keck and Sikkink 1998; O'Brien et al. 2000; Scholte 2004; Smith and Johnston 2002; Smith, Chatfield and Pagnucco 1997).[7]

Building on the ample evidence provided by such cases of transnational networks, let us now turn to the context and characteristics of their activities that appear as common features of most transnational networks.

NETWORKING

Transnational networking is a form of organization characterized by voluntary and horizontal patterns of co-ordination, which are trust-centred, reciprocal and asymmetrical. Networks are in fact eminently non-static organizations: flexibility and fluidity are two major features of the network organizational form. A flexible organizational structure enhances the capacity to adapting effectively to changing social circumstances and political situations at the global level. Fluid organizational structure, conversely, allows for porous organizational boundaries that do not require enrolment ratified by formal membership, but are able to cross national and cultural borders. Network structure also varies in that connections can be direct as well as indirect, and linkages can be centralized or decentralized with differing levels of segmentation (Anheier and Katz 2005; Diani 2003). Main activities of transnational networks include spreading information, influencing mass media and raising awareness. In this vein, they constitute a sort of 'global infrastructure' for global social movements. By sharing information, resources and costs, transnational networks generate value-added for all their participants in terms of innovation, responsiveness and mutual support, thus achieving greater legitimacy and power in a positive sum manner. At the same time, lobbying, protest and supplying of services to constituency are also main functions and objectives of transnational networks.

A network among organizations from a large number of countries is formed when a set of preconditions exist, in terms of values, identities and political projects, and when a convergence develops on the importance of a specific global issue, on the agreement on a common issue frame and on the appropriate strategies to tackle it. The procedures according to which the consensus on values, identity and strategy is negotiated, affirmed and reproduced among independent members that decide to work together on global issues are crucial in order to achieve convergence. The production of a statute, charter or programme is usually crucial in the network formation process that is then approved following different procedures, both formal and informal, consensus being the most frequent method.[8]

The 'internal' dynamics of a global network are determined by the strategic decisions of national social and political actors to enter, stay or leave a network. Underpinning these decisions are a number of reasons which can be interpreted according to a model of acquisition of shares of 'ownership' in the network, where the investment of political capital and resources by each participant is negotiated with the network co-ordinator and other key members, in order to obtain political gains both at the international and national level, in ways that may differ substantially across member organizations. Networks are thus constantly evolving through processes of internal discussion, contestation and resistance, which produce either a new 'constitutional' character or a new membership. Here the power dimension of transnational networks is clearly evident. In transnational networks, the key principled dimension (to be examined in the next section) is always pragmatically combined to a strategic or instrumental dimension, which can be roughly labelled *do ut des* conditionality. Although the normative content is of paramount importance in the structuring of transnational networks, it is equally significant to reveal the instrumental side of the network relationships in terms of political drive, leadership and interest pursuit. The instrumental reading of the network organizational structure is nowhere more evident than in the mechanism of participation and 'ownership' of the network. Members are not part of the network until they decide to what extent to take part, which is directly dependent on what the member receives back from its participation. This results in differing degrees of participation of each member, and thus in asymmetrical roles in the network.

This strategic aspect of the network organizational form, however, should not be overemphasized, for it is moderated by both the discursive process within the network which keeps changing members' interests and by the original background in reference to common principles and values. In this regard, members should be simultaneously considered stakeholders and shareholders. They are stakeholders insofar as they have in common—before entering a network or as a consequence of the internal discursive practice—a number of general principles and values that refer to concrete stakes in the struggle on global politics (the moral side of the network relationship). But they are also shareholders as they bargain the degree of their engagement according to the degree of the satisfaction of their specific interest (the strategic, power-related side of the network relationship). Both strategic and normative components are then balanced by an outcome-oriented attitude, according to which achieving concrete results and building credibility constitute important elements underpinning networks' strength, growth and legitimacy.

VALUES AND IDENTITIES

Transnational networks within GJMs are characterized by a set of common beliefs and values which define their political identity. Whereas other kinds of networks are constituted around different principles (economic, scientific, etc.), network activists are usually motivated by shared principled ideas and interpret their role as a fully political, non-profit attitude (Keck and Sikkink 1998; Ness and Brechin 1988). Transnational networks are dependent on shared values and, at the same time, are key organizational instruments for building such shared values, identities, mutual trust, common visions and strategies among organizations of different countries (Olesen 2005; Risse-Kappen 1994; Schulz 1998; Smith, Pagnucco and Lopez 1998; Smith 2002). Differently from the national case, the members of transnational networks do not originally share the same issue frames, political cultures or repertoires of action, nor do they generally share a language. Within a national civil society, the common language, culture and experience make the rise of collective action easier, involving both organizations and individuals, with a highly informal pattern and fuzzy edges of the movement. At the global level, such common ground cannot be taken for granted and has to be slowly built by deliberate, long-term efforts of organizations with substantial resources. In the case of GJMs, the complexity of global issues and the resources needed for acting on them are major barriers to entry in the field of global activism. Transnational networks have represented a major way for lowering such barriers and allowing a broader participation to global campaigns.

The normative aspect of transnational networks and, more generally, of social movements is crucial in defining their identity. In particular, the normative component of this kind of organizations illustrates a double and reciprocal dynamics, in which universal principles encounter values and norms generated from below, resulting in an unpredictable and creative normative combination. Transnational networks foster a number of fundamental principles which, despite being originated in a specific cultural context, can be shared by culturally diverse actors. These principles typically include equality, justice, peace, human rights, autonomy and environmental protection (Boli and Thomas 1999; de Sousa Santos and Rodríguez-Garavito 2005; Risse, Ropp and Sikkink 1999; Smith, Pagnucco and Lopez 1998). Alongside these fundamental principles, value pluralism is expressed by the differing norms emerging from below, from grass-roots movements, which serve as sources of credibility for the project of normative persuasion pushed by transnational networks. The interaction between the global and local perspectives on values can be highly effective for creating new spaces for political action (such as in the case of the WSF).

However, the asymmetries among members' political cultures, commitments and resources should not be underestimated and may lead to power positions and unbalanced decision-making within networks, often in favour of Western countries (extreme cases may be the international 'franchising' strategies of Friends of the Earth [FoE] or Transparency International; the latter, however, could hardly be considered as part of global social movements). The important role that civil society organizations from the North have played in past decades in the establishment of major transnational networks has even led to charges of 'cultural imperialism' and of under-representation of voices and interests of the South in some contexts (Doherty and Doyle 2005; Smith and Wiest 2005). An increasing awareness of such risks is emerging in most networks, and some are experimenting with novel forms of transnational links involving popular organizations from the South (Sen et al. 2004). In recent years, however, the influence of South-based global networks has increased; in the case of trade issues and mobilizations against World Trade Organization (WTO) policies, groups such as Via Campesina, Third World Network and Focus on the Global South have come to play a dominant role in shaping global activism and interacting with policymakers (see Chapter 5, this volume).

When the matching of values and principles is problematic, a common normative strategy to disseminate fundamental principles and to enhance the encounter between universal and local values consists of deploying the adjacency principle (Tilly 2001). Accordingly, an appeal is made to fundamental principles that are already accepted in other spheres and cases, and an extension to new circumstances is proposed through an appeal to an impartial analogy. Such value transportation provides a mechanism that allows for influence over other spheres of action, both domestically and transnationally. However, because each cultural context is modelled on different values, results vary because the encounter generated by the norm's transportation does not guarantee an unconditional acceptance in the receiving community. Moreover, even the cultural domain where the principle has originated can be influenced in turn, thus changing those principles that are claimed to be universal. In both cases of change, the normative interaction between diverse cultural–political contexts produces a new identity, which is fundamental for the promotion of normative change in the political realm (Finnemore and Sikkink 1998).

The coexistence of the appeal to common ideals and to specific local norms and values, in fact, explains also the possibility for activists with different nationalities, personal motivations and social background to be involved in a common transnational collective action without having to belong to a specific organization. By producing a common interpretation of reality that generates feelings of a shared destiny and solidarity, transnational networks nurture a common identity, which is inclusive of very different economic and social conditions, uniting, for instance, poor farmers of the South and affluent consumers of the North as in the Via Campesina network, or groups from indebted countries and from creditor countries as in the Jubilee networks. Such a development represents a major novelty in the forms of political action, as it overcomes the 'us' against 'them' opposition and moves beyond a strictly antagonistic perspective of the 'other'. Such a complex redefinition of identities and interests across national borders results from the ability of transnational networks to develop a common interpretation of global realities—typically with a critique of neoliberal globalization—to shape common targets in an autonomous way and to offer prospects for concrete actions and effective change. This shared identity, however, does not preclude the preservation of diversity, as political visions are always entrenched in grass-roots political experiences. Pluralism within networks is then allowed by the simultaneous presence of differing perspectives of action, informed by local motivational sources and a shared appeal to ultimate values.

GLOBAL POLITICAL OPPORTUNITIES AND THE POLITICS OF CHANGE

At the core of mechanisms leading to the emergence and operation of transnational networks resides the perception of the possibility of change in one specific global issue area. Whereas the perception of an unjust situation necessarily constitutes a precondition for action, it is only when the actor recognizes the possibility to have a positive impact on such a situation that mobilization may start. Necessary for such a mobilization are two elements: conceptualization and political commitment.

Transnational mobilization on global issues should be interpreted as the result of several steps. A crucial challenge for any transnational network is the ability to present the issue at stake in a way that it is perceived as problematic, urgent and soluble (Bob 2005; Carpenter 2007; Keck and Sikkink 1998). The first step in cross-border mobilizations is, therefore, the production of knowledge and the creation of frames presenting the issue in such terms. A second step consists of the external dissemination and strategic use of such knowledge (Kolb 2005). This is the crucial stage for it is here that information acquires a fully public dimension, thus a political significance. Global public opinion needs to be attracted and its imagination captured for framing the terms of the conflict in such a way that the issue at stake becomes associated to a general interest which requires a public engagement. Often, when networks become active players in the 'epistemic communities' of experts of global issues, they tend to be perceived by public opinion as credible sources of information and increase their influence on policy-making.

However, in order to promote change a third step is necessary in terms of acquisition of legitimate representation of the general interests at stake (Brown 2008; Collingwood 2006; Jordan and van Tuijl 2000; Van Rooy 2004). Contrasting the situation of international affairs in which states monopolize power and social actors are structurally excluded, the task consists here in the appropriation of a recognized role in the public sphere, as rightful advocates of general interests. To the question 'in the name of whom do you speak?', transnational networks need to offer a response in terms of reclaiming for themselves the representation of a more general interest than the one relevant for economic and political decision-makers (Florini 2000; Hudson 2001; Rajagopal 2003). Once transnational networks succeed, through the process here summarized, in shaping a challenge associated to particular global issues, the political opportunity for mobilizing and network building arises.

The global political opportunity structure within which transnational networks act is complex and multilayered (della Porta and Tarrow 2005; Kolb 2005; Tarrow 2001, 2005; Thomas 2002). Although the issues that motivate mobilization can be ultimately global (though often mediated by the national or local dimensions), the possibility of successful mobilization is rooted in the structure of political opportunities combining the national and transnational domain of political action. Whereas success necessarily depends on international circumstances, an important role in the rise of global social movements is often played by national conditions (McAdam, McCarthy and Zald 1996; Schulz 1998; see Chapter 5, this volume). In national contexts, social movements are rooted in a thick web of social relations and common identities and have access to important resources (human, financial, etc.), but operate in highly formalized political systems that shape and constrain their mobilization and impact. Conversely, at the global level, transnational networks face major obstacles and costs in building up cross-border relationships among civil society organizations with different cultures and languages, and they have access to highly limited resources. At the same time, however, transnational networks face a political system where the lack of democracy and the innumerable failures to address global problems represent as many opportunities for cross-border mobilizations. The lack of a rigid, well-defined institutional setting similar to the national one widens the options for political action. In different ways, international organizations such as the United Nations or the European Union may provide opportunities for creating political spaces and mobilizing resources to the advantage of transnational networks and national activism (Joachim and Locher 2009; McKeon 2009).

In fact, transnational networks may contribute to expand the political opportunities that are present in national contexts; they often serve as facilitators for providing space to actors who are usually voiceless and excluded (Evans 2000). Transnational networks can also amplify local voices through global 'bridges' and 'boomerangs', setting them in the context of global issues and policies and providing in this way greater strength to local or national activism (Keck and Sikkink 1998, Tarrow 2001; Thomas 2002). At the global level, transnational networks can provide 'discursive representation' to global interests that remains unrepresented in the political system (Keck 2004).

In the more fluid space of global politics, the wider opportunities for political action may lead to a variety of strategies by transnational networks. When there is a low degree of conflict and institutional alliances are possible, 'vertical coalitions' on selected global issues may emerge. In these, civil society organizations may cooperate, or at least establish a dialogue, with particular supranational organizations (Willets 2006) and with some 'progressive' governments or regional bodies (as in the cases of the International Criminal Court, landmines, child labour or the Cancún WTO conference). When conflict is strong, on the other hand, it can be easily directed to the highest level, to the core of global decision-making (as in the case of G8 protests), with a highly visible and effective challenge. In both cases, the results are greater opportunities for transnational networks to emerge as a legitimate and authoritative voice for global interests, extending their impact on public opinion and on civil society organizations interested in joining transnational networks and mobilizations.

Transnational networks can thus be understood as functional organizational responses to the new global socio-political environment in which political opportunities, on the one hand, and scarce resources (finance, knowledge, etc.), on the other, create conditions in which a network structure can perform better than other organizational forms (Pfeffer 1997). As this combination is inherently contingent, transnational networks tend to have a limited political life. On the one hand, networks are created on specific issues; it is very difficult to change and 'reprogramme' them towards a different issue, and in many cases it is just easier to create a new network. On the other hand, social movements and especially networks are cyclical phenomena. The interaction between the set of values shared by social movements and global political opportunities leads to the emergence of different projects of political change, reflecting also the heterogeneity of actors, for instance, balancing more 'reformist' and more 'radical' attitudes (Marchetti 2009; Pianta 2001b). Individual networks, therefore, fit a specific set of conditions internal and external to global movements, but when some of them change, the factors that led to their rise may dissolve, mobilization may decline rapidly and networks are unlikely to readapt to new political contexts.

ACTIONS

The major instrument of action available to transnational networks is the development of campaigns. They involve co-ordinated activities, at the global, national and local levels, including a wide repertoire of actions from protest to information and education of public opinion, from lobbying to advocacy of alternative policies. Such actions are made possible, organized or encouraged by transnational networks and derive an important part of their significance and impact from the very presence of co-ordinated transnational activism.

Typically, a global campaign requires a clear message able to mobilize activists, supporters and sympathizers against a blatant injustice and a well-defined adversary or in solidarity with the victims. Campaign activities tend to be carried out by the network itself in the case of global events, and by its member organizations or sub-networks when they take place at the country or local level. A successful campaign requires the right choice of action repertoires, levels of mobilization and targeting of adversaries, in order to maximize both activism and the potential impact on the policy process.

The activities of transnational networks are summarized in Table 4.1 in terms of i) the nature of activism—focused on civil society itself, educating public opinion, targeting specific institutions or developing alternative practices, and ii) its scope—truly global actions, transnational or regional actions, or national/local actions with a global significance. An important part of actions is directed 'internally' to network members and global movements, or to the 'proximate' world of civil society groups that may be attracted to the issue at stake; this is the case, typically, of the WSF. Other forms of activism specifically target the 'external' world of public opinion or global political and economic powers; this is the case of mobilizations on trade, debt, democracy or wars. Actions by transnational networks have a differentiated impact on their internal, 'proximate' and external constituencies, and respond to specific needs, challenges and opportunities emerging in different contexts. The examples provided in Table 4.1 show that major global mobilizations have in fact focused on different types of activities with distinct objectives; therefore, their outcomes need be assessed with different benchmarks. However, the examples

Table 4.1 Types and Scope of Activities of Transnational Networks

	Truly Global Actions	*Transnational or Regional Actions*	*National/Local Actions with a Global Significance*
Activities Internal to Civil Society	World Social Forum (WSF)	European Social Forum (ESF)	Local Social Forum
Public Opinion-Oriented Actions	Global day of action against war in Iraq	Actions on EU External Human Rights Policy	National actions on climate change
Institutions-Oriented Actions	Campaign for reforming the United Nations	Anti-Bolkestein campaign in the EU	Campaigns on national debt relief for third world countries
Concrete Alternative Practices	Corporate accountability	Fair Trade	Zapatismo in Chiapas

also show the difficulty of establishing clear-cut divisions between types of action that may have an impact on several 'targets', and may involve mobilizations at several levels.

Finally, in terms of activities targeting institutions, three different models of interaction with power may be identified: (a) acceptance, integration and co-optation in existing power centres; (b) external dialogue and criticism, aiming at reform; (c) rejection and conflict aiming at radical change. Whereas the models of integration and critical dialogue entail the possibility of reframing the institutional discourse from, alternatively, inside or outside the policy process, the model of rejection leads to political contestation. The differences in the nature and locus of the strategies pursued by transnational networks and social movements in addressing global issues reflect the variety of actors within social movements, their visions and attitudes, as well as the specific opportunities that they try to seize. Such differences, however, are not necessarily a factor of weakness; in fact, successful change in global issues requires a combination of differing capacity of resistance, radical visions, alternative practices, policy proposals and instruments able to introduce specific reforms when favourable political opportunities open up (Pianta 2001b; Pianta, Marchetti and Zola 2009).

CONCLUSIONS

In this chapter, political mobilizations on global issues have been interpreted through a transnational perspective that allowed us to grasp the novelty of global social movements as contentious global political actors. Within them, transnational networks have been identified as key innovatory forms of political mobilization, able to effectively address global justice and other international issues.

Building on the conceptualizations of global activism by different streams of literature, and on the evidence from a large number of case studies, we have proposed a definition of the key common features that define transnational networks associated to global social movements. They include the nature of networks as organizations, values, political opportunities and types of action. In the last two decades transnational networks have played a major role as backbones of global social movements, mobilizing grass-roots activists and influencing world public opinion, developing transcultural common identities, formulating multiple campaigning strategies and carrying out political struggles, both against and inside international institutions. Transnational networks have developed a sophisticated political formulation of global issues and have challenged the legitimacy and policies of global economic and political powers. They have given voice to demands for global justice and opened up spaces for public participation in global decision-making, demanding greater international democracy.

When policy changes on global issues have been implemented on debt, trade, food, finance, human rights, human security or the environment it has usually been influenced by the long-term efforts of transnational networks associated to global social movements. If we are to understand how change may happen in global policy, transnational networks have to be recognized as an increasingly important player in the arena of global politics.

NOTES

1. The authors wish to thank Martin Koehler for extensive discussions on the themes of this chapter, and Donatella della Porta, Peter Utting and Daniela Barrier for their comments.
2. See Bandy and Smith (2004); Cohen and Rai (2000); della Porta, Kriesi and Rucht (1999); della Porta and Tarrow (2005); Khagram, Riker and Sikkink (2002); Smith, Chatfield and Pagnucco (1997); Smith and Johnston (2002).
3. See Cohen and Rai (2000); Glasius (2005); Joachim and Locher (2009); Keck and Sikkink (1998); Khagram, Riker and Sikkink (2002); O'Brien et al. (2000).
4. See Arrighi, Hopkins and Wallerstein (1989); Brecher, Costello and Smith (2000); della Porta et al. (2006); della Porta (2007); Pianta (2001a); Pianta and Silva (2003); Waterman (2001).
5. The present analysis is based on our previous empirical research (Pianta 2001b; Pianta and Silva 2003; Pianta 2005; Pianta and Zola 2007) and on work for the DEMOS project (della Porta 2007, 2009a, 2009b; della Porta Pianta, Marchetti and Zola 2009; Pianta and Marchetti 2007). Whereas these works provide extensive empirical analyses, in this chapter we aim to offer a broader theoretical formulation of the key features of transnational networks in global social movements.
6. In particular, 'in organisational studies networks are conceptualised as relationships based on forms of exchange and distinct from markets and hierarchies. Networks are regarded as an intermediary between markets and

hierarchies as they have less uncertainty than the former and less complexity than the latter' (Henry, Mohan and Yanacopulos 2004: 842). However, social networks entail differing power and thus some degree of implicit hierarchy, as explained in a later section.

7. In some cases transnational networks, rather than being the backbone of global mobilizations, may play a more peripheral role, with a 'bridging function' between civil society and global politics, providing national groups with experts' competences, resources and access to international institutions. Examples include UN-related networks favouring civil society participation to UN activities or World Summits (Pianta 2005), or networks favouring consultation and dialogue with corporations on environmental sustainability or corporate social responsibility (see Chapters 4 and 9, this volume). Networks with a bridging function are peripheral to the dynamics of global social movements and may lose autonomy and legitimacy as they move closer to cooperation with centres of power, thus running the risk of co-optation.
8. The different procedures may include simple majority voting, qualified majority voting, consensus, unanimity and no objection base. Additional key elements in this process include internal debate, entitlement to speak and entitlement to vote.

BIBLIOGRAPHY

Alcalde, Javier. (2009). *Changing the World. Explaining Successes and Failures of International Campaigns by NGOs in the Field of Human Security*, PhD thesis, European University Institute.

Anheier, Helmut, Glasius, Marlies, and Kaldor, Mary. (eds) (2001). *Global Civil Society 2001*, Oxford: Oxford University Press.

Anheier, Helmut, and Katz, Hagai. (2005). 'Network Approach to Global Civil Society', in Helmut Anheier, Marlies Glasius and Mary Kaldor (eds), *Global Civil Society Yearbook 2004/5*, London: Sage.

Armstrong, David, Farrell, Theo, and Maiguashca, Bice. (eds) (2003). *Governance and Resistance in World Politics*, Cambridge: Cambridge University Press.

Arrighi, Giovanni, Hopkins, Terence, and Wallerstein, Immanuel. (1989). *Antisystemic Movements*, London: Verso.

Bandy, Joe, and Smith, Jackie. (eds) (2004). *Coalitions across Borders: Transnational Protest and the Neoliberal Order*, Lanham, MD: Rowan and Littlefield.

Bob, Clifford. (2005) *The Marketing of Rebellion: Insurgents, the Media and International Activism*, Cambridge: Cambridge University Press.

Boli, John, and Thomas, George M. (eds) (1999). *Constructing World Culture: International Non-Governmental Organizations since 1875*, Stanford, CA: Stanford University Press.

Brecher, Jeremy, Costello, Tim, and Smith, Brendan. (2000) *Globalization from Below. The Power of Solidarity*, Cambridge: South End Press.

Brown, L. David. (2008). *Creating Credibility. Legitimacy and Accountability for Transnational Civil Society*, Sterling, VA: Kumarian Press.

Bunch, Charlotte. (2001). 'International Networking for Women's Human Rights', in M. Edwards and J. Gaventa (eds), *Global Citizen Action*, London: Earthscan.

Carpenter, R. Charli. (2007). 'Setting the Advocacy Agenda: Theorizing Issue Emergence and Non-Emergence in Transnational Advocacy Networks', *International Studies Quarterly*, 51 (1): 99–120.

Cohen, R., and Rai, S. (eds) (2000). *Global Social Movements*, London: Athlone Press.

Coleman, William D., and Wayland, Sarah. (2006). 'The Origins of Global Civil Society and Nonterritorial Governance: Some Empirical Reflections', *Global Governance*, 12 (3): 241–261.

Collingwood, Victoria. (2006). 'Non-Governmental Organizations, Power and Legitimacy in International Society', *Review of International Studies*, 32:439–454.

de Sousa Santos, Boaventura. (2006). *The Rise of the Global Left: The World Social Forum and Beyond*, London: Zed Books.

de Sousa Santos, Boaventura, and Rodríguez-Garavito, Cesar A. (eds) (2005). *Law and Globalization from Below: Toward a Cosmopolitan Legality*, Cambridge: Cambridge University Press.

della Porta, Donatella. (ed) (2007). *The Global Justice Movement: A Cross-National and Transnational Perspective*, Boulder, CO: Paradigm.

———. (2009a). *Another Europe. Conceptions and Practices of Democracy in the European Social Forums*, London: Routledge.

———. (2009b). *Democracy in Movement. Conceptions and Practices of Democracy in Contemporary Social Movements*, London: Palgrave.

della Porta, Donatella, Andretta, Massimilian, Mosca, Lorenzo, and Reiter, Herbert. (2006). *Globalization from Below: Transnational Activists and Protest Networks*, Minneapolis: University of Minnesota Press.

della Porta, Donatella, Kriesi, Hanspeter, and Rucht, Dieter. (eds) (1999). *Social Movements in a Globalizing World*, London: Macmillan.

della Porta, Donatella, and Tarrow, Sidney. (eds) (2005). *Transnational Protest and Global Activism*, Lanham, MD: Rowan and Littlefield.

Diani, Mario. (2003). 'Networks and Social Movements: A Research Programme', in M. Diani and D. McAdam (eds), *Social Movements and Networks: Relational Approaches to Collective Action*, Oxford: Oxford University Press.

Doherty, Brian and Doyle, Timothy (2005) 'Friends of the Earth International (FoEI): Negotiating a North-South Identity', Paper presented at the ECPR's Joint Sessions in Granada, Spain, April 2005.

Donnelly, E.A. (2002). 'Proclaiming Jubilee: The Debt and Structural Adjustment Network', in S. Khagram, J.V. Riker and K. Sikkink (eds), *Restructuring World Politics: Transnational Social Movements, Networks and Norms*, Minneapolis: University of Minnesota Press.

Edelman, Marc. (2003). 'International Peasant and Farmers Movements and Networks', in M. Kaldor, H. Anheier and M. Glasius (eds), *Global Civil Society 2003*, Oxford: Oxford University Press.

Evans, Peter. (2000). 'Fighting Marginalisation with Transnational Networks: Counter-Hegemonic Globalisation', *Contemporary Sociology*, 29:230–242.

Faulkner, Frank. (ed) (2007). *Moral Entrepreneurs and the Campaign to Ban Landmines*, New York: Rodopi Press.

Finnemore, Martha, and Sikkink, Kathryn. (1998). 'International Norms Dynamics and Political Change', *International Organization*, 52 (4): 887–917.

Florini, Ann. (ed) (2000). *The Third Force: The Rise of Transnational Civil Society*, Tokyo: JCIE and CEIP.

Gills, Barry K. (ed) (2000). *Globalization and the Politics of Resistance*, Basingstoke: Macmillan.

Glasius, Marlies. (2005). *The International Criminal Court: A Global Civil Society Achievement*, London: Routledge.

Held, David, and McGrew, Anthony. (eds) (2002). *Governing Globalization: Power, Authority and Global Governance*, Cambridge: Polity.

Henry, Leroi, Mohan, Giles, and Yanacopulos, Helen. (2004). 'Networks as Transnational Agents of Development', *Third World Quarterly*, 25 (5): 839–855.

Hudson, Alan. (2001). 'NGOs' Transnational Advocacy Networks: From Legitimacy to "Political Responsibility"?' *Global Networks*, 1 (4): 331–352.

Joachim, Jutta, and Locher, Birgit. (eds) (2009). *Transnational Activism in the UN and the EU*, London: Routledge.

Jordan, Lisa, and van Tuijl, Peter. (2000). 'Political Responsibility in Transnational NGO Advocacy', *World Development*, 28 (12): 2051–2065.

Juris, Jeffrey S. (2008). *Networking Futures: The Movement against Corporate Globalization*, Durham, NC: Duke University Press.

Katz, Hagai, and Anheier, Helmut. (2006). 'Global Connectedness: The Structure of Transnational NGO Networks', in M. Glasius, M. Kaldor and M. Anheier (eds), *Global Civil Society 2005/6*, London: Sage.

Keck, Margaret. (2004). 'Governance Regimes and the Politics of Discursive Representation', in N. Piper and A. Uhlin (eds), *Transnational Activism in Asia: Problems of Power and Democracy*, London: Routledge.

Keck, Margaret, and Sikkink, Kathryn. (1998). *Activists beyond Borders: Advocacy Networks in International Politics*, Ithaca, NY: Cornell University Press.

Khagram, Sanjeev, Riker, James, and Sikkink, Kathryn. (eds) (2002). *Restructuring World Politics. Transnational Social Movements, Networks, and Norms*, Minneapolis: University of Minnesota Press.

Kolb, Felix. (2005). 'The Impact of Transnational Protest on Social Movement Organizations: Mass Media and the Making of ATTAC Germany', in D. Della Porta and S. Tarrow (eds), *Transnational Protest and Global Activism*, Lanham, MD: Rowan and Littlefield.

Marchetti, Raffaele. (2008). *Global Democracy: For and Against. Ethical Theory, Institutional Design, and Social Struggles*, London: Routledge.

———. (2009). 'Mapping Alternative Models of Global Politics', *International Studies Review*, 11 (1): 133–156.

McAdam, Doug, McCarthy, John. D, and Zald, Mayer N. (1996). *Comparative Perspectives on Social Movements: Political Opportunities, Mobilizing Structures, and Cultural Framings*, Cambridge: Cambridge University Press.

McKeon, Nora. (2009). *The United Nations and Civil Society: Legitimating Global Governance—Whose Voice?* London: Zed Books.

Mittelman, James H. (2000). *The Globalization Syndrome, Transformation and Resistance*, Princeton, NJ: Princeton University Press.

Moghadam, Valentine. (2004). *Globalizing Women: Gender, Globalization and Transnational Feminist Networks*, Baltimore, MD: Johns Hopkins University Press.

Ness, Gayl D., and Brechin, Steven R. (1988). 'Bridging the Gap: International Organizations as Organizations', *International Organization*, 42:245–273.

O'Brien, Robert, Goetz, Anne Marie, Scholte, Jan Aart, and Williams, Marc. (2000). *Contesting Global Governance: Multilateral Economic Institutions and Global Social Movements*, Cambridge: Cambridge University Press.

Olesen, Thomas. (2005). *International Zapatismo. The Construction of Solidarity in the Age of Globalization*, London: Zed Books.

Pfeffer, Jeffrey. (1997). *New Directions for Organisation Theory*, Oxford: Oxford University Press.

Pianta, Mario. (2001a). *Globalizzazione dal basso. Economia mondiale e movimenti sociali*, Rome: ManifestoLibri.

———. (2001b). 'Parallel Summits of Global Civil Society', in H. Anheier, M. Glasius and M. Kaldor (eds), *Global Civil Society 2001*, Oxford: Oxford University Press.

———. (2005). *UN World Summits and Civil Society. The State of the Art.* UNRISD Programme -Working Paper No.18, UNRISD, Geneva.

Pianta, Mario, and Marchetti, Raffaele. (2007). 'The Global Justice Movements: The Transnational Dimension', in D. Della Porta (ed), *The Global Justice Movement: A Cross-National and Transnational Perspective*, Boulder, CO: Paradigm.

Pianta, Mario, Marchetti, Raffaele, and Zola, Duccio. (2009). 'Crossing Borders. Transnational Activism in European Social Movements', in D. Della Porta (ed), *Democracy in Movement. Conceptions and Practices of Democracy in Contemporary Social Movements*, London: Palgrave.

Pianta, Mario, and Silva, Federico. (2003). *Globalisers from Below: A Survey on Global Civil Society Organisations, Globi Research Report*, Rome: Lunaria.

Pianta, Mario, and Zola, Duccio. (2007). 'La montée en puissance des mouvements globaux 1970–2005', in I. Sommier, O. Fillieule and E. Agrikolinasky (eds), *La généalogie des mouvements altermondialistes*, Paris: Karthala.

Rajagopal, B. (2003). *International Law from Below: Development, Social Movements and Third World Resistance*, Cambridge: Cambridge University Press.

Risse, Thomas, Ropp, Steve, and Sikkink, Kathryn. (eds) (1999). *The Power of Human Rights. International Norms and Domestic Change*, Cambridge: Cambridge University Press.

Risse-Kappen, Thomas. (1994). 'Ideas Do Not Float Freely: Transnational Coalitions, Domestic Structures, and the End of the Cold War', *International Organization*, 48:185–214.

Risse-Kappen, Thomas. (ed) (1995). *Bringing Transnational Relations Back In: Non-State Actors, Domestic Structure and International Institutions*, Ithaca, NY: Cornell University Press.

Scholte, Jan Aart. (2004). 'Civil Society and Democratically Accountable Global Governance', *Government and Opposition*, 39 (2): 211–233.

Schulz, Markus S. (1998). 'Collective Action across Borders: Opportunity Structures, Network Capacities, and Communicative Praxis in the Age of Advanced Globalization', *Sociological Perspectives*, 41 (4): 587–616.

Sen, Jai, Anand, Anita, Escobar, Arturo, and Waterman, Peter. (eds) (2004). *World Social Forum: Challenging Empires*, New Delhi: Viveka Foundation.

Seyfang, Gill. (2003). 'Environmental MEGA-CONFERENCES from Stockholm to Johannesburg BEYOND', *Global Environmental Change*, 13 (3): 223–228.

Silliman, Jael, and King, Ynestra. (eds) (1999). *Dangerous Intersections. Feminist Perspectives on Population, Environment and Development*, Cambridge: South End Press.

Silva, Federico. (2008). *Do Transnational Social Movements Matter? Four Case Studies Assessing the Impact of Transnational Social Movements on the Global Governance of Trade, Labour and Finance*, Ph.D. Thesis, Fiesole, European University Institute.

Smith, Jackie. (2002). 'Bridging Global Divide? Strategic Framing and Solidarity in Transnational Social Movement Organizations', *International Sociology*, 17 (4): 505–528.

Smith, Jackie, Chatfield, Charles, and Pagnucco, Ron. (eds) (1997). *Transnational Social Movements and Global Politics: Solidarity beyond the State*, Syracuse, NY: Syracuse University Press.

Smith, Jackie, and Johnston, H. (eds) (2002). *Globalization and Resistance: Transnational Dimensions of Social Movements*, Lanham, MD: Rowan and Littlefield.

Smith, Jackie, Pagnucco, Ron, and Lopez, George A. (1998). 'Globalizing Human Rights: The Work of Transnational Human Rights NGOs in the 1990s', *Human Rights Quarterly*, 20:379–412.

Smith, Jackie, and Wiest, Dawn. (2005). 'The Uneven Geography of Global Civil Society: National and Global Influences on Transnational Association', *Social Forces*, 84 (2): 621–652.

Tarrow, Sidney. (2001). 'Transnational Politics: Contention and Institutions in International Politics', *Annual Review of Political Science*, 4:1–20.

———. (2005). *The New Transnational Activism*, Cambridge: Cambridge University Press.

Teivainen, Teive. (2006). *Democracy in Movement. The World Social Forum as a Process of Political Learning*, London: Routledge.

Thomas, Daniel C. (2002). 'Boomerangs and Superpowers: International Norms, Transnational Networks and US Foreign Policy', *Cambridge Review of International Affairs*, 15 (1): 25–44.

Tilly, Charles. (2001). 'Mechanisms in Political Processes', *Annual Review of Political Science*, 4:21–41.

Van Rooy, Alison. (2004). *The Global Legitimacy Game: Civil Society, Globalization and Protest*, Basingstoke: Palgrave.

Waterman, P. (2001). *Globalisation, Social Movements and the New Internationalism*, London: Continuum.

———. (2004). 'The Global Justice and Solidarity Movement and the World Social Forum: A Backgrounder', in J. Sen, A. Anand and P. Waterman (eds), *World Social Forum: Challenging Empires*, New Delhi: Viveka Foundation.

Willets, Peter. (2006). 'The Cardoso Report on the UN and Civil Society: Functionalism, Global Corporatism, or Global Democracy?' *Global Governance*, 3 (12): 305–324.

Part II

The Activism–Policy Nexus in Practice

5 Global Networks on Trade Policy

The Case of the WTO Conference in Cancún[1]

Federico Silva

INTRODUCTION

In recent decades civil society has become an increasingly active player in global affairs. Its role, long confined to the national level, has expanded transnationally in the context of globalization and the reallocation of state sovereignty. The creation of supranational institutions like the European Union (EU) and the World Trade Organization (WTO) have major implications for the activist–policy nexus, as trade and other policy is designed and negotiated beyond the nation-state and as activists have to craft new tactics and strategies to gain policy influence. This chapter contributes to the debate on civil society's impact on international policy-making by exploring the role of global advocacy networks in challenging trade liberalization and the policies of the WTO. Special attention is given to the WTO Ministerial Conference held in Cancún in 2003.

Since its foundation in 1995, the WTO has been a key actor in trade liberalization policies and, as a result, has been constantly challenged by major civil society protests. The WTO Ministerial Conference in Seattle in 1999, which was expected to be the launching pad of the so-called Millennium Round, is widely considered as the 'birthplace' of the movements against neoliberal globalization of the last decade. Civil society organizations' (CSOs) protests and criticisms and the growing divide between policy attitudes of the 'North' and the 'South' contributed to make global trade a major arena of contestation of the economic agenda of the North and resulted in the collapse of the Ministerial Conference. Key questions raised by opponents included the unfair nature of 'free' trade among highly unequal trade partners, the unequal distribution of the benefits from trade between North and South, the questionable impact of trade liberalization on development and the lack of democracy in the rules and procedures for WTO decision-making.

The subsequent WTO Ministerial Conference in Doha took place just after 11 September 2001 and at the start of the war in Afghanistan. In that context, civil society was unable to capitalize on its strong mobilizations of 2000 and 2001 and had to reframe the terms of the trade debate in light of the changed geopolitical circumstances. The Doha Ministerial ended with a final declaration which, according to the opponents, further advanced the liberalization agenda. In the run up to Doha, the EU had mobilized to set up an organized coalition that included powerful Northern nations like the United States and Japan and other 'friends of investment countries'. The EU was particularly interested in the revival of negotiations on the so-called Singapore issues, which include, amongst others, investment liberalization.

The next Ministerial Conference of the WTO took place in Cancún, Mexico, in September 2003. Although far less publicized than the two previous WTO Ministerial Conferences, the event was equally, if not more, important. In fact, the dynamics which emerged in Cancún have set the stage for the stalemate in which the WTO and its Doha Round agenda are still trapped a decade later. At Cancún, a counterweight to the power of the EU and other Northern countries clearly emerged and negotiations broke down on 12 September 2003. The conference ended with neither an agreement nor a final declaration. The 'post-mortem' ascribed responsibility to both civil society and developing countries.[2]

In this chapter I investigate the role played by civil society organizations at Cancún itself and in the run up to it, and the impact that global advocacy networks had on the failed negotiations of the WTO Ministerial Conference.

WTO AND GOVERNMENTS' POSITIONS IN THE WTO CONFERENCE IN CANCÚN

In most of the media and in the collective memory, Cancún is associated with the appearance on the global stage of the alliance among emerging powers of the South, such as China, India, Brazil and South Africa, and their challenge to the North on issues of agricultural subsidies and market access. Although divisions on agriculture played a role in heightening tensions among WTO member countries, the most proximate cause for Cancún's collapse was the disagreement on the 'Singapore issues', the negotiating table to which WTO members turned after the stalemate on agriculture. Although less known than other themes, such as tariff barriers and Trade-Related Intellectual Property Rights (TRIPS), the Singapore issues had been in the pipeline for a long time. They refer to the deregulation of financial flows (especially liberalizing foreign direct investment), greater competition, transparency on procurement practices and reductions in the cost of trade. After the creation of the WTO, some of the early members believed that it was necessary to address these issues in a systematic way. The first appearance in the WTO of the issues of investment, competition, transparency in government procurement and trade facilitation dates back to the Ministerial declaration of 1996. Then, the WTO Ministerial

Conference was held in Singapore, which is why these four issues are also known as the 'Singapore issues'.

After the conference of Singapore, WTO working groups on the Singapore issues carried out preliminary work of clarification on the different matters, with the plan to later launch a round of negotiations. After Seattle, decisions on this matter were postponed to Doha. The package of Singapore issues was regarded with particular suspicion by CSOs, because it contained one of the most problematic issues in relation to globalizing processes, namely, foreign direct investment (FDI), which accounted for a large share of financial flows and was considered strategic in trade liberalization. In the eyes of civil society, the issue of investment and its role in the Washington Consensus was at odds with many of the concerns and values linked to rights-based development and social justice.

The liberalization of FDI had been promoted by the Multilateral Agreement on Investment (MAI) sponsored by the OECD in the late 1990s. The collapse of the MAI—partly due to the opposition of France—was widely seen as the first important success of the anti-globalization movement (Anheier, Glasius and Kaldor 2001). The MAI had tried to set up a uniform set of rules protecting FDI from what could be construed as unfair treatment in national law. Generally, civil society viewed the liberalization of FDI as detrimental to developing countries as it would favour multinational corporations over local economies, lower environmental and labour standards and increase inequalities (Clarke and Barlow 1997).

This is why the resurfacing of the trade and investment issue sounded an alarm bell for civil society groups. There was the risk that the general heading 'relationships between trade and investment' might open the way for like-minded Western countries to restart negotiations on investment. At the Doha Ministerial, the final declaration stated that negotiations on the Singapore issues 'will take place after . . . the Ministerial Conference [Cancún] on the basis of a decision to be taken, by explicit consensus . . . on modalities of negotiation'. In other words, it was decided that the work on the Singapore issues should continue in the form of a 'study' (and not be included in the Doha Round), but that an 'opening of negotiations' should soon follow. This call for negotiations responded to the strong pressure exerted by the EU, Japan and the United States, supported by others in the coalition of 'friends of investment countries'.[3] The decision was highly disputed, as were many others at the Doha Ministerial. Thus, the Singapore issues became a symbol of the growing conflict between the North and the South, rather than representing an 'ordinary' multilateral trade dispute.

In the aftermath of Doha, disagreements increased, and a coherent political front was created among developing countries through a series of meetings involving trade ministers. On the whole, ninety developing countries from the Africa, Caribbean and Pacific (ACP), the African Union (AU) and the group of Least Developed Countries (LDC) were officially opposed to the launch of negotiations on the Singapore issues in Cancún. Out of these ninety countries, sixty were members of the WTO, which overall, at the time, counted 148 members.

Against the South, there was the so-called Quad (United States, EU, Japan and Canada) plus some other countries, notably South Korea. It is worth noting that their unity was only apparent; the positions of the EU and the United States were not the same. Differences arose over the antitrust question, where the United States was sceptical about delegating the power of judging on antitrust decisions to a competition policy board in Geneva (*Economist* 2003a),[4] This was probably due to the U.S. consideration that other forums such as NAFTA were a better negotiating place for North American interests than the WTO. The EU was also divided. Confronted with the mounting pressure of developing countries, some states (notably, UK, France and Germany[5]) were downplaying the importance of the Singapore issues and argued against the EU Commission's interpretation of the Doha declaration.[6] Finally, additional pressures on the Commission originated from important groups in the European Parliament, namely, the Greens and socialists, who were explicitly opposed to the launch of negotiations.

The question before the Cancún Ministerial Conference was not so much whether there was opposition to the Singapore issues, but rather how far the opposing block of developing countries would go to resist under the pressure of negotiation. Furthermore, there was the question of whether the Singapore issues would really be at the centre of the Ministerial negotiations or, as in Seattle, whether other issues would be in the spotlight.

GLOBAL ACTIVISM ON TRADE

Major Civil Society Actors, Networks and Organizations

Over the last decade, civil society activities at the transnational level have taken the form of coalitions, networks, alliances and campaigns, combining the strength of nationally based organizations with the international experience and collaboration of development NGOs and specialized networks of experts, amongst others. These actors have represented the core of the rapid emergence of social movements challenging neoliberal globalization.[7]

The rapid growth of global mobilizations has been investigated by several studies.[8] Key civil society actors that have played a major role in building cross-border activism and the global networks on trade policy that have challenged the WTO include the following.

Our World Is Not For Sale (OWINFS)

Created after Seattle, OWINFS was the major global network on trade issues, including over two hundred major organizations from a large number of countries, North and South. It operated as one of the 'general web headquarters' of activism and expertise on trade, providing documents, reports and co-ordinating actions. OWINFS campaigned on different WTO issues, including TRIPS, agriculture, GATS, the Singapore issues and investment. In Europe, a sister platform of OWINFS was created, the Seattle to Brussels Network (S2B), that was particularly active on GATS and co-ordinated some of the major activities and protest events that took place in the run up to Cancún.[9] Most of the organizations and networks listed in the following were also part of OWINFS.

Third World Network (TWN)

Founded in 1984 and based in Malaysia, TWN is an international network of Southern organizations engaged on development issues. It was one of the first organizations to deal with the WTO[10] and its impact on developing countries. TWN includes also *TWN Africa*, which was founded just before Doha and whose activities at the time of Cancún were important in extending the Southern platform. TWN Africa gave rise to the *Africa Trade Network*, which co-ordinates some of the major African organizations active on trade.

Focus on the Global South

Founded in Bangkok in 1995, it has country programmes in India, the Philippines and Thailand. It had played an active role in building civil society competences on trade issues and promoting international networking.

Southern and Eastern African Trade Information and Negotiations Institute (SEATINI)

Linking civil society groups and institutions from several African countries, SEATINI organized specifically to address WTO policies. In the run-up to Cancún it played an important role in establishing links with African governments.

European Organizations

Among European actors, an important role was also played by the major UK civil society organizations, which included CAFOD, Christian Aid, Action Aid, World Development Movement (WDM), Oxfam, War on Want and New Economics Foundation. Cooperating closely in the run-up to Cancún, they provided trade mobilizations with competences, resources and global links, and animated other networks, addressed in this volume, associated with debt relief and trade justice.

International Forum on Globalization (IFG)

Among North American groups, this network with global links, created at the time of NAFTA,[11] played a prominent role in developing strategies and competences. Through teach-ins, conferences and publications it supported the idea that a global co-ordination of efforts was the most effective way to mobilize a critical response to corporate globalization. Major contributions to trade activism came from Public Citizen, Center of Concern, the Institute for Policy Studies, Institute for Agriculture and Trade Policy (IATP), Polaris Institute and the Council of Canadians.

The Dynamics of Transnational Networks

The role of networks in global activism is crucial. This has been identified since the early works on social movements. Collective actions have been compared to the 'reticular and polycephalous' image of a network (Gerlach 1976). With globalization, this 'relational aspect' has been stressed even more (Anheier, Glasius and Kaldor 2001; Reinicke 1999), and the network metaphor came to cover any collective action in modern societies, including knowledge production and fruition (Castells 1996). In this book, Chapters 3 and 4 explore parallel dimensions of the importance of networks for global activism.

The development of more structured alliances through networking in order to reinforce the 'internal' dynamics of civil society is a quality CSOs have always invested in. In Diani's (1995) analysis, networks are the 'precondition' not only for collective actions but often also for their 'outcome'. First, networks increase the capacity to mobilize material resources (money and people), which is an urgent need for organizations operating at the transnational scale; second, global issues require a certain amount of expertise (immaterial resources) that can be more easily provided collectively through the horizontal flows of information that characterizes networks. This is why it has been argued that, the more CSOs are linked, the more likely they are to survive (Smith, Chatfield and Pagnucco 1997: 55).

Empirical research on the UN parallel summits and other civil society events have pointed out that these venues are perceived by CSOs both as an occasion to deploy their 'external' strategies of protest and lobbying and an opportunity for addressing their 'internal' needs of strengthening and developing their relations (Benchmark Environmental Consulting 1996; Pianta 2001; Van Rooy 1997). As it is often argued, networking at the transnational level has been favoured by the revolution in communication technology that has greatly increased the possibility of exchanging information and organizational capabilities for mobilization or recruitment of members (Starr 2005).

Network analysis has been widely used in recent years for investigating such developments. It makes it possible to understand the collective and relational aspects by looking at general structural patterns of a group, instead of focusing on the characteristics of each single unit (see, for example, Anheier and Katz 2005; Diani 1995; Diani and McAdam 2003). Concepts drawn from network analysis theory have proved particularly useful at assessing the impact of civil society organizations, because results are often obtained collectively. Specifically, scholars have successfully linked certain specific relational properties of a group with the consequences of its actions.[12] So-called 'non-segmented', 'optimized' or 'dense' networks are the most effective in terms of political impact (Anheier and Katz 2005; Caniglia 2002; Diani 1995; Diani and McAdam 2003). In fact, networks with the preceding characteristics appear to favour an optimized flow of information and resources, enhancing the effectiveness of its actions.

The higher the density of the network, the higher the number of linkages, which means that there are more (alternative) paths for the different actors to exchange resources and information (knowledge, expertise, competences) with other actors. The lower the average distance, the shorter the paths through which information and resources have to flow; thus, more resources are saved, and resources and information flow more quickly. The more compact the network, the more easily resources and information will be diffused and shared among *all* the nodes and not only by those which are closer to each other. Conversely, highly segmented networks have very few possibilities of surviving, simply because their actors have difficulties in exchanging the information and resources necessary to foster their cooperation. A new linkage is not a costless task, because it requires an effort to establish and maintain it. If the network structure is not able to 'return' these costs in terms of cooperation enhancement, the network risks collapsing with respect to its very *raison d'être*.

From the analysis of the relationships amongst the CSOs engaged in the Cancún process, what emerges is a highly non-segmented network (Silva 2008). The network is not only wide and variegated in its memberships, but the actors are densely connected and the low average distance among them shows an overall picture of compactness. Furthermore, powerful actors, such as TWN, Focus and the UK CSOs, were the most central ones, playing a crucial brokerage role and helping in bringing all the nodes together. Confirming the aforementioned view of networks, this structure has been beneficial for civil society activism as it has allowed the construction of an epistemic-like community, effective lobbying and widespread protests, examined in the next paragraphs.

THE EMERGENCE OF AN EPISTEMIC COMMUNITY

If the network can be considered the 'hardware' of collective action, resources running across it can be considered its 'software', including both material (money and people) and immaterial (frames, knowledge and information) elements. The importance of the latter type of resources has been underlined by sociologists pointing out that network structures create a sense of collective identity that is a justification and an incentive for collective action (della Porta and Diani 1999). In fact, the constant exchange of information and identities contributes to create a substratum of common understanding, frames and goals that keeps the network together.

However, the importance of such immaterial resources in conceptualizing a civil society network can be better captured through the idea of 'epistemic community'. An epistemic community has been described as a group of people united by a series of principled beliefs reflecting the beliefs of the wider community, which is characterized by a well-known reputation and a high level of expertise, and oriented towards promoting these shared beliefs in the policy process (see Haas 1990, 1992). Although Haas' definition was originally developed for 'technocratic' or academic groups, the definition applies well to some CSOs networks.[13]

Keck implicitly achieved similar conclusions in studying NGOs in the World Bank project of Planaforo: 'NGOs channel information, make contacts, write reports and briefing papers [. . .] the role NGOs play involves brokerage rather than representation. In it, the necessary political resources are not those we associate with traditional forms of political mediation—ability to mobilise, attract votes distribute patronage–but rather access to information [and] the ability to *produce* information' (Keck 1998: 198). In this perspective, it is crucial to note that the exchange and sharing of information is not an end in itself. Espousing Haas's idea that the information produced by epistemic-like communities is oriented towards policy change, Keck and Sikkink (1998) noted that the information social movements produce and diffuse is their 'most valuable currency' to influence political processes.[14]

At the global level, access to information and knowledge appears as a key factor for the effectiveness of civil society activism, especially when they consist of competences such as mastering the technical jargon, analysing policies and their consequences and the ability to develop detailed counterproposals. In fact, civil society organizations capable of producing such knowledge can be considered as *experts* by interested parties such as policymakers, media and public opinion, thus increasing their influence on the policy process. Risse (2000) defines this relevant information as 'authoritative knowledge' to remark the role that *expertise* plays in augmenting CSOs' leverage in politics. Generally, CSOs capitalize on their more general knowledge deriving from past experiences, and this knowledge-experience takes different forms. The *knowledge-experience of the political process* (for example, knowledge of how an IGO works, up-to-date information on the negotiation stages, knowledge of the channels of influence) means being familiar with the 'rules of the game'. The *networking knowledge-experience* is the capability of CSOs, based on personal relationships, to know each other's qualities and competences and the 'right' officials and policymakers. Finally, the *communicative knowledge-experience* is CSOs' capability to handle the media, to know how communication mechanisms work and how to reframe an issue in order to make it palatable and comprehensible for the media and the public and not least to CSOs themselves.

According to available data (Silva 2008), the civil society network of organizations active in Cancún can be regarded as a vibrant epistemic-like community if we consider the role that information and knowledge played in their strategies. CSOs produced a remarkable variety of materials on the Singapore issues, ranging from technical documents to firsthand information on the negotiations' status, to media releases, to educational material, that were circulated online to reach wider audiences (Silva 2008). In parallel, several workshops and conferences were held on these issues, including events at the first (2001) and second (2002) World Social Forum in Porto Alegre. These conferences played an important role in spreading ideas, strengthening network ties and enlarging the network of organizations and groups involved in transnational activism.[15]

REFRAMING TRADE ISSUES FOR GLOBAL PUBLIC OPINION

A major outcome of this epistemic-like community was the ability to influence public opinion. The richness of web-based activities diffusing knowledge on the problems of liberalization of trade and investment influenced the framing of the public debate. Additional work was carried out by CSOs with regard to the need of turning complex technical issues into something that the public and the media would find ethically and politically relevant and worth engaging in. The Singapore issues were linked to the experience of the MAI—on which a solid base of public opinion had already formed—and were incorporated into a broader social justice discourse, which presented them as a means for the North to strengthen the divide with the South. Finally, the Singapore issues were linked to other high profile themes in WTO negotiations, such as the agreement on trade in services (GATS).[16] Choosing to campaign on different issues at the same time and producing declarations that mention the two together stimulated the reflection of public opinion on the potential linkages between them.[17]

Reframing the issues was important in order to make the public aware of how crucial they were and to render the issues relevant for a broader range of CSOs. At the time of the Ministerial in Doha, concern about the Singapore issues was very much limited to a vanguard of Southern organizations. By linking them to GATS, a greater involvement of Northern organizations was possible, building on their experience since Seattle on GATS issues. The result was a new North–South partnership on a common agenda that enlarged the platform of civil society mobilization.

In drawing attention to the Singapore issues, CSOs have often replaced the media in providing a link between the political process and the public sphere. In 2003 the African Union organized a conference in Grand Baie, Mauritius, which ended with a final declaration identifying the Singapore issues as a potential deal-breaker in Cancún. CSOs set up a media centre sending journalists to Mauritius, which helped to give the conference due attention. CSOs managed to use the outcome of the event to strengthen their positions and build alliances with developing countries.

The effective use of expertise raised the profile and reputation of CSOs, resulting in greater influence on public opinion, more effective collective action and stronger policy impact through lobbying of governments' representatives.

LOBBYING ON GLOBAL TRADE

Cancún was the second time in a decade of WTO history that the biennial Ministerial Conference collapsed. Although both Seattle and Cancún shared the same critique of liberalization of the trade system, the paths to their outcome differed. In Seattle, the impact of civil society activism on the official summit was obtained in the streets; in Cancún the key move was gaining access to the official delegations and the negotiations. This did not mean that the traditional repertoire of CSOs' actions—carried out in an innovative manner in Seattle—was not present in Cancún. Protests took place in the streets of Cancún, but these actions were supplemented by a systematic work around and inside conference rooms. Key players in lobbying efforts were the international networks of civil society groups that had been strengthened or newly established, some large Northern-based NGOs, and the CSOs more closely involved with some delegations of countries of the South.

Four years after Seattle, some of the organizations that had marched in its streets were now part of official delegations. Extensive lobbying was pursued as a deliberate strategy long before the days of the conference. As Walden Bello, an important figure in OWINFS, has argued, a specific objective of CSOs involved 'intensifying our efforts to assist developing country delegations in Geneva to master the WTO process and formulate effective strategies to block the emergence of consensus on the areas prioritized by the trading powers and reassert the priority of implementation issues [and] pushing developing countries to create a block in support of the Chairman's Statement on the new issues and explicit consensus as the key legal document, and to push countries not to extend explicit consensus' (Bello 2003).

Lobbying through Parallel Summits

In the previous WTO Ministerial Conferences one of the major problems for Southern CSOs was that, mainly due to lack of resources, their lobbying activities were limited to the Ministerial event. In the run-up to Cancún, CSOs became increasingly aware that the chance of being effective was in the variety of pre-conference meetings where nation-states define their negotiating position. In April 2003, a Southern network of civil society organizations, SEATINI, organized a workshop on the Singapore issues, which was held in Arusha (Tanzania) with the participation of trade ministers of eight WTO member countries.[18] In the same fashion, the Dhaka meeting held in May 2003, which involved more than thirty trade ministers of the least developed countries, was paralleled by an international civil society forum.[19] Lobbying efforts by Southern organizations were carried out also at the African Union Ministerial Conference in Grand Baie, Mauritius. The meeting was accompanied by an NGO forum, which was the first meeting of this kind to be open to CSO representatives. All these shadow-meetings shared the same intent: advising and lobbying Southern national delegations, with the aim of constructing a common agenda of action for Cancún (Tetteh 2003).

The Geneva permanent missions at the WTO were also targets of lobbying efforts, as at the seminar on investment organized by TWN in Geneva in March 2003, involving major North-based NGOs, trade unions and official delegates. Moreover, TWN and other civil society groups participated to the public symposium in Geneva organized by WTO. The aim of these initiatives was to get a grasp on ongoing negotiations and to strengthen relations between CSOs and Southern member countries of the WTO.

Lobbying through Consultations

Sometimes, in the preparation of international events, CSO representatives are called in as external 'professional experts' by countries that do not have the resources or the necessary competences to carry out research and develop a policy perspective on specific issues. International CSOs and their experts provided substantial technical assistance on the multilateral trade system to various small developing countries, advising the national delegations in the run-up to the Cancún Ministerial. After Cancún, officials from Western countries have made reference to this 'hidden' work, accusing Northern CSOs, notably Oxfam, of having worked against a possible agreement in Cancún by imposing their agenda on Southern countries.[20]

Major lobbying results have been obtained by Southern CSOs in dedicated government bodies such as those resulting from the implementation of the Joint Integration Technical Assistance Programme (JITAP).[21] The programme, jointly developed by ITC, UNCTAD and WTO in 1998, involved eight African countries in its first phase and aimed to provide them with the resources for building up research and policy capabilities on multilateral trade issues. In all of the countries, the programme led to the creation of inter-institutional committees (IICs) addressing WTO policy and supporting Ministerial activities. In seven out of eight cases, the programme engaged CSOs as relevant stakeholders in its operations. The programme proved particularly effective in Kenya and Uganda, where CSO participation in the institutional decision-making processes of trade policies expanded significantly, enhancing their legitimacy.

The result was that at the Cancún Ministerial, CSOs were strongly present in the Uganda and Kenya delegations that played a central role in the conference dynamics. Kenya was elected representative for the group of seventy-one countries against the Singapore issues. Kenya and Uganda were both present in the first green room meeting on the Singapore issues, and Kenya was amongst the nine countries discussing the Singapore issues on the night of 11 September. The morning after, both Kenya and Uganda were among the thirty countries in the last green room meeting. Finally, Kenya was the first delegation to walk out of the negotiating table.

Lobbying in Cancún

In Cancún, the presence of CSOs was significant. Almost two thousand CSOs participated in the days of the Cancún Ministerial, representing eighty-three countries (Cevallos 2003). One-fourth were African CSOs, and among them more than two hundred CSOs[22] were officially accredited to the conference.[23] More importantly, as noted earlier, some NGO representatives were included in national delegations, such as Kenya, Uganda and Tanzania. Among them were various representatives of SEATINI and Action Aid.[24] At prior Ministerial Conferences, the presence of CSOs had never reached these figures.

Despite the fact that CSOs are officially excluded from the WTO decision-making process, over the years participation has increased through informal mechanisms. Historically, national delegations have been composed of members of governments and the private sector. From Seattle on, trade unions and CSOs representatives were included in the delegations of some countries. The status of being included in a national delegation is significant. An accredited organization is allowed access to the media room and some of the plenary conferences and workshops, and to meet with delegates. The participation in the national delegations allows CSO representatives to get much closer to the policy-making process, through various means.

First, a privileged, sustained and direct contact with the national delegations makes it easier for CSOs to have impact on their position. Developing countries' delegations are usually small, composed by an average of twenty people,[25] which enables members of the delegation to be in constant dialogue. Even during the last hectic hours of the Cancún conference, when access was restricted to trade ministers, meetings between them and CSOs of African countries occurred during the breaks (Gregow 2003).

Second, through national delegations CSOs had the possibility to access primary information on the status of the negotiation. In Cancún CSOs gained knowledge of the official EU position on the draft declaration with the major proposed amendments well before some of the EU member-states themselves.[26] This access to information contributed to making CSOs' technical knowledge effective. Their understanding of all of the steps in the negotiation process and of the interplay of different forces helped focus CSO advocacy work.[27] Moreover, they became the primary node linking the political and the public sphere, with major media relying on information provided by NGOs.[28]

Being part of a national delegation also led to a third crucial improvement in the position of CSOs, that is, the possibility of holding their national delegations accountable both within the negotiating process and in front of public opinion. This 'watch-dog' role for democratic accountability and transparency was an important component of the legitimacy and effectiveness of CSOs.

Protests in Cancún

In the days of the Cancún Ministerial, protest events—from street demonstrations to 'alternative summits'—took place outside and inside the conference, with a key role played again by the international networks of civil society groups and large NGOs. The two events with the greatest visibility were the Farmers' and Indigenous Peoples' March held on 10 September,[29] and the concluding March held on 13 September.[30]

A series of meetings (in the tradition of civil society parallel summits) offered opportunities for public discussions and for the development of common strategies and counterproposals on trade policy. Between 6 and 14 September, around fifty forums, assemblies and teach-ins took place in Cancún, involving more than ten thousand activists from more than one hundred countries.[31] The events conveyed a broad range of arguments, covering all the trade issues at stake in WTO negotiations. They also offered the opportunity for activists and CSOs who were not 'insiders' to trade negotiations to become informed, engaged in the debates over the movement's strategies, and more active in CSO networks critical of trade liberalization policies. Such events were a key factor for extending mobilizations at the national level on trade issues in a very large number of countries.

To coincide with protests outside the Cancún conference, accredited organizations held symbolic events of protest inside the Ministerial. This helped to show that protest and lobbying moved together and were part of a collective enterprise.[32] The strategy agreed by international networks was that CSOs should appear as cohesive as possible, with people inside and outside the conference working towards the same objective, although relying on different strategies and forms of action.[33]

THE COLLAPSE OF THE WTO CONFERENCE AND THE IMPACT OF ACTIVISM

Civil society preparation, intentions and actions had an impact in Cancún in conjunction with the course of events and the evolving alignment of different interests and strategies of key players in the conference.

A summary of events at the Ministerial sheds some light on its outcome. The conference opened on 10 September 2003 with the establishment of a table of negotiations on agriculture by the chairman, Luis Ernesto Derbez, the Mexican Minister of Foreign Affairs. After three days of negotiations, the US and the EU found themselves in a well-documented impasse, vis-à-vis the firm opposition of the G21 block. Probably under the advice of the EU, which was the main force pressing for discussion of the Singapore issues, the chairman turned to them before the question of agriculture was resolved (see Ketkar 2003; ICTSD 2003a, 2003b). Arguably, the idea of the EU was to get a good bargaining deal on the Singapore issues before granting concessions on agriculture.

A revised version of the Ministerial text was issued Saturday around noon, probably in the hope of instilling new life into the negotiation process. The opposite happened. The new draft exacerbated existing tensions instead of dismantling them. The section on the Singapore issues did not reflect the Southern delegates' view. Whereas previous draft versions of the Cancún Ministerial text included double-option brackets (continue the 'study' period versus commence the negotiation process), in this latest version the 'study option' was left out. Moreover, the text included an annex discussing modalities for government procurement and trade facilitation as if negotiations were already opened. After a long meeting of the heads of the delegations on the revised Ministerial text on the night of 11 Saturday, where the Southern delegates did not hide their disappointment and frustration,[34] Derbez decided to continue negotiations of the Singapore issues and scheduled a meeting with nine ministers (from Kenya, China, South Africa, Brazil, India, Malaysia, EU, the United States and Mexico), which lasted from 1:00 to 3:00 a.m. (Redfern 2003). This meeting was followed in the morning by a larger meeting involving thirty countries. At all three meetings the developing countries maintained their position on the Singapore issues, resisting the mounting pressure from Western countries and refusing to open up negotiations. The EU and Japan played their last card, declaring to be prepared to drop two issues. Despite this move, the negotiations collapsed in the late afternoon, and Derbez officially closed the conference. The day after, a brief Ministerial statement was released instead of the usual Ministerial text. The group of countries of the South claimed victory.

What lies behind this outcome is a complex set of conflicting interests. The major divide on the Singapore issues in Cancún was the North–South divide between the Quad and the 'Group of 90', whereas in Doha the division was between the Quad and a 'crumbling' group of developing countries. Moreover, other divisions were at stake in Cancún, within the EU itself and, more importantly, in the Quad between the United States and the EU. Well before the beginning of the negotiations, the United States was taking a much softer position than the EU with regard to the Singapore issues. A few weeks before the conference, the United States declared that they could be 'unbundled'; the EU only envisaged this possibility in the last day of the conference.[35] Moreover, during the Cancún Ministerial, the United States did not insist on turning from agriculture to the Singapore issues. And at the last green room meeting, when the EU and Japan were ready to make concessions, South Korea, another country supporting the Singapore issues, insisted on the 'all four or nothing' position, adding complications to an already complex negotiation (see Elliott, Denny and Munk 2003; ICTSD 2003a). In this regard, the aggressive negotiation strategy of the EU—wanting to negotiate the Singapore issues before granting anything on agriculture—made the U.S. spokesperson argue that the EU was, with its conduct, 'isolating itself from an entire planet' (ICTSD 2003b).

A crucial factor is that in Cancún, in contrast to previous events, the 'Group of 90' proved to be united and cohesive. Therefore, the major U.S.–EU 'divide and rule' strategy proved ineffective. The first reason for this unity was the weaker power of the 'you are with us or against us' argument that the United States had used in Doha in the aftermath of 11 September 2001, as well as the widespread criticism in the South of the U.S. war in Iraq that had started a few months before. Secondly, several large countries of the South, such as Brazil, India and South Africa, supported the G90 position to the end, whereas other countries, which in Doha had backed down, resisted external pressure. Third, and more important, the negotiation strategy of the Quad did not work out. The *Economist* commented a few days after the Ministerial Conference that: 'the instant post-mortem blamed rich countries most. NGOs accused them of wrecking the talks by pushing poor countries too far on the Singapore issues and giving too little on agriculture. There is much truth to both claims'.[36] The aggressiveness of the EU had the boomerang effect of weakening the Quad and reinforced the fears of developing countries. As an African delegate observed:

> Doha was slightly different from Cancún. When developing countries from the ACP and LDC groups went to Doha, we told our Ministers that the Ministerial had problems, but there were two issues—(the ACP waiver plus TRIPS and health)—that allowed the EU to get what they wanted. In Cancún, there wasn't any fanfare that 'we are not going to accept this until we get that'. The entire text was rejected. There wasn't anything for developing countries in the entire text'.[37]

In this intricate tale of power politics, the role of CSOs was significant, albeit identifying this role is far from an easy task. A useful framework is provided by the concept of 'political opportunity structure' introduced by Tarrow (1998) to explain the interplay between the external conditions and collective action.[38] Even though there is wide agreement on the fact that institutions and the political context matter for the dynamics and outcomes of collective actions, much less agreement exists about the relevant set of variables that can explain this.[39]

Key in this regard is the concept of alliances and the presence of possible negotiators acting on behalf of another group (Tarrow 1998). Because CSOs do not hold any decision-making power, the possibility for CSOs to promote a policy relies on their ability to find policymakers that can endorse it.

In Cancún, CSOs developed a strong alliance with Southern governments as a result of the extensive consultation, lobbying and advocacy work discussed in previous paragraphs. Moreover, they tried to weaken the alliance between the United States and the EU, reporting latent conflicts to the press and creating awareness on the possibility of a collapse if developing countries were able to remain united. Key conditions for an alliance were present. First, developing countries formed a common front on the Singapore issues (especially on investment) that was highly confrontational with the Quad's position. Second, their position was very similar to the one advocated by civil society networks. Even if there were differences between the two sides, they had never been so close before in their history. The speech given by the South African president, Thabo Mbeki, on the eve of the Ministerial pointed out the proximity of their positions: '[CSOs] may act in ways you and I may not like (. . .) but the message they communicate relates to us' (*The Straits Times, 3 September 2003*). Afterwards he argued that the alliance with civil society groups of North and South could help developing countries to get a better deal in Cancún.

This alliance was crucial in creating a shared awareness of the decisive character of the Singapore issues. In the run-up to Cancún, official government documents referred to the contributions of CSOs, with ministers asking for consultancy activities and meetings with CSOs. On the other side, CSOs held forums and workshops in collaboration with institutional actors, advocated policies and provided technical analysis to governments. Not only did many of the positions held by the national governments resemble the conclusions of CSO briefings and declarations; there was also a genuine interplay and exchange of ideas between the two sides. Second, this alliance was crucial for holding national delegations more accountable than they were in Doha. Being in the advantageous position of working close to governments, but not being subordinate to them, CSOs had the ability to monitor, prod and support Southern delegations.

However, this model of alliance between CSOs and Southern governments also had its potential weaknesses. First, it was 'tactical' in nature, linked to the contingent interests of the 'Group of 90'. It has been argued that Southern negotiators were not as committed to their demands on the Singapore issues as CSOs were, and they could have dropped their resistance if a significant concession on agriculture had been made by the North. Second, CSO strategy relied on important dynamics within the 'Group of 90' itself, in particular the unity between the emerging powers of Brazil, India and South Africa, not to speak of China and other countries of the South, which had increasingly heterogeneous trade interests. Both weaknesses were to be fatal four years later. The 2007 WTO Ministerial Conference in Hong Kong ended with modest progress of the trade liberalization agenda but with a collapse of the unity of the South, as major countries negotiated their acceptance on the basis of individual 'deals' with the North that favoured their trade interests.

ASSESSING THE POLICY IMPACT OF GLOBAL ACTIVISM ON TRADE

The WTO trade liberalization agenda encountered a major setback at the Cancún Ministerial Conference, and the activism of international networks of civil society organizations played a significant role in this outcome. A very large coalition of CSOs from over one hundred countries was involved in a cohesive and non-segmented network that developed a common identity and strategy, offered information and expertise on relevant issues, built viable alliances with key governments of the South, carried out extensive lobbying and advocacy and continued with large-scale protests against the WTO agenda. From the evidence provided by this chapter, and from current literature on the impact of CSOs, three major insights emerge.

The first concerns the evolution of civil society strategies with regard to the WTO: from protest to multiple strategies, combining contestation with lobbying and alliance building with like-minded governments. The traditional way for CSOs to respond to WTO conferences, like other global summits, has been through parallel events that shadowed official gatherings, which would take place at the same time and place, address the same issues from a different political perspective and propose different solutions (see Pianta 2001; Pianta and Silva 2003). However, with few exceptions—notably the NGO forums during the UN thematic conferences—civil society events lacked an established interaction with the official summit. In many cases, a confrontational attitude with strong forms of protest has characterized civil society activism, as in Seattle at the Third WTO Ministerial Conference and at the G8 summit in Genoa in 2001. There was a shared reluctance among most CSOs to get 'compromised' by going into dialogue with international institutions accused of being unaccountable and undemocratic.

Global activism, sustained by international civil society networks in the run-up to the Cancún WTO conference, experienced an evolution of attitudes. A broad understanding emerged that in order to be effective, protests had to be complemented by extensive lobbying of national delegations, with more of an 'insider' strategy than in the past. This move has to be put in the context of the political climate that followed the terrorist attack of 11 September 2001, when movements against neoliberal globalization had to avoid being conflated with violence. The specific reason, however, was the increasing awareness of the distinctive nature of WTO governance. In contrast to many other intergovernmental organizations, the WTO is based on a power structure in which the decision-making power of officials is more limited than the power of the national delegations. Although there are cases of draft conventions issued by the Geneva Secretariat (as in Doha), the main decisions in the negotiating rounds are made by the national delegations. Furthermore, although CSOs have always been very critical of the democratic deficit of the WTO, they have also been aware that, in a favourable situation, the negotiating table of a 'green room' meeting can be broken by a single state, if it is able to withstand the pressure from the other states. Consequently, lobbying towards like-minded national delegations became not only a necessary strategic choice, but also the most effective way CSOs could disrupt WTO negotiations.

International civil society networks active on trade issues came to understand these factors and opportunities. They had the resources, knowledge and contacts with officials and governments that were required to develop and carry out such a strategy. Furthermore, they were successful in building a consensus on this strategy by a very large base of CSOs in a large number of countries. Finally, they were able to implement it in an effective way, thereby contributing to the collapse of the Cancún Ministerial.

The second insight concerns the relevance of the external environment in which CSOs pursue their goals. One of the major hypotheses in the sociological literature on the structure of political opportunities is that the policy gains obtained at the transnational level by CSOs change (also) according to the 'openness' of the international governmental organization involved. The idea that openness matters for civil society trajectories figures in all of the major definitional attempts to conceptualize political opportunities (Eisinger 1973; Kriesi et al. 1995; McAdam, McCarthy and Zald 1996; Tarrow 1998). In comparative research carried out on environmental social movements in France, Germany, Sweden and the United Kingdom, Kitschelt (1986: 59) has proved that the openness of the political regimes was 'a filter between the mobilization of the movement and its choice of strategies and its capacity to change the social environment'. Nevertheless, in light of the comparison carried out in the preceding, 'openness' should not be taken to include the idea of formal 'inclusiveness', such as a *de jure* system that allows for CSOs to be able to take part in a global event.

As the case of Cancún demonstrates, what counts for CSOs' effectiveness is the extent to which they are able to build relationships of trust and alliances with those that participate in the decision-making process, or at least have some influence on it. Trust and alliances, as the Cancún case suggests, can *de facto* transform a global institution into a sort of 'open system', despite it *de jure* remaining closed. This concept of openness is not far from that proposed by Kitschelt (1986), emphasizing the notion of alliances in picturing what an 'open system' consists of (see also Tarrow 1998). Thus, we can argue that the policy gains by CSOs are related to 'openness' of the system, meaning not just its formal inclusiveness, but rather their capacity to find trustable allies among institutional players and to exploit divisions amongst elites.

The idea that 'alliances' matter is, of course, not a new finding, given the stress placed on the concept of alliances by social movement scholars in numerous case studies at the national level (Gamson 1991; Kriesi et al. 1995), as well as in several studies addressing the transnational level.[40] Still, the case of Cancún allows new insights.

Within the 'realist' approach in the field of international relations, alliances are thought of mainly in reference to the most powerful states, because these are ones believed to be able to affect outcomes in world policy-making. In this frame, CSOs and other actors are more likely to succeed when they succeed in changing the preferences of the most powerful states (Krasner 1993). However, the Cancún case supports the exception to this hypothesis, showing that CSOs are able to have an impact *despite* the opposition of powerful states. Other studies have provided similar evidence, as the case of the Campaign to Ban Landmines (Mekata 2000) and different cases of disarmament and human security investigated by Alcalde (2009). Although some states, in accordance with the predictions of the 'realist' approach, are indeed capable of influencing the course of international events and challenging the multilateral arena through bilateral agreements, coalitions between (less powerful) states may often also prove politically effective. In the case of Cancún, the G90, the African Union, the ACP and the LDC counterbalanced the political weight of Northern states with their numbers, cohesion and competences (see Narlikar 2001, 2003). Again, in establishing such alliances between civil society and like-minded governments, a crucial instrumental role was played by international networks of CSOs.

This brings us to our third point, which concerns the importance of the *national* level in CSOs' strategies. As globalization proceeded, nation-states were considered to be losing power relatively to an emerging multilayered, decentralized transnational system, with multinational corporations as key actors. In this perspective, the collapse of the WTO conference in Seattle has often been seen as the moment when 'national' politics was put on the sidelines and civil society protest directly targeted international governmental institutions as the 'appropriate' level of decision-making on global issues (see O'Brien at al. 2000). Although this perspective offers fascinating insights, one should not hasten into a 'hyper-globalist' position. Domestic structures have indeed experienced a loss of power to the transnational level, but they have also maintained a relevant degree of power, especially with regard to an institution such as the WTO, where member states play a key role. Unlike in Seattle, where the protests outside the conference fuelled the idea of a 'CSOs versus IGO relation' with no room for states, a more state-centric view regained its importance in Cancún, also in relation to the new CSO strategies discussed earlier. In Cancún civil society sought to achieve an impact on WTO decisions through lobbying and cooperating with national delegations.

The idea that the national level can be a crucial leverage for CSOs' access to the realm of the global polity is not completely new. In the most simple 'boomerang effect'—when CSOs try to influence the national level through action in the transnational sphere (Keck and Sikkink 1998), or in the more complicated 'spiral model' (Risse, Ropp and Sikkink 1999), the national and transnational levels interact to a considerable degree. It can be argued that in Cancún there occurred a 'reversed boomerang effect', that is, CSOs sought to affect the transnational sphere represented by the WTO by relying on the power of states and on political relations developed at the national level.

In conclusion, the case of the Cancún WTO conference shows that civil society groups have been able to adapt their strategies, integrate several forms of action and establish extensive relations with governments, while maintaining their autonomy and their agenda for policy change. In the end, they contributed to the collapse of the WTO negotiations for further liberalization of trade and investment. The crucial actors within civil society that made this possible were the international networks, which provided the essential knowledge and competences to develop a common strategy and which were widely supported by many CSOs in most countries of the world. They built alliances with like-minded Southern states and were able to sustain the confrontation with Northern country positions. International civil society networks therefore emerge as an important new player in the global scene, capable of having an impact on decision-making on global issues when conditions are favourable.

NOTES

1. This chapter is based on my PhD thesis (Silva 2008), which assessed the relevance of social movements in terms of their impact on global public policy-making associated with the WTO and the United Nations. The research combined qualitative and quantitative tools, such as interviews with key activists and policymakers, aimed at identifying the internal dynamics of complex international mobilizations and network analysis aimed at understanding the linkages and the degree of interconnectedness among civil society organizations (CSOs).
2. Franz Fischler from the EU, the second most important negotiator after Pascal Lamy, declared that 'One of the biggest problems [in Cancun] was that too many people were not interested in the success of the round and the second problem was that there was a misperception of what negotiations mean . . . This was led partly by NGOs, they conveyed the message to developing countries that no deal was better than a bad deal.' AlertNet, 19 September 2003, http://www.trust.org/alertnet/
3. In January 2001, the EU and ten other countries (Japan, Korea, Switzerland, Argentina, Australia, Brazil, Egypt, South Korea, Mexico and Nicaragua) asked the WTO director-general to launch a full new round of negotiations. The Singapore issues were explicitly mentioned as an important part of this broad agenda. In the same period, an EU submission to the Working Group on Competition Policy mentioned the Singapore issues and advised the WTO members to put them on the agenda.

4. Furthermore, unlike the EU, the United States was from the very beginning disposed to 'unbundle' the Singapore issues (*Washington Trade Daily* 2003).
5. See 'Chips Off the Bloc: Disunity within the EU on the Singapore Issues', August 2003, Action Aid Report.
6. *International Trade Daily*, 23 July 2003; see also House of Commons International Development Committee (2003).
7. As Diani (1995: 5) writes, social movements can be conceptualized 'as networks of informal interactions between a plurality of individuals, groups and/or organizations, engaged in a political or cultural conflict, on the basis of a shared collective identity'.
8. See, for example, Della Porta 2007, 2009; Pianta and Silva 2003; Pianta and Zola 2008. An early analysis of parallel summits is in Pianta 2001.
9. A series of demonstrations were held across Europe to coincide with the EU Council of Trade ministers meeting held in Palermo on 5–6 July 2003.
10. TWN was one of the first CSOs to set up an office in Geneva to better follow the work of the WTO, the permanent missions of member states and key intergovernmental organizations, such as the South Centre.
11. The composition of the IFG board included well-known activists and organizations, including Martin Khor (TWN), Lori Wallach (Public Citizen), John Cavanagh (Institute for Policy Studies), Walden Bello (Focus on the Global South), Maude Barlow (Council of Canadians), Tony Clark (Polaris Institute), Vandana Shiva (Resource Foundation) and Mark Ritchie (Institute for Agriculture and Trade Policy). http://www.ifg.org/about/bod.htm
12. It is true, as Diani has correctly underlined, that organizational characteristics of single units can have an influence on the network structure. Variables such as degree of professionalization and resources might be expected to influence the structure and centrality of the organizations within the network (Diani and McAdam 2003). Nevertheless, from a network perspective, it is the characteristics of the network that matter in the end.
13. I use the term 'epistemic-*like* community' in order to denote the difference in the application of the original concept.
14. For analysis of how research can be used to influence policy, see the work of ODI-RAPID at http://www.odi.org.uk/work/programmes/rapid/default.asp and IDRC at http://www.idrc.ca.
15. These events were also opportunities to open up to the outside world. The public symposium on the 'Doha Development Agenda and Beyond' (Geneva, 29 April–1 May 2002) and the seminar on investment (Geneva, March 2003) are successful cases of encounters between leading activists of CSOs, academics, experts and policymakers.
16. An example is the work of the Corporate Europe Observatory (see Investment Watch 2003). Other related work was also carried out by the WDM. Its expertise was crucial for CSOs' advocacy when the EU proposed to treat the Singapore issues in a 'GATS-style' negotiating mechanism.
17. For instance, a motion of the SPD in a session of the German Bundestag (Published Record 15/1317, 15th Legislative Session Status: 01/07/2003) links the Singapore issues to GATS expressing concerns on the implications of foreign investment measures for developing countries' economies.
18. Tanzania, Zambia, Kenya, Namibia, Uganda, Mauritius, Mozambique and Angola were the countries from which trade ministers attended the workshop.
19. See www.cpd-bangladesh.org. This seminar was held 29–30 May 2003, and was organized by the Centre for Policy Dialogue (CPD)—a Bangladesh think tank—in association with Consumers International, the EU-LDC Network, Oxfam International, South Asia Watch on Trade, Economics and Environment (SAWTEE) and SEATINI.

20. See http://www.pbs.org/newshour/bb/international/july-dec03/wto_9–15.html. See, for instance, the views of Josetta Shiner, a deputy U.S. trade representative. These accusations have been rebutted by CSOs, pointing out that they are an attempt to escape from the responsibility for the collapse of the Cancún Ministerial.
21. See Ddamilura and Abdi (2002).
22. See http://www.wto.org/english/forums_e/ngo_e/ngo_e.htm. I did not consider BINGOs (business and industry NGOs), GONGOs (government organized NGOs) or similar organizations in this calculation, based on the WTO's official NGOs participant list.
23. See http://www.wto.org/english/forums_e/ngo_e/ngo_e.htm. A full list of NGOs eligible to attend the Fifth WTO Ministerial Conference can be found (under Cancún 2003) here.
24. See http://www.chamber.org.hk/memberarea/chamber_view/WTO_min_attd_Rev2.pdf. See also interviews with Action Aid, in Silva (2008).
25. For instance, the Canadian delegation was close to one hundred people. See http://www.dfait-maeci.gc.ca/tna-nac/WTO-del-en.asp.
26. This fact led to official complaints by many EU countries.
27. In previous events CSOs complained about the delay with which they obtained information on the negotiations from governments; under such conditions, it was difficult to carry out effective lobbying.
28. For example Reuters asked CSOs about information during the days of the Cancun ministerial (see Silva 2008).
29. It is estimated that fifteen thousand to twenty thousand people participated in protests, although some reports indicate a much larger presence. The march ended at the fences protecting the area of the hotels and Convention Centre, which was 10 kilometres inside at the so-called 'Km 0' of the coastal area. Acts of civil disobedience or highly symbolic actions occurred in front of the fences.
30. The demonstration involved ten thousand people.
31. For further information, see Silva (2008).
32. See interview in Silva (2008), 'The Campaign to Reform the World Bank'.
33. During the conference the strong presence of CSOs was acknowledged by many political leaders.
34. The minister of trade for Botswana, Nkate, declared at the Heads of Delegation meeting: 'Our understanding of the Doha mandate is that negotiations would commence on the basis of a decision to be taken, by explicit consensus, on modalities for negotiations. The text before us has actually departed from that mandate and what it represents is unacceptable to us since it is not based on explicit consensus. Therefore, there cannot be negotiations on these issues'. Kenya stated: 'The draft modalities that were annexed to the text and that have found their way into the text were not negotiated nor discussed in any meaningful way . . . Kenya cannot accept to the launching of negotiations on issues that we do not clearly understand and whose implication on our economies have not been assessed' (see Gregow 2003).
35. See *Washington Trade Daily* (2003).
36. *Economist*, 19 September 2003.
37. African delegate quoted in ActionAid International (2004: 10).
38. The political opportunity structure is defined as the 'dimension of the political environment that provides incentives for collective action by affecting people's expectations for success or failure' (Tarrow 1998: 77).
39. At the transnational level, variables such as inclusiveness, alliances/divided élites, trust and relative power, might be relevant for assessing CSOs' impact on global institutions (see Silva 2008).

40. See Florini (2000); Fox and Brown (1998), Keck and Sikkink (1998); and Chapter 4, this volume.

BIBLIOGRAPHY

ActionAid International. (2010). *Divide and Rule: The EU and US Response to Developing Country Alliances at the WTO*. http://actionaid.org.uk/doc_lib/30_1_divide_rule.pdf.

Alcalde, J. (2009). *Changing the World. Explaining Successes and Failures of International Campaigns by NGOs in the Field of Human Security*, PhD thesis, European University Institute.

Anheier, H., Glasius, M., and Kaldor, M. (eds) (2001). *Global Civil Society 2001*, Oxford: Oxford University Press.

Anheier, H., and Katz, H. (2005). 'Global Connectedness: The Structure of Transnational NGO Networks', in H. Anheier, M. Glasius and M. Kaldor (eds), *Global Civil Society 2005*, Oxford: Oxford University Press.

Bello, W. (2003). 'The Road to Cancún: Towards a Movement Strategy for the WTO Ministerial in Cancún', Focus on Trade, 86 (April). http://www.focusweb.org/publications/FOT%20pdf/fot86.pdf (accessed August 2011).

Benchmark Environmental Consulting. (1996). Democratic Global Civil Governance. Report of the 1995 Benchmark Survey of NGOs. UD Evaluation Report 4.96, Royal Ministry of Foreign Affairs, Oslo.

Caniglia, B. (2002). 'Elites Alliances and Transnational Environmental Movement Organisations', in J. Smith and H. Johnston (eds), *Globalisaton and Resistance*, Lanham, MD: Rowman and Littlefield.

Castells, M. (1996). *The Rise of a Network Society*, Oxford: Blackwell.

Cevallos, D. (2003). 'Conference Draws 2,000 NGOs from 83 Countries', Inter Press Service News Agency. http://www.ipsnews.net/africa/interna.asp?idnews=20019.

Clarke, T., and Barlow, M. (1997). *Mai: The Multilateral Agreement on Investment and the Threat to Canadian Sovereignty*, Toronto: Stoddart.

Ddamilura, D., and Abdi, H.N. (2002). *Civil Society and the WTO: Participation in National Trade Policy Design in Uganda and Kenya*. Policy Paper, London: CAFOD.

della Porta, D. (ed) (2007). *The Global Justice Movements: A Cross-National and Transnational Perspective*, Boulder, CO: Paradigm.

———. (ed) (2009). *Democracy in Social Movements*, London: Palgrave.

della Porta, D., and Diani, M. (1999). *Social Movements: An Introduction*, Oxford: Blackwell.

della Porta, D., Kriesi, H., and Rucht, D. (eds) (1999). *Social Movements in a Globalising World*, London: MacMillan Press.

Diani, M. (1995). *Green Networks: A Structural Analysis of the Italian Environmental Movement*, Edinburgh: Edinburgh University Press.

Diani, M., and McAdam, D. (eds) (2003). *Social Movements and Networks: Relational Approaches to Collective Action*, Oxford: Oxford University Press.

Economist (The). (2003a). "Tequila Sunset in Cancún", 17 September. http://www.economist.com/node/2065723 (accessed 8 August 2011).

———. (2003b). 'The WTO under Fire', 18 September. http://www.economist.com/node/2071855 (accessed 8 August 2011).

Eisinger, P. (1973). 'The Conditions of Protest Behavior in American Cities', *American Political Science Review*, 81:11–28.

Elliott L., Denny, C., and Munk, D. (2003). 'Blow to World Economy as Trade Talks Collapse', *Guardian*, 15 September.

Florini, A.M. (ed) (2000). *The Third Force. The Rise of Transnational Civil Society*, Tokyo: JCIE and CEIP.

Fox, J.A., and Brown, D.L. (1998). *The Struggle for Accountability*, Cambridge, MA: MIT Press.

Federal Trust (The) (2003) 'Expanding WTO rules? A Federal Trust Report On Singapore Issues'. London: The Federal Trust, http://mayapur.securesites.net/fedtrust/filepool/FedT%20Expanding%20WTO%20rules.pdf

Gamson, W. (1991). *The Strategy of Social Protest*, 2nd ed., Belmont, CA: Wadsworth.

Gerlach, L. (ed) (1976). 'La struttura dei nuovi movimenti di rivolta', in A. Melucci (ed), *Movimenti di rivolta*, Milan: Etas.

Gregow, Karin. (2003). 'Brief Analysis of the Cancún Ministerial from an African perspective', *Econews Africa*, 9 September.

Haas, P. (1990). *Saving the Mediterranean: The Politics of Environmental Cooperation*, New York: Columbia University Press.

———. (1992). 'Epistemic Communities and Mediterranean Pollution Control', *International Organisation*, 46:1–35.

House of Commons International Development Committee. (2003). 'Trade and Development at the WTO: Issues for Cancún', Seventh Report of Session 2002–3 (Vol 1/HC400–1), London. http://www.publications.parliament.uk/pa/cm200203/cmselect/cmintdev/400/400.pdf.

International Council for the Settlement of Investment Disputes. (2003a). 'At Eleventh Hour, Divergences All Over Again', *Bridges Today* 5–6 (September): 14–15.

———. (2003b). 'New Ministerial Text to be Issued Today', *Bridges Today* 7 (September–October).

Investment Watch. (2003). 'Corporate Conquistadors in Cancún: The EU Offensive for WTO-Investment Negotiations'. http://archive.corporateeurope.org/mai/conquistadors.pdf.

Keck, M. (1998). 'Planafloro in Rondonia: The Limits of Leverage', in J.A. Fox and D.L. Brown (eds), *The Struggle for Accountability*, Cambridge, MA: MIT Press.

Keck, M.E., and Sikkink, K. (1998). *Activists beyond Borders: Advocacy Networks in International Politics*, Ithaca, NY: Cornell University Press.

Ketkar, Prafulla. (2003). *Deadlock at Cancún: A New Beginning.* IPCS Issues Brief, No. 12, Delhi, India.

Kitschelt, H. (1986), Political Opportunity Structures and Political Protest: Anti-Nuclear Movements in Four Democracies, *British Journal of Political Science*, 16: 57–85.

Krasner, S. (1993). 'Sovereignty, Regimes, and Human Rights', in V. Rittberger (ed), *Regime Theory and International Relations*, Oxford: Oxford University Press.

Kriesi, H., Koopmans, R., Duyvendak, J., and Giugni, M. (1995). *New Social Movements in Western Europe*, London: UCL Press.

Marchetti, R., and Pianta, M. (2007). 'Global Justice Movements: The Transnational Dimension', in D. Della Porta (ed), *The Global Justice Movements: A Cross-National and Transnational Perspective*, Boulder, CO: Paradigm.

McAdam, D. McCarthy, J., and Zald, M. (eds) (1996). *Comparative Perspectives on Social Movements*, Cambridge: Cambridge University Press.

Mekata, M. (2000). 'Building Partnerships toward a Common Goal: Experiences of the International Campaign to Ban Landmines', in A.M. Florini (ed), *The Third Force: The Rise of Transnational Civil Society*, Tokyo: JCIE and CEIP.

Narlikar, A. (2001). *WTO Decision Making and Developing Countries.* South Centre Trade Working Papers, No. 11 (November), Geneva.

———. (2003). *International Trade and Developing Countries: Bargaining Coalitions in GATT and WTO*, Oxford: Routledge.

O'Brien, R., Goetz, A.M., Scholte, J.A., and Williams, M. (2000). *Contesting Global Governance: Multilateral Economic Institutions and Global Social Movements*, Cambridge: Cambridge University Press.

Pianta, M. (2001). 'Parallel Summits of Global Civil Society', in H. Anheier, M. Glasius and M. Kaldor (eds), *Global Civil Society 2001*, Oxford: Oxford University Press.

Pianta, M., and Silva, F. (2003). *Globalisers from Below: A Survey on Global Civil Society Organisations*, Rome: Globi Research Report.

Pianta, M., and Zola, D. (2008). 'La montée en puissance des mouvements globaux 1970–2005', in I. Sommier, O. Fillieule and E. Agrikoliansky (eds), *Généalogie des mouvements altermondialistes en Europe*, Paris: Karthala.

Redfern, P. (2003), "Kenya's Major Role in WTO Debacle," *Daily Nation*, September 17, 2003.

Reinicke, W.H. (1999). 'The Other World Wide Web: Global Public Policy Networks', *Foreign Policy*, 117:44–57.

Risse, T. (2000). 'The Power of Norms versus the Norms of Power: Transnational Civil Society and Human Rights', in A.M. Florini (ed), *The Third Force: The Rise of Transnational Civil Society*, Tokyo: JCIE and CEIP.

Risse, T., Ropp, S.C., and Sikkink K. (1999). *The Power of Human Rights: International Norms and Domestic Change*, Cambridge: Cambridge University Press.

Silva, F. (2008). *Do Transnational Social Movements Matter? Four Case Studies Assessing the Impact of Transnational Social Movements on the Global Governance of Trade, Labour, and Finance*, PhD thesis, European University Institute.

Smith, J., Chatfield, C., and Pagnucco, R. (1997). *Transnational Social Movement and Global Politics*, Syracuse, NY: Syracuse University Press.

Starr, A. (2005). *Global Revolt*, London: Zed Books.

Tarrow, S. (1998). *Power in Movement*, Cambridge: Cambridge University Press.

Tetteh, Hormeku. (2003). 'African Ministers Against Negotiations of New Issues', in *TWN-Africa,* Grand Baie, Mauritius, 20 June.

Van Rooy, A. (1997) 'The Frontiers of Influence: NGO Lobbying at the 1974 World Food Conference, the 1992 Earth Summit and Beyond', *World Development*, 25 (1): 93–114.

Washington Trade Daily. (2003). 12 (48), 25 July.

6 Advocacy for Corporate Accountability and Trade Justice

The Role of 'Noble Networks' in the United Kingdom

Jem Bendell and Anne Ellersiek

INTRODUCTION

Following several decades of globalization and liberalization, the grounds for social contestation and civil society advocacy on global justice issues seem as strong today as in the past. Perverse trends in global inequality, the ongoing scale of global poverty and multiple crises—related to food, energy, the financial system, unemployment and climate change—are just some of the underpinnings of contemporary activism.

As an expression and catalyst of civil society mobilization, non-governmental organizations (NGOs) in Britain have been working to reduce global inequalities for many decades and are paying increasing attention to policy advocacy (Bryer and Magrath 1999; Edwards 2003). Today, non-governmental and community groups address every conceivable policy issue and operate in virtually every country as well as beyond national borders (Evans 1999). Transnational NGOs, such as Amnesty International, Oxfam, Greenpeace, Christian Aid, World Vision or Friends of the Earth (FoE) address civic claims in various national and global policy forums (Smith 2005) in an attempt to influence the policies and practices of states, international institutions, companies and customers (Hudson 2001).

Practitioners and scholars alike describe 'networks' of NGOs as a key mechanism for their advocacy on these issues (see Chapter 3, this volume). In this chapter we refer to 'civic networks' to describe a social structure of organizations or individuals apparently working toward a common good, and connected by interdependencies or interests, such as campaign aims, finance, visions and values, whether recognized and formalized by participants or not.

Building upon the preceding conceptual discussion of promises and risks involved in networked activism in Chapter 3, the potential of networks both to influence the external policy environment and do so in ways conducive to global justice, are examined by the means of case studies of three United Kingdom (UK)-based NGO networks concerned with issues of trade justice and corporate accountability. The research involved extensive interviews with network participants and other stakeholders, a survey of activists and policymakers and other data-gathering methods.[1] The networks studied include:

- The Corporate Responsibility (CORE) Coalition, which calls for greater accountability of senior corporate management, openness and transparency of company activities that impact different stakeholders, and mechanisms for redress. Until it was passed in November 2006, the Companies Law Reform Bill was a key focus for CORE's campaigning which called for increased directors' duties to stakeholders, mandatory reporting on social and environmental issues, and improved access to justice for those affected by corporate irresponsibility.
- The Publish What You Pay (PWYP) campaign, which was launched by the Open Society Institute and Global Witness with a coalition of more than seventy other civic groups. The campaign aims to help citizens hold their governments accountable for how resource-related funds are managed and distributed and calls for the mandatory disclosure of the payments made by oil, gas and mining companies to all governments for the extraction of natural resources. PWYP is widely reported as instrumental in the setup of the voluntary Extractive Industries Transparency Initiative (EITI), launched at the World Summit for Sustainable Development in September 2002 by UK Prime Minister Tony Blair.
- The Trade Justice Movement (TJM), which is concerned with making the international trading system more supportive of reducing global inequality. Focusing in particular on UK and European Union (EU) trade policies, the TJM is a coalition of more than eighty civic society groups, mostly British NGOs or the UK branches of international NGOs, and 9 million members.[2] It includes trade unions, aid agencies, environment and human rights campaigns, fair trade organizations, faith and consumer groups. The TJM is known for its tactic of mass public mobilization in support of its goals. The TJM worked closely with CORE on the Companies Bill Law Reform.[3]

The cases chosen relate to different dimensions of the interface between economic policy and global inequality, and represent different states of networking and levels of connection to broader social mobilization agendas. They were chosen for these differences, so as to give a broader view of the issues.

NETWORK IMPACTS

Before examining the question of impact it should be noted that it is difficult to attribute the cause of a particular event in complex societal systems like public policy processes. In natural science, a particular intervention can be shown to correlate and likely cause a particular effect. In social science, the extrapolation of cause from correlation is complicated by the infinite connections to other factors. An NGO may campaign for a policy change and a policy change may occur, but a third factor may have caused the latter or have influenced both the development of the campaign objectives and the policy change. Thus a correlation of campaigns and policies does not necessarily imply an autonomous power within civic society. However, for the purposes of the discussion, we assume that a policy change in line with civic network goals was partly the result of that network's activities, especially when this is supported by opinions from network participants and the civil servants involved.

A particular change in policy may seem significant or insignificant depending on the view of the observer. Thus impacts can be assessed in terms of the network's own goals; the participant organizations' goals; opinions from the intended beneficiaries themselves; other stakeholders and, finally, an analyst's perspective of the beneficiaries' interest based on prior analysis can become necessary when the intended beneficiaries are diffuse, such as all poor people, or all people affected by environmental degradation, as in the case of the networks studied. This does not reduce the importance of bringing forth views from specific groups of affected persons when assessing the importance and appropriateness of any campaign or policy change, but that level of analysis is beyond the reach of this particular study.

CORE

In late 2000, a group of NGOs called the Corporate Accountability Network (CAN-Network), agreed to form the CORE coalition as a way to feed into the Company Law Review and challenge its contents. In 2001, Peter Frankental, from Amnesty, Simon McCrae, from Friends of the Earth UK, and Niall Watson from the World Wide Fund for Nature (WWF-UK), confirmed CORE's establishment and provided funds to hire Brian Shaad as a part-time co-ordinator. Deborah Doane at New Economics Foundation chaired, with Christian Aid and Traidcraft soon joining the new coalition. CORE turned its attention to the Department of Trade and Industry's (DTI) proposal that company boards should consider 'intangible assets of the company', such as the value of the brand and reputation, as well as intellectual copyrights and patents (DTI 2002). This would be done through an Operating and Financial Review (OFR) (DTI 2003).

Initially, the activists criticized the DTI recommendations that would leave it up to individual directors to decide what is material to their companies, providing no real prospect of an actual, uniform standard for reporting, such as companies having to publish an environmental and/or social report to shareholders. However, the agenda began to shift, with not only NGOs but also financial institutions such as Cooperative Financial

Services (CFS), supporting a more defined protocol for reporting. Subsequently the DTI announced a draft of the new law where the OFR 'shall include information about the employees of the company and its subsidiary undertakings, environmental matters and social and community matters'; and 'shall include analysis using financial and other key performance indicators, including information relating to environmental matters and employee matters'.[4] The draft was widely seen as a successful outcome of a multi-stakeholder input into the policy process. However, just before its conclusion, Gordon Brown, the Chancellor of the Exchequer at the time, cancelled the OFR. Reports suggested that he had done this after direct lobbying by the Confederation of Business and Industry (CBI), which played to his interest as being seen as 'pro-business' and reducing the administrative burdens on enterprise (Saha, 2006). The decision came as a shock to those in the financial industry who had been participating in consultations developing the proposals, as well as to the NGOs. Together they strongly criticized the decision and announced that they would focus their efforts on the Company Law Review.

This was the context for extensive mobilization by CORE on the Company Law Review, including a partnership with the TJM to mobilize massive letter writing to Members of Parliament (MPs) by their constituencies. Some MPs reported that they had never received so many letters about a single issue (TJM 2006).

A companies bill was written and concluded its passage through Parliament to become law as the Companies Act 2006, receiving Royal Assent on 8 November 2006. The extensive lobbying of MPs on the issue may have contributed to some becoming expert on the issues at hand. Some MPs, from various political parties, even went further than the NGOs in the requirements on companies. This level of awareness meant that additional requirements were made on the bill as it passed through Parliament, namely, stronger social and environmental reporting requirements. The resulting Companies Act 2006 now requires that the thirteen hundred or so publicly listed companies in the UK report on the following issues where they are necessary to understanding the company's business:

- Environmental matters (including the impact of the company's business on the environment)
- The company's employees
- Social and community issues
- Risks through company supply chains

The Companies Act 2006 also increased directors' duties to take account of stakeholders other than shareholders. However, it has been left to directors to determine what it means to take account of other stakeholders and also what social and environmental issues are material to the business and the nature and extent of reporting on these issues. The new law is allied to a concept of 'enlightened shareholder value' whereby social and environmental performance are considered to have some material impact on corporate financial performance and therefore of interest to some shareholders.[5] The new duties on directors and the new reporting requirements are thus not about the importance of stakeholders or social and environmental issues in their own right but in terms of how they impact on business performance. The quality of the decisions and the reporting will thus be limited to what is relevant to financial performance. Much will depend on the guidance the government provides on the meaning of this new law. Given the concerns, the government announced it would review in two years whether compulsory reporting standards are needed, and to ask NGOs what they think.[6] Another important mechanism for defining what this law means in practice will be any subsequent jurisprudence based on court decisions when a company or a director is challenged for breaking this new law.

The change in UK corporate law brought it up to date with what had already been agreed in other European countries like Denmark, France and the Netherlands. The 'success' of the campaigning by CORE needs to be tempered by the knowledge that far lower levels of public mobilization and campaigning were required to achieve mandatory social and environmental reporting in other European countries. Given the Anglo-Saxon approach to shareholder freedoms, and a strongly neoliberal government that was basing UK economic strategy on a financial services sector thriving through greater financial freedoms and innovations, CORE had a tougher task than its European counterparts. The resulting legislation was, however, reflective of the neoliberal ideology in the UK.

The law reflects a growing consensus in British business community that corporate responsibility is a financially sound approach to business. This consensus developed in the late 1990s as the concept of companies voluntarily accepting more responsibilities for social and environmental issues spread. However, research does not support this claim as a general principle. Instead, it finds that there are cases where social and environmental malpractice is financially damaging and some where it is not, and some cases where social and environmental excellence is financially rewarding and some where it is not (Maron 2006). The industry sector, the profile of the corporate brand, ownership structure of the company and nature of a societal issue are all key to whether that issue is material to financial performance or considered to be so by shareholders. The rise of private equity and hedge funds during the start of the twenty-first century is a reminder of the incoherence in basing a public policy for corporations on enlightened shareholder value when there are only so many 'enlightened' shareholders with an interest in social and environmental dimensions of business performance. The only means of ensuring the coherence of a law would be if it were coupled with a law that regulated shareholder behaviour. This is unlikely as the Companies Act was based on a desire to maintain the primacy of unfettered private property rights in corporations, that is, shareholder autonomy and control, while encouraging more strategic attention to social and environmental issues by corporate executives. A law that encouraged enlightened shareholder value, such as by rewarding investors with long positions in companies, holding stock over many years, would challenge that approach.

This neoliberal approach to corporate law was not something we found shared by the NGOs in CORE. They sought greater corporate accountability to society, rather than to more enlightened shareholders, or, as one civil servant put it,[7] 'We had "enlightened shareholder value"—CORE and others didn't like the "shareholder value", business didn't like the "enlightened" part of it.'

However, in general CORE sought whatever mechanisms would deliver more commitment from companies, including using financial arguments. Therefore, we found little evidence in the case of CORE that a third factor was involved in influencing both CORE's campaign and the associated public policy change. Perhaps its interest in the pragmatic use of any arguments that would advance corporate accountability could be interpreted as an aversion to political economic approaches involving a principled stand on the importance of stakeholders rather than shareholders. Perhaps NGOs' interests in being able to report some successes to their managers, advisory boards, trustees and members meant that the participant NGOs focused more on the practical 'win' of achieving some form of mandatory reporting, rather than the political 'loss' of a further restatement of the primacy of shareholder freedoms that the new Companies Act represented. To condemn a law that appeared to many as a step forward, on the grounds of political principle, would not sell well to an NGO's various constituencies, as well as the fragile epistemic community of investors, civil servants and other stakeholders, who had worked toward the new law. Instead, CORE organized a party to celebrate the new law.

The emphasis on a neoliberal approach to shareholder primacy is not a peculiarly British phenomenon. The European Commission had been pushing for the removal of many regulations restricting shareholder freedoms (Burkart and Lee 2008; George 2008). Ongoing economic EU integration meant that the EU became more important to the objectives of CORE. The fundamental lack of direct representative power at the heart of the EU structure, with the European Commission being the main legislative body that works closely with national civil services, particularly trade and industry ministries, and the European Parliament being largely a ceremonial talk shop, manifests itself in the case of corporate accountability. With growing consensus among civic society across Europe of the need for new rules on corporations, in June 2002, the European Parliament passed a resolution stating that companies should be required to supply information on the social and environmental impact of their operations (Bendell 2002). However, the European Commission continued to promote a neoliberal agenda. Five years later, the European Parliament passed a similar resolution based on the *Report on Corporate Social Responsibility: A New Partnership*, which 'urged' the European Commission to create legal obligations regarding directors' duties, mechanisms of redress for foreign affected persons and environmental and social reporting to reinforce corporate accountability. Achieving that resolution required a major input of time and resources from civic society groups across Europe, and was claimed as a success by groups like CORE. However, a more significant development in corporate accountability that year was the decision of the European Commission not to require a public registration of the activities of lobbyists, including their financial arrangements and clients (Huw 2007). Given that corporate lobbying of Eurocrats is a key mechanism in the policy process affecting corporate governance across the European Union, this was a major failure, and it indicated a weakness in the ability of national NGOs to quickly mobilize on EU matters that affect the frameworks within which they seek to achieve their public missions. Part of the reason for this may be that UK NGOs seek to be perceived as apolitical, in order to not alienate potential donors and to avoid audits and challenges from the UK Charities Commission, which requires NGOs to be apolitical to the extent that they focus on their mandates and base any advocacy on evidence from their on-the-ground experience.

CORE participants reflected that in 2006 they had already achieved some aims, including:

- Building a wide base of support for corporate accountability regulation.
- High level of awareness of CORE in Parliament and government (it was recognized as a serious player).
- Media awareness of company law (and CORE).
- Raised the stakes for government on company law, and community and environment were made explicit statements in the bill.
- A significant 'multiplier' effect—more cooperation between NGOs on these matters, achieving other outcomes, such as increased transparency on corporate lobbying and increased finance sector engagement. The multiplier effect applied also to Europe, where many coalitions were launched with CORE support.

Despite that CORE's members were interested in generating a movement for greater corporate accountability within the United Kingdom and across Europe, however, the strategy of the network was not developed toward the creation of a social movement. Some of the shortcomings of the network in its ability to build a movement were already becoming apparent in 2006. Some participants considered that their evidence base was weak and that their analysis of the issues was not strong enough and that the financial sustainability of CORE was not clear. The financial situation became more acute so that CORE could no longer afford to pay its chairperson, who then resigned and later took on a role in senior management within one of the participating organizations.

The lack of finances illustrates the dependence of CORE on the ability and interest of participants on the steering group (SG) to access internal funds and spend them on CORE. The continued success of CORE was therefore dependent on the personal commitment of existing SG members. Subsequently, after the new Companies Act, two key organizations downscaled their involvement in CORE. In 2007, FoE, which had been key to convening the network, decided to place less emphasis on corporate accountability campaigns and focus more on clear environmental issues such as climate change. This was explained by one former FoE staff member as a feeling that 'there is only so far you can go with corporate law, either in attaining policy changes or in bringing your members along with you'. The upsurge in interest in environmental issues due to rising concern with climate change in the United Kingdom since 2006 meant that FoE wanted to both offer itself as *the* environmental organization to support as well as influence the climate change agenda more directly. Compared to reducing one's carbon footprint, corporate law campaigns were not that easy to sell to supporters, or to get them involved. Christian Aid also decided to scale back its involvement as it underwent a reorientation of its policy advocacy. Emerging themes included finance and climate change, both of which could relate quite clearly to CORE, because of the need to move the duties and reporting agenda into the financial services sector, as discussed in the preceding, and the role that mandatory reporting of carbon emissions might have in encouraging their reduction. However, old-fashioned approaches to realignments of organizational strategies involve restructuring of departments and budgets, and so existing activities can be suspended even though they might relate to the new strategy. These developments indicated that CORE participants had not been able to embed the dual importance of corporate accountability work and continuity of participation in networks into their own organizations' strategies that would then necessitate continued budgetary and staff commitments. How a network might help its participant organizations to achieve such a strategic long-term commitment and thus stabilize the network's future is discussed in the following.

This insecurity of funding and participant commitment means that the lasting impact of CORE on British civic society is debatable. Evidence for the impact on European and international civic society is rather weak. CORE participants are involved in efforts at creating Europe-wide and international collaborations on corporate accountability. However, these meetings have been poorly attended, and have struggled to find a common agenda amid concerns about limited resources and the need for funding.

PUBLISH WHAT YOU PAY

Since the formation of the Publish What You Pay (PWYP) network in 2002, the main industry it has focused on, extractives, has experienced an unprecedented boom. In 2005 alone, public mining companies experienced a 72 per cent increase in their total capitalization from 2004, with net profits increasing by 59 per cent, representing an increase of U.S.$45 billion (Standing 2007: 1). This was good news for their shareholders, who received $18 billion in 2005, up 82 per cent from the previous year. The increase in profits being made by the major oil and gas producing companies was also extraordinary. The five major U.S. companies reported profits of $342.4 billion between 2001 and 2006 (PricewaterhouseCoopers 2006). During this time the evidence of corruption continued to increase, while most anti-corruption prosecutions of business people faltered and all the main goals of the PWYP network remained unfulfilled. Corruption in Africa was estimated by the African Union to be costing the continent nearly $150 billion a year (Webb 2008).

Despite this general picture of a global boom of resource consumption racing ahead, while policy implementation on corruption and good governance stumbles behind, there is evidence that the PWYP network had some impact on policy-making that may eventually reduce levels of corruption and improve accountable governance.

The network helped reshape the political opportunities for civic society action on good governance and corruption in four key ways: raising the agenda, framing the agenda by identifying agency, inspiring processes for engagement and influencing processes that might regulate. Each will be discussed in turn, before looking at the failures to achieve the specific policy goals of the network.

First, PWYP raised the agenda. The level of mobilization the network facilitated and represented has made corruption a key international policy issue, particularly in relation to resource extraction in Africa (Standing 2007: 1). International financial institutions (IFIs), global corporations and donor and recipient governments all claim that the fight against corruption is a major priority.

Second, PWYP helped reframe the issue by identifying corporations as key agents that should bear responsibility. During the 1990s, the World Bank emphasized public sector corruption as part of its good governance agenda and 'depicted the private sector as one of the primary victims' (Standing 2007: 1). By 2005, some in the Bank were acknowledging that companies operating in weak or transition states were not passive victims but active parties to corruption (Kaufmann and Vicente 2005). 'Corruption is not only the abuse of public office for private gain, but also the use of public office for private gain by third parties: the grabbing hand of the state is joined by the grabbing hands of private companies' (Standing 2007: 1). This was a shift toward the way the problem was framed by members of PWYP, who chose to focus on the responsibilities of those who make the various payments to governments. Thus the network had opened up a new political opportunity to influence corruption and good governance through corporate practice.

Third, this influence meant that PWYP helped shape the creation of new processes for organizations to engage on these issues. The NGOs' role in subsequent policy processes was expanded and institutionalized, particularly through the creation of the Extractive Industries Transparency Initiative (EITI). The PWYP campaigns led the UK government to announce the creation of the EITI at the World Summit for Sustainable Development in September 2002. The EITI is a multi-stakeholder initiative that addresses how to promote the transparency of government revenue streams ('publish what you receive'). Members of EITI agree on a broad set of principles, including the need for double disclosure between companies and governments to allow for figure comparison. The EITI has garnered the support of international institutional investors with combined trillions of dollars under managements, such as Fidelity Investments and Merrill Lynch Investment Managers (Ballentine and Nitzschke 2005). Statements from delegates at successive G8 meetings since 2003 have also expressed support for the initiative.

Aspects of its functioning, discussed in the following, that relate to civil society are key in understanding how civic society mobilization ostensibly helped institutionalize and protect such mobilization.

The fourth area where PWYP influenced the political opportunities for action was its contribution to the pressure for the establishment of mechanisms that could regulate governments worldwide. The United Nations Convention against Corruption (UNCAC) was adopted by the United Nations General Assembly on 31 October 2003 (Resolution 58/4). The agreement of such a convention was not an explicit aim of PWYP, but its campaigning for government action helped speed the negotiations. Five years after its agreement, no process had been agreed by which governments could be assessed for their compliance with the Convention. Lilian Ekeanyanwu, chairperson of Nigeria's Zero Corruption Coalition and a member of Transparency International (TI) Nigeria, explained at the UNCAC conference that 'many of us, from countries where this is a life or death issue, will be heading home having heard little more than rhetoric' (TI 2008).

Beyond these broad changes in policy contexts, PWYP has not achieved its initial immediate policy aims, each of which would involve the British government adopting new legislation to compel different parts of the financial sector to behave differently in the transparency they require from corporations. The main policy aim that launched the campaign was for stock market listing rules to be changed so all listed companies would need to disclose what they paid to governments. No progress has been made either directly with the stock markets or the UK government on this matter.

A second policy task relates to methods for reporting on such payments. PWYP has called for new accounting standards that would require the disaggregation of payments to governments so that investors and other interested parties could see where the funds are going. A key focus for this has been the International Accounting Standards Board (IASB), which promotes mandatory standards globally for 'profit-oriented' bodies. It is a nongovernmental body independent of formal accountability to governments and intergovernmental bodies. Now globally influential, its stated aim is 'to develop, in the public interest, a . . . set of high quality . . . enforceable global accounting standards' (Gallhofer and Haslam 2007: 633).

PWYP decided to engage with the IASB during the development of the International Financial Reporting Standard (IFRS) eight Operating Segments, a document that would help integrate aspects of U.S. accounting practice with other accounting standards. PWYP managed to marshal the most number of submissions to any such standard development process of the IASB (Gallhofer and Haslam 2007: 652). An advisor to PWYP, Richard Murphy, formerly with KPMG explained that:

> After 20 to 30 letters . . . a head of steam was building up . . . [we] wrote to indicate . . . we wanted to meet . . . we were happy to arrange a . . . visit to take them to Africa . . . to see the scale of the issue and talk to local tax officials. The reply came . . . the relevant person was going on maternity leave. We wrote . . . that surely we must have a meeting . . . the answer came back that we are not going to talk. There was no constructive engagement . . . We realised there was no real point in the consultative process. (Gallhofer and Haslam 2007: 653)

He said that they had already decided to adopt an approach that would not require detailed disaggregation of payments to governments. In addition he claimed there was 'an organized counter campaign' to encourage submissions to the IASB to challenge the calls from PWYP participants:

> The number of letters in favour of . . . IFRS8 . . . jumped up dramatically after the flurry of submissions from [PWYP]. There have never been so many submissions in favour . . . we still managed to get over half the submissions but only just . . . IASB considered all our letters to be the same. This was not true. Each party submitting was encouraged to include their own issues . . . several did. (Gallhofer and Haslam 2007: 652–653)

The existence of the network was used by a resistant organization to actually undermine the collective influence of its members. The implications are that PWYP would have benefited from more supporters in the wider accountancy profession without formal ties to the PWYP network itself becoming engaged in the IASB. After years of attempts from PWYP to engage, the trustees of IASB finally met them in July 2007 for initial discussions.

Gallhofer and Haslam (2007: 646) conclude that the resistance of the IASB to PWYP highlights the political nature of processes masquerading as technical:

> The IASB may claim to be neutral and 'merely' a technically/scientifically expert, but actually it is political. In making some things visible

> and others not, it has consequences beyond the confines of a narrow economics. In ostensibly serving the latter . . . it substantively fails to realize its potential as information for democracy and society as well as for economic resource allocation.

They suggest that either the IASB's understanding of its public purpose is 'less than sound' or it knowingly disguises underlying commercial interests of the accountancy profession that are 'diverging from reasonable notions of the public interest' (Gallhofer and Haslam 2007: 646). To help expose the political nature of the work at IASB, PWYP lobbied the European Parliament on the issue. In November 2007 the Parliament voted for a new international accounting standard requiring oil, gas and mining companies to report payments to governments on a country-by-country basis.

In addition to calling on governments to intervene with stock markets and accounting standards bodies, PWYP was campaigning to see action from governments within existing legal frameworks, in particular within the context of obligations under the Convention on Combating Bribery of Foreign Public Officials of the Organisation for Economic Co-operation and Development (OECD). On this there has been complete failure. TI publishes a report card once a year on how the OECD Convention is being applied. It showed there are very few investigations and prosecutions on business bribery in at least half of OECD countries. The United Kingdom was one of the worst ranked for starting investigations but failing to prosecute. Of the fifteen foreign bribery investigations in 2007 and the four in 2006, the United Kingdom brought one prosecution (Webb 2008).

'It is hypocritical that OECD–based companies continue to bribe across the globe, while their governments pay lip-service to enforcing the law', said David Nussbaum, former chief executive of TI (TI 2006). The OECD itself has been critical of the United Kingdom's implementation of the Convention. A high-profile instance of non-compliance is the al-Yamamah case. The UK government cancelled an investigation into a major arms deal with Saudi Arabia involving BAE Systems on national security grounds. It was 'seen by many as a national scandal setting back the UK's reputation in the international arena' (Webb 2008). At the time of writing, the case is still in the UK's High Court, which ruled in 2007 that the case should be reopened.

Given the lack of progress in these areas, it is not surprising that PWYP participants focused on the creation of the EITI as a key success of the network. They even link to it from the central frame of the PWYP homepage. The strengths and weakness of the EITI in encouraging the transparency of government revenues that PWYP seeks is important to explore.

EITI is not the governmental response that PWYP called for. It does not focus on new regulations on international corporations, but provides a voluntary system for governments and businesses to improve the transparency of payments related to extractive industries. PWYP was founded on a rejection of the possibility that voluntary action would be sustainable,

EITI on the proposition that a voluntary approach could deliver benefits for participants.

A success of the EITI has been to attract many candidate countries and supporting companies to commit to greater transparency, and to begin working out mechanisms for this. However, by the end of 2007 only a couple of the supporting companies had published information on their governmental payments and no candidate country has been endorsed for the transparency of its accounts.

Despite EITI being founded on a concept of voluntary change that PWYP had rejected at the outset, the latter recognized that EITI is one of the most active mechanisms on the issue and that its existence provides the members of PWYP with greater political opportunities for their action. By giving NGOs a place in its organizational structure and role on its board, EITI provides access to higher policy levels than some NGOs would have had before. In addition, it provides new means for protecting civic society action at national levels, by requiring countries that seek endorsement from EITI to respect civic society rights to information, association and advocacy; and by mobilizing powerful groups in the defence of specific NGOs when governments retaliate against their campaigning on transparency-related issues. This was illustrated in early 2008 when the government of Gabon suspended a number of NGOs, including some members of PWYP, for being critical of the government's use of oil revenues. Within a week of PWYP and EITI secretariats and members expressing concern, the country revoked its ban.

The fact that PWYP members benefit from EITI's existence suggests some confluence of interests between the instigators and funders of these initiatives. PWYP and EITI share a similar approach in four areas, each of which could be contested for its inability to promote governance to reduce global and national inequalities.

First, neither EITI nor PWYP have sufficiently engaged the newly emerged powers, particularly India and China, which are major investors across the Global South. TI's 2006 Bribe Payers Index illustrates one aspect of the problem, with China and India the worst performers.

Given questions about voluntary initiatives and the highly restricted political opportunities for advocacy NGOs in China and elsewhere, focusing more attention on new or enhanced intergovernmental arrangements seems a promising strategy. Both the EITI and PWYP, however, have lacked a focus on lobbying for such intergovernmental mechanisms. A case in point is the UN Convention against Corruption, which lacks an effective enforcement procedure. The absence of such mechanisms is considered by many scholars to be a result of the power of corporations on the foreign and trade relations policies of national governments (Bendell 2004). This led to defeatism among many civic society organizations about the possibility of encouraging new rules for global trade (Murphy and Bendell 1999), which was reflected by some of the participants in PWYP.

A third area of common approach between the initiatives is the proposition, perhaps assumption that transparency can deliver good governance.

This is questionable, given the analysis of countries where there is transparent corruption. In the Philippines the media has consistently revealed instances of corrupt politicians arranging payments for themselves in return for award contracts for building roads and airports and other activities. Inquiries in the Senate have also helped reveal the level and routine nature of corruption, and how debates in and around government focus on what is an acceptable level of corruption rather than its outright condemnation. Despite this transparency, little has changed in the governance of the country. In the most recent circumstance under the government of Gloria Arroyo, this appears to be because the various sectors of society that could challenge such practices—the church, courts, military, police and civic society—are politicized and have financial self-interests in maintaining the current political order. Transparency is the focus of both initiatives because it appears as a first step toward good governance and because it appears as a more technical rather than political measure. However, to achieve good governance requires dealing with issues of power and how the information can then be used. PWYP avoids this issue as a result of the interests of its members, who seek to maintain an apolitical profile for purposes of their charitable status and broad memberships.

Fourth, both initiatives focus on extractive industries. However, some research suggests that today corruption is most prevalent in the building of power stations, roads, airports, hydroelectric dams and waste management systems, as well as in basic services such as justice, health, education and energy supplies; corruption in public procurement in many countries is also found to be widespread (Webb 2008). This suggests that EITI should not be a main focus for PWYP. However, extractive industries provide a clear and visible link to the constituencies of PWYP memberships, through the involvement of companies headquartered in the West, such as the oil and mining majors. In addition, the social and environmental impacts of such projects are highly visible and provide a connection between the broader corruption issue and the specific concerns of participant charities, such as humanitarian action, deforestation and so on.

These four areas of overlap raise questions about the effectiveness of these initiatives to promote good governance of business and investment. These limitations are the result of the same structural factors that relate to the power of corporate interests over foreign affairs and the limited ability of civic society groups to tackle causes of societal problems free from interests of their own organizational mandates and funding streams.

TRADE JUSTICE MOVEMENT

The TJM points to the change in UK company law as its key impact on UK public policy. Although it played an important role in this process by helping to mobilize people through its NGO members, the corporate accountability agenda had not been the central focus for TJM or the reason for its creation. The CORE coalition was created for that purpose. Instead, TJM was initially created to organize what could be called 'high-street NGOs' (large and well known to many people in the UK) to continue and expand the agenda and tactics pursued by the Jubilee 2000 coalition (see Chapter 3, this volume), which focused on debt cancellation for poor countries. It played a key role in the late 1990s in bringing thousands of people onto the streets in the cities hosting the major summits of institutions it considered responsible for the debt situation and its impacts, specifically the World Bank, the International Monetary Fund (IMF) and the G8. TJM involved many of the same organizations in the Jubilee campaign and sought to apply similar pressure on another aspect of the global economy—international trade agreements. Individual members of the public, media and protesters were already making the connections, with the protests at the 1999 World Trade Organization (WTO) Ministerial meeting in Seattle occurring a year before the TJM was formed. Therefore, the TJM impact on public policy should really be assessed on the basis of the framework of trade agreements that has arisen post-Seattle. On those terms, the TJM has failed to make an impact. Worse, it could be argued that a historic opportunity to embrace and organize a groundswell of public interest and commitment at the turn of the millennium was lost by the members of TJM. Both points are explained in the following.

The WTO plays an important, although not encompassing, role in international trade rules. The protests in Seattle and the collapse of those talks amid resistance from delegates from the Global South meant that a new, ostensibly more developmental, agenda had to be found. This resulted in the Doha agenda for future negotiations, which had still not been completed by 2008. Therefore, the argument put forward by TJM that development has been made central to international trade policy at WTO is questionable.

One of the successes that TJM points to is the delays in rich countries obtaining agreements on liberalizing finance and investment via the WTO. However, this fails to mention how the forum for rich countries, which includes the United Kingdom, has now shifted to bilateral agreements to pursue its aims for liberalization of finance and investment. In the case of the United Kingdom, the European Union has taken on ever-greater leadership in trade policy through negotiating Economic Partnership Agreements. By 2008, dozens of African, Caribbean and Pacific countries had signed trade deals with the European Union that included agreements on issues such as investment and trade in services. By 2002, it was already clear to trade analysts that other mechanisms than the WTO would be used by corporate interests to seek changes in regulatory frameworks, including the use of bilateral and regional agreements (Peterson 2002). Given this understanding, one might have expected a major mobilization around EU policy-making processes, to ensure they would be open to civic society scrutiny and pressure. However, the initial consultations from the European Commission on requiring disclosure of the funding and activities of lobbyists did not receive a major response from trade campaigners, including the TJM secretariat, and a voluntary register was adopted by the European Union. The European branch of TJM member FoE did take a lead in creating a network to pressure for greater disclosure in future.[8]

This success is, however, about resisting rather than advancing an agenda on these matters. A member of TJM expressed his sense of the challenge: 'How successful have we been in all that? Not very so far, but we've only been working five years, and it's a bit of a big thing to try to overthrow the neoliberal economic order—but we're getting there.'

This economic order, and particularly the global financial system, is recognized by many NGOs as posing problems for the reduction of poverty and the achievement of greater equality. There are important development concerns arising from tax havens, currency speculation, leveraged buyouts, short-selling stocks and near-term focused asset management. Tax evasion and offshore banking secrecy cost developing country governments up to U.S.$500 billion a year in lost revenues. Currency speculation at over a trillion dollars a day has destabilized currencies so that there is a mismatch between loans priced in rich country currencies and repayments in domestic currencies. The world's top twenty banks account for 80 per cent of this currency speculation, and thus benefit disproportionately from the use of this power to influence currency prices.

Given this systemic influence on the global economy, merely slowing down the policy agendas of some of the major financial firms is not very significant. The 2005 G8 summit reaffirmed its commitment to global financial liberalization even though many developing countries questioned the benefits of capital liberalization; particularly those like China, Chile and Malaysia that had not liberalized their financial sectors and had managed to ride out regional financial crises. No commitment was forthcoming from the UK government on a new approach to the financial system on the issues mentioned earlier, and none was being formulated or requested by TJM, apart from some reports on specific issues like tax evasion by its members, such as Christian Aid. Even the Western financial crisis, brought on by a crash in confidence in financial derivatives in the real estate sector in 2007, did not lead to initiatives from TJM on what an economic justice agenda would look like for finance. This is surprising if one remembers how a campaign on a financial issue—poor country debt—inspired the creation of TJM.

Another claim of success made by the TJM was the increasing attention given by trade negotiators to eliminating export subsidies by rich countries. The concern expressed by some British international development NGOs, Southern governments and large agricultural producers is that they are unable to compete on price with subsidized products from rich countries that enter their markets, nor can they sell their products freely in rich country markets. In 2005 an agreement to include this issue in the future was reached at the WTO. The development NGO position was questioned by some, such as Vandana Shiva, who focused more on small-scale and environmentally appropriate solutions to food supply (Shiva 2002).

An awareness of the resource dependency of the long-distance trading of large-scale farming of cash crops, and an argument for more local production and trade, underpins the criticism of the development NGO position on market access. As the implications of climate change for agricultural production become more widely understood, particularly the growing cost of oil-dependent agricultural inputs, such as fertilizers and the cost of transportation, this analysis is more widely recognized (Ho, 2008). Consequently, any policy changes that encourage more mechanized forms of production and longer transportation of supplies conflict with attempts to promote climate change mitigation and adaptation.

Another dimension to the criticism of the market access argument of development NGOs is that it is unclear how such changes would deal with the fundamental drivers of hunger and malnutrition. These drivers are disputed but are generally understood to include the quantity and quality of food, levels of income and income inequality in society and the diversity of both food supplies and incomes available to communities. Greater access to Northern markets for developing country producers will benefit those companies able to take advantage of such trading opportunities. However, this will not affect the poor producers, who often experience rising prices for land and inputs as commercial cash-cropping grows in their locale. As annual discussions at the World Social Forum and advocacy by global movements like Via Campesina repeatedly emphasize, liberalization of trade can generate inequality, which can be a key driver of hunger.

Such concerns suggest that British development NGOs might have focused on matters other than agricultural trade liberalization. In early 2007, as food prices worldwide rocketed due to problems with production combined with spiralling demand from Asia, so TJM's criticism of rich country policies that kept down international prices for foods like rice, corn and wheat, seemed redundant. Instead, any policy that would keep prices down, including export subsidies would help to alleviate the global problem with food prices.

TJM lacks a coherent philosophy about the root cause of malnutrition and maldevelopment. The mission of TJM reads like a long list of specific policy concerns rather than an overarching analysis of the nature and cause of maldevelopment. A lack of a cohering political vision also means that the NGOs in TJM did not relate effectively to the upwelling of public interest in systemic critiques of globalization in the late 1990s and early twenty-first century. TJM claims it 'has established a reputation for public mobilization in support of its goals' and cites that over twenty-five thousand people 'filled Whitehall at an all-night vigil'.[9] However, it is important to remember that in Genoa in 2001, over one hundred thousand people protested at the G8. Only a few thousand were organized by the TJM, and in general there was little evidence of any connection between the people protesting and the NGOs who were focused on lobbying politicians and speaking to the media. Given that absence on the ground, the protestors were approached and recruited by traditional left-wing organizations, such as the Socialist Workers Party and its front group called Globalise Resistance. The upwelling of protests was described as anti-globalization or anti-capitalist movements. That neither phrase appeared on the TJM website highlights the fact that TJM members did not feel comfortable working with an explicitly political framing of the problems. The subsequently popular term of *Global Justice Movement* was mentioned only once, in passing. This lack of connection to the wider movement of individuals critiquing global capitalism was illustrated by a fall-out between TJM and the organizing committee for the European Social Forum in 2004.[10]

In the absence of a groundswell of activists, the TJM used another means of generating mass participation—celebrities. The Live 8 musical event, held to coincide with the G8 summit in Scotland, helped create media attention and public participation, but also reshaped the message being conveyed to the world. The message became one of charity not justice, with the powerful leaders of the world asked to help the unfortunate rather than being challenged to correct their own countries' involvement in oppressive trading and financial relations with poor countries. Many of the celebrities congratulated the politicians, although the movement on trade issues was non-existent, and the debt cancellation deal was not comprehensive.

The lack of connection to grass-roots activists, absence of a coherent political philosophy, the ease with which celebrities could influence the message and the lack of impact on public policy suggest that the TJM is not actually a movement in the true sense of the word. Perhaps the financial crisis that broke in 2008 may change that by giving TJM member NGOs a political opportunity to advance more radical critiques of and proposals for the financial system. Time will tell whether they manage to bridge their institutional NGO concerns by engaging at the grass-roots level as a new wave of activism calling for financial justice rose in 2009.

Collective Impacts on Global Inequality

Several themes emerge from the preceding discussion on the impacts of the different networks. First, the policy goals of the networks are conservative, even when compared to the nature of the problem defined by the networks and their participants. For instance, it is not certain that the greater disclosure of corporate activities sought by PWYP and CORE would actually deliver a change in irresponsible behaviour. The agenda is conservative largely because the NGOs identify policy goals that they think could be attainable within existing power structures and past experience. However, other moderating influences may include: the sources of funding for participant organizations, including governments, corporations and established middle-class individuals; concerns with the restrictions on political action due to the NGO's charitable status; and the class of the NGO professionals themselves, many of whom will work in government or corporate management at some stage in their career.

Second, the achievement of these conservative policy goals is limited. Only 3.9 per cent of survey respondents reported that public policy changes on the issues the network was campaigning on were 'substantive' without further qualification. Another 53.9 per cent considered that such policy changes were 'substantive but didn't sufficiently address structural issues', and 30.8 per cent that they were 'superficial'. The remaining 11.5 per cent reported no changes in policy. PWYP and TJM cannot point to many concrete policy outcomes that align with their original campaign goals. The CORE coalition has achieved changes in the law, but with no clarity about how these will be interpreted and implemented.

Third, when these policy goals are achieved, it appears to exhaust rather than energize the network. Since the change in UK company law, CORE's funding and participation tailed off, it lost staff and ceased campaigning. Some NGOs expressed they felt they had gone as far as they could within their own organizations on a corporate reform agenda.

Fourth, when the policy goals of the networks were achieved, the translation of these policy innovations into the practice of business, investment or trade has been minimal, at least in the time horizon of this project. For over eighteen months, the UK government did not provide guidance, let alone a standard, for what the new law on corporate social reporting and directors' duties actually would mean. This leaves it up to companies to determine what they think the law means, as well as the courts, when a case is finally brought that uses this legislation. That highly paid corporate lawyers will likely influence the substance of new laws on corporate accountability, through an effective defence of their clients, is not a positive reflection on the democratic process.

Fifth, the existence of numerous networks on aspects of economic policy has not made a generic impact on the economic policy agenda in the United Kingdom. The early twenty-first century has witnessed a continuing emphasis on the liberalization of trade and finance at home and abroad, in pursuit of the illogical aim of continual economic growth within a finite natural environment. The inability to shift the broad agenda could be the result of a reluctance to elucidate a comprehensive political analysis of the problems with, and causes of, inequality. Although one of the networks calls itself a movement for justice, the networks have not clearly identified themselves as part of a common effort for economic justice or articulated how they relate to the concept of such a movement that has spread worldwide—the GJM. The importance of this gulf is only accentuated by the global financial crisis that developed in 2008. The ability of these networks to enable NGOs to develop common critiques and push common proposals may determine the relevance of these NGOs to the emergence of a new global financial order that will shape inequalities for years to come.

FROM NOBLE TO GLOBAL

The preceding case studies of civic networks have revealed a number of major challenges for global justice activism, in terms of the limited impact on public policy processes, and the limited role of the networks and NGOs in people's daily struggles against unequal power relations. The term 'noble' usefully describes different aspects of these networks as they existed during the early years of the twenty-first century. The Encarta definition of noble comprised five dimensions: having excellent moral character (possessing high ideals or excellent moral character); aristocratic (belonging or relating to an aristocratic social or political class); relating to high moral principles (based on high ideals or revealing excellent moral character); magnificent (impressive in quality or appearance); and in chemistry, non-reactive (chemically inactive or inert). The civic networks studied here demonstrate something of each of these five aspects of this concept. 'Noble networks' are networks with apparently noble objectives that involve people whose relationship to their intended beneficiaries can put them in an elite position, but fairly inert in terms of their impact on society.

Rather than being forces in a social movement that transform power relations in a society or the wider world, networks may be enabling the status quo by providing a place where educated, intellectual and ethically concerned people can convene and express this concern without challenging power structures. The fact that many NGO professionals end up working in business or government highlights how they may be helping institutions to adapt and reform, rather than transforming them. Given the growing rates of global inequality and the role of economic and political power in shaping that inequality, it appears that UK civil society is far too civil and there is far too much 'society', in the elite socializing form of that term. In historical studies, the term *noble networks* has been used to describe trans-European elites of the past (Sandberg 2006). The contemporary forms of civic network are not powerful in this sense; in fact, they are far from it. However, this historic parallel highlights that, to be an agent of global equality, their challenge is both to embody democratic ideals themselves and secure them in global power structures, rather than creating new buffers around power structures.

Our analysis has not covered other forms of civic organization, such as trade unions and grass-roots community organizations. Networks of those organizations may or may not experience some of the opportunities and problems outlined in this chapter. We conclude that civic networks similar to those examined here should move from being noble to global, in a range of different ways. An obvious way is to become more internationally connected, involving groups from around the world and seeking to influence actors and policies in different countries and at international forums, depending on the opportunities that arise. They can also become more global by espousing universal values as a way of articulating a common agenda rather than reacting to national government policy and donor interests. Another way would be by involving more diverse participants from different races, genders, places, sectors and classes, as well as ensuring that the networks are increasingly legitimate in what they say and do. They can become more global also through their notion of the person: to see how the processes that create problems for intended beneficiaries are the same processes that create problems for themselves, their organizations and even their donors. Although charity will never be an inclusive global concept, solidarity can be. Networks could focus more on systems that are universal, particularly finance and entertainment media, which are the most global systems of power in the world today.

The implications of this analysis for donors and for progressives in government and business are complicated. Donors could explore how to enable Southern constituencies to advocate for themselves and shift policy-related funding away from Western groups and to the South. However, large donor attempts to influence civil society mobilization from below have been found at times to undermine existing legitimate channels that arise from local contexts (Mouffe 2005). Therefore, a form of solidarity donorship may be required, where donors look to service the needs of peoples' organizations in ways that do not require continued foreign intervention to succeed, and that do not create new independent channels of resource flow and agenda setting. Unfortunately, the approach of the UK Department for International Development (DFID) in giving far larger sums of funding to large United Kingdom–based NGOs may work against this and further undermine the ability of NGOs to work as social movement organizations. Given the role of large donors, particularly as part of governments, in maintaining the power structures that drive much inequality and injustice, more time should be spent on internal organizational change within the bureaucracies of government and intergovernmental institutions.

Another area where large donors could support change on economic justice issues is to help those professionals in business and finance, who left NGOs, yet work on related issues. Such people have become good technicians at particular aspects of the social and environmental performance of business and finance but are not able to create as much change as they might, due to limited time and mandates from their employers. The implications of this analysis for such people in the private sector is that they support and engage in more informal networks on these issues that cut across organizational sectors, seek to involve more civic society organizations in their own multi-enterprise associations and support the training of NGOs in the North and South on matters of private finance.

These recommendations all relate to a shift in mindset among professionals in NGOs, companies and donors, who are interested in pursuing an economic justice agenda. The shift is away from an organization-centric mindset to a movement-centric one, where an individual's and their organizations' role in strengthening a network's impact becomes a priority

(Bendell et al. 2009). The relationship of NGOs to social movements has been a difficult one, as processes of professionalization and donor interests have often led NGOs away from more systemic critiques of economic systems and processes of grass-roots mobilizing to build countervailing powers. In the United Kingdom, many mainstream NGOs have significant resources and profile, and so there is little need to join networks to work on their core mandates, unless they wish to address the systemic causes of the issues they focus on. An interesting question is whether such NGOs have the ambition and courage to work on a more transformative agenda and, if so, whether networks could bridge the gap between themselves and the wider public of active citizens and social movement adherents.

As the networks studied were fairly new, the limitations we point to could merely be the birthing pains of new forms of organizing that traverse boundaries of nation, sector and public concern. As experience grows and connections are made, the somewhat 'noble' networks chronicled in this chapter have the opportunity to become truly global forces for the common good. Given intensifying national and international inequalities and the violence that this situation can breed in communities across the world, it is an opportunity we hope they seize.

NOTES

1. For more information on the methodology used for this study, see Chapter 3 in this volume.
2. See http://www.tjm.org.uk.
3. Ibid.
4. See http://newsweaver.co.uk/accatas/e_article001248641.cfm?x=b11,0,w.
5. See http://www.tjm.org.uk.
6. See http://www.foe.co.uk.
7. These and the following citations used in this chapter are taken from the interviews of this research. For more information on the methodology of this study, see Chapter 4 in this volume.
8. See the Alliance for Lobbying Transparency and Ethics Regulation at the European Union (ALTER-EU), available at http://www.alter-eu.org.
9. See http://www.tjm.org.uk.
10. An open letter from NGOs to the organizing committee was posted on the Indymedia website at http://www.indymedia.org.uk/en/2004/09/297118.html.

BIBLIOGRAPHY

Ballentine, K., and Nitzschke, H. (2005). *Profiting from Peace: Managing the Resource Dimensions of Armed Conflict*, Boulder, CO: Lynne Rienner.

Bendell, Jem. (2002). 'World Review', *Journal of Corporate Citizenship*, 7:43–56.

———. (2004). *Barricades and Boardrooms: A Contemporary History of the Corporate Accountability Movement.* Programme on Technology, Business and Society, Paper No. 13, UNRISD, Geneva.

Bendell, Jem, Visser, Wayne, Peck, Jules, Cohen, Jonathan, Moon, Jeremy, Young, Mark, Bendell, Mark, Kearins, Kate, Concannon, Tim, Shah, Shilpa, Ives, Kate, Abrahams, Desirée, Gibbons, Paul, Shah, Rupesh, and Manoochehri, John. (2009). *The Corporate Responsibility Movement*, Sheffield: Greenleaf Publishing.

Bryer, David, and Magrath, John. (1999). 'New Dimensions of Global Advocacy', *Nonprofit and Voluntary Sector Quarterly*, 28 (1): 168–177.

Burkart, Mike, and Lee, Samuel. (2008). 'One Share—One Vote: The Theory', *Review of Finance*, 12 (1): 1–49.

Ho, Mae-Wa. (2008). *GM–Free Organic Agriculture to Feed the World*, International Panel of 400 Agricultural Scientists Call for Fundamental Change in Farming Practice, ISIS Report 18/04/08. http://www.i-sis.org.uk/GMFreeOrganicAgriculture.php (accessed July 2008).

Department of Trade and Industry. (2002). *Modern Company Law for a Competitive Economy: Final Report*. www.bis.gov.uk/files/file23279.pdf (accessed July 2008).

———. (2004). *The Operating and Financial Review*. DTI and Working Group on Materiality Publications. http://www2.accaglobal.com/pubs/general/activities/research/research_archive/rr-089–001.pdf (accessed July 2008).

Edwards, Michael. (2003). NGO Legitimacy—Voice or Vote? Bond: Global Policy Forum. http://www.globalpolicy.org/ngos/credib/2003/0202rep.htm (accessed July 2008).

Evans, Huw. (1999). 'Debt Relief for the Poorest Countries: Why Did It Take So Long?' *Development Policy Review*, 17 (3): 267–79.

Gallhofer, Sonja, and Haslam, Jim. (2007). 'Exploring Social, Political and Economic Dimensions of Accounting in the Global Context: The International Accounting Standards Board and Accounting Disaggregation', *Socio-Economic Review*, October: 1–32: 633–646.

George, Susan. (2008). *Europe Deserves Much Better Than the Lisbon Treaty*, Transnational Institute, 16 May. http://www.tni.org/archives/george_lisbon-treaty (accessed December 2008).

Hudson, Alan. (2001). 'NGOs and Transnational Advocacy Networks: From Legitimacy to Political Responsibility', *Global Networks*, 1 (4): 331–352.

Kaufmann, Daniel, and Vicente, Pedro. (2005). *Legal Corruption*, Washington, DC: World Bank Institute.

Maron, IsaiahYeshahu. (2006). 'Toward a Unified Theory of the CSP–CFP Link', *Journal of Business Ethics*, 67:191–200.

Mouffe, Chantal. (2005). *On the Political*, New York: Routledge.

Murphy, David F., and Bendell, Jem. (1999). *Partners in Time? Business, NGOs and Sustainable Development*. UNRISD Discussion Paper No. 109, UNRISD, Geneva.

Peterson, Luke Eric. (2002). 'Dusted-off Trade Treaties Ensure There Is No Such Thing as a Free Riot', *The Guardian*, 6 May. http://www.guardian.co.uk/business/2002/may/06/2 (accessed July 2008).

Publish What You Pay International. (2002). *George Soros and NGOs Call for Rules to Require Corporations to Disclose Payments*, Press Release, 13 June, London: PWYP International.

PricewaterhouseCoopers. (2006). *Mine: Let the Good Times Roll. Review of Global Trends in the Mining Industry*, London: PricewaterhouseCoopers.

Jones, Huw. (2007). *Lobbyists Throw EU Transparency Plan into Doubt*, Reuters via Transnational Institute, 11 June. http://www.tni.org/article/lobbyists-throw-eu-transparency-plan-doubt (accessed July 2008).

Saha, Poulomi Mrinal (2006). The Operating and Financial Review—Testing Transparency. 4 January. http://www.ethicalcorp.com/content/operating-and-financial-review-testing-transparency (accessed July 2008).

Sandberg, Brian. (2006). *'Through Naval Practice and the Association with Foreigners': French Nobles and Religious Struggle in the Mediterranean, 1598–1635*, Journal of Mediterranean Studies 16: 219–227.

Shiva, Vandana. (2002). 'Deconstructing Market Access', *Znet Communications, November02*.http://www.zcommunications.org/deconstructing-market-access-by-vandana2-shiva (accessed July 2008).

Smith, Jackie. (2005). 'Globalization and Transnational Social Movement Organisation', in G.F. Davis, D. McAdams, W.R. Scott and M.N. Zald (eds), *Social Movements and Organization Theory*, Cambridge: Cambridge University Press.

Standing, Andre. (2007). *Corruption and the Extractive Industries in Africa: Can Combating Corruption Cure the Resource Curse?* Occasional Paper 153, October, The Institute for Security Studies, Pretoria.

Transparency International. (2006). *Bribe Payers Index 2006*. http://www.transparency.org/policy_research/surveys_indices/bpi/bpi_2006#pr (accessed July 2008).

———. (2008). *UN Corruption Conference: Failure to Act on Critical Issue a 'Major Setback' for the Fight against Corruption*, Press Release, 01 February. http://www.transparency.org/news_room/latest_news/press_releases/2008/2008_02_01_uncac_final (accessed July 2008).

Trade Justice Movement. (2006). *Right Corporate Wrongs: The Companies Act (Formerly the Companies Bill). An Update for Supporters on the Outcome*, November. http://corporate-responsibility.org/wp/wp-content/uploads/2009/09/Companies_Bill_Supporter_Verdict__Long_Nov06.pdf (accessed July 2008).

Webb, Toby. (2008). *Strategy and Management: Transparency International—Counting Corporate Corruption*. 13 February. http://www.ethicalcorp.com/communications-reporting/transparency-international-—-counting-corporate-corruption (accessed July 2008).

7 Reforming Agricultural and Trade Policy in France

The Limits of Multi-Actor Coalitions[1]

Benoit Daviron and Tancrède Voituriez

INTRODUCTION

The gradual liberalization of France's trade policy has been under way for over two decades. The reaction from French producers and civil society, as well as certain governmental institutions, has been strong, reflecting concerns not only about farmers in France and elsewhere in Europe, but also in relation to farmers in developing countries who have been negatively affected by 'neoliberalism'.

This chapter examines the extent to which non-state actors concerned with issues of trade justice are attempting to influence agricultural policy in France. Specifically, we shall examine:

1. The different types of discourse and proposals generated by non-state actors related to the reform of agricultural policy for the purpose of reducing North–South inequalities
2. The nature and form of relationships between non-state actors, as well as between these and the state
3. The influence of these relationships on policy reforms

Our research primarily involved interviews with individuals in NGOs, agricultural organizations and government agencies in France concerned with agricultural and trade policy issues (see Annex 7.1).

The sections that follow present our findings. First we outline the context of the European Common Agricultural Policy (CAP) and the reforms that it has undergone, as well as early antiliberal protests against these reforms. The next section examines the different perspectives of the main actors concerned with agriculture and trade policy: the NGOs, the agricultural professional organizations (APOs) and certain government institutions. Considerable convergence around an antiliberal position emerges from this examination. The third section addresses the question of why this antiliberal coalition has had such little influence on public policy. We conclude by summarizing the findings of the research.

THE COMMON AGRICULTURAL POLICY AND TRADE LIBERALIZATION

At a seminar on the Doha Development Round in Washington in February 2006, the director-general of the World Trade Organization (WTO), Pascal Lamy, summarized the strengths and weaknesses of the WTO member countries engaged in the negotiation: 'The EU knows it will have to move on agriculture market access, the U.S. knows it will have to move on agriculture domestic support and emerging countries like Brazil, India or South Africa know they will have to move on industrial tariffs and services'(Lamy 2006). He also stressed the fact that, among all of the sectors subject to liberalization, the agricultural sector is the one that 'holds the key to unblocking and revitalizing the negotiations and ensuring substantive progress across the board'. Implicit was the suggestion that the impasse on this 'problem sector' was due to two parties, Europe and the United States.

Despite the campaigns of NGOs calling for international solidarity in opposing Europe's double standards (Oxfam 2002), and the apparent academic consensus that access to the agricultural markets of the North would be more useful than reform of the support system (Hertel and Winters 2006), ultimately it was Europe, particularly France, that constituted the first obstacle to negotiation and to the success of the so-called 'development' round at the WTO. In the words of the director-general, France's position was 'excessively defensive on the agricultural question'.[2]

Over forty years ago, a 'French' policy on agricultural markets ceded ground to a European one: the CAP. It is the CAP that essentially determines prices and revenues for French farmers and that regulates trade with outside countries. The evolution of the CAP, from its origin up to recent reforms, is outlined in the following.

On 25 March 1957, the Treaty of Rome solidified the creation of the European Economic Community (EEC), and laid the groundwork for the establishment of a common agricultural policy. Article 39, paragraph 1, of the treaty (now article 33 of the treaty creating the European Community) defines five fundamental objectives of the CAP:

1. Increase agricultural productivity by promoting technical progress and ensuring rational development of agricultural production and optimum use of the factors of production, in particular labour.
2. Ensure a fair standard of living for the agricultural community, in particular by raising the individual incomes of those working in agriculture.
3. Stabilize markets.
4. Ensure secure availability of supplies.
5. Provide consumers with food at reasonable prices.

The principal objectives of the Treaty of Rome were 'quite effectively fulfilled by the CAP between 1960 and 1990' (Bureau 2007: 27). Productivity grew considerably, with price stability providing producers a predictable economic horizon. This encouraged investment, innovation and productive development (Bureau et al. 1991). The ability of the CAP to provide consumers with products at reasonable prices is more debatable and varies from sector to sector (Butault 2006). Although the CAP did not succeed in providing a high overall standard of living to those making a living in the agricultural sector in 1960, it nevertheless did facilitate the transformation of an agrarian economy into an industrial and service-sector economy.

The CAP that prevailed until the late 1980s clearly led to a number of dead ends—all, however, the result of the very mechanism designed to encourage production. Problems included surpluses, budgetary slippage (particularly in the context of channelling the surpluses) and conflicts with other countries (the latter being a result of the downward pressure on prices triggered by subsidies and surpluses). Africa, strongly linked to the European market as a result of its colonial past, was the continent that suffered most from the CAP. Despite the Yaoudé and Lomé Accords, Africa essentially lost the preferential access it had enjoyed under policies of imperial autarky. In fact, these agreements initially functioned through the 'aid, not trade' type of compensation. Africa's share of total world exports of food products fell from 11 per cent to 4 per cent between 1960 and 1990. At the same time, the continent found itself compelled to specialize in single tropical products such as coffee and cacao (Daviron 2008).

In the early 1990s, the CAP became a source of serious international tension and delayed the conclusion of a trade agreement under the General Agreement on Tariffs and Trade (GATT) framework. Leading the CAP protest, the Cairns group, which included the competitive agricultural export countries such as Australia, New Zealand, Brazil, Argentina and South Africa, was formed in 1986 to accelerate the multilateral liberalization of agricultural trade. It was the fact that most the group's countries were developing countries that prompted the front-page article in *Le Monde,* on 29 November 2002, by Mark Vaile, then New Zealand's Minister of Agriculture, with the explosive title 'Agriculture: Europe Strangles the Poor Countries'(Vaile 2002). Nevertheless, the actual rationale for Europe's reforms, and for its progressive market deregulation, was first and foremost a domestic one.

France argued against the Commission's point of view, stressing the domestic cost of the CAP and the importance of new expenditures, particularly for research. It dissociated itself from responsibility for Europe's role in the GATT and WTO negotiations. The constraints on negotiations, which were anticipated by the Commission, gave the CAP reform a decidedly liberal hue (Fouilleux 2003).

In the context of stalled GATT negotiations, EU Agriculture Commissioner Ray MacSharry launched the reform of the CAP in 1992, reducing support prices for several commodities, but compensating farmers with direct payments. Through the Blair House Accord that year, the United States and Europe broke the impasse in the agricultural negotiating group of the Uruguay Round, which finally concluded in December 1993. Subsequent reforms to the CAP in 1999 and 2003 further liberalized EU trade policy, with more substantial cuts in support prices and the decoupling of direct payments and production levels. There was also an increased focus on rural development and the environment.

In France, the Blair House Accord subsequently provoked irate protest, in which it was difficult to differentiate antiliberal from anti-American elements. The monthly publication of the alter-globalization farmers' organization, *Confédération Paysanne*, complained: 'European Commissioner MacSharry diverged from his mandate and also made some important concessions on animal feed'(Confédération Paysanne 2001). According to *L'Humanité*: 'We know that this agreement was "negotiated" by two European commissioners at the end of their terms, with Carla Hills serving the interests of the Bush administration. It may be recalled that these two officials, in a rush to catch their return flight to Brussels, left the final redaction of the text to the Americans. We also know that one of the two commissioners—Irishman Ray MacSharry—was acting as an official negotiator at the very time that he was contemplating a return to private-sector work in agriculture in the United States'(L'Humanité 1993). In a debate that pitted Luc Guyau, president of the main farmers' organization, the *Fédération nationale des syndicats d'exploitants agricoles* (FNSEA) against Philippe Vasseur, Deputy of the *Union pour la Démocratie Française* (UDF) in December of 1993, Guyau declared that 'the perverse spirit of Blair House still haunts' the Brussels agricultural arrangement in the framework of the GATT negotiations. *Coordination Rurale* believes that 'the Blair House Accord cannot ensure quantitative and qualitative food security and create jobs, and . . . will lead to a change in the landscape and to the destruction of farms' (Deneux and Emorine 1998: 47). In the view of *Confédération Paysanne*, the sharp drop in prices slated to take effect for cereals, milk and beef 'shows that by proposing to dismantle market organizations, the Commission has chosen to fall in line with American agricultural policy, rather than defending the European model' (Deneux and Emorine 1998: 49).

Opposition from the agricultural farmers' associations (although not as universal as that provoked by the Blair House Accord) was, in the opinion of Dominique Barreau, secretary-general of the FNSEA, triggered by a transition instrument 'along liberal lines, under which Europe was to decrease production and turn for its food to the more competitive countries, such as Brazil and Australia' (Barreau 2006). The Commission saw the opposition as a reaction to a formative instrument for a new European model, the Single Payment Scheme (SPS). Although the decoupling proposal brought farmers together in opposition, its implementation called for intense negotiation and lobbying. The FNSEA and Jeunes Agriculteurs

(JA), the two historic modernizing unions, were best equipped for this task. Between the announcement of the decoupling and its implementation, there was a split in the unions' opposition. The fiercer opponents, such as *Confédération Paysanne*, voiced sharper condemnation of the instrument, whereas FNSEA and JA, working together within the French Agricultural Council (CAF, *Conseil de l'Agriculture Française*), emphasized pragmatism, attempting to stem the losses caused by the reform. They succeeded in ensuring that aid would be allocated on the basis of historical yields. This rule gave the most productive operations an advantage. Satisfied in the end, the FNSEA secretary-general stated that 'FNSEA and JA mobilized to ensure that this new system would involve the least possible harm and unfairness for farmers'(Barreau 2006). In the WTO negotiations, too, the group insisted on securing from the negotiations every possible concession favourable to supporting the agricultural revenue of 'steadfast France'. The *Confédération* demurred, denouncing the inclusion of agriculture in the WTO and protesting that 'agriculture is not goods'.

The battle over the Single Payment Scheme (SPS) is symptomatic of the schism in the French farmers' associations. In the minority is *Confédération Paysanne*, supportive of alter-globalization and calling for remunerative prices that cover production costs to protect small farms, along with global regulation for overall control of supply, while opposing both Brussels (EC) and Geneva (WTO), which it tars with the same liberal brush. In the majority are FNSEA and JA, supportive of the third world via prices that reward activity and production and advocating that farmers be remunerated at a level corresponding to their effort, productivity, individual initiative and entrepreneurial spirit. They oppose Brussels and its 'paper shuffling', but are determined to win whatever they can in each negotiation. Finally, they support the WTO to the extent that regulations are negotiated in that context, rather than supporting a simple reduction in tariffs.

AN ANTILIBERAL CONVERGENCE

The incorporation of the issue of North–South inequalities in arguing for the reform of France's agricultural policy lent special interest to the WTO Doha negotiations, which began in 2001. Designated the 'development round', the negotiations made inclusion of this topic obligatory, or nearly so, and forced every organization, group and union to take an explicit position on the question of North–South inequalities. In the remainder of this chapter, therefore, we focus in particular on the Doha Round and the WTO negotiations, in an attempt to spotlight the discourse and proposals of professional organizations such as *Confédération Paysanne*, FNSEA and JA, as well as NGOs; particularly, the NGO-co-ordinating organization, *Coordination Sud*, and the ministries of foreign affairs and agriculture. The Ministerial meetings (Doha in 2001, Cancún in 2003,

Hong Kong in 2005), in particular, provided opportunities to establish and articulate positions.

The Agricultural Professional Organizations (APOs)

Confédération Paysanne

Confédération Paysanne resulted from the merger, in 1987, of three different entities: the *Confédération Nationale des Syndicats de Travailleurs Paysans* (CNSTP), *Paysans Travailleurs*, which itself was the product of a schism in the *Centre National des Jeunes Agriculteurs* (CNJA) in the early 1970s, and the National Federation of Smallholders' Unions (FNSP, *Fédération Nationale des Syndicats Paysans*), a 'leftist' agricultural union that was came into being with the advent of the first socialist government in 1981. *Confédération Paysanne* is a member of *Coordination Paysanne Européenne* and of the international rural producers' movement, *Via Campesina.*

The position of the *Confédération*, which changed little as the negotiations progressed and regressed, was to denounce export subsidies for their: 'disastrous effect not only on the South, but also on the small farmers of the North. These subsidies, which come from European taxpayers, go directly into the pockets of the shareholders of the multinational agribusinesses. FNSEA and agribusiness lobbies are very happy with this agreement; we are not'.[3] Opposing agricultural negotiations in the WTO, the goal of the *Confédération* was 'to break them' and to demand 'with the farmers of the South, the application of a food sovereignty rule that allows each country to define its own agro-food policy, to place priority on supplying its own domestic market, and to implement prices that take account of production costs and decent remuneration for farmers. The priority is to feed the population, not to export' (Confédération Paysanne 2007: 12).

The position opposing the WTO's liberal model consists of a demand to adopt the principle of 'food sovereignty'; defined by Via Campesina as 'the peoples', countries' or state unions' right to define their agricultural and food policy, without any dumping vis-à-vis third countries'. Food sovereignty is presented as a necessity in the face of the specific nature of the agricultural sector (for example, inelastic short-term supply and demand, unequal distribution of information, and constant changes in the nature of international trade), all of which make it impossible for agricultural markets to self-regulate.

The specific proposals for policy reform are primarily aimed at providing for:

- Assured revenue, as a result of remunerative prices.
- Compensatory aid for disadvantaged areas and operations.
- Self-sufficiency, as a goal of the European Union, i.e., the EU should meet its own essential needs for quantity and quality, and this

should be achieved through import controls, namely, import taxes in the form of a variable levy on imports, and a preferential product-specific agreement.

- A production quota system.

It should be noted that food sovereignty is at times presented as being primarily a European demand, with consequences that could be expected to benefit various world regions. Thus, the Hacktivist News Service, in describing the arrest of the *Confédération* spokesperson in Hong Kong a few hours before the start of the WTO Ministerial meeting in December 2005, pulls no punches:

> Gérard Durand, spokesperson for *Confédération Paysanne,* was arrested while peacefully advocating European food sovereignty, the only agricultural policy that can guarantee a future for Europe's smallholders and for those of other world regions (Hacktivist News Service 2005).

The Majority Agricultural Unions: FNSEA and JA

At first glance, the FNSEA and JA position seems more puzzling. Viewed by the public as the organizations representing large farms and operators, their base is more diverse than that of the *Confédération.* They defend the interests of a mix of protected activities (grain production, livestock farming), subsidized activities (oilseeds) and export activities (wines and spirits). Once they recovered from the disappointment of the Blair House Accord, FNSEA and JA continued to use and participate in the WTO negotiations to 'prevent the worst' and to defend 'the French and European agricultural model'. The reaction of these organizations to agricultural trade liberalization also brought them closer to farmers in developing countries, not least through their participation in agricultural or rural development organizations and networks with strong links to developing countries. These included, for example, *Agriculteurs Français et Développement International* (AFDI), *Formation pour l'Epanouissement et le Renouveau de la Terre* (FERT), the *Fondation pour l'Agriculture et la Ruralité dans le Monde* (FARM) and *Mouvement pour une Organisation Mondiale de l'Agriculture* (MOMA).

JA, which serves as a fertile ground for selecting and training future FNSEA leaders, traditionally shows a degree of sensitivity to the third world that is less visible among their elders. The policy report of the 2001 conference (CNJA 2001) makes this particularly evident. The report extended the debates that had taken place a few months earlier with a number of NGOs, including the *Comité Français pour la Solidarité Internationale* (CFSI), and the platform representing French NGOs before the European Union. These discussions had culminated in the signing of the 'Vaumeilh Manifesto', which was designed to define 'the shape of an agricultural development policy whose fundamental objective is food security for all'. The 2001 report was strongly influenced by the thinking of Professor Marcel Mazoyer (see the following), whose basic ideas were reflected in the manifesto: the massive gaps in productivity between agriculture in the developed countries and agriculture in the developing countries; the effect of the race for labour productivity on agricultural prices; declining profits; and under-consumption and the resulting market crisis. In a work published in 2002, Jean-Luc Duval, president of the CNJA from 2000 to 2001, emphasized the influence of Mazoyer: 'He opened our eyes to a reality that we were totally unaware of' ((Duval 2002: 53).

Following the logic of this analysis, the report denounces 'a counter-productive liberalism' and calls for 'strong policies' that make it possible for farmers to 'make a living from their work, with dignity, based on remunerative prices'. Accordingly, it proposes the following measures:

- Establish or gradually increase the tariffs of poor countries.
- Create an organized market (customs union) on the regional level to bring together agricultural sectors that have equivalent levels of productivity.
- Create a world organization to regulate trade, in order to control the world volume and inventory for certain products.

The report of the 2007 meeting (Jeunes Agriculteurs 2007: 48) revives these issues, stating that 'the dismantling of agricultural policies and the liberalization of the agricultural sector do not improve the fate of the poorest countries or of smallholders, but, rather, do quite the contrary!', and asserting that food sovereignty is a right. The report was innovative in putting forward a series of proposals for the global organization of agriculture. The principal missions would be, on one hand, to define 'principles for the regulation of agricultural markets and for the organization of international agricultural trade between regional groups' (Jeunes Agriculteurs 2007: 48), and on the other, to co-ordinate the action of international institutions active in the sector (FAO, the World Bank, the IMF, WHO and WTO). The influence of MOMA can be clearly seen in these ideas.

As the negotiations progressed, the FNSEA position, in relation to the South, adopted phrasing and proposals that would not be objectionable to *Confédération Paysanne*. To dispel the image of an organization of 'fat cats', the FNSEA held a high-profile event fifteen days before the WTO Ministerial meeting in Hong Kong, in December of 2005. With support from AFDI and FARM, it brought together ministers and smallholders from both the North and South. In his closing speech before the start of the Ministerial meeting, Jean-Michel Lemétayer, president of FNSEA, set forth the organization's final positions. They featured an insistence on the particularities of agriculture, opposition to unbridled liberalism and pricing based on a global 'race to the bottom', the promotion of food sovereignty and replication of the European model. These principles and conditions addressed the interests of all of the world's smallholders, on whose behalf Lemétayer spoke in the introductory portion of his remarks:

> I am especially happy today. Along with our colleagues from different Southern countries, we felt, in discussions in Ouagadougou, Dakar, Bobo Dioulasso and Cancun, that it was urgent to make our voice heard. On the eve of this event [the Ministerial meeting in Hong Kong], we, the smallholders of the North and the South, have held firm to the intention of expressing ourselves, in hopes that all that has been said will not prove to have been in vain (Lemétayer 2005).

Later in his speech, Jean-Michel Lemétayer stressed the singularity of agriculture in guiding:

> our number one mission, that of nourishing human beings. We have insisted on the importance of family farming, which is essential to ensure the occupation and development of cultivable area throughout the world, to ensure that our societies are economically and socially balanced, that economic activity and jobs grow, and that our cultures, and women's place in society, are respected. That is why an agricultural product is not an object of trade like any other. It deserves different treatment (Lemétayer 2005).

And then he condemned 'unbridled liberalism. We are for globalization with a human face. Globalization in which the human dimension is more important than goods'. This echoes the 'agriculture is not goods' position of the *Confédération Paysanne*. Lemétayer continued with:

> Here the dogma of trade liberalization has run aground. Everyone has said so, our African friends in particular. Systems of protection are vital to avoid ruining farmers, to permit remunerative prices, to guarantee and ensure respect for our social and cultural differences. Each country or group of countries must have the freedom to assert its food sovereignty, to decide on its agricultural policy, with all the economic and social consequences this implies (Lemétayer 2005).

Like the *Confédération Paysanne*, FNSEA condemned export subsidies because of their effects on the South. Moreover, in a swipe at the Americans, it also condemned 'in-kind food assistance'. The remaining propositions are more ambiguous. If the imperative of national or regional food sovereignty is reaffirmed, the means of getting there should 'link support with production controls, support with supply regulation, support with organizing markets'. The creation of regional spaces is presented as 'legitimate'.

Directly related to developing countries, Lemétayer referred to the development projects of AFDI, 'whose thirtieth anniversary we [the organization] are celebrating. This is little known, because we stress effectiveness over communication. We are smallholders, we live in solidarity, a pleonasm that must be repeated often' (Lemétayer 2005). Furthermore, he put forward proposals that addressed two issues: cotton and market access consistent with the European 'Everything But Arms' model. These proposals involved, respectively, (a) the reform of U.S. aid policy and (b) the opening of the relevant U.S. markets. These proposals are aimed less at 'our African brothers' than at the United States as a rival.

The NGOs

As the first group of NGOs in France devoted to international solidarity, *Coordination Sud* was created in 1994. Today it includes over one hundred NGOs in a confederation consisting of six direct member groups and NGOs. Its objective is to help the French NGOs participate in the debate on international issues by working with the French government, the European Commission and the international institutions, as well as with national groups of NGOs in the North and South. The French government regards the positions of *Coordination Sud*, which are endorsed by some or all of its members, to be representative of the French NGOs concerned with international solidarity on agricultural issues. In what follows, we will present the organization's analysis of the overall situation and positions, and then proceed to explain the nuances that distinguish it from—and sometimes place it in opposition to—some of its members.

Rather than denouncing export subsidies, as does the discourse of the APOs, *Coordination Sud* emphasizes the issue of dumping. The link between North–South inequality and trade is not limited to export subsidies. More generally, it involves the sale on the world market of any product at less than its production cost. This definition of dumping, however, differs from that of the WTO (which defines it as a difference between two prices, rather than the difference between price and cost), and it explicitly targets direct aid, which, it says, forces farmers to seek survival through activities that are not really profitable and to artificially increase the amounts they produce and export. To reduce these inequalities generated by international trade, *Coordination Sud* recognizes the right to food, the principle of food sovereignty, the principle of special and differential treatment for low-income countries and the creation of mechanisms to stabilize international prices.

These positions and demands are detailed in a report co-signed by *Agir Ici*, *Artisans du monde*, *Comité Catholique contre la Faim et pour le Développement* (CCFD), CFSI, *Groupe de Recherche et d'Echange Technologique* (GRET) and *Peuples Solidaires*, with support from France's Ministry of Foreign Affairs (MAE). Entitled 'Agriculture: Regulating World

Trade—Putting Development at the Centre of Negotiations on the Agriculture Agreement in the WTO', the text presents the recommendations of the French international solidarity NGOs on the occasion of the December 2005 sixth Ministerial meeting of the WTO in Hong Kong.

Coordination Sud points its finger at the nefarious effects of liberalization—not of the CAP—on the world's poorest people. Emphasizing those who end up on the losing end of globalization, and its inequitable effects on growth, the report warns: 'In the context of over-production in all agricultural sectors—given the effective demand—and possible significant productivity gains, the creation of a world market that integrates all of the national markets is truly going to wreak rural carnage'. It cites 'negative effects for States . . . unequally distributed benefits . . . multinationals as big winners . . . endangering the rights of man', and points to a dire scenario, one supported by studies on rice, sugar, bananas, chicken, milk and cotton'(Coordination Sud 2005: 5) . The form and organization of the text show two influences: Oxfam and its reports on the injustices of trade and policy, and (once again) Marcel Mazoyer. The seven recommendations, characteristic of the organization, emphasize rights:

1. Place priority on human rights.
2. Recognize the principle of food sovereignty.
3. Recognize the right of agricultural sectors to develop.
4. Clean up and regulate global agricultural markets.
5. Recognize the social and environmental value of agricultural products.
6. Contribute to more balanced power relationships within the agro-food chains.
7. Adopt policies consistent with the fight against hunger and poverty.

These demands contained strong echoes of those put forward by many small farmers' organizations in developing countries, such as the ones affiliated with *Via Campesina* and the *Reseau des Organizations Paysannes et de Producteurs de l'Afrique de l'Ouest* (ROPPA). There are multiple links between the French agricultural community (in the broad sense) and these two organizations. In formal terms, *Confédération Paysanne* is a member of *Via Campesina* through its participation in *Coordination Paysanne Européenne*. Less formally, the links are intellectual and ideological. A number of figures in the French debate (among them M. Mazoyer, J. Berthelot, H. Rouillé d'Orfeuil and B. Hermelin) have actively contributed to constructing these organizations' positions by taking part in the events that they organize. The influence is clearly illustrated by the book, *Via Campesina: Une alternative paysanne à la mondialisation néolibérale* (Via Campesina 2002), which contains chapters authored by the French scholars M. Mazoyer, L. Roudart and J. Berthelot.

Our interviews indicate that although differences of opinion between the government and the agricultural organizations are virtually non-existent,

Table 7.1 Proposals of French NGOs on International Agricultural Trade

Proposals	*C2A*	*CoorSud*	*IRAM*	*GRET*	*Oxfam*	*Hulot*
Food sovereignty	X		X	X		
Policy space					X	
Community preference	?		?	?		
Right to protection	X	X	X	X	X	X
Controlling supply	X		X	X		X
Organization of regional markets	X	X	X	X		
Regulation of world markets	X	X	X	X		
Short chains						X

Source: Based on authors' interviews.

some variations are apparent among the international solidarity NGOs. Table 7.1 shows the positions of some of the most visible NGOs' regarding key recommendations.

Although there is consensus on the right to protection, certain principles or proposals, such as controlling supply and food sovereignty, are not included in the individual positions of all of the NGOs. Although there is some variance in preferences for one measure or another, APOs also tend to support the set of propositions listed in Table 7.1.

Table 7.2 confirms that the prevailing analysis in France of the "true problems" underpinning North–South inequalities essentially looks outside the province of the CAP, although the CAP is seen as having some

Table 7.2 Position of the NGOs on the 'True Problems' behind the Inequalities

		C2A	*Coor-Sud*	*IRAM*	*GRET*	*Oxfam*	*Hulot*
Developing country problems	Productivity gap	X		X	X		
	Rural employment		X				
	Rural poverty			X		X	
Universal problems	Agricultural prices (low)	X	X	X	X		X
	Risk of shortages						
	Sustainability						

Source: Based on authors' interviews.

responsibility (the APOs stress export subsidies, whereas the NGOs' broad definition of dumping includes direct income support as a mask for production support). The central problems relate to low productivity, under-employment and rural poverty in developing countries, as well as universal problems, involving agricultural prices (which, in real terms, are considered to be on an irreversible downward course), the risk of shortages (these latter two problems do not, of course, occur simultaneously) and environmental problems.

Government

We turn now to positions within the French government administration: first to those of the ministry with responsibility for foreign affairs and development cooperation, and then to those of the Ministry of Agriculture. The position of the Ministry of Finance, which helps explain the influence of the NGOs and APOs, are referred to in subsequent sections.

The Aid Establishment

France's agricultural policy has traditionally been based on positions that are very close to those of the NGOs and the agricultural community. These include, among others, a preference for regional protection and a belief in regulating international trade and stabilizing prices. This similarity of views is no mere coincidence. The offices in charge of these portfolios in the Ministry of Foreign Affairs (Rural Development Division and the Office of Agricultural Policies and Food Security in the Directorate-General for International Cooperation and Development—DGCID) outsource work to a limited number of research institutions/NGOs (*Solidarité Agro-Alimentaire*—SOLAGRAL; *Institut de Recherche et d'Application des Méthodes de développement*—IRAM; *Centre de Coopération Internationale en Recherche Agronomique pour le Développement*—CIRAD and GRET) because their own human resources available for analysis have been cut back. SOLAGRAL, which disbanded in 2003, played an important role in trade issues. Even at the time of conducting this study, the only document available on the Ministry of Foreign Affairs website regarding the issue of Southern farmers and the WTO was a series of files produced by SOLAGRAL in 2002.

French development cooperation, however, has undergone numerous transformations over the last two decades.[4] The reforms included incorporating the Ministry of Cooperation within the Ministry of Foreign Affairs in 1998. This change was accompanied by the creation, within the Ministry of Foreign Affairs, of the DGCID. As of the merger, the role of the Ministry of Foreign Affairs has tended to be that of providing strategic guidance to the French Development Agency (AFD), which assumed a pivotal role in the French development aid system. The victory of AFD over Cooperation is also a victory of Finance over Foreign Affairs. As Meimon (2007: 47) points out: 'This power relationship between Finance and Cooperation is nothing new. However, the 1998 reform, which returned to an older process, further accentuates this "power grab" on the bureaucratic battlefield'.

Until recently, however, the MAE/DGCID maintained direct control over management operations related to 'institutional and sovereignty-related sectors'. Thus, the agricultural policy and agricultural trade portfolios remained within their purview. This role, however, was somewhat weakened following the transfer to AFD of institutional support activities (including support for agricultural policy formulation). This could affect the convergence of views with the NGOs and the agricultural community.

Within AFD itself, personnel working in the field of agricultural and rural development whose positions coincide with the 'French agricultural consensus' tend to be marginalized, and are struggling to develop a sectoral strategy (at the time of writing, this is the only sector without a strategy). They seem largely unable to influence the mainstream views. When this study was conducted, Jean-Michel Severino had been AFD director since 2001. He had served as France's General Inspector of Finances and, previously, as World Bank vice-president. With a chief economist (Pierre Jacquet) he established an office in charge of strategy, but it lacked connection with the agency's operational staff.

Different perspectives clearly exist between those at the top of AFD and many of the operational staff. The tenth edition of the *AFD Economists' Letter*, which appeared in December 2005 and dealt with agricultural policies in Africa, reflects the ambiguities of the current situation. An editorial by Pierre Jacquet, chief economist of AFD, recalls that liberalization is 'necessarily the driving engine' of a multilateral trade system. In his view, 'to protect is to introduce discrimination in favour of certain groups and countries to the detriment of others', and 'this discrimination is inevitably questioned, and feeds rancour and tensions'. The editorial is followed by a paper by Philippe Chédanne, of the Steering and Strategic Relations Department (which reports to Jacquet). His paper offers a diagnosis of the agricultural problem closely in line with that of the NGOs (featuring the constantly changing nature of trade, the downward trend in prices resulting from productivity gains, concentration in the agro-food sector, export subsidies in the developed countries and a North–South agricultural productivity gap of one to one thousand). This assessment, however, serves as prelude to proposals that are either highly orthodox or vague: the need for strong commitment on the part of decision-makers in developing countries and implementation of public policies as 'indispensable to supporting the rural economies and eliminating major constraints on research, land, taxes, funding of transfers and private investment'. Thus, it calls for bolstering the 'coherence of public policy in both North and South'(Chédanne 2005). By way of counterbalance, the letter concludes with a review by Jean-Claude Devèze (formerly a major player at the Ministry of Agriculture and Rural

Development, and now strategy chief) of a work by Marc Dufumier, entitled *Agricultures et Paysanneries des Tiers Mondes*. Devèze makes a point of stating that Dufumier, who holds the Chair of Comparative Agriculture and succeeds Marcel Mazoyer (see the following) and René Dumont in this post, advocates a protectionist point of view that is favourable to the creation of regional groups, made up of countries with comparable levels of productivity.

The Ministry of Agriculture

The diagnosis and positions of France's Ministry of Agriculture throughout the Doha Round have changed little. The 'specific' and 'multi-functional' nature of agriculture is a recurrent theme, as indicated in the following quote:

> The declaration [of Hong Kong, at the WTO meeting in December 2005] introduces the possibility of an ambitious agreement as a conclusion to the round. Our objectives, formulated before the negotiation, remain current: to frame globalization within equitable rules, to encourage growth and job creation in France, to preserve a multi-functional agriculture and, above all, to encourage the development of the poorest countries through trade (Bussereau and Lagarde 2006).

Also recurrent is the logically implied need for agricultural policy. According to the Minister of Agriculture, Hervé Gaymard (2002–2004): 'Agriculture serves to nourish people. It also serves to occupy and maintain space in all of the social, territorial and environmental dimensions involved. As a result of this dual function, it cannot be devoted exclusively to the market'(Gaymard 2004).

The French government also responded to concerns of the emerging agricultural exporters, such as Brazil. A key concern was that agriculture in various Northern countries depends on high levels of government support, whereas certain countries have a high-return agricultural sector without relying on public spending. The French Ministry of Culture emphasized, however, other benefits that derive from the multi-functional character of the European agricultural model, such as its contributions to rural employment, land management and food security (Aumand, Le Cotty and Voituriez 2001).

A second objection from the profitable agricultural exporting countries was that Europe refused to agree to more than very limited reductions in its domestic supports and tariffs, thus harming the developing countries. The Ministry of Agriculture responded that 'the Doha Round is, pre-eminently, the development round, and France's participation is precisely to help the developing countries, not to encourage the ultra-liberal development of world trade. Moreover, Europe and France require lessons from no one when it comes to development. This continent already imports more of the output of the Third World than any other'(Bussereau 2005). The terminology 'Third World' is notable here. In short, agriculture is a specific sector, at least in European public opinion, and, among the rich countries, Europe contributes more effectively to development than any other by being the biggest buyer of products from the countries of the third world.

The Ministry's position at the start of the Doha Round was to insist on the principle of multi-functionality, while attempting to maintain, among its negotiating partners, the coupling of aid and tariffs. This position was deemed unacceptable and found few adherents among the developing countries.[5] The European Commission scuttled 'multi-functionality' after the Doha Ministerial, although the French Ministry of Agriculture continues to use the term. On the issue of multi-functionality, France and Europe were compelled to withdraw behind a very pragmatic line of reciprocity and, after reforming the CAP in 2003, demanded that agriculture not serve as a bargaining chip in the negotiation.

It was proposed that the less-advanced countries should enjoy expanded duty-free market access to developed country markets (with Europe setting the example in this respect); that regional trade should increase (with Europe leading the field by signing the Economic Partnership Agreement, or EPA); and that the right to protect production for the sake of food security and development be re-established. In this regard, Hervé Gaymard recalled the origins of the CAP: 'It is necessary, therefore, to encourage the development of subsistence farming and the adoption of consistent trade policies, passing, if necessary, through stages of protecting the domestic market, as Europe did when it implemented the common agricultural policy'(Gaymard 2004). Note, finally, that the Ministry proposed to distinguish countries according to their level of development, in order to adjust the margin for government intervention that countries would preserve within the WTO framework, with that margin being inversely proportional to income. Accordingly, there would be developed countries, emerging countries and 'truly poor countries', with the latter having the right to implement protections and enjoying greater access to the markets of other countries.

POINTS OF CONVERGENCE

The preceding analysis suggests a strong convergence in the analysis and proposals of international solidarity NGOs, APOs and some government agencies. This convergence, which could be called 'antiliberal', involves the following points:

- Agricultural policy in the North is partially responsible for North–South inequalities.
- This partial responsibility specifically involves export subsidies.

- Nevertheless, current policies in the North are not the true source of North–South inequalities—the source of the problems lies elsewhere.
- The problems are primarily the result of productivity gaps, poor governance in the South and a lack of autonomy and freedom in the formulation of sovereign agricultural policy.
- The solutions to problems of North–South inequality thus depend less on reforming policy in the North than on asserting and enforcing the right to protective measures and to the formulation of agricultural policies that regulate domestic and regional markets in developing countries, similar to what was established by the CAP in the 1960s.
- What is good for the developing countries today is also good for Europe. The rights to implement protective measures and a degree of food self-sufficiency are legitimate rights of all countries.

Furthermore, the actors interviewed for this study endorse agricultural exceptionalism, according to which the features of agriculture (market failures and social and strategic functions) intrinsically justify public intervention in both the North and the South. However, although different organizations and actors may emphasize different aspects when translating this 'agricultural exception' into specifics, 'food sovereignty' remains a common denominator in the vast majority of positions expressed. The term has both implications for policy in the South and conveys a sense of 'community preference' which one finds in the official French discourse.[6]

The Historical and Intellectual Foundations of Convergence

The foundations of the antiliberal coalition were laid in the 1960s. The story has been told many times.[7] In the early 1960s, a group of young farmers represented by *Jeunesse Agricole Catholique* took over the CNJA and allied itself strongly with Edgard Pisani, a Gaullist Minister of Agriculture of the left. This alliance led to the Framework Law on Agriculture of 1960–1962, which defined the principal tools for modernizing French agriculture. The approach was to eliminate a great number of farms and promote a sector of entrepreneurial smallholders (Muller 1984).

Pisani's analysis, like that of CNJA, did not, however, stop at the borders of the European Economic Community. During the 1960s, the two allies developed very similar messages and proposals on the organization of international trade. Product-specific market organizations and protection mechanisms vis-à-vis non-European producers were put in place (such as deductions/reimbursements or direct supports).

The historical critique of agricultural liberalism was to benefit from a 'scientific' line of argument and from a broad and strategic audience in the French agricultural community, thanks to its appropriation by two professors of agronomy in France's higher education system: Marcel Mazoyer and Jean-Marc Boussard. These two played an intellectual role that is far more than anecdotal, given the importance of agronomists in the sector's various organizations (NGOs, APOs and government).

For a long time, Marcel Mazoyer occupied the Chair of Comparative Agriculture and Agricultural Development. As René Dumont's successor, he educated several generations of French agronomists who were particularly interested in North–South relationships and development issues. Today, these people occupy many senior positions within government and in research institutions, NGOs and professional organizations. The 'Mazoyer frame of reference' brings together the diverging splits in opinion. His name can also be found in the publications of the Via Campesina (2002) and Confédération Paysanne (2007), as well as those of *Jeunes Agriculteurs* (CNJA 2001).

The comparative analysis of labour productivity is at the heart of the Mazoyer frame of reference (Mazoyer and Roudart 1998). When different forms of agriculture embody such varying levels of productivity side by side, the result is rural exodus, unemployment and poverty. This limits the growth of world demand, and hence industrial and agricultural development. Therefore, the solution to the agricultural crisis, as well as to the overall crisis, 'necessarily depends on a policy that is coordinated at the global level, permitting poor agriculture that is in danger of being eliminated to maintain itself and develop'(Mazoyer and Roudart 1998: 493).

This analysis led to a series of proposals concerning agricultural trade policy:[8]

- A major increase in agricultural prices in the poor countries—gradual, so that 'the negative effects for buyers do not outweigh the positive effects for producers' (Mazoyer and Roudart 1998: 492).
- A major wage increase in the poor countries.
- Implementation of a hierarchical organization of markets that makes it possible to set differentiated prices—and thus differentiated levels of protection—by large regions, in inverse proportion to the levels of agricultural productivity. This 'presupposes negotiation and international product-specific agreement on prices and on the quantities to be produced in each region, implementation of one or more international funds to cross-subsidize prices, and the establishment of stabilization funds' (Mazoyer and Roudart 1998: 494).

Jean-Marc Boussard, who was an economic researcher at the *Institut National de la Recherche Agronomique* (INRA) and professor at the *Ecole Nationale du Génie Rural, des Eaux et des Forêts* (ENGREF), is recognized as a major figure in France's rural economics. Emphasizing two particularities of agricultural markets—on the one hand, risk and expectations in production decisions and, on the other, rigidity of demand—Jean-Marc Boussard developed mathematical models showing that when the two come together in competitive markets, the result is constant and unpredictable price fluctuations that hurt consumers, particularly poor consumers. Agricultural markets are therefore fundamentally chaotic, and it is poor consumers who pay the bill. Boussard's work has served as a scientific basis for the arguments against liberalization put forward by the Ministry of Agriculture during the Doha Round, as well as by the large producers (such as PluriAgri). The policy recommendations that emerge from this analysis emphasize the need to stabilize prices within a market protected by tariffs, and to control supply through quotas—regardless of a country's level of development.

The Highly Permeable Borders between Organizations

The organizations and individuals involved in issues of agricultural trade and development constitute a very small world. As a result, interactions between the individuals are numerous. There are various forms of permeability between (and within) the NGOs, the agricultural professional community and government.

One of these is the financial link between the organizations. We have already cited the importance of the relationship between the development cooperation arm of the Ministry of Foreign Affairs and various NGOs and research institutions, such as GRET, IRAM and, earlier, SOLAGRAL. Also of note here are the various salaried posts made available to GRET by CIRAD, a public research institution.

Another form of organizational linkage is the movement of individuals from one organization to another. Two important examples of this deserve mention:

1. The first illustrates permeability between government administrations. Bruno Vindel worked for a long time at the Ministry of Foreign Affairs' Division of Rural Development. At the time of writing, Vindel was the Deputy Director of Evaluation, Forecasting, Research and Orientation (DPEI/SDEPEO) at the Ministry of Agriculture and Fisheries.
2. The second illustrates the relationship between NGOs and government. Marie Cécile Thirion worked for a long time as head of research at SOLAGRAL before moving to the Ministry of Foreign Affairs' Office of Agricultural Policy and Food Security (DGCID). The authors of this chapter also illustrate this permeability, both having worked at SOLAGRAL before joining CIRAD.

A third case involves individuals serving simultaneously in multiple organizations. Those serving elected positions representing agricultural producers are themselves, no doubt, champions of this practice. One of many examples of this is Xavier Beulin, who serves as President of the *Fédération française des producteurs d'Oléagineux et Protéagineux*

(FOP) and of the *Société Financière de la Filière des Oléagineux et Protéagineux* (SOFIPROTEOL), as well as being a member of the FARM board of directors. Also at FARM, serving as head of the Rural Development, Environment and Natural Resources Department of AFD, is Jean-Yves Grosclaude. Henri Rouillé d'Orfeuil is another case in point; he is president of *Coordination Sud* as well as being a personal member of the Board of Directors of AFD and a CIRAD official (where he is director of European and International Relations).

THE LIMITS OF POLICY INFLUENCE

As we have attempted to show in the preceding, the agricultural debate in France and the issue of the causal link between agricultural policy and North–South inequalities show a strong antiliberal convergence among NGOs, APOs and government. The paradox of this situation is that these forces seem to have little effect on policy. In fact, as has been seen, the CAP has in recent years undergone a series of clearly liberal reforms.

This final section attempts to explain this paradox, analysing on the one hand the types of action that these organizations undertake and, on the other, the evolution of economic policy-making and public decision-making in France over the last twenty-five years. During this period, France's economic policy has become increasingly liberal, albeit in a particular way. This has been described as 'pragmatic liberalism', which involves both gradual implementation and reluctance on the part of the government to officially acknowledge the liberal turn.

As indicated earlier, the limits of influence are explained partly by the small size of the agricultural trade and development community in France. Furthermore, among certain key societal actors in the field of development, agricultural and trade policy issues were not central concerns. In diametrical opposition to the great permeability between organizations specializing in agriculture, the relations of these organizations to the 'rest of the world' are marked by an airtight membrane and a lack of bridges. The near absence of the agricultural issue in the *Association pour la taxation des transactions financières pour l'aide aux citoyens* (Attac—see Chapter 12, this volume) illustrates this phenomenon. Since its formation, Attac has conducted no campaigns on CAP or on agricultural trade. Moreover, at the time of writing, the 'knowledge' section of its website—which presents analytical documents by subject (such as water, territory and 'living beings')—does not include headings on agriculture or agricultural trade.

The limited influence of the antiliberal coalition can also be explained by the discrepancy between the modes of action of the organizations in the agricultural sector—which target the general public and/or technical ministries—and the nature of the public decision-making process associated with France's new neoliberal trajectory.

Modes of Action

In a document on the French NGO Sector,[9] *Coordination Sud* shows the diversity of approaches taken by international solidarity organizations. The general lines of that analysis are presented here.

A number of broad sets of NGOs can be distinguished:

- NGOs dealing with emergencies
- NGOs devoted to supporting development
- Fair trade NGOs
- Advocacy NGOs
- NGOs working in education geared to development and international solidarity

This categorization must be interpreted cautiously, however, because most of the groups are active in more than one area. For example, the so-called emergency NGOs are involved in development activity (for example, *Action Against Hunger*, *Doctors of the World* and *Handicap International* devote a large portion of their budgets to this type of operation) and are also increasingly active in advocacy. CCFD, which is a major actor in development support, has long played an important role in education for development, and is active in advocacy on numerous fronts.

The *Coordination Sud* document also notes that:

> the presentation would not be complete without mentioning another family which, while very heteroclite, includes the membership of certain NGOs, namely, those in the alter-globalization movement. Here, too, there is no unanimously accepted definition of an 'alter-globalization organization', unless it is perhaps those rallying around the slogan 'another world is possible' (with which many NGOs may relate to). In any case, the alter-globalization family of organizations includes a highly diverse set of actors: unions, citizens' movements, groups for international solidarity, organizations devoted to protecting human rights or the environment, etc. Membership in this family is at the discretion of the NGOs. Some claim it, others reject it (thus, some emergency organizations consider themselves alter-globalization, while others carrying out the same activities do not wish to identify themselves that way) (Coordination Sud 2003).

There are no precise and reliable statistics on the thematic distribution of activities among French NGOs. Based on the survey by the Commission for Cooperation and Development (CCD, *Commission coopération développement*) on money and NGOs concerned with international solidarity, *Coordination Sud* concludes that the largest area of action is emergency aid (which may represent approximately one-fifth to one-quarter of the

NGOs' budgets). At the same time, four broad areas of action are evident, with roughly equal budgets for health, education (including training), rural development and economic development.

The group has also noted that regardless of the theme of the work, the NGOs have no unique mode of intervention or influence. They can be grouped as follows:

- Pamphlet campaigns (for example, the 'Campagne Poulet') particularly by NGOs, such as Oxfam-Agir Ici, that from their start have specialized in this type of activity
- Expertise made available to decision-makers (such as the work of GRET and IRAM on the EPAs)
- Advocacy: speaking on behalf of a group (*Coordination Sud*)
- Civil disobedience (*Conference sur les OGM*)
- Violent obstruction (French agricultural unions), notably during periods of surpluses
- Lobbying (APOs)

A reading of the interview findings reveals both (a) the full commitment to lobbying activities by the APOs, which target decision-makers or their staff, and (b) campaigning, advocacy and expertise on the part of NGOs and various organizations and groups (such as AFDI) closely associated with APOs, designed to influence governmental decisions through individuals who, although not the ultimate decision-makers, are involved in policy-making.

Agriculture as a Caricature of French-Style Neoliberalism

Neoliberal policy in France has taken a form very different from that in Anglo-Saxon countries. In 1983, after two years of 'single-country Keynesianism', the socialist government made a decisive turn in the trajectory of France's economic policy (Jobert and Théret 1994). However, the reform process was slow and was less brutal than in Great Britain or in countries such as Chile or Mexico (Fourcade-Gourinchas and Babb 2002).

There was, indeed, a turn towards the market (greater competition, accompanied, however, by more profit for firms), while the state's role shifted from *dirigisme* and production to support, as well as (partial) compensation for the losers. This shift went officially unrecognized, if not denied entirely. This is what Palier, Hall and Culpepper (2006) underline when they speak of a 'France in the middle of the markets, with no compass'. In the view of these authors, the changes were imposed without discussion, explanation and legitimization were totally lacking and 'most of the governments since the late 1980s concluded that it was impossible for them to truly defend market-oriented policies' (Palier, Hall and Culpepper 2006: 26). Since that period, no government or political party has explicitly espoused a neoliberal programme. Madelin, who attempted to do so, remained at the head of the Finance Ministry for a mere three months. Most often, whatever market policies were implemented were justified in terms of building Europe, which was presented as both a constraint and an ideal.

The neoliberal change in course illustrates the perpetuation of technocratic decision-making in the French government. It was imposed by an administrative elite that had converted to economic liberalism in the 1970s as the best way to pursue the modernization of France. In the view of Jobert and Théret (1994), France's neoliberal shift 'constitutes the last stage of the great invasion of the principal centres of economic and political power by a managerial elite coming from senior governmental positions in the main centres of economic and political power'(Jobert and Théret 1994: 47) . Drawn from the ranks of the *École Nationale d'Administration* (ENA) and the *École Nationale de la Statistique et de l'Administration* (ENSAE), this elite became truly hegemonic, eliminating the planning approach that was in place in the Ministry of Finance and marginalizing the research services of the technical ministries.

CONCLUSION

Readings and interviews on the positions of NGOs, APOs and various French government agencies regarding the relationship between North–South inequalities and agricultural trade policy indicate a convergence on a core of principles, proposals and ideas. The central notions, here, concern agriculture's inherent need for policy to regulate markets, the right to a certain level of food self-sufficiency ('food sovereignty') and a joint affirmation of the right to protect national and regional markets. Reducing North–South inequalities thus depends less on reforming agricultural policy in the North than on restoring sovereignty in the South, so that the Southern countries can formulate agricultural policies to regulate domestic markets, just as the CAP did in Europe in the 1960s. This is not to deny that there are diverging views—marginally so in terms of what the South should do, more prominently so with regard to Northern policy. The differences essentially involve the fate of domestic supports, centred, however, around a consensus that direct export subsidies should be eliminated and non-zero tariffs maintained.

The French position, which is generally shared by the NGOs, APOs and some government agencies, diverges sharply from the European mainstream, which saw a clear liberal shift in 1992 and then again in 2003. The weight, significance and inertia of French agricultural thinking that crystallized in the 1960s around the 'Pisani-Baumgartner' plan provide one explanation. A second is that agronomists educated in the context of that approach still have a strong presence in the NGOs and APOs and in government. A further factor is the financial and human porosity of boundaries between government and the world of the NGOs. A final element is the role of the Ministry of Finance in policy reform. Although not a highly visible player in this regard, it has direct access to the European Council in Brussels. Thus, it could marshal budgetary arguments to support liberal reform of the CAP and apply discreet but effective pressure against the positions of the Ministry of Agriculture, the NGOs and the agricultural community, whose converging views ultimately were isolated and weak.

The various components of France's agricultural community, sharing the same perspectives on the CAP and capable of acting collectively when the opportunity arises, lack the ability to exert influence because of their own limitations and the extreme difficulty of making headway vis-à-vis the Ministry of Finance. It is worth noting, in this connection, the weak modes of action favoured by these organizations. Further study is needed regarding the way in which the organizations have locked themselves into a discourse centred on the specificity of agriculture, with the end result of 'ghettoizing' it. Clearly, a Minister of Agriculture, today, has no discourse or analysis with which he or she can prevail upon the Ministry of Finance—as Pisani had done with his colleague Baumgartner—in an effort to organize international agricultural markets. Just as clearly, the NGOs find it difficult to mobilize their 'colleagues' in the workers' unions, the political parties or even Attac.

Annex 7.1 Institutions and Individuals Interviewed, mid-2007

NGOs	• Coordination Sud (Henri Rouillé d'Orfeuil) • Fondation Nicolas Hulot (Marc Dufumier) • GRET (Bénédicte Hermelin) • IRAM (Benoit Faivre Dupaigre) • OXFAM-Agir Ici (Caroline Dorémus-Mège) • SOLAGRAL (Roger Blein)
Agricultural community (unions, associations, foundations)	• Agriculteurs Français et Développement international (AFDI, Gérard Renouard) • Association Générale des Producteurs de Blé et autres céréales (AGPB, Hervé Le Stum) • Fédération Française des Producteurs d'Oléagineux et Protéagineux (FOP, Philippe Dusser) • Fondation pour l'Agriculture et la Ruralité dans le Monde (FARM, Bernard Bachelier) • Pluriagri (Jean-Christophe Debar)
Government	• French Development Agency (AFD, Claude Torre) • Ministry of Foreign Affairs—Directorate-General for International Cooperation and Development (DGCID, Marie-Cécile Thirion) • Ministry of Agriculture (Bruno Vindel)

NOTES

1. This chapter was translated from its original French version.
2. Interview with Pascal Lamy, *Le Monde*, 25 February 2006 (see Clavreul, Lemaître and Ricard 2006).
3. Interview with Jean-Marc Desfilhes, who oversees international issues for *Confédération Paysanne*, at Novethic on 16 November 2001.
4. For an account of these changes, see Meimon (2007).
5. Note the case of Mauritius, anxious to preserve its sugar's preferential access to the European market.
6. See for example the speech by the president of France at Rennes, 11 September 2007, 'France opposes 'any agreement contrary to the interests of France . . . France demands reciprocity, France demands balance, France demands community preferences'. .
7. See Fouilleux (2003); Gervais, Jollivet and Tavernir (1978); and Muller (1984).
8. This analytical framework continues, in part, to be taught by Marc Dufumier, who now holds the Chair of Comparative Agriculture.
9. See http://www.coordinationsud.org/ongrama/le-secteur-des-ong-francaises/, 'Le secteur des ONG françaises'.

BIBLIOGRAPHY

Aumand, Anthony, Le Cotty, Tristan, and Voituriez, Tancrède (2001). *Quels instruments de valorisation de la multifonctionnalité?* Nogent sur Marne: CIRAD.

Barreau, Dominique (2006). 'FNSEA and JA mobilized'*Le Jura agricole et rural*, 13 November

Bureau, Jean-Christophe. (2007.) *La politique agricole commune*, Paris: La Découverte.

Bureau, Jean-Christophe, Butault, Jean-Pierre, Hassan, D., Lerouvillois, P., and Rousselle, J.M. (1991). 'Formation et répartition des gains de productivité dans les agricultures européennes', *Cahier d'Economie et de Sociologie Rurales*, 20:63–90.

Bussereau, Dominique. (2005), Response of the Minister of Agriculture and Fisheries in the Senate, Paris, 20 October

Bussereau, Dominique and Lagarde, Christine. (2006). 'La multifonctionnalité de l'agriculture', *Le Monde*, 3 January.

Butault, Jean-Pierre (2006). 'La baisse des revenus et l'essoufflement de la productivité dans l'agriculture française depuis 1998', *Inra Sciences Sociales*, 2, 8 p. .

Centre National des Jeunes Agriculteurs. (2001) *Paysans du Monde: le prix de notre avenir. Rapport d'orientation*, Annecy-le-Vieux: CNJA.

Chédanne, Philippe(2005). L'agriculture et le commerce. *La Lettre des Economistes de l'AFD*, December

Clavreul, Laetitia Lemaître, Frédéric, and Philippe Ricard. (2006) 'Pascal Lamy: en cas d'échec, l'OMC joue sa crédibilité politique', *Le Monde*, 25 February.

Confédération Paysanne. (2001). 'European Commissioner MacSharry diverged from his mandate'. *Campagnes Solidaires*, no. 156, October.

Confédération Paysanne. (2007). *Pour une autre politique agricole européenne*, Paris: Confédération Paysanne.

Coordination Sud (2003),'Le secteur des ONG françaises'Paris : Coordination Sud,

Coordination Sud (2005). Agriculture : pour une régulation du commerce mondial. Mettre le développement au cœur des négociations de l'Accord sur l'Agriculture à l'OMC. Recommandations des ONG françaises de solidarité internationale à l'occasion de la 6e Conférence ministérielle de l'OMC Hong Kong, Chine, 13–18 décembre 2005. Paris : Coordination Sud.

Daviron, Benoit. (2008). 'The Historical Integration of Africa in International Food Trade: A Food Regime Perspective', in N. Fold and M. Larsen (eds), *Globalization and Restructuring of African Commodity Flows*, Uppsala: Nordic Africa Institute.

Deneux, Marcel, and Emorine, Jean-Paul. (1998). *Rapport d'information du Sénat français fait au nom de la commission des Affaires Economiques et du Plan par la mission d'information chargée d'étudier l'avenir de la réforme de la Politique Agricole Commune*, *No. 466*, Paris: Senat.

Duval, Jean-Luc. (2002). *Faim des paysans, faim du monde*, Paris: Le Cherche Midi.

Fouilleux, Eve. (2003). *La politique agricole commune et ses réformes: une politique à l'épreuve de la globalisation*, Paris: L'Harmattan.

Fourcade-Gourinchas, Marion, and Babb, Sarah L. (2002). 'The Rebirth of the Liberal Creed: Paths to Neoliberalism in Four Countries', *American Journal of Sociology*, 108 (3): 533–579.

Gaymard, Hervé. (2004). Speech at the Chair for Inter-Ethnic and Intercultural Teaching and Research (CERII), Paris, 7 October.

Gervais, Michel, Jollivet, Marcel, and Tavernir, Yves. (1978). *Histoire de la France Rurale, Tome 4: La Fin de la France Paysanne de 1914 à nos jours*, Paris: Seuil.

Hacktivist News Service (2005) 'La défense de la souveraineté alimentaire bâillonnée', WTO Hong Kong: Hacktivist News Service. December. http://www.hns-info.net/article.php3?id_article=7401 (consulted in September 2007)

Hertel T.W., Winters, L.A. (eds) (2006). *Poverty and the WTO: Impacts of the Doha Development Agenda*, Basingstoke: Palgrave Macmillan and the World Bank.

Jeunes Agriculteurs. (2007). *Pour un pacte alimentaire, le défi d'une agriculture durable*, Epinal: Jeunes Agriculteurs.

Jobert, Bruno, and Théret, Bruno. (1994). 'France: La consécration républicaine du néo-libéralisme', in B. Jobert (ed), *Le tournant néo-libéral en Europe*, Paris: L'Harmattan.

Lamy, Pascal. (2006). 'The Doha Development Agenda: Sweet Dreams or Slip Slidin' Away?'—Speech at the Peterson Institute for International Economics, Washington, 17 February.

Lemétayer, Jean-Michel.(2005) 'Discours de clôture ', Paris, 1 December. http://www.fdsea08.fr/sites/webfnsea/actu/comm/avant2006/2005/12/hong_kong__mes_pour_une_mondialisation___visage_humain_.aspx

L'Humanité. (1993). 'An agreement "negotiated" by two European commissioners at the end of their terms', *L'Humanité* 22 November

Mazoyer, Marcel, and Roudart, Laurence. (1998). *Histoire des agricultures du monde: du néolithique à la crise contemporaine*, Paris: Edition du Seuil.

Meimon, Julien. (2007). 'Que reste-t-il de la coopération française', *Politique Africaine*, 105:27–50.

Muller, Pierre. (1984). *Le technocrate et le paysan*, Paris: Les Editions Ouvrières.

Oxfam International. (2002) *Rigged Rules and Double Standards: Trade, Globalisation*

and the Fight against Poverty, New York: Oxfam. http://www.maketradefair.com/assets/english/report_english.pdf (Consulted in September 2007)

Palier, Bruno, Hall, Peter, and Culpepper, Pepper. (2006). 'La France sans boussole au milieu des marchés', in P.D. Culpepper, P.A. Hall and B. Palier (eds), *La France en mutation, 1980–0–2005*, Paris: Presses de Science Po.

Solidarité Agro-Alimentaire. (1999). *La multifonctionnalité de l'agriculture dans les futures négociations de l'OMC*, Paris: Ministère de l'Agriculture et de la Pêche.

Vaile, Mark. (2002) 'Agriculture: l'Europe étrangle les pays pauvres', *Le Monde*, 29 October.

Via Campesina. (2002) *Une alternative paysanne à la mondialisation néolibérale*, Geneva: CETIM.

8 Debt Relief and Trade Justice in Italy

Paolo Gerbaudo and Mario Pianta[1]

INTRODUCTION

Third world debt and international trade have been at the centre of the policy debate in the last two decades, a period marked by a process of neoliberal globalization and deepening inequalities between North and South. Such a debate has not been confined to governments and economic decision-makers; civil society in Europe has strongly voiced its concerns on the economic and social injustice associated to debt and trade liberalization, leading to strong mobilizations, public opinion campaigns and, in some cases, changes in government policies. In Italy, such activism has been widespread, rooted in the country's political cultures, and has integrated debt and trade issues within the broader values and frames underpinning mobilizations on global justice, peace and the environment.

In order to investigate the evolution and policy impact of Italian mobilizations on debt and trade, we rely on the analytical framework of the politics of contention.[2] The *framing* of issues is the first question to be addressed in order to set mobilizations in their context and explore the ways in which the issue is conceptualized, perceived and acted upon. Second, the ability of mobilizations to develop, exert influence and achieve their goals depends on the *political opportunities* that open up at the national and international level, creating spaces for activism, widening public opinion support, building alliances with sections of the elites and putting pressure on policymakers. Third, we consider the *mobilizing structures*, including the forms of organization and the strategies pursued by activists, which shape mobilizations and their interactions with political power. Three different, but often complementary, dimensions are relevant here: the presence of an 'epistemic community' with a shared conceptualization of the issues, the lobbying of decision-makers on specific themes and the strength of protest that may challenge the legitimacy and content of policies.

These questions, in the case of debt and trade, are not confined to national political systems. The *transnational* nature of the issues has led to conflicts involving supranational actors, such as the IMF, the World Bank, the WTO and the European Union, and the policies of the most powerful states, such as the United States. Civil society groups have developed transnational links; built cross-border networks; supported the rise of global movements that have questioned the legitimacy of supranational institutions; demanded the cancellation (or reduction) of third world debt, new forms of international finance, a stop to trade liberalization and more equitable economic relations between the North and the South of the world.[3]

Following such a perspective, in this chapter we move from the reconstruction of the contexts of mobilizations to a study of debt and trade activism in Italy, linking developments at the domestic and transnational levels. Our key findings on Italian activism include the following:

- Activism over debt and trade has emerged out of concerns on global justice issues—North–South inequalities, neoliberal globalization, ecology and peace—and has maintained close links to such broader themes. In other words, it has been framed in terms of global justice.
- There is a continuity in the mobilizations over debt and trade, with an involvement of a variety of forces in Italian civil society; specific campaigns have been relevant in particular periods, with favourable political opportunities.
- Links to international networks on debt and trade have been important from the early years, confirming the transnational dimension of mobilizations.
- The organizational form adopted tends to be the coalition of civil society groups, building on the activism of many small groups with little resources and an established culture of collaboration; although this has favoured the spread of public awareness, it has limited the effectiveness of 'professional' lobbying for change.
- The strategies adopted combine the use of protest, with frequent (and often large) demonstrations, the search for policy alternatives with some interaction with policymakers, but rather weak lobbying activity.

The policy impact of Italian mobilizations on debt and trade is assessed in the final section. We consider how important the search for policy change was in the development of mobilizations and which strategies have been effective. Mobilizations have led to a law on debt cancellation for poorer countries with a budget of six billion euros and to slowing down the trade liberalization agenda.

THE CONTEXTS OF MOBILIZATIONS

Debt and trade issues have been conceptualized in different ways by political and social actors, including solidarity groups, development NGOs, environmental and peace groups, trade unions and Catholic organizations. The framing of debt and trade in Italy has emerged from the political cultures that have influenced social mobilizations, from the political opportunities opening up at national level and from transnational activism on such issues. In post-war decades both left and Catholic political cultures devoted a substantial attention to international solidarity. Three experiences emerging in the 1970s highlight this background.

The first Italian initiative that raised awareness on global injustices—from a left perspective—is the *Permanent Peoples' Tribunal*, established in 1979 by the Lelio Basso International Foundation for the rights and liberation of peoples in Rome, and based on the 'Universal declaration of the rights of peoples' launched in Algiers in 1976. Two sessions of the Permanent Peoples' Tribunal have concerned the policies of the IMF and the World Bank, in coincidence with their summits in West Berlin in 1988 and Madrid in 1994 (Fondazione Internazionale Lelio Basso 1998).[4]

A second experience—emerging from a Christian perspective—was that of the *International Documentation and Communication Centre* (IDOC) based in Rome,[5] which had acted since the 1960s as an independent clearinghouse on global justice issues. IDOC had extensive links with liberation movements in the third world and progressive Christian communities, and opened the way to the encounter with Marxist activists.

A third Italian experience concerns the rapid growth of NGOs active in development cooperation, with an increase from forty in 1979 to one hundred in 1988 and 154 in 2002. They emerged from both Catholic and left political cultures, led to the presence of thousands of Italian 'cooperation workers' in developing countries and maintained a strong grass-roots orientation. Much of their work supported social and economic change at the local level in poor countries and had an advocacy dimension that addressed also debt and trade issues.[6]

From these experiences, rooted in solidarity activism with third world countries, different frames emerged in the 1980s that could be used in order to mobilize over the issues of debt and trade, including the values of economic and social justice and rights, the structural nature of global inequalities, the need to respect the sovereignty of poor countries and the looming ecological crisis.

The political opportunities for mobilizations on debt and trade in Italy were shaped by major events. The third world debt crisis first exploded in 1982 and trade liberalization accelerated in the mid-1990s. A specific impact on Italian activism came from the presence of G7/G8 summits in Italy in 1994 and 2001, and from the 2000 Catholic Jubilee (Pianta 2001b).

The diversity of the multilayered governance systems that are relevant in the cases of debt and trade needs to be pointed out. For debt, national governments were key players alongside the IMF; financial obligations were mainly between public agencies, under political responsibilities. The role of supranational bodies, such as the Paris Club of major creditor nations and private banks, was limited. Decisions by national governments therefore remained crucial. In such a context, social mobilizations did engage in extensive transnational networking, but could develop following the traditional model of civil society campaigns targeting the national government and demanding a specific policy change.

For trade, with the foundation of the WTO and the transfer of trade negotiating power to the European Union from EU member countries, the role of national governments was drastically reduced. Key decisions on EU trade policy proposals were taken in Brussels, closer to the interests of major states and powerful business lobbies than to the deliberation of national Parliaments. Therefore, national policies lost their relevance and much of the mobilization over trade took a transnational or local direction. On the one hand, Italian activism was linked to international civil society networks campaigning against the WTO and its Ministerial meetings, with limited visibility in the domestic political arena. On the other hand, the spreading of awareness among public opinion and the search for practical initiatives that could be carried out on trade issues led to a large diffusion of 'fair trade' alternative shops that became centres of activism over North–South inequalities. These specific structures of political opportunities help explain the patterns of mobilizations that can be found in Italy on the issues of debt and trade from the 1980s to the present.

THE EVOLUTION OF ITALIAN MOBILIZATIONS

Sources and Methods

For the investigation of Italian mobilizations on debt and trade we have used a variety of sources, including the academic literature; the literature produced by activists and the documents of organizations and campaigns;[7] specialized journals, magazines and newspapers with a coverage of such issues;[8] an analysis of the websites of nine major organizations and campaigns;[9] and detailed interviews with nine key activists and experts involved in mobilizations on debt and trade (see Annex 8.1). The combined use of these sources makes possible a systematic coverage of major events, presented in the following, and in-depth understanding of the dynamics of mobilizations over debt and trade as discussed in later sections.

Key Events in Italian Mobilizations

Building on these sources, the major events of the Italian mobilizations on debt and trade are summarized in Table 8.1. An analysis of the two campaigns is carried out in the next sections. The sequence of events shows a slow start of initiatives in the early 1990s, an acceleration since 1997 and a peak in the years 2000–2003. At first, mobilization on debt and trade were intertwined, due to the overlapping of groups and initiatives, and framed (rather generally) in terms of global justice. Since the late 1990s the two

Table 8.1 Key Events in Italian Mobilizations on Debt and Trade (1990–2005)

Year	*Event*	*Organizers*
1990	Sud chiama Nord, International convention on debt cancellation	Campagna Nord-Sud
1992	Cinquecento anni bastano (500 years are enough) conference	Campagna Nord-Sud, Terre del fuoco
1994	G7 Countersummit by Il Cerchio dei popoli, The Other Economic Summit	Forty Italian civil society organizations
1995	Assembly of the Peoples' UN in Perugia	Tavola della pace—Peace Roundtable
1997	Assembly of the Peoples' UN for an economy of justice in Perugia	Tavola della pace—Peace Roundtable
1997	First International Forum on Debt	Sdebitarsi
1998	Second International Forum on Debt	Sdebitarsi
1998	Meeting of Eurodad, International Forum	Eurodad
1998	Meeting of Jubilee 2000, International Forum	Sdebitarsi, Jubilee 2000
1999	The Pope meets the Jubilee 2000 campaign	Vatican—Jubilee 2000
1999	Third Assembly of the Peoples' UN 'Another world is possible' in Perugia	Tavola della pace—Peace Roundtable
2000	Sanremo Music Festival, Jovanotti's rap on debt	Sdebitarsi, RAI
2000	New rules for the new millennium, International Forum	Mani tese NGO
2000	World Forum on Ethic Banks and Armed Banks	CRBM
2000	World Forum on Alternatives: After Seattle Conference	Attac—Italy, Le Monde Diplomatique
2000	Bologna OECD countersummit	Ad hoc coalition
2000	Rete Lilliput national activists meeting	Rete Lilliput
2001	Naples No Global Forum Countersummit	No Global network
2001	Genoa G8 Countersummit	Genoa Social Forum
2001	Fourth Assembly of the Peoples' UN in Perugia	Tavola della pace—Peace Roundtable
2002	First European Social Forum in Florence	ESF co-ordinating committee
2003	Forum alternativo per un'europa sociale	ESF co-ordinating committee
2003	Naples: Mediterranean Social Forum	Fsmed organizing committee
2003	Protest against Euromed summit	CRBM
2003	Protest against European ministerial meeting on Cancún WTO summit	CRBM, Fair
2003	National Day on common goods against Cancún WTO summit	Fair, CTM Altromercato, CRBM
2003	International conference Europe and the debt of poor countries	Sdebitarsi
2005	World Mobilization Week on International Trade	Lilliput, CTM Altromercato
2005	Rome: AltraEconomia public meetings, seminars	Lilliput, CTM Altromercato
2005	VII international forum of Sdebitarsi	Sdebitarsi

campaigns acquired their own specificity, with different forms of organization (mainly coalitions of civil society groups) and types of action (mainly protest events).

The major characteristics of Italian activism include the following:

1. Debt and trade issues are often integrated within broader themes, such as North–South inequalities, ecology and peace. This has led, on the one hand, to a framing of these issues in terms of global justice and, on the other hand, to an ability of social mobilizations to integrate different themes related to global issues; debt and trade mobilizations were in fact at the core of the protests against neoliberal globalization in 2000–2002.
2. There is a strong continuity in the activism over debt and trade, with a large variety of forces in Italian civil society involved. However, when mobilizations reach a critical point of contention and favourable political opportunities appear, organizational structures change, leading to specific campaigns and highly focused events.
3. The international participation is important from the early years, signalling the presence of persistent and strong links to international networks on global issues. Italian and international mobilizations on debt and trade emerge in parallel.
4. Organizers of events are almost always coalitions of civil society groups, building on a well-established political culture of collaboration; this model of activism is also the consequence of the presence of a very large number of small civil society groups with few resources. This favours the spread of public awareness and protest, but tends to limit the effectiveness of 'professional' lobbying for change.
5. The nature of events combines frequent (often large) protest events and meetings searching for alternative proposals, where the interaction with policymakers is important. Actions related to lobbying, or targeted to 'epistemic communities' are less visible and weaker in the Italian mobilizations.

MOBILIZATIONS OVER THIRD WORLD DEBT

Debt and the Environment: The *Campagna Nord-Sud*

During the 1970s and early 1980s the debate on North–South inequalities was mainly a matter of political discussion with a limited outreach to public opinion. The first Italian initiative on debt has been the *Campagna Nord-Sud: Biosfera, Debito e Sopravvivenza dei Popoli* (North–South Campaign: Biosphere, Debt and People's Survival), launched in 1988 by the environmental and peace activist Alexander Langer, who had become member of the European Parliament for the Greens. The campaign proposed bridging economic and environmental issues, identifying the question of debt as the centrepiece of a system of global injustice, leading to dramatic economic and environmental consequences. It did not start with a well-developed set of policy proposals to address the issue; it raised public awareness and helped put pressure on international financial institutions—such as the IMF and World Bank—and develop alternative policy approaches (Langer 1992; Regidor and Binel 2002).

This also influenced the way in which the question of international trade was framed in this period. Giorgio Dal Fiume, who was involved in the campaign, argues that:

> in the 1980s the question of debt was more prominent than the question of trade, but they were connected. The question of natural resources, the fact that third world countries were obliged to increase exports to pay their debt. Talking about debt entailed an analysis also of international trade. The campaign raised awareness in Italy, in the world of NGOs, and it also began to work with institutions. (Interview, 21 February 2008)

At the political level, an opportunity for action opened up when Italian socialist leader Bettino Craxi was chosen as special UN envoy on third world debt. An international convention of the Campagna Nord-Sud was held in Rome on 16–17 October 1990, with speakers from third world countries and the participation of Bettino Craxi, who argued that part of the debt had to be cut in order to allow third world countries to access new borrowing from private banks. This dialogue did not reduce the large distance between official policies and the views of the campaign (Langer 1992: 140).

Challenging the G7 in Naples, 1994

An important opportunity for addressing the problems of the global economy came with the G7 meeting held in Naples in July 1994. In the months before the summit a coalition of forty civil society groups, supported by left political forces and trade unions was created, with the name of *Il Cerchio dei Popoli* (Peoples' Circle). It linked up with the London-based *New Economics Foundation*, which had organized parallel summits at G7 meetings since 1984 in London, calling them 'The Other Economic Summit' (TOES). The events organized in Naples included a series of conferences on global issues (with speakers such as Samir Amin, Susan George and Serge Latouche); a meeting of social movements (held in the large dismantled steel plant of Bagnoli, with a strong involvement of trade unions); and a symbolic summit of the 'Seven Poors', representatives from grass-roots and indigenous groups of seven countries of the South.

A letter signed by the 'Seven Poors' contesting the strategy of rich countries against the world's poor was sent to the prime ministers participating to the G7 summit; they were also received by the mayor of Naples, Antonio Bassolino, recently elected by a centre-left coalition. Cultural events and a street demonstration with fifteen hundred people were also organized.

The agenda of the countersummit comprised the broad range of issues that would in later years be addressed by civil society gatherings such as the World Social Forum (WSF). Particularly prominent were issues related to development, work, environment, human rights, food, trade and debt. An emphasis was put on the need for democratic control of the processes of globalization. The countersummit provided Italian civil society with an important opportunity for making links with the incipient international networks working on global issues. A result of the event was an effort to develop a well-defined series of proposals submitted to the prime ministers attending the G7 summit. The proposal on debt requested:

1. Reduction in the whole stock of bilateral debt for severely indebted low-income countries of between 80 and 100 per cent by the end of 1995.
2. Extension of debt reduction to commercial and multilateral debt (financed by new Special Drawing Rights, the sale of gold stocks by the IMF or a more creative use of reserves and profits of multilateral development banks).
3. Reform of the Paris Club of creditors to provide a more open forum which could take wider resource flows and development financing needs of debtor countries into account.

This and other proposals would develop in later years to inform the strategies of national and international campaigns on debt.

A Positive Peace: An Economy of Justice

As the United Nations celebrated its fiftieth anniversary in 1995, in Perugia the first meeting of the Assembly of the Peoples' United Nations was held. This conference was attended by civil society representatives from more than one hundred countries, each invited by an Italian local authority. The assembly heard witnesses of world problems and called for reform and democratization of the United Nations. Organized by *Tavola della Pace* (Peace Roundtable), co-ordinating five hundred Italian local and national groups and 350 local authorities, the assembly has since then been convened every other year, focusing in 1997 on economic justice, in 1999 on the role of global civil society—arguing that 'another world is possible'—and in 2001 on 'globalization from below'. A major event which has ended every session of the assembly has been the 15-mile march from Perugia to Assisi, a historic peace movement route, attended on average by fifty thousand people (Lotti and Giandomenico 1996; Lotti, Giandomenico and Lembo 1999).

In the assemblies held in 1997 and 1999 global economic issues—debt and trade in particular—were put centre stage, using a frame of global justice. From the Perugia events, final documents emerged with specific proposals including the cancellation of third world debt, the reform of the World Bank, the introduction of the Tobin tax on international financial transactions, a world contract on water and the defence of labour rights at the international level. Such experiences anticipated the rise of Global Justice Movements (GJMs).

Globalizz-Azione dei popoli

Building on the high-profile events of Naples and Perugia, a campaign of awareness around global issues named *Globalizz-Azione dei Popoli* (Global Action by the People) was launched in Rome in 1997 by Alberto Castagnola, who had been active in IDOC, with the support of Progetto Continenti, Comunità di Capodarco and Kairos. It produced twelve booklets on global issues whose aim, Castagnola argues, was:

> to spread awareness about the fact that the serious issues affecting the South involve the North as well, and to promote a change in the peoples' behaviour in the North in order to allow a change in the mechanism of trade with the South. (Interview, 18 February 2008)

Grass-roots mobilizations at the local level followed, and such experiences would grow into the *Rete Lilliput*,[10] an important player in later campaigns.

The Creation of Sdebitarsi and the Activism of the Catholic Church

In 1996–1997 the *Sdebitarsi* campaign was created, with initial financial support from the city council of Rome, which was controlled by a centre-left coalition. The Catholic Jubilee of 2000 had been convoked and debt remission was a traditional element of jubilees. In parallel, in the UK, the international campaign Jubilee 2000 was launched (see Chapter 9, this volume), building on the previous activity of the Debt Crisis Network. The opening conference of Sdebitarsi in Rome coincided with the meeting of the European Debt and Development network (EURODAD).

At the time, Italy lacked a culture of professional campaigns. Luca De Fraia, the first co-ordinator of Sdebitarsi, underlines that:

> there was no sophisticated culture of campaigning. Before that, there had been the campaign for the ban on landmines, the other successful campaign in Italy. The only thing we had was an appeal on debt cancellation and a petition for which we collected signatures of support. (Interview, 28 February 2008)

Campaign speakers would tour Italy to present the issue and collect signatures for the petition, relying on grass-roots activism, including that of Rete Lilliput, the Catholic organization *Caritas* and missionary groups. In 2000, a communications campaign was started that aimed to influence public opinion, with spots on local radios. This media-oriented approach led to the appearance of the singers Bono and Jovanotti at the Sanremo Italian Song Festival in February 2000 with a message on debt relief.

At the same time, the Catholic Church, on the eve of the Jubilee of the year 2000, intensified its mobilization on third world debt. Pope John Paul II made a series of speeches in favour of debt relief, and the encyclical 'Tertio Millenio Adveniente' addressed the issue. In September 1999 the Pope showed his support to the international campaign Jubilee 2000 by receiving a delegation including the singers Bono and Bob Geldof, and a representative of the Italian campaign Sdebitarsi.

Although catholic activism broadened the consensus around debt relief, it also created problems for the consistency of the frame of mobilization. At the beginning of 1999 the Italian Catholic Church set up its own *Campagna ecclesiale per la riduzione del debito dei paesi più poveri* (Church Campaign for the Reduction of Debt of the Poorest Countries). As Luca De Fraia highlights:

> initially it was quite traumatic, because groups that were initially part of Sdebitarsi joined that campaign. Catholics were divided and it became very difficult to manage a situation with two campaigns on debt. (Interview, 28 February 2008)

The Catholic Church campaign framed the issue in terms of 'debt reduction' rather than 'debt cancellation', demanding a revision of the IMF-sponsored agreement on Highly Indebted Poor Countries (HIPCs). The main initiative organized, *Tu in azione* (You in Action) emphasized individual involvement and aimed at collecting one hundred billion lire for a buy-back of the credit Italy had with two highly indebted African countries.

Sdebitarsi maintained a focus on requests for policy change but avoided criticism of the new campaign and tried to cooperate; the head of the Catholic campaign, Riccardo Moro, responded to criticism from the missionary world arguing that 'the campaign of the Catholic Church is not an alternative to analogous initiatives at the Italian and international level [. . .] rather it aims at a pastoral action [. . .] that cannot be done by lay organizations' (Moro 1999, p.25).

Success and Decline of Debt Relief Activism

The coexistence of the two campaigns extended the reach of mobilization, but watered down its demands. Sdebitarsi had first demanded the cancellation of debt through a government decree, but later asked for legislation to be approved in Parliament. Under mounting pressure from the Vatican and the Catholic Church, in April 1999 the Italian government, led by a centre-left coalition announced an initiative on third world debt. According to Luca De Fraia:

> at that time, the scene changed. We moved from petitions to a more institutional work on the law. We had won the recognition of the principle of debt relief, but government proposals did not satisfy us. We started to lobby Parliament to influence the elaboration of policy. (Interview, 28 February 2008)

The result was the law 209/2000 on debt cancellation, approved in 2000, whose content and outcome is examined in the final section of this chapter. The high visibility of the issue of third world debt, which resulted from years of campaigning and the intervention of the Catholic Church, had eventually led to an important policy change, a pioneering initiative among European countries and a major turning point for Italian activism (De Fraia and Chiodo 2001; Pettifor 2001a, 2001b).

The campaign on third world debt maintained a high profile during the protests against the G8 in Genoa in July 2001, organized by the Genoa Social Forum. Debt was presented as a major issue of conflict in a radical critique of neoliberal globalization. During the days of the G8, the city was covered with posters representing a starving black woman breast-feeding a fat white child, with the caption 'didn't you have enough?' Sdebitarsi hoped to use the event to showcase the Italian initiatives and legislation on the international stage. The outcomes of the G8 summit in terms of policy decisions around debt and other global justice issues were disappointing; the only initiative was the creation of a global fund against HIV-AIDS. The violent repression of the protests in Genoa weakened the mobilizations on debt and on other global issues. For Raffaella Chiodo:

> During the G8 in Genoa, the issue of debt was central, everybody was paying attention to it. Then it went out of fashion. People started to believe it had been solved because a law about it had been approved. This impression was reinforced by Tony Blair's declaration at the G8 summit in Gleneagles in 2005 that debt had been cancelled. But they were talking about just 10 per cent of third world debt. (Interview, 27 February 2008)

Other initiatives have also taken place; third world debt and trade agreements with Europe have been addressed by the Campaign *Chiama l'Africa*, launched in 1997 by 147 Italian NGOs, with a strong presence of Catholic organizations.[11] An assessment of the outcomes of mobilizations is provided later in the chapter.

MOBILIZATIONS ON INTERNATIONAL TRADE

During the 1980s and the early 1990s international trade was not an issue of political contention in Italy. Around the mid-1990s, the rounds of trade liberalization, the creation of the World Trade Organization (WTO) and the OECD proposal for a Multilateral Agreement on Investment (MAI) that would protect foreign investment turned trade into an issue of social mobilization.

From MAI to Seattle

The first initiative addressed the OECD proposed MAI agreement. An ad hoc campaign *Mai al mai* (Never MAI) was set up by Associazione Botteghe del mondo, Bilanci di Giustizia, GlobalizzAzione dei popoli, Chiama l'Africa, Mani Tese, Nigrizia, Campagna per la Riforma della Banca Mondiale, Sdebitarsi, Centro Nuovo Modello di Sviluppo, WWF and Pax Christi. These groups were the ones that had coalesced around the *Tavolo intercampagne* promoted by the Lilliput network. This experience contributed to the co-ordination of different campaigns on global issues, giving shape to one of the backbones of the emerging global justice movement in Italy.

The campaign against MAI stressed the increased power of multinational corporations and the loss of sovereignty of countries that would follow the MAI agreement. Actions for raising awareness were carried out at the local level, with some international links. Eventually, European mobilizations led the French government to withdraw support for the proposal; the collapse of the OECD MAI agreement was a first case of success of global movements against neoliberal globalization (Pianta 2001a).

In 1999 attention turned to the WTO, its Millennium Round of trade liberalization and its Ministerial meeting in Seattle. The huge protests held in Seattle at the end of November 1999 are widely considered as the birth date of the GJM. The Italian participation in the events was limited to a representative of the MAI campaign and the Lilliput network, Maurizio Meloni, and to a representative of the fair trade organization *CTM Altromercato*, Giorgio Dal Fiume—evidence of the scarce resources available to Italian groups and the modest attention that trade issues had so far received. However, about fifty events in support of the protest in Seattle were organized in different cities by the Lilliput network and other groups (Meloni 2000).

The Seattle protests launched opposition to trade liberalization as a new area of activism, building on the rich Italian experiences of mobilizations associated with peace, the environment and North–South issues. There was also rapid learning from international experiences, with participation in the cross border networks that started to challenge the global financial order and, in particular, the IMF and the World Bank. The French mobilization against MAI had led to the creation of a new organization, *Attac*, proposing the Tobin Tax on currency transactions and alternatives to neoliberalism (see Chapter 12, this volume). The Italian section, Attac Italia, was soon established.

The specificities of trade issues had to be learned by Italian activists, and several groups become actively involved in campaigning for trade justice. Among them, the *Campaign for the Reform of the World Bank* (CRBM), whose co-ordinator, Antonio Tricarico, explains that:

> the WTO is a complex structure, you need to understand how it works, you need a high level of technical expertise. All this was initially difficult to translate into a public campaign, as later happened with the Italian mobilizations against the WTO Cancún summit. (Interview, 26 February 2008)

These experiences, however, never coalesced around a single campaign, as in the case of Sdebitarsi; the groups active on trade justice remained more dispersed, broadly divided between 'elite' groups involved in international advocacy networks—large NGOs or specialized campaigns with high technical competences on trade issues—and the constellation of locally active groups—fair trade cooperatives and associations such as those of the Lilliput network. Several reasons explain these developments. First, the scope for mobilizations for policy change at the national level was limited, as decisions were made in Brussels and at the WTO. Second, the need for competences, the complexity of issues and the difficulty to turn them into objectives of activism easy to communicate to public opinion and civil society made the launch of focused mobilizations difficult. Third, the more radical frame for mobilization, involving the critique of trade liberalization developed within the context of protest against neoliberal globalization, was not shared by moderate and Catholic groups, and their involvement remained limited.

Genoa, Florence and Cancún

In the Genoa protests against the G8 summit of 2001 the issue of trade became relevant for the global justice movement as a whole, but no specific campaign was in place. After the terrorist attacks of 11 September 2001 and the start of the war in Afghanistan, the Doha meeting of the WTO in late 2001 was met by limited mobilization at the national level. Mobilizations reorganized with the European Social Forum held in Florence in 2003. According to Antonio Tricarico:

> the international campaign against the trade liberalization agreement planned for the WTO meeting in Cancún of 2003 was launched at the European Social Forum in Florence and had a strong impact in Italy, with a large number of initiatives. Italy probably had one of the most successful mobilizations on this issue. (Interview, 26 February 2008)

Italian NGOs had also become more knowledgeable and active on the international scene. As Monica Di Sisto of *Fair* points out:

> initially the campaigns on WTO and on bilateral agreements were rather generic and limited to slogans such as 'stop subsides', 'no agriculture in the WTO', 'water is a common good'. Then the movement came to acquire an expertise on these issues and it was able to develop proposals, especially on bilateral agreements that are more technical. We moved from opposition to the WTO to trying to understand what we wanted, with less media impact but with more effectiveness on specific points. (Interview, 1 March 2008)

A crucial development at the international level was the creation of the global network *Our World is Not for Sale*[12] (OWISFS), which attracted widespread participation from Italian civil society groups and effectively shaped the patterns of trade mobilizations in many countries of the North and South. Its activities in the European context were co-ordinated through the Seattle to the Brussels network. As decision-making on trade issues was taking place in Brussels, Geneva and at WTO conferences, such global and regional networks became the appropriate place for organizing protest, lobbying and developing alternatives to the neoliberal trade regime. The scope for activism at the national level was reduced to raising consciousness on the importance of issues and spreading the agenda developed by international networks.

Other activities on trade issues in Italy included the *No Dumping* campaign. Carried out by the federation of Catholic NGOs, FOCSIV, with the support of twenty other organizations, the campaign called on the EU to end subsidies for agricultural exports (FOCSIV 2003). In more recent years activism has focused on bilateral trade deals, the European partnership agreements (EPA) with developing countries that include trade liberalization requirements. More specific actions have focused on trade in food products, with campaigns to assert the principle of food sovereignty against the logic of global markets that has led to speculation and rising food prices (McKeon 2009).

Facing the lack of opportunities for introducing policy change at the national level, concerns over trade as a source of North–South inequalities have led to a search for different ways of achieving change. Links between poor producers in the South and responsible consumers in the North have developed outside the logic of global markets through the rapid growth of 'fair trade'. This involves promoting production processes that respect the rights of workers and the environment, support for local development, and the payment of above-market prices. In parallel, the model of opulent consumption in the North has been questioned, searching for more sustainable and sober behaviours; in Italy this has led to the growth of collective purchasing groups (GAS) linked to specific producers certified to be environmentally and socially friendly. Giorgio Dal Fiume argues that:

> The emergence of fair trade in Italy towards the end of the 1980s and its establishment during the 1990s with hundreds of *botteghe del mondo* (world shops) as places for social action and education has made the question of international trade more visible at the national level. Fair trade has become not just a form of alternative consumption, but a concrete action for fairer trade rules. (Interview, 21 February 2008)

The specific outcomes that such models of activism have had in Italy are assessed next.

ASSESSING OUTCOMES AND POLICY CHANGES

Comparing Mobilizations and Outcomes

The previous sections have shown that from the mid-1990s, the questions of debt and trade became increasingly separate. Table 8.2 summarizes the main differences. In terms of organization, the debt campaign was styled on Northern European models, with a focused mobilization. On trade, the mobilization maintained a more dispersed form, as different groups were active at the national level and participated in the same OWINFS coalition at the international level.

Table 8.2 A Comparison of Debt and Trade Mobilizations

	Debt	*Trade*
Structure	National coalition, linked to international campaigns	International network with national nodes
Strategy	Lobbying, raising awareness (mass mobilization)	Raising awareness, protest, proposal of alternatives, lobbying (elite campaign)
Frames	Global justice	Anti-neoliberalism
Mobilization cycle	Focused and sustained	Intermittent
Key events	1990: Early campaigns on debt 1997: Sdebitarsi founded 1999: Law on debt enters parliamentary discussion 2000: Approval of the law 2001: Debt is central in the Genoa G8 protest	1997: Italian participation in the campaign 'Stop MAI' 1999, 2003, 2005: Minimal Italian participation to WTO protests in Seattle, Cancún, Hong Kong; national days of action on trade, GATS, etc. 2006: mobilization against EPA
Scale of action	National, transnational	Transnational, local, national

This differentiation is associated to two main factors. First, in the analysis of political opportunities we already pointed out that debt mobilizations could target and make demands on the Italian government, whereas trade entailed a complex system of international governance with a reduced power of national governments.

Second, a divergence in the framing of issues emerges, with debt being conceptualized in terms of global justice and trade being framed in terms of anti-neoliberalism. Antonio Tricarico, co-ordinator of CRBM, observes that:

> The mobilization on debt has been broader and had more of an ethical character. The mobilization on trade, instead, had to be more political, being crucial for the critique to neoliberalism. Debt is historically the consequence of a series of neoliberal economic policies, but it can also be approached from a more ethical and conciliatory standpoint and this is why the Church has always concentrated on this initiative. Conversely, the movements on debt in the South have always been more political. But if you look at the Italian context you see that—also through the use of celebrities in media-oriented events—a de-politicization was brought about; this allowed to mobilize larger support, but banalized the problem. (Interview, 26 February 2008)

The policy outcomes of the campaigns on third world debt and international trade are coherent with the frames and political opportunities that have come to characterize these two streams of activism. The centralized, focused character and wide reach of debt mobilization is matched by an important policy outcome: the law on debt relief approved in 2000. The more dispersed nature of the campaign on international trade has led to different results of smaller relevance, including steps that have slowed down the trade liberalization agenda pursued by all Italian governments—of both centre-right and centre-left—in the last decade.

Table 8.3 Assessing the Impact on Policy of Debt and Trade Mobilizations

	Debt	*Trade*
Local level	None	None on international trade On fair trade: regional laws (Liguria 2007; Tuscany 2005)
National level	Law on international debt relief allowing for cancellation of six billion euros of bilateral debt	Slowing the pace of the trade liberalization agenda
Transnational level	Italy favours debt relief in multilateral institutions; pioneering role of debt cancellation law	Slowing the pace of the trade liberalization agenda

The National Law on the Cancellation of Third World Debt

The policy outcome of the Italian campaign on third world debt has been, at first sight, quite important. The parliament introduced a law for the cancellation of debt (legge 209/2000),[13] which eliminated six billions euros of bilateral debt with third world countries. The result is particularly significant because it was the first law among Western countries regulating the cancellation of debt, and for a long time the only one. After six years, Spain produced a similar law during the first government led by socialist leader Zapatero. Luca De Fraia, who was involved in the campaign during the period between 1997 and 2001, asserts that:

> the campaign aimed at a legislative initiative. The law was approved. A number of billions euros of debt have been cancelled and we also have instruments of transparency to monitor the cancellation of debt. I think that we can be satisfied by that. (Interview, 28 February 2008)

The law was produced in a period of favourable political opportunities. Besides the interest of the Catholic Church, the government of the centre-left coalition, headed by the post-communist leader Massimo D'Alema came to consider the cancellation of debt an important political initiative.[14] However, a series of problems ensued during the implementation of the law. The electoral victory of Silvio Berlusconi's centre-right coalition in 2001 changed the political climate. An executive regulation by the new government slowed down the distribution of debt relief funds and they were used to mask a deep cut in foreign aid.[15] Raffaela Chiodo, who co-ordinated the campaign in recent years, points out that:

> during Berlusconi's government the time-frame of debt cancellation was distorted. According to the law six billions euros should have been cancelled in three years. In five years only half of those have been actually cancelled. This has been a problem especially for the countries which were relying on Italian plans of debt cancellation. This did not happen by chance, it was coherent with Berlusconi's political plans. (Interview, 27 August 2008)

If we consider the implementation of debt legislation, we find a more modest impact. But in terms of the conventional relationship between social activism and government policy-making in Italy, the debt campaign was an important breakthrough in the ability to influence Italy's legislation and international action. In the international context, the passing of Italian legislation was a pioneering achievement in Europe and Italy in some occasions used its modest influence in multilateral institutions to favour debt relief projects.

The Impact on Italian and EU Trade Policy

In the case of trade, we find nothing similar in terms of policy impact. The commitment to trade liberalization by all Italian governments since the creation of the WTO, the bipartisan consensus among major political forces and the EU responsibility on trade issues meant that the political opportunities for change in trade policies were minimal. However, patient lobbying by specialized civil society groups and trade unions has tried to influence the Italian government's negotiating positions and the implementation of specific bilateral and multilateral agreements. According to Monica Di Sisto of Fair, a member of the international network OWINFS:

> Italian trade activists have acquired more expertise of the specificity of trade negotiations, have been effective in some cases in putting pressure on the government and have now credibility not just because we take people to the streets, but because we are able to advance policy proposals. In this way, we managed to slow down the neoliberal agenda, or at least to point out its contradictions, opening up a public debate. Moreover, international networks are now stable and provide a constant flow of ideas and strategies to those who want to develop policy alternatives. (Interview, 1 March 2008)

Trade unions have played an active role on trade issues, with a close collaboration with civil society groups. In particular, unions emphasize the need to include labour standards in trade agreements. Cecilia Brighi, international secretary of the CISL trade union and member of the board of the International Labour Organization (ILO) points out:

> Our work for introducing social, labour and environmental concerns in trade agreement has been very difficult. Governments and policymakers were impermeable to our pressure, and even more so was the bureaucracy of negotiators committed to trade liberalization. Even though the current negotiations are at an impasse, there is a lot of work we still have to do. Perhaps there are more political opportunities at the supranational level; the global system is in crisis and needs to address some key issues in order to regain credibility. At both levels, however, the problem is the lack of coherence between what politicians say and what they do. (Interview, 26 February 2008)

In assessing the policy impact of trade mobilizations, the supranational dimension emerges as the critical one for shaping (and contesting) trade arrangements, with limited political opportunities left at the national level.

LESSONS FROM POLICY OUTCOMES

A number of lessons on the relationships between activism and policy-making on debt and trade issues can be drawn from the Italian experience. First, the heritage of national political cultures has remained strong and influential on the ways mobilizations have developed, and on the forms of interaction with institutions and policymakers. This is coherent with the findings of several comparative studies on the growth of global justice movements in the last decade (della Porta 2007, 2009). The high degree of political awareness of Italian civil society (compared to other European countries) has influenced the development of mobilizations and the integration of these issues with the broader themes of North–South inequalities, with debt mainly framed in terms of global justice, and trade in terms of resistance to neoliberal globalization.

Second, the way Italian mobilizations have been organized highlights strengths and weaknesses of the country's political cultures. The typical actors of Italian activism are a large number of small groups with few resources, linked in networks and campaigns, building on a strong 'political and social capital' of previous activism and on extensive practices of collaboration. Such a model has few parallels in European countries. These actors favour the spread of public awareness, the integration between different themes and have proved to be effective in mounting very large and frequent protest events. They have also favoured the integration between traditional advocacy activism and the development of alternative practices and grassroots initiatives, such as fair trade and responsible consumption.

However, their small scale and limited resources often prevented the development of a 'critical mass' in terms of commitment, competence and activism on specific and complex themes. In relation to issues such as debt and trade, there is a strong need for sustained active participation in global advocacy networks and for developing a 'professional' ability to lobby national and international decision-makers for change in policies. The weakness of Italian mobilizations in these aspects has contributed to the limited impact we have identified.

Third, the context of political opportunities—at the national and supranational level—helped the success of the debt mobilization and limited the impact of trade activism. In the case of trade—as previously shown in Chapter 5, this volume—what can make a difference in civil society impact is the presence of stable, large and well-organized global networks, capable of countering trade liberalization policies at several levels. They have to combine an ability to organize large protests events, access decision-makers and carry out highly competent lobbying on the details of trade agreements.

Such a landscape of political opportunities for policy change highlights the great potential that the EU could have if European policies opened up to arguments of civil society. Europe could assert itself as an arena for deliberating policies on global issues, linking the intense activism of civil society, the role of national governments and the major influence the EU has at the global level. This 'virtuous circle' of democratic debate between activism, national and supranational politics in the EU context has taken place in cases concerning human rights (such as in the creation of the International Criminal Court), the environment (for example, on climate change) or selected disarmament treaties (such as the landmine or cluster bomb bans), but never on issues concerning the global economy. In a context of decreasing legitimation of the project of European integration, the opening up of EU policies to mobilizations on social and economic justice could represent an important possibility for reconstructing a widely shared vision of Europe's role in a less unequal world.

Annex 8.1 Interviews

1. Marco Bersani, co-ordinator of Attac Italia, 21 February 2008.
2. Cecilia Brighi, international secretary of CISL (Catholic Trade Union), 26 February 2008.
3. Alberto Castagnola, member of IDOC, Sdebitarsi and Rete Lilliput, 18 February 2008.
4. Raffaella Chiodo, second co-ordinator of Sdebitarsi (Campaign for Debt Relief), 27 February 2008.
5. Giorgio Dal Fiume, co-ordinator of CTM Altromercato (fair trade shops), 21 February 2008.
6. Luca De Fraia, first co-ordinator of Sdebitarsi (Campaign for Debt Relief), 28 February 2008.
7. Monica Di Sisto, FAIR (trade justice campaign), 1 March 2008.
8. Francesco Martone, founder of CRBM (Campaign for the Reform of the World Bank) and former senator, 4 March 2008.
9. Antonio Tricarico, co-ordinator of CRBM (Campaign for the Reform of the World Bank), 26 February 2008.

NOTES

1. We want to thank all those who shared with us their experiences of activism, and in particular the interviewees listed in Annex 8.1, as well as Martin Koehler, Giulio Marcon and Nora McKeon for their comments and advice.
2. See the introduction to this volume. On social movements and the politics of contention, among a large literature, see McAdam, McCarthy and Zald (1996); McAdam, Tarrow and Tilly (2001), della Porta and Diani (2006); della Porta (2007, 2009). The impact of mobilizations has been studied by Giugni, McAdam and Tilly (1999) and Giugni (2004). See also Chapters 4 and 5, this volume.
3. Cases of conflict with supranational institutions are investigated, among others, in Keck and Sikkink (1998) and O'Brien et al. (2000).
4. This Public Opinion Tribunal was launched by the Italian Socialist politician Lelio Basso, building on his experience in the Tribunal against war crimes in

Vietnam, organized in 1967 by the British philosopher and peace leader Bertrand Russell, and chaired by French philosopher Jean Paul Sartre. Since its foundation, the Tribunal has met more than thirty times, involving dozens of judges selected from well-known experts and Nobel laureates. It has examined cases of violation of rights of individuals and peoples, raised by civil society groups—from Latin America to Tibet, from Afghanistan to former Yugoslavia—and it has also addressed questions related to economic, social and environmental rights.

5. IDOC had originally been founded by the Protestant churches to monitor the Second Vatican Council, opened under Pope John XXIII in 1962 and closed under Pope Paul VI in 1965, that contributed to modernize the liturgy and social doctrine of the Catholic Church.
6. In 1979 and 1987, new laws opened the way for large development cooperation expenditure by the Italian government, with a significant role of NGOs. This policy was reversed, however, in the mid-1990s (Marcon 2002).
7. The amount of booklets, documentation files, infosheets and report produced by different campaigns, organizations and journals in order to popularize the complex issues of debt and trade is remarkable. It includes the newsletters of *Idoc internazionale* and *GlobalizzAzione dei popoli*; the publications of the Centro internazionale Crocevia, including *Semi*; the Bologna-based journal *Terre del fuoco*; trade union publications such as *Azimut*; various publications of individual NGOs such as *Terra Nuova Forum*, *Volontari per lo sviluppo*, *Solidarietà internazionale* and *Missione Oggi*. See also Campagna per la riforma della Banca Mondiale (CRBM) et al. (2005); FOCSIV (2003); George (2002); Lotti, Giandomenico and Lembo (1999); Marcon (2002); Regidor and Binel (2002); Tavola della Pace (2000).
8. The themes of North–South solidarity, the question of debt and later the trade challenges raised by the creation of WTO have been addressed since the 1980s by a wide range of radical media, including the daily newspaper *Il Manifesto*, *Onde Lunghe* (a free magazine on social movements published between 1993 and 1995), the magazine *Carta* (published since 1998), the journal *Capitalismo, Natura, Socialismo*, etc.
9. They include: Sdebitarsi, Rete Lilliput, Associazione Botteghe del Mondo, Unimondo, Ctm Altromercato, Campagna per la Riforma della Banca Mondiale, Fair, Attac Italia.
10. See Rete Lilliput (2001).
11. For an official description of the campaign Chiama l'Africa, see http://www.cipsi.it/nuovo/cipsi/documenti/yearbook/124.pdf.
12. See http://www.ourworldisnotforsale.org/.
13. See http://www.esteri.it/MAE/IT/Politica_Estera/Economia/Cooperaz_Econom/Debito_Estero/Legge_25_luglio_n_209.htm.
14. The approval of the law was extremely rapid for Italian standards. It just required six months of discussion in the two chambers, and at the final vote was approved with overwhelming bipartisan support.
15. By counting the funds destined for debt cancellation as a form of foreign aid, the government claimed that aid had increased to 0.16 per cent of GDP.

BIBLIOGRAPHY

Campagna per la riforma della Banca Mondiale and Manitese (2005). *Tutte le bugie del libero commercio*, Milan: Terre di Mezzo, Supplement to Altraeconomia.

De Fraia, L., and Chiodo, R. (2001). 'Sdebitarsi, una campagna di successo', *Limes, I popoli di Seattle*, 3:143–150.

della Porta, D. (ed) (2007). *The Global Justice Movements: A Cross-National and Transnational Perspective*, Boulder, CO: Paradigm.
———. (ed) (2009). *Democracy in Social Movements*, London: Palgrave.
della Porta, D. and Diani, M. (2006). *Social Movements: An Introduction*, 2nd ed., Oxford: Blackwell.
Federazione Organismi Cristiani Servizio Internazionale Volontario. (2003). 'No Dumping', *Concorrenza sleale,* Supplement to *Vita*, Rome.
Fondazione Internazionale Lelio Basso. (1998). *Tribunale permanente dei popoli. Le sentenze: 1979–1998*, Lecco: Stefanoni.
George, S. (2002). *Fermiano il WTO*, Milan: Feltrinelli.
Giugni, M. (2004). *Social Protest and Policy Change*, Lanham, MD: Rowman and Littlefield.
Giugni, M., McAdam, D., and Tilly, C. (1999). *How Social Movements Matter*, Minneapolis: University of Minnesota Press.
Keck, M.E., and Sikkink, K. (1998). *Activists beyond Borders: Advocacy Networks in International Politics*, Ithaca, NY: Cornell University Press.
Langer, A. (ed) (1992). *Sud chiama Nord. Proposte e soluzioni alla crisi del debito.* Proceedings of the conference of Campagna Nord-Sud: biosfera, sopravvivenza dei popoli e debito and Provincia di Roma, Rome, 16–17 October.
Lotti, G., and Giandomenico, N. (eds) (1996). *L'Onu dei popoli*, Turin: Edizioni Gruppo Abele.
Lotti, G., Giandomenico, N., and Lembo, R. (eds) (1999). *Per un' economia di giustizia*, Perugia: Tavola della Pace.
Marcon, G. (2002). *Le ambiguità degli aiuti umanitari. Indagine critica sul terzo settore*, Milan: Feltrinelli.
———. (2004). *Le utopie del ben fare*, Naples: L'ancora del Mediterraneo.
McAdam, D., McCarthy, J.D., and Zald, M.N. (1996). *Comparative Perspectives on Social Movements: Political Opportunities, Mobilizing Structures, and Cultural Framings*, Cambridge: Cambridge University Press.
McAdam, D., Tarrow, S., and Tilly, C. (2001). *Dynamics of Contention*, Cambridge: Cambridge University Press.
McKeon, N. (2009). *The United Nations and Civil Society: Legitimating Global Governance, Whose Voice?* London: Zed Books.
Meloni, M. (2000). *La battaglia di Seattle. L'Organizzazione mondiale del commercio e la rete che l'ha imbrigliata*, Piacenza: Editrice Berti.
Moro, R. (1999). 'Dossier sul debito', *Missione Oggi*, 8 (October): 25–27.
O'Brien, R., Goetz, A.M., Scholte, J.A., and Williams, M. (2000). *Contesting Global Governance: Multilateral Economic Institutions and Global Social Movements*, Cambridge: Cambridge University Press.
Our World Is Not for Sale Network. (2002). 'WTO: Shrink or Sink', *Peace Research Abstracts*, 39 (5): 611–755.
Pettifor, A. (2001a). 'Jubilee 2000 e il problema del debito', in Mani Tese (ed), *Nuove regole per il nuovo millennio*, Bologna: EMI.
———. (2001b). 'Why Jubilee 2000 Made an Impact', in H. Anheier, M. Glasius and M. Kaldor (eds), *Global Civil Society*, Oxford: Oxford University Press.
Pianta, M. (2001a). *Globalizzazione dal basso: Economia mondiale e movimenti sociali*, Rome: ManifestoLibri.
———. (2001b) 'Parallel Summits of Global Civil Society', in H. Anheier, M. Glasius and M. Kaldor (eds), *Global Civil Society*, Oxford: Oxford University Press.
Regidor, R.J., and Binel, A. (eds) (1992). *Dissenso sul mondo*, Rome: Campagna Nord-Sud and Terra Nuova.
Rete Lilliput. (2001). *La rete di Lilliput: Alleanze, obiettivi, strategie*, Bologna: EMI.
Tavola della Pace. (2000). *Another World Is Possible: The Experience and Proposals of the Assemblies of the UN of the Peoples*, Perugia: Tavola della Pace.

9 Dropping the Debt?

British Anti-Debt Campaigns and International Development Policy

Clare Saunders and Tasos Papadimitriou

In July 2005, an astounding 225,000 people, mostly clad in white, took to the streets of Edinburgh to form the largest demonstration Scotland has ever known. The demonstration demanded that the leaders of the G8 countries 'Make Poverty History' (MPH) by 'dropping the debt', 'providing more and better aid' and ensuring 'trade justice'. The MPH demonstration and accompanying Live 8 concerts were so significant that the Roman Catholic Primate, Archbishop Cormac Murphy O'Connor, called it 'the greatest moral upheaval since the campaign against the slave trade' (Rootes and Saunders 2007: 128).

Although MPH was, by most accounts, an astounding demonstration, it should not be viewed as a stand alone moral shake-up, or one that—at least on its own—necessarily had a significant effect on British international development policy. All of MPH's three demands had previously been expressed in the campaigns of humanitarian, aid and development organizations (HADOs). Prevailing campaigns for 0.7 per cent of gross national income to be spent on aid, for example, began in the 1970s, with the Campaign for Real Aid. Although trade justice did not emerge as a *campaign* until the late 1990s, organizations like Oxfam have been working on fair trade since the 1960s. And debt has been a key campaign issue since the Jubilee 2000 coalition (J2000) emerged in 1996 (Saunders 2009).

In this chapter, we focus on just one of the themes of MPH—dropping the debt. We begin by summarizing the challenge of the debt issue as raised by British HADOs. We then offer a commentary on the emergence and development of the debt campaign precedents to MPH. We move on to discuss British policy developments that appear to have emerged as a result of debt campaigns.

FRAMING THE ISSUE OF DEBT

To a large extent, British HADOs have developed a division of labour in which each produces specialist material on key topics upon which they focus. At the time of this writing, the main HADOs working on and framing the debt issue are Jubilee Debt Campaign (JDC) and the New Economics Foundation (NEF), which hosts the Jubilee Research New Global Economy team in the Centre for Global Interdependence. Consequently, the websites of these organizations host many briefings on the debt issue, and the organizations are responsible for producing master-frames on debt to which other organizations, that form part of the Jubilee coalition, subscribe.[1] In comparison, the Christian Aid website hosts only one or two recent discussion documents that are indirectly related to the debt issue, the Catholic Agency for Overseas Development (CAFOD) tends to produce shorter synopses which do not diverge from the master frames, the World Development Movement (WDM) only has information dating from the turn of the millennium, and the website of MPH, which is now a moribund network, is perhaps better described as a tool for mobilization rather than for public education. Although Oxfam's website hosts a number of discussion documents on debt, they are mostly outdated.

However, it has not always been this way. Prior to the emergence of J2000 at the end of the 1990s, other HADOs had begun to grapple with the issue of debt. Oxfam, perhaps now the most influential of British HADOs, had raised the issue of debt during the 1980s, but it was not an especially strong agenda during that decade; rather it was ancillary to its relief work in famine-stricken Africa. It revealed, for example, in 1987, that for every £1 that the world contributed to famine relief in Africa in 1985, the West took back £2 in debt repayments. CAFOD and other British HADOs followed a similar trajectory, touching upon controversial aid and development issues, but never fully engaging with them until J2000 raised the profile of debt in the late 1990s, and even then only with trepidation.

The WDM, initially formed as a coalition that would work on the politically oriented *Manifesto for World Development*, was different. Eventually set up as a limited company, it was, unlike its counterparts constrained by charity law, able to make overtly political demands for, among other things, an increase in third world aid budgets and repayments of the debt burden of poorer countries (Macdonald 1972). But it was J2000 that was the most successful at framing the issue of debt in such a way that made it a significant public and political issue. Hence, we focus this section of the chapter on the successful and resonant framing of J2000 (later reinvented as Jubilee Debt Campaign/JDC). How, according to J2000/JDC did the debt crisis emerge? Why did it become a problem? And how can it be solved?

JDC (2008) suggests that the debt crisis emerged in a series of phases, beginning with colonialism in the 1920s and moving through independence in the 1940s and 1950s. According to JDC, it was at this time, during the Cold War, that ruthless lending to poor countries began. But debt, they suggest, only began to develop into crisis proportions during the oil crisis in the 1970s, which resulted in plummeting interest rates and consequently lavish borrowing and lending. But when financial markets recovered, interest rates soared, commodity prices crashed and poor countries began earning less on exports than on loans, making it difficult for them to afford necessary imports and trapping them in poverty.

Worse still, unpaid—and increasingly unpayable—debt grew. New loans, administered by multilateral institutions and funded by taxpayers in rich countries, were given to allow poor countries either to repay old debts or simply to keep them afloat. But these new loans were granted on condition that specific economic policies were adhered to under highly controversial Structural Adjustment Programmes (SAPs), widely assessed as having had seriously negative impacts on the lives and prospects of the poorest people (J2000 1999: 32–33). Cuts in public spending and overall deflationary policies, required by SAPs, protected the value of creditor assets while simultaneously exacerbating poverty (Pettifor 2001: 43–44). This has served to uphold the power and wealth of rich countries at the expense of poor, and has also meant that debt service payments often outstrip spending on social services, such as health care and education (JDC 2008).

Although Poverty Strategy Reduction papers have succeeded SAPs, and the Heavily Indebted Poor Countries (HIPC) Initiative and the Multilateral Debt Relief Initiative (MDRI) have been introduced and broadened (see section on British policy responses to anti-debt campaigns), HADOs remain concerned about the economic policy conditions that continue to be imposed on countries seeking debt relief (JDC 2008). This, they argue, is undemocratic, and locks poor countries into a perpetual cycle of poverty. They bemoan that those countries that, usually with good reasons, refuse to follow the Washington consensus are effectively denied debt relief and can be declared 'off track' for the HIPC, even if their failure to comply is due to the country seeking to meet its population's basic needs. HIPC is also criticized for being too exclusive, due to what is deemed to be an inappropriate equation used to determine eligibility, and for being too slow at reducing debt burdens—the whole process can take up to six years. The calculation for determining eligibility is based on the notion of 'sustainable debt', of which HADOs are highly critical. Only when debt is unsustainable—determined by the existence of a ratio of over 150 per cent of debts to annual export earnings—will a country qualify. JDC (2008) reports that by April 2008, 'only' U.S.$45.4 billion's worth of debt had been written off for twenty-three countries, contrasting with the estimated U.S.$400 billion for the one hundred countries that NEF had identified as in need of debt relief.

As well as assisting too few needy countries and being unfair, British HADOs also argue that the debt repayment schemes are unjust and that they need to be extended to other lending institutions beyond the public sector (JDC 2008). JDC (2008) is critical of the MDRI because it covers only four of twenty-three existing multilateral institutions that hold debts. Furthermore, it argues that debt relief should be extended beyond bi- and multilateral relief, to relief from debt accrued from private companies and banks and export credit agencies. This, they argue, would prevent 'vulture

Table 9.1 British HADO's Frames on Debt

Diagnostic		*Prognostic*	
Problem	*Culprits*	*Solution*	*Agents*
Unpayable, unjust, illegitimate debt	Commercial banks Rich governments World Bank/International Monetary Fund (IMF) Neoliberal policies	Cancel > $400 million debt for one hundred countries Redefine 'sustainable debt' Extend schemes to all types of creditors; end vulture funds End economic policy conditions Develop a framework for fair lending and processes	HADOs and public for awareness and mobilization Research for knowledge production A transparent, impartial agency for administering new loans and existing debt relief

funding'—whereby private companies pay off a country's debt at a reduced price, but charge the debtor the full price, making a net profit. In addition, JDC (2008) draws on Alexander Sack's work on 'odious debt', to argue that irresponsibly lent loans should be written off if they do not benefit a debtor nation's population, do not have citizen consent and if the creditors were aware that funds might be nefariously used (see also Mandel 2006). According to these principles, the millions of pounds worth of outstanding developing country debt that was accumulated by dictatorships should be cleared. A summary of British HADOs' framing of the debt issue is shown in Table 9.1, distinguishing between diagnostic and prognostic frames.

BRITISH ANTI-DEBT MOBILIZATIONS AND ORGANIZATIONS

In this section of the chapter, we explore the emergence of the anti-debt coalition, J2000, as an overtly political force. We also examine the conflicts and tensions that arose in the HADO sector over the emergence of J2000. The section moves on to a discussion of the HADO sector in the aftermath of J2000, which ceased to exist at the turn of the millennium.

The British HADO sector has a long history rooted in philanthropic agencies, but significant HADOs did not emerge until the early nineteenth century. The HADO sector has developed in five main phases, each significantly more politicized than its forerunner (Saunders 2009). It was only in the fourth phase, 1970s–1980s, that HADOs publicly declared that poverty was 'political'. The politically overt high-profile mass-mobilizing coalitions that are now routine to the HADO sector were almost unknown prior to the mid-1990s. J2000 was not the first, but was certainly one of the most significant. Why, then, were the forerunners to J2000 so tame? In short, it was due to a confluence of factors, including restrictions emplaced by charity laws that prevented them from becoming overtly political (Black 1992), their roots in religious or social philanthropy, the complex nature of the issues they tackled (Bryant and Lindenberg 2001: 2), fear of alienating their conservative supporters and the constant distraction of emergency and relief missions. Needless to say, several things changed. Charity laws were relaxed in 1995, protest became more acceptable among the electorate, and the Disasters' Emergency Committee formed, taking the strain off individual agencies at times of humanitarian crises. In addition, J2000 worked hard to unravel the complex issue of debt into bite-size pieces suitable for a public audience. As a well-resourced, entrepreneurial organization, which used innovative campaigning styles and strong leadership, J2000 reinvigorated the HADO sector.

The first attempt to form a politically oriented coalition was in 'phase 4' of the development of the HADO sector. The WDM, established in 1972, brought together Oxfam, Christian Aid and others in an active campaign coalition to tackle poverty. However, the charities involved in the coalition were soon warned by Charity Commissioners that, should they continue to work with the coalition, they would be 'in breach of trust' and that 'those responsible could be called upon to recoup to the charity any of its funds which have been spent outside of its purposes' (Black 1992: 154). Thus, WDM, unlike its charitable predecessors, became an independent limited company. By keeping emergency relief and on-the-ground development projects out of its remit, and purposefully avoiding charitable status, WDM was one of the best-placed British HADOs for engaging in overt campaigning for global economic justice. Its first manifesto of 1972 stated that its aims were to 'recognise the need for a determined and vigorous programme to establish international economic justice' (MacDonald 1972: 4), with debt cancellation featuring heavily on its agenda.

One of WDM's most significant campaigning events of the 1980s was its twenty-thousand-strong mass lobby of Parliament in 1985, which called on Members of Parliament (MPs) to demand improvements on trade and food debts. Although the founder charitable organizations themselves were constrained by Charity Commission regulations, the supporters of Oxfam, Christian Aid, CAFOD and War on Want attended in droves. Even so, due to the complexity of the issues it sought to address, WDM was unable to mobilize the public as much as it had hoped. As Black states, the launch of WDM:

> was something of an anti-climax. There was no echoing roar as there had been . . . for emergencies. A hundred or so committed development action groups . . . beaver away, trying to disentangle growth rates from commodity agreements, unearth the mysteries of ODAs [Overseas

> Development Agencies] and GATT, unhook multilaterals from inter-governmentals, and work out where the poor fitted in . . . But for all the achievements of the emerging development lobby, no-one could pretend that [it] . . . evoked in the public mind the passionate concern that a Biafran child could conjure. (1992: 159)

Consequently, the large demonstration of 1985 was a one-off, not only for WDM, but also for the HADO sector at large, with such publicly visible demonstrations disappearing from public view until the late 1990s, when J2000 emerged.

The less-well-known forerunner to Jubilee, the Debt Crisis Network, was led by the New Economics Foundation, Christian Aid and the WDM. This was engaged in intense lobbying for debt cancellation, and a Britain-wide 'road show' that featured talks from African leaders on effects of heavy debt burdens. HADOs were critical of the modest improvements in debt relief that were made under the HIPC, and the lack of progress motivated them to engage in a campaign to give debt a higher public profile. In April 1996, the Debt Crisis Network began taking the Jubilee campaign forward, with some tentative support from CAFOD and Tearfund. The J2000 campaign was officially launched later in 1996, supported by Christian Aid, CAFOD, Tearfund, Oxfam and WDM. In October 1997, it became a coalition (J2000 1999: 8), with over seventy supporting non-governmental organizations (NGOs), including HADOs, trade unions, women's organizations, the Green Party and faith-based organizations (Peters 2000). The prominence of the latter cannot be understated. Jubilee's 'guiding principles were grounded in Judaic and Christian biblical ethics on human rights, opposition to usury, and the need for periodic correction to imbalances—the Sabbath and Jubilee principles' (Pettifor 2001: 48). In line with such principles, the initial priority of J2000 was to ensure that unpayable debts were written off by 31 December 1999 and other debts were reduced to levels allowing sustainable human, environmental and economic development (Pettifor 1998: 121).

One important factor in the emergence of J2000 was finance. Concerned that HADOs lacked direction and leadership, a philanthropic millionaire named Ian Marks funded the Debt Crisis Network and the initial work of J2000. But effective leadership was also important. Ed Mayo, who previously worked on debt exposition at WDM, and Ann Pettifor, ex-advocacy worker for the mayor of London, were key initiators of J2000. Pettifor, in particular, worked hard to present the complex debt issue in an easily comprehensible form to a public audience, spending almost four years addressing meetings across the country—from town halls to churches and community centres—at first addressing meagre audiences, but eventually large crowds. The concept of 'pre-cut-off point' debt was driven home, resulting in thousands of campaigners writing to complain to the British Treasury about its misleading claims to have cancelled 100 per cent of unpayable debt. Nearly seven hundred thousand postcards, letters and emails on the issue of debt were estimated to have been sent (J2000 2000: 23), resulting in the treasury hiring two additional workers just to handle the additional mail. Apart from the sheer numbers, what made particular impact was the knowledge and commitment of anti-debt campaigners that could clearly not be classified as 'the usual suspects' of political activism (Mayo 2005: 148). Ordinary citizens sent handwritten letters or telephoned their MPs and government departments with informed opinions and questions, utilizing the very successful collection and dissemination of information that J2000 had generated.

It was the coalition's accessible information dissemination and critique of the G8, IMF and World Bank as contributors to the debt problem (for example, the IMF expected to receive at least $600 million more from Africa in 1998 than it gave it in 1997) that assimilated the HADO sector into the developing global justice movement, which critiques international financial institutions (IFIs), the agenda of neoliberalism and lack of democracy in global governance. Indeed, in 1998, the participants in J2000's symbolic human chain action, timed to coincide with a G8 meeting in Birmingham, came from a range of NGOs and radical activist networks that have since been considered to be part of the broader global justice or, as it is more commonly known, the anti-globalization movement (Rootes and Saunders 2007).

Over seventy thousand people from all walks of life participated in the symbolic human chain, from bishops to radical environmental protesters. The action was designed to raise the profile of the debt issue in the Birmingham G8 discussions (Anheir, Glasius and Kaldor 2001: 331). The preceding People's Summit—a series of talks and workshops to spread awareness of the role of the G8 in relation to debt issues—took place in a church with a capacity to hold 800, but the participants soon spilled out into surrounding areas, clamouring to hear the speakers (Pettifor 1998: 116).

The human chain demonstration was immediately followed by a street party organized by a small group of radical activists with some help from London Reclaim the Streets, the network that had previously organized road blockades for street parties in protest against capitalism and car culture. To the dismay of most attendees, several partygoers helped themselves to fruit and vegetables from a market stall and began firing them at police, who were provoked into shutting down the party, causing it to have a much less happy and considerably earlier ending than planned (Trapese 2005).

Some of the organizers of the J2000 human chain action were disheartened by what they considered an apparent lack of cooperation with the street party organizers, regarding them as being in direct competition for supporters and expressing concern that the street party would ruin the integrity of their action. According to the street party organizers, J2000 had pressured at least one of the bands due to play to pull out. Although a minority of J2000 staff realized the street party organizers shared the same politics (some even attended the party), most believed the police warning that partygoers were intent on sabotaging the human chain action. Despite the conscious effort of street party organizers to choose a time and location that would not disrupt it, as well as encouraging people to participate in it (Trapese 2005), anyone publicizing the street party during the J2000 action was asked to leave. Even though J2000 had a fairly radical outlook on debt, it was still careful not to jeopardize its reputation with the public and decision-makers—preferring some engagement with the secretary of state for International Development (see next section) and eschewing potentially violent actions.

There was not only conflict between J2000 and its more radical counterparts, but also between J2000 and other HADOs. This included Oxfam and Christian Aid, which both initially considered J2000 to be too radical. Just five years before the human chain demonstration, Burnell (1993) had warned that, as a result of loosely escaping sanctions in the aftermath of being investigated by the Charity Commission, politically minded charities would likely 'be more cautious, at least for the time being' (Burnell 1993: 78). He had also noticed that Oxfam had begun to focus on less contentious issues, and was more frequently consulting the Commissioners in advance. At the end of the 1990s, with charity laws only recently relaxed, Oxfam remained in the habit of working closely with the government. According to Pettifor,[2] Oxfam thought J2000 was:

> Too left wing, too radical and anti-Blair . . . And we had a huge demonstration in Birmingham and they told their staff that anybody who participated in our demonstration would be sacked.

Christian Aid was also initially sceptical, urging J2000 to cancel the action because of conflicts with its own fundraising strategy. Christian Aid also questioned J2000's mobilization strategy, believing that its enlistment of evangelical organizations (Tearfund and Traidcraft) was purposefully designed to out-compete Christian Aid. Nonetheless, eventually, both Oxfam and Christian Aid joined J2000, realizing that the almost entirely peaceful action in Birmingham (excluding the street party) was a missed opportunity to get on board a hugely popular campaign.

J2000 did much more than organize a street demonstration and encourage people to write to government ministers and MPs. Its most significant achievement was its capacity for international networking, reflected in the huge success of its international petition, which asked world leaders to cancel the unpayable debts of poor countries. Between 1998 and 2000, the petition was signed by over twenty-four million people from 166 countries and entered the *Guinness World Records 2001* as the largest known petition (J2000 2000: 17).

THE NEW MILLENNIUM

At the turn of the millennium, J2000 ceased to exist. Realizing that there was still much work to do, some of its key campaigners set up a successor organization, JDC. Although it has a significantly smaller budget and different staff, JDC continues to avidly campaign against debt, and attends protests at G8 summits, including at Prague in 2000, where it raised its concerns about the IMF's relaxed conditions on its debt scheme (Ford and Poolos 2000), and Gleneagles in 2005, where it sought firmer commitments to Millennium Development Goals (MDGs). Furthermore, it seeks to influence British policy. Ann Pettifor and Ed Mayo continued work on the debt issue at the New Economics Foundation (NEF). From there they monitored the IMF to ensure that it would deliver on its promises, and then filtered their research work into a new organization called Jubilee Research, which, now under the auspices of NEF, continues to produce cutting-edge research on the debt issue, even though its founder members now campaign on other related issues.

In 2002, the main HADOs (including Oxfam and Christian Aid) launched a new campaign coalition called the Trade Justice Movement (TJM), which called 'for fundamental change to unjust rules and institutions governing international trade, so that trade is made to work for all'.[3] The TJM was formed as a result of inter-organizational discussions about how best to influence the British government's stance during and after the Doha Round of trade negotiations. However, key members of J2000 regarded TJM to be an attempt by established HADOs to take the reins back into their own hands, by returning the focus to trade—an issue they had sought to promote before J2000 stole the show.

But TJM certainly did not signal the death knell for debt campaigns. The Make Poverty History (MPH) coalition was a more recent attempt to campaign for, 'in nine words: trade justice, drop the debt, [and] more and better aid' (Make Poverty History 2005a). Gorringe and Rosie (2006: 11.1) note MPH's similarity to J2000, calling it 'the closest echo of J2000'. At its peak it consisted of over five hundred British NGOs, including JDC and a host of other charities, campaigns, trade unions, faith groups and celebrities. As the British branch of the Global Coalition Against Poverty (GCAP), the coalition believed that 2005 provided an unprecedented opportunity for tackling trade, aid and debt issues given that, among other things, Britain hosted the G8 summit (at which poverty in Africa was a key theme) and held the chair of the European Union. The pinnacle of its existence was the 225,000-strong protest march in Edinburgh, timed to coincide with the commencement of the G8 summit at nearby Gleneagles. Formally existing only throughout 2005, MPH is now only a nominal entity. The fact that MPH had constrained itself to campaigning for a little longer than one year reduced its ability to impact upon the public and decision-makers so much as J2000, even though Jubilee itself could have been even more effective should it have had longevity.

Thus, it is not surprising that both J2000 and MPH have been criticized for having 'expiry dates'. According to Susan George, the short expiry dates meant that the momentum of popular mobilization and the pressure on world leaders that the J2000 had generated was tragically deflated (George 2004). But there are also advantages to having a short life span. It gave both campaigns a highly motivating dynamic, and prevented them from becoming obsessed with organizational maintenance—long-term advertising and paying staff and taxes, and so on, can become demanding and, in the longer term, work against the overall aims of coalitions.

Since MPH in 2005, debt campaigning has once again taken a lower profile in Britain. The Your Voice Against Poverty Coalition, which organized a solidarity anti-G8 action to coincide with the July G8 meeting in Germany in 2007, attracted only a few thousand protesters. The Put People First demonstration, conterminous with the G20 meeting in London in April 2009, did not explicitly have debt on its agenda. However, although large-scale demonstrations appear to have fallen back into the ether, campaigners are still working behind the scenes and via their websites to influence British and international policies on debt, with, as we shall see, some degree of success. Electronic-based campaigns, like JDC's Pick Up the Pace campaign, which encouraged its website visitors to send an email to the international development secretary, are becoming increasingly common. The ready-to-send email recognized that only 20 per cent of poor country debts had been 'dropped' since the Jubilee campaign started, and asked that Britain provide multilateral relief to all poor countries, that all unpayable debt be dropped and that Britain should also persuade other countries to do the same. Similarly, the Stop the Vulture Culture campaign, which drew on Oxfam's earlier Clipping the Vulture's Wings campaign, involved JDC supporters emailing MPs *en masse* in an attempt to ensure that British legislation prevents vulture funding. HADOs have responded in-depth to a consultation on this.

Despite peaks and troughs in visible protest, the key British HADOs that campaign on debt continue to have high levels of public support. Christian Aid has 87,500 members; Oxfam has 650,000; WDM has 12,500; War on Want has 5,500; and CAFOD has 70,000. Collective memberships (or organizational affiliations) are also large. Christian Aid has over twenty thousand churches affiliated to it; WDM has seventy-eight supporter organizations; War on Want has 303; and MPH had, at its peak, around five hundred. In addition to formally subscribed members, each organization has voluntary supporters, ranging from around ten for War on Want and WDM, through to thousands of local volunteers that work as part of the JDC's network of 120 local groups. Christian Aid has approximately thirty thousand active supporters. This suggests that British anti-debt organizations have considerable resources at their disposal, and this is reflected also in their relatively large budgets. Estimated annual budgets range from £147 million (CAFOD) and £138 million (WDM), down to £800,000 for MPH and £200,000 for JDC. However, campaign coalitions like JDC and MPH are funded by key membership organizations in addition to their background budgets (Saunders 2006).

A survey of MPH demonstrators (Rootes and Saunders 2007) found that of the key HADOs discussed in the preceding, Christian Aid and Oxfam were the most frequently listed organizations in response to a question asking participants to list the top five most important organizations of which they were a member (one hundred listed Christian Aid, and ninety-three listed Oxfam). Others were listed considerably less frequently: WDM (forty times), MPH (sixteen, despite it not being a 'proper' organization with membership), CAFOD (fifteen) and War on Want (just six). War on Want has never recovered from financial mismanagement at the end of the 1990s, and its downfall may have been exacerbated by the decline in socialism in Britain (Burnell 1993: 68). Interestingly, the reconstituted version of J2000/JDC has clearly fallen from prominence, having been listed by only seventeen respondents. Indeed, 54.8 per cent of respondents claimed to have *never* had any contact with JDC, under one-fifth had collaborated in a campaign with JDC, just 15.1 per cent had received some of JDC's campaign information and only 7 per cent were members. Other prominent organizations (listed at least twenty times) were Amnesty International (123), Greenpeace (sixty-three), Friends of the Earth (FoE, fifty-seven), Tearfund (thirty-seven), Traidcraft (thirty-six) and Campaign for Nuclear Disarmament (CND, twenty-two). This can be viewed as an expression of the diversity of the MPH coalition, stretching the coalition boundaries further than J2000 had done.

BRITISH POLICY RESPONSES TO ANTI-DEBT CAMPAIGNS

Only fifteen years ago, politicians and officials routinely dismissed debt cancellation as impossible, unnecessary or undesirable. Now, in 2009, politicians in countries around the world have worked together to provide significant, even if not totally adequate, amounts of bi- and multilateral debt relief. What brought about this change? Mike Foster, Parliamentary Under Secretary for State and International Development recently claimed that 'the contribution of campaigners and the general public has been instrumental in this success' (Foster 2009).[4] But, of course, given the international scope of the campaign, it is difficult to tell whether it was this, or pressure from other countries, that wrought the change in British policy. In this section, we chart the development of British policy in this area, noting how it has interacted with campaigns. It will be shown that, although giant steps have been made in cancelling debt, there is, according to HADOs, still a long way to go.

The initial stance of Margaret Thatcher, (British Prime Minister 1979–1990), also demonstrates how much progress has been made. To date, around U.S.$100 billion of debt relief has been granted under the HIPC and MDRI, and pledges have been made to increase international aid to 0.7 per cent of annual gross domestic product (GDP). In contrast, during the Thatcher administration Britain's aid budget fell from 0.59 per cent in 1979 to 0.23 per cent in 1997. Adrian Hewitt,[5] founder of, and research advisor to, the United Kingdom (UK) Parliamentary All-Party Group on Overseas

Development (APGOOD), with extensive knowledge of Westminster policy-making circles, discusses the stance of the Conservative governments toward international development in the following terms:

> NGOs . . . in those days weren't so important, weren't consulted about policy-making . . . in the 1980s, certainly under Thatcher who didn't want to listen anyway to them . . . they just weren't big enough. Certainly in the early Thatcher period, she really wasn't keen on aid spending and development wasn't a very important subject in Britain.

As discussed previously, the international debt crisis of the 1980s had set in motion various attempts by the IFIs and the major creditor countries to 'deal' with the problem. Within that process, the position of the Conservative governments moved from proposals to lower interest rates on rescheduled loans (late 1980s), to cancellation of half of the debt owed to creditor countries by the lowest income countries (while rescheduling the rest), to a two-thirds remission, which was finally agreed at the 1994 G7 summit in Naples. However, in practice, this level of reduction was only applied to a small proportion of poor countries' debts, which, in addition, had to meet stringent SAP conditions to get debt relief and were not exempt from any repayments to the IMF or World Bank (Jubilee USA 2009).

The launch of the J2000 coincided with the 1997 landslide electoral victory of the Labour Party, led by Tony Blair. Within months of coming into office, the first Labour government, true to its manifesto pledge, established a new Department for International Development (DFID), headed by Clare Short, who was driven to make DFID a success. Later that year the first White Paper on International Development, *Eliminating World Poverty: A Challenge for the 21st Century*, was published (DFID 1997). For the first time, a British policy paper stressed the need to relieve poor countries of unsustainable debts, and J2000 was commended for raising the issue. However, to the dismay of campaigners, the paper stressed that countries in receipt of debt should meet 'international development targets [by] following sound economic policies which benefit the poor, and which promote responsive and accountable government, encourage transparency and bear down on corruption' (DFID 1997: 72). It endorsed SAPs and omitted to mention harmful conditionalities.

In his speech to the Commonwealth Finance Ministers meeting in September 1997, Gordon Brown, then Chancellor of the Exchequer, reiterated the Labour Party's Manifesto promise to support further measures to reduce the debt burden borne by the world's poorest countries. He determined that HIPC eligible countries 'should at least have embarked on the process of securing a sustainable exit from their debt problems by the year 2000' (Brown 1997), by which time the extent and terms of debt relief envisaged for at least three-quarters of these countries should also be cleared. Although the need for joint international action was stressed, including reforms of HIPC that would expand and accelerate the process of debt relief, Britain also announced unilateral actions, such as the provision of technical assistance and the targeting of export credits at productive expenditure. Despite reforms, today HADOs remain critical of the HIPC.

1998 saw Gordon Brown allegedly taking the international lead on the debt, pushing for progress on the HIPC. However, there was not a single mention of debt in the conclusions of the Finance Ministers produced ahead of the Birmingham G8 summit (University of Toronto G8 Information Centre 1998). Subsequently, tensions between the government and the campaign arose. The government, citing security concerns, unsuccessfully sought to persuade J2000 to cancel the mobilization. Because this failed, they decided that leaders would meet outside the city, in an attempt to diffuse the protest. The high profile of the human chain action, however, forced a U-turn. Remarkably, Blair made hasty arrangements to leave the summit to meet with campaign leaders and, literally at the last minute, the issue of debt was given a higher profile. Blair was not the only politician to engage with campaigners. Short, leader of DFID, was one of the keynote speakers at the People's Summit in Birmingham in 1998, and maintained a close relationship with campaigners throughout the Jubilee campaign. However, her willingness to cooperate should not be read as evidence of convergence of interests between campaigners and Labour politicians. As Short herself states in her autobiography:

> The campaigners were calling for unconditional cancellation of debt and pointing out that it had often been incurred by previous regimes and should not obstruct reforming governments. But we in DFID were clear that if debt were cancelled unconditionally, it was likely that the old problems would recur, and new debt would stack up and the problem would come round time and time again. (Short 2005: 82)

Whereas J2000 wanted conditionalities scrapped, DFID remained committed to Poverty Reduction Strategies—SAPs in all but name. As Short (2005: 82) puts it in her memoir, 'we decided to support the campaigners but tried to ensure that more generous debt relief should generate serious economic reform and a focus on poverty reduction'.

The Birmingham G8 summit marked a turning point in the attitude of major creditors and gave the campaign new strength in stepping up its critique of HIPC and proposing alternative solutions (Collins, Gariyo and Burdon 2001: 138). Until that point, and certainly before the 1996 Lyon summit where the HIPC Initiative was launched, development issues used to be very low on the agenda at G7 summits. This has been considerably altered since. As Gordon Brown later acknowledged, J2000:

> forced Third World debt on to the agenda. It was your determination and commitment and vision that forced the G8 to respond, for a simple

> conviction that the burden of unpayable debt on the poorest of the world is simply morally wrong. (Collins, Gariyo and Burdon 2001: 138)

He also made a special mention to the impact of the three hundred thousand postcards received by the Treasury from anti-debt campaigners and concluded by saying that popular pressure is absolutely necessary for anything to be done.

By April 1999, every G7 government had announced its own proposals for debt relief, and Canada had committed itself to cancelling 100 per cent of bilateral debt. At the G8 summit, the Cologne Debt Initiative was launched, almost doubling the amount of pledged debt cancellation to U.S.$100 billion as part of the Enhanced HIPC. The language of the initiative and subsequent official statements was markedly influenced by the discourse put forward by J2000. It acknowledged that 'recent experience suggests that further efforts are needed to achieve a more enduring solution to the problem of unsustainable debt burdens' and was full of references to 'faster, deeper, and broader debt relief', 'the threshold of a new millennium', and the need for 'poverty reduction plans for the effective targeting of savings derived from debt relief' developed through 'consultation with civil society' (Collins, Gariyo and Burdon 2001: 140; University of Toronto G8 Information Centre 1999). The announcement was welcomed by J2000 although the conditionalities and limited scope of the initiative were criticized. After the summit, Blair mentioned at the House of Commons that the debt initiative was the most important achievement of the summit. It is interesting to note how the position of the British government had shifted from a full endorsement of the first HIPC Initiative to calls for substantial extension of the scheme, becoming increasingly congruent with the stance of campaigners. At the IMF-World Bank annual meeting in September, U.S. President Bill Clinton announced that the United States would cancel 100 per cent of bilateral debt, for HIPC-completed countries. Britain soon followed suit, adding in total a further U.S.$11 billion of debt relief (J2000 2000: 8).

The second DFID White Paper on International Development *Eliminating World Poverty: Making Globalisation Work for the Poor* (2000), restates the British position as a world leader on debt relief. It explicitly acknowledges J2000's impact on the agreement for the 1999 Enhanced HIPC and the G7 pledge of U.S.$100 billion debt relief. The government claims to have 'pressed strongly for the process to be accelerated [with] greater flexibility . . . in assessing countries' eligibility for debt relief' (DFID 2000: 90). It emphasizes the importance of 'nationally owned' or 'country-led' Poverty Reduction Strategies (PRS), that move away from 'over prescriptive aid conditionality', which, DFID claims 'has a poor track record in persuading governments to reform their policies' (2000: 91–92). This is hardly an explicit condemnation of conditionalities, but talk of 'an enormous conceptual shift from the structural adjustment of the 1980s and early 1990s' (DFID 2000: 92) shows that some progress has been made since the 1997 White Paper.

As promised in the White Paper, the International Development Act, which replaced the first Thatcher government's Overseas Development and Co-operation Act of 1980, was passed in parliament in 2002 (UK Parliament 2002). It states that the overarching aim of development assistance of financial, technical, material or any other nature is poverty reduction and the improvement of the welfare of the population. And in September 2002, the Treasury pledged a further U.S.$95 million of debt remission, plus its U.S.$30 million share of European Commission money, becoming the second largest (after the United States) bilateral contributor to the HIPC Trust Fund, having also contributed U.S.$43 million to assist the IMF with its costs of delivering HIPC debt relief (Select Committee on International Development 2003).

By May 2003, HADOs acknowledged that despite some progress, many promises on debt relief had not been kept. Four years after the Cologne summit, just a third of pledged debt relief had actually been cancelled (U.S.$36.3 billion). The challenge for campaigners was to keep the issue alive against false government claims that debt had been 100 per cent relieved. Despite much government rhetoric, Blair was remarkably candid about it. His 2003 statement to campaigners chimed a number of chords in tune with HADO framing of the issue:

> this is simply not enough; there is much more that has to be done and still needs to be done. We remain committed to additional debt relief and the international community has pledged to do more. To ensure that debt relief provides a sustainable exit from the burden of unpayable debt, to find ways to assist countries who . . . have been unable to benefit . . . to minimise the impact of creditor litigation . . . and to secure a change in the rules so that the calculation of any topping-up at completion point excludes any additional voluntary debt relief. (Church Times 2003)

However, HADOs remained critical about his stance on conditionalities. In return for debt relief, developing countries must, Blair stated, demonstrate commitment to poverty reduction, anti-corruption policies, good governance and 'sequenced opening up of markets to global investment and trade' (Curtis 2007). So when he was asked about PRSs, which are used by the World Bank/IMF to impose economic policies, he evaded the question and talked rather vaguely about the progress from the 'rightly criticized [and] discredited' SAPs and the challenge of making PRSs work.

At the Labour Party conference in 2004, the chancellor spoke at a fringe meeting organized by the TJM, where he announced that Britain would pay off money owed by thirty-two of the world's poorest countries to the World Bank and the African Development Bank. The move, worth £100 million a year until 2015, was intended to increase pressure on other G7 countries to follow. Although he stressed the limitations of unilateral action, with regard to multilateral debt, he claimed that:

> too many countries are still being forced to choose between servicing their debts and making the investments in health, education and infrastructure that would allow them to achieve the millennium development goals and so we must do more. (Hall 2004)

Under the proposal, fourteen countries that had qualified for debt relief under HIPC and eighteen low-income countries that are not part of the scheme would be entitled to financial help from Britain. JDC described the announcement as an 'audacious move' and highly praised Brown's leadership (Hall 2004). However, WDM's reaction was considerably more measured. Although welcoming the change of policy, it stressed that the amount of money involved was paltry, the aid budget was stagnant and inadequate, conditionalities were still in place and that Britain was simply following the example set by the United States (WDM 2005). The Commission for Africa, set up by Blair to help find appropriate ways of stimulating development in Africa and to use the 2005 UK presidencies of the G8 and European Union as a platform, came to similar conclusions (Commission for Africa 2005), and was equally criticized by HADOs.

By the time of the demonstrations in Edinburgh in 2005, Britain had agreed to cancel its bilateral debt with regard to countries that had completed the HIPC initiative, to stop receiving debt payments from countries at the first stage of HIPC and put payments from countries eligible for HIPC but not yet qualified in a trust, to be returned later (JDC, Action Aid and Christian Aid 2005). Celebrities associated with MPH, who to the annoyance of many campaigners came to dominate media coverage of the MPH campaign, initially hailed the outcome of the G8 summit—the Multilateral Debt Relief Initiative (MDRI)—as a huge campaign success. Yet as a number of British HADOs stressed, although MDRI was welcomed as a significant step forward, particularly for the eighteen countries that had reached completion point under HIPC, thus qualifying for immediate debt cancellation, government spin was projecting the misleading idea that the debt problem had been solved. In reality, its scope was narrow in comparison to MPH demands, the issue of HIPC stringent conditions was not addressed and there was no comprehensive strategy to avoid any future debt crisis. In summary, MDRI was considered to be 'charity not justice' (Nash 2008: 176), failing to deal with structural issues and continuing to be limited in scope. The Debt, AIDS, Trade Africa (DATA) report of 2007 illustrates that there is still a long way to go before the MDRI can be hailed a success (DATA 2007).

However, many commentators have deemed MPH a success to the extent that it encouraged all three major parties to commit to international development in their 2005 general election manifestos. For example, the Conservatives, as part of their action on global poverty, supported the 'principle of 100 per cent cancellation of debts to multilateral institutions' (Conservative Party 2005). In their Manifesto for International Affairs, the Liberal Democrats committed to 100 per cent debt cancellation for the poorest countries and opposed 'inappropriate economic conditions, such as the privatisation of basic services' (Liberal Democrats 2005).

In the beginning of 2006, Gordon Brown admitted that debt relief needed to extend beyond HIPC to include all sixty-seven countries eligible for concessional lending from the World Bank, if they were to meet the MDGs. In an article in *The Guardian* newspaper, he stated:

> if 2005 was the year of commitments, 2006 must be the year of delivery . . . By paying our share of their debt service, we will unilaterally lead debt cancellation for up to another 30 countries, and we will urge others to follow. (Elliot 2007)

But one can only presume that Brown deliberately muddled the facts when he claimed that '100 per cent multilateral debt relief was finally achieved for 19 HIPC—and, despite prior worries, with no extra conditionality' (Elliot 2007).

In June 2006, Blair established a monitoring group, chaired by Kofi Anan, seeking to ensure that the Gleneagles' momentum would be maintained, and in July, under the new Secretary of State for International Development Hilary Benn, the third DFID White Paper on International Development, *Eliminating World Poverty: Making Governance Work for the Poor*, was published. In the foreword, Blair states that the Gleneagles G8 summit 'backed by enormous public support . . . agreed a comprehensive, detailed plan to fight poverty' (DFID 2006: ii). The paper affirms the intentions of the government to deliver the promises made in 2005 to fight poverty, by responding to 'the four big challenges for international development': the promotion of national and global good governance; ensuring security, sustainable growth and universal health and education; tackling climate change; and the improvement of the international development system (DFID 2006: xi). This emphasizes the progress on debt relief since the Gleneagles summit, reiterates the government pledge to push for the full implementation and financing of HIPC and 'work towards 100 per cent multilateral and bilateral debt cancellation for all the poorest countries that are committed to using savings to reduce poverty' (DFID 2006: 14).

In 2007, a year in which Africa was once again highly featured at the G8 summit in Germany and where popular mobilization was rekindled, the British government tried to block a controversial debt relief plan in five of the poorest Latin American countries that is being pushed by the Inter-American Development Bank. The government opposed this because of the economic conditions that would be applied. It is debatable whether this apparent commitment to decouple economic development programmes from debt relief would have happened in the absence of anti-debt mobilizations.

Yet the government response still falls short of HADOs' demands, particularly in relation to understanding resistance to debt relief, which is usually resistance to *conditionalities* rather than debt relief per se, and in relation to odious debts. For example, in response to the electronic Pick up the Pace campaign, Mike Foster, Parliamentary Under Secretary of State for International Development, wrote a blanket reply in which he makes it clear that the British government believes that broader debt relief will prevent funds being allocated to the poorest countries, that many countries 'do not want to receive debt relief', and that the British government does not consider any debt owed to us to be 'illegitimate' or 'unjust' (Foster 2009).

More recently, progress on removal of conditionalities and on recognition and cancellation of 'odious' debts has continued to be slow. But other campaigns have successfully influenced British policy. JDC's Stop the Vulture Campaign, for example, resulted in over 150 MPs signing an early day motion in parliament, which called for the government to make the use of British courts to recognize vulture funds as illegal (Lewis 2007). This campaign has recently (in July 2009) led the government to release draft legislation and a public consultation in an attempt to prevent vulture funding.

CONCLUSION

Popular mobilization for the cancellation of unpayable debts has a relatively long history. A number of British HADOs started working on this issue in the early 1980s, when the first major debt crisis emerged. Up to the mid-1990s, HADOs and faith-based organizations increasingly documented and analysed the impact of the debt burden on poor countries, as well as the negative effects of SAPs and conditionalities that went hand in hand with any new loans or debt relief schemes (such as the HIPC Initiative).

Although the British HADO sector was slow to engage in mass mobilizations, freedom from charity constraints, the success of previous coalitions and the consolidation of the Disasters Emergency Committee helped give it more leverage to engage in such activities. This facilitated organizational participation in J2000 and more recently in MPH. These two relatively large campaigning coalitions certainly helped to raise the profile of the debt issue by demonstrating overwhelming public support for debt cancellation, commonly encapsulated by the slogan 'Drop the Debt'. Although there has been some competition for ownership of issues among British HADOs, and a new fair trade agenda has emerged, debt still remains a cornerstone.

Without a doubt, progress on debt relief worldwide has been significant; U.S.$88 billion of debt has been cancelled for twenty-five countries between 1998 and 2008. During that time, the British Labour government has been at the forefront of the issue, and British HADOs have been very adept in accepting and commending improvements while simultaneously expanding their demands for creditors to go further. But it has also been extremely slow and is still far from amounting to a comprehensive and lasting solution to the debt problem of poor countries. Critics continue to stress that debts that have been written off were largely impossible to be repaid anyway, and that the process has enabled global financial institutions to put in place a framework of neoliberal policies that perpetuate a non-level playing field between rich and poor countries.

We have provided a narrative of campaigns against debt and of policy responses. It has, however, been difficult to determine the extent to which policy responses amount to rhetoric over action, and also whether policy responses are a direct response to campaigns when other factors might have played a role. For example, on bilateral debt relief, it could be argued that Britain was simply following the example set by the United States, rather than responding to campaigners. Therefore, it is impossible to effectively determine whether the campaigns have been the critical factor in some of the policy changes. Establishing a direct causal effect between campaigning and policy is notoriously difficult, and the issue of debt is no exception. However, we hope to have demonstrated that at least one thing is certain: the debt issue would most certainly not have such high resonance with policymakers and the public alike were it not for campaigns such as J2000 and MPH. As Hilary Benn, then Secretary of State for International Development, said in 2005 (cited in Happold 2005):

> What moved the world from where it was to where it is today [on debt]? The answer is it was people lobbying, campaigning, holding hands around Birmingham and other cities in the world, combined with politicians who got the message, heard and acted. And what seemed utterly impossible one minute becomes possible the next.

NOTES

1. Edwards, head of Campaigns and Policy at JDC, interview, 15 August 2008.
2. Pettifor, interview, 12 March 2007.
3. Please see the TJM website at http://www.tjm.org.uk.
4. Certainly the public are now very favourable toward debt relief for poor countries. An opinion poll in 2000, as J2000 was reaching its climax, found that over two-thirds of the British public supported the campaign's goals (Jubilee 2000 Coalition 2000: 3). In the months leading up to the Gleneagles G8 summit, a MPH commissioned YouGov survey found that 75 per cent of those asked agreed ('strongly' or 'tend to') that 'rich countries and institutions should cancel the unpayable debts of the poorest countries' (Make Poverty History 2005).
5. Hewitt, interview, 3 July 2007; see also Hewitt (2001).

BIBLIOGRAPHY

Anheir, Helmut, Glasius, Marlies, and Kaldor, Mary. (2001).'Introducing Global Civil Society', in H. Anheir, M. Glasius and M. Kaldor (eds), *Global Civil Society 2001*, Oxford: Oxford University Press.

Black, Maggie. (1992). *A Cause for Our Times: Oxfam the First 50 Years*, Oxford: Oxfam and Oxford University Press.

Brown, Gordon. (1997). The Rt Hon Gordon Brown MP Statement to Commonwealth Finance Ministers Meeting: Mauritius—'DEBT 2000: The Mauritius Mandate'. http://www.hm-treasury.gov.uk/speech_chex_160997.htm (accessed 4 May 2011).

Bryant, Coralie, and Lindenberg, Marc. (2001). 'Responding to Globalization', in M. Lindenberg and C. Bryant (eds), *Going Global: Transforming Relief and Development NGOs*, Bloomfield, CT: Kumarian Press.

Burnell, Peter. (1993). 'Debate: Third World Charities in Britain towards 2000', *Community Development Journal*, 28 (1): 66–81.

Church Times. (2003). *Keep Your Word on Debt, Says Sentamu'.* http://www.churchtimes.co.uk/content.asp?id=20535&print=1 (accessed 4 May 2011).

Collins, Carole J.L., Gariyo, Zie, and Burdon, Tony. (2001). 'Jubilee 2000: Citizen Action across the North-South Divide', in Michael Edwards and John Gaventa (eds), *Global Citizen Action*, London: Earthscan.

Commission for Africa. (2005). *Our Common Interest: Report of the Commission for Africa*, London: Penguin Books.

Conservative Party. (2005). *Are You Thinking What We're Thinking? It's Time for Action.* Conservative Election Manifesto 2005. http://news.bbc.co.uk/2/shared/bsp/hi/pdfs/11_04_05_conservative_manifesto.pdf(accessed 4 May 2011).

Curtis, Mark. (2007). *Britain and Africa: The Aid Dividend.* http://markcurtis.wordpress.com/2007/01/10/britain-and-africa-the-aid-dividend (accessed 4 May 2011).

Debt, AIDS, Trade, Africa. (2007). *DATA Report 2007.* http://data/d202.org/issues/debt.htm (accessed 4 May 2011).

Elliot, Larry. (2007). 'Britain Seeks Better Debt Relief Deal for Latin America's Poorest', *Guardian*, 19 March.

Ford, Peter, and Poolos, Alexandra. (2000). 'Protesters Speed up Debt Relief', *Christian Science Monitor*, 92:215.

Foster, Mike. (2009). *Response on Jubilee Debt 'Pick up the Pace Campaign'.* Open letter to those who participated in the campaign. http://webarchive.nationalarchives.gov.uk/+/http://www.dfid.gov.uk/Getting-Involved/Campaigns/Campaign-Responses/Response-on-Jubilee-Debt-Pick-Up-the-Pace-Campaign (accessed 4 May 2011).

George, Susan. (2004). *Taking the Movement Forward.* http://www.tni.org/es/archives/act/1457 (accessed 21 April 2011).

Gorringe, Hugo, and Rosie, Michael. (2006). 'Pants to Poverty? Making Poverty History, Edinburgh 2005', *Sociological Research Online*, 11 (1) http://www.socresonline.org.uk/11/1/gorringe.html.

Hall, Sarah. (2004). 'Chancellor Puts the Economy to the Fore: Brown Offers Debt Relief to World's Poorest Nations', *Guardian*, 27 September. http://www.guardian.co.uk/politics/2004/sep/27/uk.labourconference4/print (accessed 4 May 2011).

Happold, Tom. (2005). 'Things Can Change, Things Do Change', *Guardian*, 18 January.

Hewitt, Adrian. (2001). 'Beyond Poverty? The New UK Policy on International Development and Globalisation', *Third World Quarterly*, 22 (2): 291–296.

JDC, Action Aid and Christian Aid. (2005) *In the Balance: Why Debts Must Be Cancelled Now to Meet the Millennium Development Goals.* Joint NGO Briefing Paper. http://www.jubileedebtcampaign.org.uk/In per cent20the per cent20balance+659.twl (accessed 4 May 2011).

Jubilee 2000 Coalition. (1999). *Breaking the Chains: The New Jubilee 2000 Debt Cutter's Handbook*, London: Jubilee 2000 Coalition.

———. (2000). *The World Will Never Be the Same Again*, London: Jubilee 2000 Coalition.

Jubilee Debt Campaign. (2008). *Unfinished Business: Ten Years of Dropping the Debt*, London: JDC. http://www.jubileedebtcampaign.org.uk/Unfinished%20business%3A%2010%20years%20of%20drop%20the%20debt+4362.twl (accessed 30 April 2011).

Jubilee USA. (2009). *Too Little, Too Late: Political Responses to the Debt Crisis.* http://www.jubileeusa.org/resources/debt-resources/beginners-guide-to-debt/too-little-too-late.html (accessed 4 May 2011).

Lewis, James. (2007). 'How Top London Law Firms Help Vulture Funds Devour Their Prey', *Guardian*, 17 October.

Liberal Democrats. (2005). *The Real Alternative*, Manifesto Text. http://news.bbc.co.uk/2/shared/bsp/hi/pdfs/LIBDEM_uk_manifesto.pdf (accessed 30 April 2011).

Macdonald, Stephen. (1972). *Action for World Development: The World Development Movement in the 1970s*, London: World Development Movement.

Make Poverty History. (2005). 'Voters Demand More Action on World Poverty', Press Release. http://www.makepovertyhistory.org/docs/votersDemandAction.doc (accessed 4 July 2008).

———. (2007) Website. http://www.makepovertyhistory.org/takeaction (accessed 4 May 2011).

Mandel, Steve. (2006. *Odious Lending: Debt Relief as If Morality Mattered*, London: New Economics Foundation.

Mayo, Marjorie. (2005. 'The World Will Never Be the Same Again? Reflecting on the Experiences of Jubilee 2000, Mobilizing Globally for the Remission of Unpayable Debts', *Social Movement Studies*, 4 (2): 139–154.

Nash, Kate. (2008). 'Global Citizenship as Show Business: The Cultural Politics of Make Poverty History', *Media, Culture and Society*, 30 (2): 167–181.

Peters, Bill. (2000). 'Jubilee 2000', *Journal of Modern African Studies*, 32 (4): 699–700.

Pettifor, Ann. (1998). *A Personal View of the Jubilee 2000 'Human Chain' Demonstration on 16 May 1998, during the G8 Summit in Birmingham.* http://www.jubileedebtcampaign.org.uk/?lid=280 (accessed 12 February 2005).

———. (2001). 'Debt', in E. Bircham and J. Charlton (eds), *Anti-Capitalism: A Guide to the Movement*, London: Bookmarks.

Rootes, Christopher, and Saunders, Clare. (2007). 'The Global Justice Movement in Britain', in D. della Porta (ed), *The Global Justice Movement: Cross-National and Transnational Perspectives*, Boulder, CO: Paradigm Press.

Saunders, Clare. (2006). 'Democratic Practices in British Global Justice Movement Organizations', in D. della Porta and L. Mosca (eds), *Organizational Networks: Organizational Structures and Practices of Democracy in the Global Justice Movement.* WP4 Report for Democracy in Europe and the Mobilization of Society, a project funded by the European Commission, Contract n. CIT2–CT2004–506026, and (for the Swiss case) by the Swiss Federal Office for Education and Science, Contract no. 03.0482.

———. (2009). 'British Humanitarian, Aid and Development NGOs (1949–Present)', in Matthew Hilton, Nicholas Crowson and James McKay (eds), *NGOs in*

Contemporary Britain: Non-State Actors in Society and Politics since 1945, Basingstoke: Palgrave Macmillan.

Select Committee on International Development. (2003). *Memorandum Submitted by the Department for International Development.* http://www.publications.parliament.uk/pa/cm200203/cmselect/cmintdev/256/2110502.htm. (accessed 4 May 2011)

Short, Clare. (2005). *An Honourable Deception? New Labour, Iraq, and the Misuse of Power*, London: Free Press.

Trapese. (2005). Website. http://trapese.clearerchannel.org/ (accessed 4 May 2011).

UK Department for International Development. (1997). *Eliminating World Poverty: A Challenge for the 21st Century, White Paper on International Development.* http://www.dfid.gov.uk/pubs/files/whitepaper1997.pdf (accessed 4 May 2011).

———. (2000). *Eliminating World Poverty: Making Globalisation Work for the Poor, White Paper on International Development.* http://www.dfid.gov.uk/pubs/files/whitepaper2000.pdf (accessed 4 May 2011).

———. (2006). *Eliminating World Poverty: Making Governance Work for the Poor, White Paper on International Development.* http://www.dfid.gov.uk/pubs/files/whitepaper2006/wp2006foreword-preface-section1.pdf (accessed 4 May 2011).

UK Parliament. (2002). *International Development Act 2002*, Office of Public Sector Information. http://www.opsi.gov.uk/acts/acts2002/ukpga_20020001_en.pdf (accessed 4 May 2011).

University of Toronto G8 Information Centre. (1998). *Conclusions of G7 Finance Ministers*, London, 9 May. http://www.g8.utoronto.ca/finance/fm980509.htm (accessed 4 May 2011).

———. (1999). *Compliance with G8 Commitments: From Birmingham 1998 to Köln 1999.* http://www.g7.utoronto.ca/evaluations/1999koln/compliance/debt.htm (accessed 4 May 2011).

World Development Movement. (2005). *Short Measures. Why UK Government Proposals Won't End the Third World Debt Crisis*, Media Briefing, 16 May.

10 The Struggle for Third World Debt Relief in France

Rodrigo Contreras Osorio

INTRODUCTION

The origin of mobilization efforts by French civil society to promote third world debt relief is closely linked to the so-called 'alter-globalization movement', which has often employed confrontational politics in its drive to combat neoliberalism. However, the discourse and nature of these efforts in France and other European countries signal the emergence of a new type of social movement, one that encompasses different forms of mobilization and social organization. In short, this movement marks the advent of a new set of social actors, a new way of formulating and defining demands, a new approach to mobilizing material and intellectual resources and a new advocacy- and negotiation-based relationship with government.

In light of these features of France's debt-forgiveness movement, this chapter examines the potentials and challenges that exist within the movement and how these relate to efforts on the part of the movement's key stakeholders to influence opinion and policy outside the movement. Of particular interest are the types of activities these actors engage in, the intellectual and material resources they bring to bear and the impact they have on French society and government policy.

The discussion is organized in three main sections. First, I examine the origins and development of the debt relief movement in France from the late 1980s to the 2005 decision by leaders of the G8 countries to substantially reduce third world debt. Next, I examine the role of the principal civil society organizations and networks involved in fighting for debt relief. Finally, I explore the relations between these organizations and the public policy process.

THE ORIGINS AND TRAJECTORY OF FRENCH MOBILIZATION EFFORTS

Between 1982 and 1990, the debt crisis provoked a series of social and political mobilizations (particularly in Latin America) that became known throughout the world as 'hunger riots'. These paved the way for international debate on the 'non-payment' of debt owed by highly indebted countries to international lending institutions.

In Europe, the debt issue gained currency in England prior to the 1984 G7 summit in London, a gathering that attracted the interest of heterodox economists and other scholars, as well as civil society organizations, with environmental groups playing the most active role. Responding to the hunger riots in Latin America and to nuclear power issues, this coalition of forces challenged the G7 countries, principally on their relationships with the countries of the South and with the environment (Merckaert 2004). Thus emerged 'The Other Economic Summit' (or TOES), the first major international gathering in which the debt question was a central topic of debate.

In France, a movement advocating debt forgiveness emerged some years later. The G7 summit in Paris, in July 1989, was accompanied by a countersummit organized by groups that mobilized around the debt issue. This countersummit featured meetings, discussion workshops and testimony by people from seven of the world's poorest countries, who had been victimized by the debt. Thus, TOES '89 addressed environmental issues and new economic relationships from two parallel perspectives: disarmament (East–West) and the third world (North–South). The latter issue set the tone for the first Summit of the Seven Poorest Peoples. In denouncing the G7 philosophy itself, TOES began by rejecting two of the cornerstones of the G7. First, the summit defined the poorest, not the richest, as being the most important figures; second, in attempting to understand current realities, it looked to the testimony of non-governmental witnesses of the peoples concerned, rather than to the statements of governments. It thus underlined 'unambiguously the exclusion and neglect to which over two thirds of humanity is relegated' (Mouchard 2003: 35).

Under the slogan 'Dette, apartheid, colonies, *ça suffit comme ça*' ('Debt, apartheid, colonies, enough already!'), the singer Renaud, along with Johnny Clegg and many other artists, organized one of the mobilization's media events: a concert that drew over one hundred thousand people to the Place de la Bastille on 8 July, in addition to the estimated fifteen thousand participating in the march. The goal of gaining forgiveness for the national debt of third world countries served as a mobilizing force for a number of organizations—not only the traditional parties of the left, such as the Communist Party and the Revolutionary Communist League (known by its French acronym LCR), but also some ten other groups and unions, including the Centre d'Études et d'Initiatives de Solidarité Internationale (CEDETIM), the General Confederation of Labour (CGT) and the Syndicat national des enseignements de second degré (SNES).

The unexpected success of the mobilization reflected interest in the debt issue within French society. Two important developments ensued. First, the mobilization led to the creation of the *Ça suffat comme ci*[1] committee, which assumed responsibility for continuing the mobilization after the activities wound down. Second, because of the interest that the mobilization aroused, and the number of non-governmental organizations (NGOs), trade unions and public figures involved, debt became an important topic in French politics and, as a result of this interest, was later incorporated as one of the thematic pillars of the alter-globalization movement.

Various organizations co-ordinated the efforts aimed at building awareness among the political elite and the general public. Technical discourse was paired with testimony from debt 'victims'. According to Agrikoliansky (2003: 87), 'moreover, the debt issue was not dealt with in isolation, but rather as part of a metadiscourse on economics, democracy and global interdependence, which already embodied the principal features of the contemporary critiques of globalization that had emerged over time'.

The degree of participation, as well as the effort's impact and consequences, is a reflection of the conditions in France's political and institutional environment during the late 1980s. First, the commemoration of the bicentenary of the French revolution played a role and evoked a certain revolutionary spirit and a sense of solidarity with respect to the world's 'third estate'. This spirit was expressed in a mobilization that was based on a discourse with revolutionary elements, one that targeted the Mitterrand government, along with the entire institutional left that held power at the time.

As an expression of opposition to the 'Mitterrandism' of the time, the 1989 mobilization also involved a reconfiguration of the political playing field within the left itself—a left in which the Communist Party was in decline and the LCR was reconstituting itself in the wake of a number of desertions and electoral defeats. The counter-celebration of the bicentenary afforded the traditional organizations of the left a unique opportunity to position themselves as an alternative to the Mitterrand left. In this context, the debt issue presented itself as a particularly propitious opportunity for action.

The Jubilee 2000 Campaign

Starting in the early 1980s, in various European countries including England, Italy and Spain, civil society organizations mobilized to advocate debt forgiveness for the poorest countries. In France, the movement gained prominence after the *Jubilee 2000* campaign. This explains a principal characteristic of the movement, both in France and in other countries where this debt-forgiveness initiative, known by the acronym MADPTM, has been implemented. Namely, it brought together Christian churches and a variety of social movements with the capacity to work together at the international level.

Responding to the demands of the national churches in poor African and Central American countries where Christianity is strongly rooted, the Catholic hierarchy took the initiative of proposing a solution inspired by the Christian tradition: forgiving the debt on the occasion of the Jubilee. The large NGOs and Christian charity organizations followed suit, mobilizing to support the campaign (Toussaint 2004: 65).

In France, the movement involved the participation of some sixty civil society organizations, of which three played a leading role: *Agir Ici* (Act Here), the Catholic *Committee against Hunger and for Development* (known by its French acronym CCFD) and *Secours Catholique* (Catholic Relief). With the slogan 'Pour l'an 2000: annulons la dette!' ('For the year 2000, let's abolish the debt'), and with its allusions to Jubilee 2000, the French movement achieved the impressive feat of gathering 550,000 of the twenty-four million signatures gathered worldwide.

The various activities that unfolded around the Jubilee 2000 campaign brought together a large number of France's civil society organizations across a wide range of interests. The principal role fell to the *Committee for the Abolition of Third World Debt* (Comité pour l'Annulation de la Dette du Tiers Monde, or CADTM), religious organizations, philanthropic organizations, the country's largest unions and social organizations such as *Attac* and *Les Amis du Monde Diplomatique*. An extensive social network thus formed around the objective of debt forgiveness. In many subsequent contexts, these actors also worked together on issues such as ethical labelling, agricultural trade, the Millennium Development Goals (MDGs) and tax havens. For a number of development-oriented NGOs, the debt-forgiveness campaign represented a politicization of their approach: awareness that education for development and support for partners must be accompanied by action that is 'political'—in the noble sense of the word—and that is designed to change the policies of the Western countries (Plate-forme Dette et Développement 2004: 87).

At the international level, when the Jubilee campaign was at its height, the Vatican decided to appoint Michel Camdessus, former director of the International Monetary Fund (IMF), to the Pontifical Council for Justice and Peace to advise on the debt. Largely opposed by non-Catholic NGOs, this decision marked the first turning point in the cohesion of the movement. In practice, the Vatican's decision led 'some large Northern NGOs, which have staff in Southern countries . . . to abandon the debt topic and deal with issues such as fair trade. In the North, staff of Christian NGOs, hired for the debt campaign were laid off or changed jobs' (Toussaint 2007). Furthermore, in 1999, some campaigns from the South decided to create the *Jubilee South* network.

The *2005: No More Excuses!* Campaign

The 2005 mobilization that took place during the lead-up to the G8 Gleneagles summit in Scotland began to take form in discussions at International Cooperation for Development and Solidarity (Coopération Internationale pour le Développement et la Solidarité, or CIDSE) in late 2003. The British NGOs thought that, because development assistance for Africa would be a central theme at the Gleneagles summit, the mobilization should confine itself to that issue. In the months that followed, the network's other NGOs and groups felt that the question of which issues should be addressed and what type of mobilization should occur were being defined and set by the British NGOs.

In preparing the mobilization, however, the discussion centred on the question of whether or not to cancel the debt of all countries whose debt would represent an obstacle to meeting the MDGs. Whereas Jubilee South and a large number of the European NGOs wanted the preparatory discussion to focus primarily on complete debt forgiveness, the British organizations did not think that conditional or unconditional debt cancellation—much less the question of assigning historical responsibility for the origin of the debt—was the appropriate topic for debate. Their perspective was more pragmatic. They believed that the importance of debt, and hence the issue of forgiving it, derives from the fact that it would prevent the debtor countries from achieving the MDGs.

The discussion became heated, with the French members of the mobilization committee accusing the British of:

> continuing the neoliberal policies that reproduce the pattern of domination exercised by the countries of the North over those of the South . . . We also wanted to broaden the discussion to the question of tax havens. This subject was impossible to discuss with the English, not only because it embarrasses them—which is why the subject was not on their agenda—but also because it was entirely beyond their objectives for the mobilization. (Interview with Jean Merckaert, 5 July 2007)

In their plans for the mobilization, the British NGOs associated the debt issue with the MDGs, a position also adopted by the Tony Blair administration. Some people interviewed for this study believed that this position was the result of pressure from the British government, and that the coincidence of views was the product of close collaboration. In the debate, the argument of the British NGOs centred around the idea that overcoming poverty in Africa depended on improving governance indices and resolving problems of corruption by strengthening institutional capacity.

The network of French organizations and groups, which had come together as the Debt and Development Platform, was responsible for preparing the campaign in France. Unlike its British partners, this entity decided to focus on the question of debt sustainability. However, after evaluating the Jubilee 2000 campaign, the Platform reached the conclusion that the disappointing results of that campaign were due to the fact that, with regard to all issues of debt, those to whom the demands were addressed were serving as both judge and jury. These were the wealthiest countries and the institutions they controlled: the G8, the international financial institutions, the Paris Club and even the French finance ministry—creditors who were simultaneously responsible for both the debt and the conduct of creditor institutions.

Given this situation, the network of French NGOs that planned the mobilization decided to focus on debt-related decision-making as one of the topics of discussion, formulating a demand that a body of international debt law be developed. This would comprise a system of rules governing loans, loan repayment and debt negotiation, to be established jointly by the debtor countries, the creditor countries and representatives of civil society and the private sector.

The proposed objective was to create rules to be applied fairly to all countries. Making this issue part of the debate meant emphasizing the responsibility of the creditors—in other words, avoiding an automatic or exclusive focus on forgiving the debt and emphasizing that creditor countries must assume responsibility for the historical origin and evolution of the debt. According to views garnered in interviews conducted for this study, the recognition of historical responsibility is an essential cornerstone for any international body of debt law, and it is a prerequisite to developing effective mechanisms that provide countries with manageable and fair borrowing conditions. Only such a course can ensure that the historical mechanism that led to over-indebtedness does not continue to operate in the future.

During the meetings to prepare for the mobilization, little progress was achieved on resolving this debate. The British NGOs (principally Oxfam) opposed more radical positions, such as that of Jubilee South, which was in favour of advocating for total and unconditional debt forgiveness. Even the position of the French NGOs—although an intermediate one which, although advocating debt forgiveness, also proposed establishing international laws to address the issue—remained unacceptable to the British NGOs.

Having established an alliance with the United Nations organizations concerned with debt relief issues, the British organizations were in an advantageous position to lead the debate given the fact that the G8, and thus the major demonstrations, were to take place in Britain. The result was an emphasis on debt relief rather than on a total and unconditional forgiveness of the debt. This hegemony of the British NGOs caused considerable discomfort for other international NGOs, and accentuated the 'ideological' differences between the British NGOs and Jubilee South, nearly leading to a breakdown in the dialogue.

The '2005: No more excuses!' campaign began in France, with the collection of 550,000 signatures of individuals supporting the Debt and Development Platform. The demands centred on three points: (a) forgiving the debt in all cases where repayment was an obstacle to achieving the MDGs; (b) creating an investigative commission in the French Parliament to shed light on the processes that led to the over-indebtedness of the countries of the South; and (c) convening an international conference, under United Nations auspices, to establish an international debt law (Plate-forme Dette et Développement 2004).

Based on these demands, the Platform launched a communication campaign featuring, among other things, a day of demonstrations in various French cities in mid-May. This was combined with ongoing efforts to gain media attention. In February and May, co-ordinated international action targeted the embassies of the G8 countries.

The members of certain networks and campaigns, such as the Debt and Development Platform and '2005: No more excuses!' met once a month with Bercy officials during the first half of 2005. At the same time, the Catholic networks remobilized for this campaign, and a number of third world churches came to meet with senior French politicians in late May (Plate-forme Dette et Développement 2004: 78).

On the international political playing field, although the French government wished to be at the forefront of efforts to foster development, it opposed the British and American idea of forgiving multilateral debt (that is, money owed to multilateral institutions such as the IMF and the World Bank). Its principal argument was that forgiving these debts would weaken these institutions' financing capacity. Its main goal was to promote its own initiative to finance development through a world tax on airline tickets. To counter the proposals of Prime Minister Blair and President Bush, in late May, France allied itself with Japan and Germany to support a counter-proposal that did little more than to marginally alleviate the debt burden of five countries (Plate-forme Dette et Développement 2004: 78).

Shortly after the meeting of the G8 Finance Ministers, the Debt and Development Platform denounced this position in the newspaper *Les Echos* as scandalous, alleging that it made France an obstacle to any progress toward forgiveness of the debt. This situation was untenable for the government of Jacques Chirac, who had made development one of the five priorities of his government. That very evening, the members of the movement met in Bercy with the officials who were to travel to London the following day to negotiate the G8 agreement. The ultimate agreement that emerged from the summit diverged significantly from France's initial position (CADTM and CETIM 2006: 98).

Debt Forgiveness in 2005

Announced on 11 June 2005 by the G8, debt forgiveness was widely featured in the media, and was generally presented as a 'historic' break that signalled a 'new approach' in dealing with the foreign debt of the poorest countries of the South. The new element in the equation was an awareness, on the part of the wealthy countries, of the need to eliminate the debt burden in order to foster growth and combat poverty in the beneficiary countries (Plate-forme Dette et Développement 2004: 34).

However, the amount of the debt to be forgiven, \$40 billion,[2] was only 5 per cent of the bilateral and multilateral debt of the South, and would not, in any case, have been repaid. Moreover, the measure did not address the beneficiary countries' major debts to international banks. Thus, the accounts were not zeroed, because the countries concerned would be obliged to continue paying the banks. In fact, what this measure did was to transfer the burden associated with the poor countries' inability to repay their debts from the private sector to the public sector, in effect socializing the costs and privatizing the profits (Plate-forme Dette et Développement 2004).

According to the analysis of the Debt and Development Platform, far from freeing up enough money to finance development in the countries in question, this heavily indebted poor countries (HIPC) initiative was essentially designed to make the 'unsustainable' portion of the debt—the portion that had little chance of being repaid—payable. Moreover, the initiative perpetuated IMF and World Bank control over the poor countries, which in the process were required to liberalize their economies in order to qualify for debt relief (Merckaert 2004: 54).

THE ROLE OF NGOS IN THE DEBT-FORGIVENESS MOBILIZATION

The mobilization of French civil society in support of forgiving third world debt was carried out primarily by a group of NGOs that had been involved in North–South issues since the 1960s. They constituted a horizontal network, comprising organizations from a variety of movements and philosophies associated with the struggle for 'another globalization', but which maintained their distance from those organizations considered 'radical' (Plate-forme Dette et Développement 2004).[3] The sections that follow describe the discourse and role of three prominent organizations: the Catholic Committee against Hunger and Debt (CCFD), the Debt and Development Platform created by NGOs for the mobilization effort; and the Committee for the Abolition of Third World Debt (CADTM).

The Catholic Committee against Hunger and for Development (CCFD)

Following a plea by Pope John XXIII, in the context of the *Rerum Novarum* encyclical, Catholic organizations organized a campaign against hunger in 1961, on the initiative of the French bishops. This was the origin of the *Catholic Committee against Hunger* (Comité Catholique Contre la Faim, or CCCF), which collected money for the effort to combat hunger each year during Lent. In 1966 the CCCF became the CCFD. Its objective is 'to help men and women who find it difficult to escape hunger by themselves become food-independent and regain their dignity' (CCFD—Terre Solidaire 1984: 85).[4]

After the Catholic Church's call for involvement in the Jubilee 2000 campaign, the CCFD intensified its work and adopted language that called for mobilization against the structural mechanisms that lead to 'maldevelopment'. It redefined its approach, focusing on fostering public awareness of globalization issues and North–South inequalities through campaigning. Underlying this was the realization that advocacy could also serve as a tool for educating the public about development.

Efforts to mobilize for the 1999 G7 meeting in Cologne brought together a number of organizations and Catholic congregations, which later worked collaboratively to organize the Jubilee 2000 mobilization in France. Initially, this co-ordination was informal and was led by the CCFD and Secours Catholique. The Cologne event attracted thirty thousand activists, with debt forgiveness as the central issue. This effort was so successful that at the end of the summit the G7 publicly committed itself to reducing the debt of the poorest countries, although conditions were attached to the process.

For this mobilization, the CCFD adopted campaign tactics that involved taking to the streets, as well as carrying out educational activities and initiatives to influence public opinion and government. In short, the focus was on raising awareness: on one hand, educating people about development and, on the other, mobilizing public opinion to secure the legitimacy needed to successfully make demands on government. The campaign was designed to begin with awareness-building activities and to later incorporate concrete actions to mobilize citizens, once the basic foundation of awareness was in place.

This was the first time that the CCFD adopted a discourse that resonated politically and carried out efforts in popular education which attacked the causes of maldevelopment rather than focusing solely on its consequences. This type of campaign came naturally to the CCFD, which had a history of participating in mobilizations in solidarity with countries of the South. However, the Jubilee 2000 campaign marked the first time that it took the initiative in co-ordinating and mobilizing, while at the same time planning future debt-related educational initiatives and engaging in advocacy to address the causes of maldevelopment.

As a Catholic NGO, the CCFD put forth the view that development requires not simply funding projects, but also attacking the causes of maldevelopment—a course that, in turn, requires engaging in advocacy with government to change the policies and processes involved.

This represented a qualitative leap in the CCFD's work within French society. The organization attempted to develop an approach that would focus a critical eye on the role that the French government assumed in debt negotiations with creditor countries. For Jean Merckaert, 'it is a matter of creating awareness and showing what is being done here—the decisions that France makes and their impact on the countries of the South' (interview, 5 July 2007).

Nearly all of the French NGOs adopted a similar shift in focus, albeit one that lagged behind British NGOs by some fifteen years. This time lag is attributable in part to the fact that, early on, British NGOs established 'policy departments'. It was in the context of the 2000 debt campaign that the CCFD recognized the crucial importance of dealing with the political aspects of development. CCFD became the first French NGO to create a policy department, looking 'not only to attack the immediate problems of poverty in the South by supporting local projects, but also [to do so] with an awareness of the need to attack the structural problems that cause the injustices and problems of maldevelopment' (interview with Bernard Pinaud, 5 October 2007).

This campaign turned out to be the largest petition campaign ever waged in France, garnering over half a million signatures. The massive number of signatures gave the Platform legitimacy in the eyes of the government and enabled it to engage the government in dialogue.

The Debt and Development Platform

In the view of the *Debt and Development Platform*, the debt-forgiveness measures of the wealthy countries had been little more than an attempt to convert borrower countries' status to one of sustainable debt. In practice, for the creditors, this meant restoring their clients' ability to pay. The philosophy of the HIPC initiative was based on this rationale. In essence, only 'unpayable' debt was removed from the books. The Debt and Development Platform expressed reservations about this approach, which ignores the impact that debt repayment has on the countries' people, as well as the political and historical dimensions of the indebtedness (Plate-forme Dette et Développement 2004). The Platform demanded total debt forgiveness for the low-income countries and forgiveness of a substantial portion of the debt of the middle-income countries (Plate-forme Dette et Développement 2004).

Initially, the Platform was characterized by two perspectives. One was associated with a current of opinion that favoured 'North–South solidarity' concerning development issues. The second was linked to groups on the extreme left and to anti-imperialist positions, such as that of CADTM. Despite the differences between these two factions, they shared a desire to work collectively.

Following the activities of the 'Pour l'an 2000: annulons la dette' campaign (1998–2000) and in the context of the international Jubilee 2000 petition, the Debt and Development Platform emerged in 2001. It was initially composed of twenty-seven French NGOs and unions that had already participated in co-ordinating the 1999 Cologne and Jubilee 2000 campaigns. The principle uniting these organizations was the quest for a 'broad, just and lasting solution to the problem of the developing countries' debt' (Plate-forme Dette et Développement 2004: 24). Thus, the Debt and Development Platform's efforts were aimed at fusing the issues of debt and development, while working to promote a definitive solution to the debt of the countries of the South. It proposed addressing the structural causes of poverty as a means of laying the foundation for lasting development in those countries.

After the Cologne and Jubilee 2000 campaigns, it was clear to the participating organizations that resolving the debt problem would not be a simple matter. Accordingly, the unions and other organizations involved decided to create a collective framework to establish an ongoing structure for their efforts, in order to share their expertise and carry out future mobilizations. This was the genesis of the Platform as a tool for disseminating information and taking action on the debt of countries of the South. To gain more thorough knowledge of the problem and to promote the implementation of the necessary measures, the Platform's organizations use their networks to influence public opinion and government in France, particularly in relation to meetings of international financial organizations.

When the Platform was created, the fact that three of France's largest unions requested to participate in the process came as a surprise to the original group. NGOs had not been accustomed to working with the unions or other social movement groups. Much discussion and negotiation ensued among the NGOs that had played an early role in the Platform. The union support arose out of the decision by the European Trade Union Confederation to support the Jubilee 2000 campaign. This decision reflected the fact that the unions' international affiliates in the South were urging their Northern partners to mobilize for debt forgiveness, based on the position that debt repayments represent a major obstacle to development. The involvement that major unions had in creating the Platform gave the effort a broadly representative nature, thus giving it the power to manoeuvre with government.

The Platform quickly became the recognized repository of expertise and citizen mobilization on debt issues. It developed the expertise needed to take part in the debt negotiation process, laying the foundation for its consultations with the finance minister and the representatives of international financial institutions. The Platform was also recognized by the government as the main civil society interlocutor for discussions on debt issues. The crux of the Platform's work centres on lobbying; developing the expertise needed to dissect and analyse initiatives, such as the HIPC initiative; engaging in advocacy vis-à-vis the government; fostering awareness and educating the public on issues relating to development; and formulating and putting forth teaching tools for activist networks and NGOs. More specifically, at the international level, it engages in collaborative activities that consist of:

- Expert work: conducting analyses, preparing reports and following international negotiations within entities such as the G8, the Paris Club, international financial institutions (IFIs) and the United Nations
- Lobbying the French government (ministries of finance and foreign affairs, office of the president, parliament) and international organizations (IFIs, United Nations)
- In association with partner groups and unions within the Platform, carrying out country-by-country monitoring of how French debt relief

is being used, and to encourage the participation of civil society in the countries involved

- Mobilization, fostering awareness and disseminating information through, for example, press releases, debt news, 'Drop the Debt' CD, concerts, websites, signature-gathering campaigns and demonstrations) (Plate-forme Dette et Développement 2005–2006: 98)

Committee for the Abolition of Third World Debt (CADTM)

The founding of CADTM in France was directly linked to the birth and development of alter-globalization groups; it grew out of the Belgian CADTM, created by Eric Toussaint in March 1990. However, the creation of CADTM-France cannot be understood without reference to the development, discourse and debates of the French alter-globalization movement and, in particular, Attac (see Chapter 12 in this volume).[5]

At the beginning of 2000, based on the accumulated experience gained by CADTM-Belgium since the 1990s, certain Attac activists were concerned about the fact that France had no organizations carrying out concrete activities and mobilizing with regard to the debt issue. They realized that, until that time, the issue had been addressed only by Catholic and Protestant organizations, which approached the subject solely from the point of view of economic and social development in the poor countries. Concern over this limitation was shared by the unions, which, in the context of the Jubilee campaign, stressed the illegitimate nature of the debt and rejected the notion of accepting it as an ongoing reality.

The Jubilee 2000 campaign had demonstrated that the issue evoked solidarity within French society and could mobilize people. However, given the deeply rooted nature of the problem and how much was at stake on all sides, the issue required more attention. This could not be undertaken exclusively by Catholic and Protestant organizations or unions, whose nature precludes them from making the debt issue the central focus of their efforts and discourse.

Despite Attac's desire to address the debt problem, it clearly did not become the central focus of its activity. Attac lacked the necessary information base for such a focus, and did not have the capacity to generate its own analyses of this complex issue. Thus, whenever Attac was called upon to take a public position on the debt problem and its consequences, it tended to rely on the analyses of the CADTM.

It was against this background, in early 2000, that a dozen people arrived at the conclusion that the debt issue could be 'a crossroads, a central issue in globalization that required attention, since prevailing on this point would make it possible to prevail on the issues flowing from it' (interview with Daniel Millet, 31 July 2007). Out of such concerns, the group decided to create CADTM-France.

The organization is composed of activists with very diverse backgrounds. Although several members of the most active core of the group are associated with the Revolutionary Communist League or are supporters of José Bové, all of those interviewed for this study considered most of the CADTM activists to be politically independent.

The fact that this group grew out of a meeting of people from different parts of France meant that the organization had a wide geographical base of support. This initially posed a serious problem for the group's formation and functioning, but over time it proved to be an advantage. The diversity of its members' origins has facilitated the creation of an extensive network throughout the country, which has proven advantageous for the dissemination of information. It also gains legitimacy from the fact that it is not a centralized group created in Paris that has imposed its views on the rest of the country.

According to those interviewed, the rapid evolution of the alter-globalization movement in France must be understood in relation to the fact that the traditional social and political institutions had lost their representativeness and credibility. It was seen as a source of real hope in a context where political parties in general, and those of the left in particular, had been discredited and had failed to address issues of global justice that were gaining international importance. France's most important unions, which have a history of solidarity with the countries of the South regarding the nature of the debt, were also losing power and influence, vis-à-vis government, with regard to decisions affecting their constituents and society in general.

Between 2001 and 2005, CADTM tried to determine the best way of organizing itself and creating a strategy that would increase its profile among the general public and in civil society, as well as among governmental decision-makers and representatives of international organizations in France concerned with the debt problem. The first step, however, was to develop a structure, create bylaws, open an office and decide on rules to govern the functioning of the organization.

In order to gain public visibility, CADTM disseminated information and created an editorial committee responsible for conducting analyses and converting these into informational and educational materials on the subject of the debt. An electronic bulletin was also created, and was issued every two or three months. At the time of writing, it reached approximately fifteen thousand individuals. One of the group's objectives for its initial period was to create an information infrastructure capable of rapidly disseminating news on the problem, as well as information on the organization's positions. Anytime important information emerges on matters involving the organization's interests or demands, it can react quickly, due to the significant public electronic presence it has established.

Another objective related to public opinion and civil society is to participate in debates and meetings, on a variety of development issues, involving various groups concerned directly or indirectly with the effects of the debt on the countries of the South, as well as with such issues as the environment, poverty and equitable trade. This involves undertaking actions to bring the issues to public attention and enhance awareness about the causes and consequences of the debt.

Whereas such activities are present throughout France, CADTM has not had the resources necessary to put in place an operational team to plan and conduct its work. The group has also lacked the continuity needed to establish a nerve centre to oversee advocacy activities and the preparation of materials for dissemination. The group's funding is limited to members' dues and the revenue from sales of publications. The funds are largely devoted to mobilizing the members of the association, either for the World Social Forum (WSF) or to underwrite the different activities emerging from the WSF.

In the absence of salaried personnel, the work has to be done on a volunteer basis by activists or members. These people must juggle their available time in order to participate in the group's activities at the national or international level. The work that the organization carries out to inform and educate the public is one of the most important aspects of CADTM's efforts and one of the main areas in which its members have been successful, having managed to make the debt problem an issue of public awareness.

MOBILIZING CIVIL SOCIETY FOR GOVERNMENT ADVOCACY

The other area in which CADTM works is that of targeting governmental decision-makers who have a voice on the debt issue at the national or international level. This means putting in motion a dynamic for dialogue—involving, on one hand, French state institutions, such as the finance ministry and, on the other hand, representatives in France of the international organizations concerned with the debt issue, such as the IMF, the World Bank and the Paris Club.

Discussions have taken place at least twice a year, in spring and fall, at the semi-annual meetings of these organizations. The dialogue involves governmental decision-makers, especially those in the finance ministry responsible for multilateral issues, as well as the deputies in the National Assembly who are members of committees dealing with France's portfolio of development assistance policies. One objective of these meetings is to provide an opportunity for exchange of views between officials and civil society (as represented by the *Platform for Public Aid to Development*) on debt-related issues and other matters of current importance. A further objective is to provide information on France's positions regarding the agenda points slated to be discussed at the semi-annual meetings of the international organizations.

These dialogues are generally organized by the Platform for Public Aid to Development. The participating government decision-makers include five staff members of the finance ministry, all senior officials with in-depth technical knowledge of the issues. The meeting is usually chaired by the Finance Ministry's deputy director in charge of 'Debt and International Affairs', who also serves as the secretary general of the Paris Club. In special cases the director of the Treasury, who acts as the president of the Paris Club, also participates. The meeting is organized around issues of concern, selected by the NGOs, related to the upcoming agenda for the meeting of the international institutions.

For the NGOs, the Paris Club meetings are perhaps one of the most difficult environments for conducting this dialogue, because the information provided to NGO representatives by Bercy officials is highly compartmentalized. One of these meetings was described by Daniel Mollet, with CADTM, as follows:

> At the beginning of a preparatory meeting, three NGO representatives generally present the points to be discussed, along with their demands. The representative of the Bercy delegation in charge of preparing the Club meeting then takes the floor to describe the ministry's position and to explain why the decision was made, as well as why the Platform's demands can or cannot be accepted. For example, at the last meeting, in preparation for a new meeting of the club, the goal of the discussion was to determine what countries would be present, since we had not had access to the list or to the points to be discussed . . . The response from Bercy was that not all of the countries were in agreement about publishing the list beforehand, and thus it could not be provided . . . In this case, Bercy is really referring to a veto by the United States and the Bush administration . . . In practice, Bercy makes them responsible for all decisions that are contrary to our demands, and tries to make it clear that the obstacles are due to the United States, while Bercy's position is generous and open. (Interview, 31 July 2007).

This, according to the interviewees, is why most of the meetings end along the following lines:

> Fine, we'll study your proposals, but in practice we'll hold to the positions that we have explained to you. But rest assured that ongoing contact is important. (Interview with Amélie Canone, AITEC, 11 July 2007)

To date, these meetings in no way herald a significant overture, let alone a change of position by the government decision-makers regarding debt. It is true, however, that the officials place real importance on the dialogue, both as an exchange of points of view between the different entities involved and as a way of keeping abreast of problems at the international level. The proof is that contact with government decision-makers and representatives of international organizations has become increasingly free-flowing, in contrast to the situation during the 1990s, when there was practically no dialogue. This was explained by Jean Merckaert of CCPD:

> In those years, when the NGOs requested a meeting to discuss any issue at all, we sometimes did not even receive a response from the national institutions, let alone from the international ones . . . There was no one to dialogue with from the government, which did not see us as legitimate representatives. Today, since the public is much more broadly familiar with our demands, the government is increasingly obliged to listen to us. (Interview, 4 July 2007)

The Limits of Policy Change

There has been significant progress, in a number of areas, in mobilizing civil society in favour of debt forgiveness. The Debt and Development Platform has succeeded in raising awareness within French society on the debt issue, by explaining its origins and implications. There have also been extensive opportunities to inform the public through the mass media, thus helping to legitimize the NGOs' actions and explain the rationale behind their objectives. Furthermore, NGOs have become essential participants in negotiations with national and international organizations. However, the road leading to debt forgiveness for poor third world countries remains a very long one—not only because of differences in the positions of the French government and international organizations, but also other reasons.

First, the debt problem is not amenable to a solution by national entities, because it is shaped by the dynamics of international negotiations. This reduces the groups' room for manoeuvring: the mobilizations, and the results of national dialogue, necessarily take second place to the international agenda and the interests of particular countries involved in the international negotiations. This does not prevent the groups from pressing the French government on the question of the debt owed to France by countries of the South. Despite all of the impediments, it is by no means impossible for France to adopt measures to overcome this problem. However, if it does so, it will be the result of the interests expressed and defended by the French government, a position which, as noted earlier, calls for conditional debt forgiveness, along with some ability to influence the national affairs of each debtor country.

The second element is that, because discussion of the debt is subordinate to the international agenda, French society's support for the demands of the Platform depends on international mobilizations and on the prominence of this problem in international discussions and initiatives. In short, although it is true that there has been progress in creating public awareness of the problem, effective mobilization of the society in favour of debt forgiveness remains an unachieved goal. One example of this is the lack of response to the call for mobilization, made by the Platform in July 2005, around the G8 meeting at which the debt of the countries of the South was a major topic. Broad support and expression of interest on the part of the general public regarding this sensitive issue was clearly absent.

This situation reflects the groups' inability to effectively enlist participation and incite action. Although the debt issue has gained a place in the public consciousness, and despite a public recognition of the complexity of the problem, the reality is that there is a lack of will to mobilize around the issue. Indeed, the weakness of the mobilization—notwithstanding support for the principles involved—demonstrates that the Platform and its constituent organizations have failed to gain traction in French society. Although progress has been made, it is the result of particular moments when the international situation has focused attention on the problem, or when natural disasters, such as the 2004 Indian Ocean tsunami, highlight the constraints affecting poor countries and their ability to solve catastrophic situations on their own.

Third, the Platform's limited success in negotiating with the national government is partly because the government entities involved have regarded meetings with the Platform as merely consultative. In contrast to the complementary relationship between the British government and civil society, groups in France face officials who are acting on the basis of an instrumental and bureaucratic logic. Government decision-makers fully understand the importance of listening to civil society, but the fact that the dialogue is merely consultative, with no concrete effect on national or international actions by the French government, diminishes its credibility and significance.

An additional factor regarding the poor progress achieved, and the weakness of mobilizing efforts, relates to the composition of the Platform itself. The core of the movement consists primarily of NGOs that have allocated resources and salaried personnel to address the debt problem, among other issues. The fact that CADTM, a key group within the Platform, has a geographically diverse base of support has done little to shape the Platform's course of action. This reflects a central reality, namely, that the movement functions technocratically, without a significant grass-roots base. As a result, its capacity to mobilize French society is limited.

CONCLUSION

By way of conclusion, let us delve a bit more deeply into the nature of today's civil society in France. The foregoing analysis points to a movement that has brought together two new elements. First, it consists primarily of the action of NGOs, which organize mobilizations and communications on the debt issue. These organizations thus represent a lobby vis-à-vis governments and international organizations. Second, closely related to this is the fact that the discourse of these groups is based on 'expertise'; that is, on intellectual and professional work within the organizations. Thus, representatives of the movement have a technical and scientific basis for arguing their cause when confronting or negotiating with government, dealing with the media, and communicating with and informing society.

Here, a distinction must be made which, although obvious, is poorly understood: a grouping of NGOs, and even the resulting mobilization effort, does not necessarily constitute a social movement. Put another way, one can hardly apply the term 'social movement' to a group of NGOs that assigns scant importance to the size of its popular base or the day-to-day mobilization of those who might be favourably disposed to its discourse. It is clear that the rhythm governing the meetings of this group of NGOs is determined by circumstances and events, that it allocates only a portion of its salaried personnel to this work and that it relies heavily on a media presence and what it calls 'taking to the streets'. This is a concept of mobilization that differs from that of groups whose activities are based on the mobilization and active, organized participation of their members.

This is a central issue, and one of the most challenging points to analyse in assessing the movement's prospects. What real possibility is there for the Debt and Development Platform to advocate for change with governmental and international entities, as well as the public at large, when the proposals are being put forward by a mere group of people, albeit technically very competent, and when, despite skilled lobbying, the group is unable to mobilize society? Whereas such a group can hardly be considered a social movement, might it be considered an expression of civil society?

What is civil society today? Could it be described as the set of adequately funded non-governmental organizations that takes action on specific issues, conducts scientific analysis, is capable of presenting technical arguments to the government and is able to create societal awareness of particular issues? If the answer is 'yes', then an even more important question presents itself: if the alter-globalization movement is a reflection of NGOs, can the movement then be defined as a social movement? Or, on the contrary, is it rather a specific actor whose nature and limits must be defined? Given the technocratic nature of many of the entities that define themselves as alter-globalization groups, and which are not built on an identity or a project of societal transformation, they can hardly be considered a social movement, let alone a political one. If this is the case, one might well ask: does the alter-globalization movement really exist?

NOTES

1. A wordplay on 'ça suffit comme ça', meaning '*more* than enough already!'

2. All references to dollars are to U.S. dollars.
3. See http://ccfdal.wordpress.com/ccfd/de-lorigine-a-aujourdhui.
4. See http://ccfdal.wordpress.com/ccfd/de-lorigine-a-aujourdhui.
5. See also Attac France (1999a, 1999b); Attac Wallonie-Bruxelles (2002).

BIBLIOGRAPHY

Agrikoliansky, Eric. (2003). *De l'anticolonialisme à l'altermondialisme: généalogie(s) d'un nuveau cadre d'action colective.* Paper presented at the international symposium 'Les mobilisations altermondialistes', GERMM/CERI, Paris, December.

Attac France. (1999a). *Attac contre les dictatures de marchés*, Paris: Syllepse Paris.

———. (1999b). *Tout sur Attac*, Paris: Mille et une nuits.

Attac Wallonie-Bruxelles. (2002). *Voix rebelles du monde*, Forcalquier: Signes d'ATTAC.

Committee for the Abolition of Third World Debt. (2004). *Les Manifestes du possible*, Liège: Syllepse.

Committee for the Abolition of Third World Debt and Centre Europe—Tiers Monde. (2006). Jubilé Sud *Menons l'enquête sur la dette! Manuel pour des audits de la dette du Tiers Monde*, Geneva: Éditions du Cetim.

CCFD—Terre Solidaire. (1984). *Le Défi de la solidarité*, Paris: Comité Catholique Contre la Faim et Pour le Développement/Fayard.

Merckaert, Jean. (2004). 'La Dictature de la bonne gouvernance, ou l'impasse des indicateurs de performance politique?' *Techniques financières et développement*, 75:23–34.

Mouchard, Daniel. (2003). *Les mobilisations contre l'AMI: un 'moment fondateur' du mouvement altermondialiste?* Paper presented at the international symposium 'Les Mobilisations Altermondialistes', GERMM/CERI, Paris, 3–5 December.

Plate-forme Dette et Développement. (2004). *Rapport 2003–2004—La Dette face à la démocratie*, Paris: Plate-forme Dette et Développement.

———. (2005–2006). *La loi de créanciers contre les droits des citoyens*, Paris: Plate-forme Dette et Développement.

Toussaint, E. (2004). *La finance contre les Peuples*, Liège: CADTM/Syllepse/Cetim.

———. (2007). *La lutte pour l'annulation de la dette dans une perspective historique, Attac newsletter, No. 560*, Paris: Attac.

11 Global Justice and/as Global Democracy

The UK Campaign for a Tobin Tax

James Brassett

INTRODUCTION

The Tobin Tax is by now a well-known proposal to place a small tax on foreign currency transactions (Tobin 1978; Ul Haq, Kaul and Grunberg 1996).[1] As it has been developed and debated within global civil society campaigns, the proposal has expanded to include rather more political than technical issues, the possibility of global redistributive justice as a result of the potentially vast revenues (Spahn 1995) and, in some articulations, it sustains a logic of emancipation via the construction of global democratic institutions (Patomäki 2001). Moreover, the Tobin Tax was at the heart of early initiatives to reform the Global Financial Architecture (GFA) and has been part of many attempts to lobby global institutions since then (Porter 2005: 146). Thus, for many working in the anti-/alter-globalization movement, the Tobin Tax has stood out and persisted as an important and credible challenge and/or alternative to neoliberal global finance. The arguments for the tax within global civil society have taken on important ethical dimensions and should therefore be analysed in terms of their contribution to debates over global justice and democracy.

This chapter seeks to address and analyse the United Kingdom (UK) Tobin Tax campaign by focusing upon these ethical questions. As such, it departs from much scholarly work on the Tobin Tax which focuses upon *feasibility*. Our argument is not that the feasibility questions are unimportant or misdirected. Rather that the scholarly analysis of the proposal has become transfixed with quite a technical set of economic debates at the expense of an appreciation of the ethical implications of the campaign per se. Even the most reflective scholars of the campaign feel the need to either prove or disprove the feasibility of the tax before they can address its broader implications. From this perspective the broader impacts of the campaign itself can sometimes be overlooked.

The guiding hypothesis is that—read through the prism of the UK campaign—the Tobin Tax has come to occupy a role within global civil society which holds strong implications for the ways in which we think about global justice and global democracy. We argue here that the UK campaign for the Tobin Tax demonstrates both the limits and the potentials of international taxation as a response to poverty in the developing world.

The chapter proceeds in six sections. The first introduces the background history of the Tobin Tax and notes how debates have moved from a fairly technical economistic debate over feasibility to a more political and ethical set of debates over the political potentials and redistributive possibilities of the proposal. The second section focuses on the UK campaign for the Tobin Tax more specifically and highlights existing critiques of it as excessively conformist, neoliberal in orientation and focused upon a charity-based conception of global justice. The third section then attempts to place the UK campaign within a broader globalizing context. It highlights the decline of the UK economy, a set of moves to open up the City of London to foreign banks, a general financialization of UK society (most clearly recently felt through increases in personal debt) and a set of laws designed to limit the political nature of non-governmental organization (NGO) campaigns. The fourth section develops an argument for a global democratic analysis of the UK campaign for a Tobin Tax. Whereas a nationally located campaign, 'War on Want/Stamp Out Poverty' necessarily speaks and acts in a way that has global impact, the campaign should be assessed in a multilevel—local, national, regional, global—fashion. Thus, the last two sections focus, in turn, upon the positive and negative impacts of the UK campaign in the context of global democracy.

THE TOBIN TAX: FROM ECONOMICS TO POLITICS AND ETHICS

When the possibility of a tax on foreign exchange transactions was first raised by James Tobin in 1972, it was firmly embedded in discussions about 'sound' economic policy. Tobin himself positioned the tax as a moderate reform which might 'throw some sand in the well greased wheels' of global currency markets (Tobin 1978: 158), slowing the damaging effects of short-term speculation divorced from the real economy. Initially, monetarist concerns with the effectiveness, enforceability and political feasibility of the tax were seen as constituting significant challenges to its feasibility. However, the augmented version of the tax advocated by Spahn (1995), which proposed a two-tier approach (where a low-level, revenue-raising tax could be coupled with a high-level surcharge that would act to break trading in the event of a speculative attack), moved beyond many of the challenges to Tobin's original formulation. Importantly, he opened space for thinking about the political dimensions and redistributive potentials contained within the tax. This has fed into broader debates about politics and ethics, and it has helped to construct new vocabularies of the Tobin Tax which move beyond questions of economic (logical and technical) feasibility in order to address issues of a political and ethical nature.

The campaign for a Tobin Tax arose in the context of discussions about the possibilities of reforming the GFA which occurred in response to the financial crises of the late twentieth century (see Eichengreen 1999). In such a context the campaign, although highly ambitious, was credible. Initial support worked at the intersection of international organizations, technical experts and, in a limited sense, some states. Civil society actors, including the Halifax Initiative, the French NGO Association for the Taxation of Financial Transactions and Aid to Citizens (Attac), the German think tank World Economy, Ecology and Development (WEED), the Network Institute of Global Democratization (NIGD) and War on Want, placed the campaign at the front of their agendas. These groups have backed the tax for various reasons, including as a tool for lobbying (as have Attac and War on Want), and as a mechanism for public discussion (such as NIGD). Importantly, they have produced and sponsored numerous expert studies of the Tobin Tax.

Whereas a straightforward economic or realist analysis could dismiss such groups, arguing that they are unlikely to be politically effective, there is more to be considered in terms of the discursive shifts within global finance governance. The campaign has engaged significantly with political and ethical vocabularies of the tax, transcending the economism which conditioned earlier understandings.

Political and ethical engagements, although not ignoring questions of economic feasibility, have appealed to issues of political autonomy, justice and democracy in the face of globalization, transcending the 'reformism' of economistic approaches in favour of a political resistance to the structural power and/or logic of markets. With respect to political autonomy, the tax has been seen as a means to reigning in the forces of global finance and restoring some room for manoeuvre to national governments, (re) opening spaces for political rather than financial deliberation. Global justice perspectives have rested on the revenue-raising potentials of the tax, which could be used to fund global development projects, subjecting global finance to basic principles of justice (Patomäki 2001: xix). Global democratic approaches see the Tobin Tax as holding the potential to build a democratic public sphere which might *politicize* global finance. In this sense the Tobin Tax campaign itself is an act of global democratization, which draws people together in a campaign against the anti-democratic nature of the prevailing GFA, opening new democratic spaces.

THE UK CAMPAIGN AND EXISTING CRITIQUES

War on Want is a development NGO founded in 1951, based in south London with close ties to the Labour Party and the *Guardian* newspaper. It enjoys links with numerous Christian groups and faith charities, and sources considerable funding from those organizations. Although its campaign objectives are wide, including the promotion of human rights, trade justice, tax justice and development, it has consistently targeted poverty as an overriding concern. The group adopted the Tobin Tax campaign at the end of the 1990s, first under the direction of Steve Tibbett and then David Hillman. It embraced the campaign more comprehensively in 2002 when it established the Tobin Tax Network: a grouping of over fifty campaign agencies, charities, faith groups and trade unions, with organizations including Oxfam, Christian Aid, Unison and the united Reform Church. In addition, it has linked up with the Make Poverty History Campaign under the title 'Stamp Out Poverty'.[2]

War on Want has used the Tobin Tax as a campaign tool for lobbying the Treasury and Department for International Development (DFID), as well as creating awareness at social forums and other public discussions. Importantly, in a number of policy documents it has actively contributed to the intellectual development of the Tobin Tax. This section introduces some key campaign activities and arguments of War on Want before outlining some of the central critiques of the UK campaign. In general, the UK campaign can be seen to fall within the moderate range of proposals related to the Tobin Tax. It seeks a low-rate tax and has (recently) come to focus on the revenue-raising function. Central criticisms of the campaign therefore suggest that it does not go far enough.

The Tobin Tax Network has focused on the revenue-raising potential of the Tobin Tax, what David Hillman describes as the 'discourse of social justice'.[3] In a number of policy briefs the NGO has funded experts to produce detailed studies of how revenues could be leveraged to fight poverty in a way that would be acceptable to governments and business (Kapoor 2003; Spratt 2005; War on Want 2002a, 2002b). In particular the key campaigners—David Hillman, Sony Kapoor and Avinash Persaud—have rapidly taken on a strategic edge, attempting to leave behind their self professed incarnation as the 'sandal wearing brigade' to promote a more hard-nosed and economically credible version of the Tobin Tax.[4]

The version of the Tobin Tax promoted by War on Want has therefore changed markedly over the course of the campaign. Under different campaign leaders the group has shifted its focus from a universal Tobin Tax at 0.1 per cent (War on Want 2002b) through a Currency Transactions Tax (Kapoor 2003), to a unilateral 'Stamp Duty' on Sterling at 0.005 per cent (Spratt 2005). As well as promoting an ambitious version of the Tobin Tax, the initial incarnation of the War on Want campaign, under Steve Tibbett, contained many of the democratizing and transformative dimensions of the Tobin Tax highlighted earlier. For instance, the keynote report (tellingly) entitled *The Robin Hood Tax* called for:

> a new body under the aegis of the UN [United Nations] to formulate policy on the tax, to oversee compliance and to decide how to spend the revenue. The body could be called the *Global Development Commission*

> and it would necessarily involve a body to distribute the revenue, made up of independent but elected advisors. (War on Want 2002a: 3)

However, as the personnel changed at the War on Want, and as David Hillman took over to form the Tobin Tax Network, many of the larger aspects of the Tobin Tax were dropped. Advocacy became focused on a more straightforward 'Currency Transactions Tax' to raise revenue for development (Kapoor 2003). Indeed, a recent report commissioned by Stamp Out Poverty even articulates a version of the tax that would be unilateral. It argues for a simple levy by the UK government via the central bank (Spratt 2005), with the aim of raising revenues to contribute toward the UK's commitment to the Millennium Development Goals (MDGs). The campaign has therefore undergone a substantive shift from Tobin's original proposal to a unilateralist augmentation of the Spahn tax to raise revenues for foreign aid.

Despite these discursive shifts, the *modus operandi* of the campaign has remained consistent throughout. The aim is to set up a simple narrative and reproduce it for diverse audiences, namely: *Bankers make vast amounts of money by betting on currency. This exacerbates poverty and there exists a simple solution—the Tobin Tax—to both calm speculation and raise funds for poverty.* This narrative is often augmented with various strategic touches. For instance, War on Want is adept at bringing in famous endorsements like Jon Snow, Baroness Shirley Williams and Bill Nighy. They have also used academic economists like Rodney Schmidt and financial market players like Jim O'Neil to add to the credibility of their proposal with technical audiences. But the basic narrative remains the same: an easily communicated account of what globalization is, followed by the Tobin Tax as a way to change it.

A clear example of the use of such narratives can be seen in the video 'The Banker 2', produced through the 'Robin Hood Tax' campaign which has recently emerged on the back of momentum generated by Stamp Out Poverty.[5] The video presents an altercation between Ben Kingsley, who is playing a stereotypical rich, white banker, and a number of threatening-looking adolescents, played by actors from Skins, The Inbetweeners and Harry Potter—all well known to young British people. After going through the banker's pockets, briefcase and wallet, the 'threatening' youths cut a small amount from one coin, and return the rest to the banker, promising him that they will 'spend it well'. The short video inverts initial perceptions of what might be expected from such a situation, presenting the banker as the 'real' threat to society. The 'solution' is branded as common sense—'small change for the banks' at the cost of 'a big difference for the world'. The video finishes by drawing viewers to the campaign website, where they can register their support, upload their own videos, and promote the campaign through Twitter, Facebook and Flickr. The tagline for the website reads 'Turning a Crisis for the Banks into an Opportunity for the World', furthering moves to inject ethical discourse into discussions about the GFA.

This recent move toward reframing the Tobin Tax as a 'Robin Hood Tax' represents a not insignificant attempt to narrate the tax and the campaign as both instantly comprehensible and immediately reasonable. Tapping into an important British cultural narrative, it attempts to make connections between increasingly widespread ethical condemnation of financial institutions and the virtue attached to the notion of 'stealing from the rich and giving to the poor'. Supporters are invited to see themselves as 'Merry (Wo) men' and attach pictures of masks, arrows and hats—all well-recognized symbols of the Robin Hood myth—to their Facebook profiles and Twitter feeds. They are participants at the intersection of supporting the tax and understanding and accepting a powerful and respected British identity; in supporting the campaign, they are invited to self-narrate as heroes of the oppressed. In this sense, the reformed campaign further advances moves to locate discussions of the GFA within ethical discourses.

At the same time, there are clear limitations with the discourse of the Tobin Tax elaborated in the War on Want campaigns. Central criticisms are that it is geared toward a charity discourse and sometimes more focused toward elite-level lobbying than issues of broad-based public democracy (Brassett 2009). Indeed the aesthetics of the campaign are sometimes particularly ambiguous. Its publications portray a stark dichotomy between 'rich', 'suit-wearing' 'bankers' and 'poor', 'starving' 'black' people. It could well be argued that the 'Stamp Out Poverty' and 'Robin Hood Tax' campaigns, which have close links with charities and faith groups, leave unquestioned financial universalism and reproduce the charity discourse of global justice. However, despite the existing critiques of the UK campaign, there is also a political adaptability in the way the campaign has developed. It has been able to target different audiences (civil society, Treasury, DFID) with a similar message. In this way, a conversation on global justice is opened within global governance. In order to address this conversation the chapter will first look at the specific structural contingencies facing British civil society, before going on to develop a global democratic analysis of the campaign which remains sensitive to local, national, regional and global levels, and the multiple audiences that the campaign addresses.

THE GLOBAL CONTEXT OF THE UK CAMPAIGN

In the context of the global campaigns and narratives of the Tobin Tax the UK campaign nominally falls into what might be termed a neoliberal or perhaps better, a conformist position. The proposal is quite modest in level and is geared toward raising revenues to be put toward existing practices of development aid. Moreover, in its recent articulations as 'Stamp Duty on Sterling', the campaign has reneged on a previous commitment to develop a global levy with a global administration perhaps via the United Nations. However, there are some contextual and historically contingent factors which underpin the UK campaign that stem from Britain's position within and orientation toward the international political economy. These do not act as apologies for the conformist nature of the campaign, but they do suggest a set of qualifications for how we understand the progress and action of the campaign.

This section deals with three points in particular: (a) Britain in decline, (b) finance and financialization and (c) the legal status of charities. The aim is to develop a clearer understanding of the role of globalization in the discussion of global civil society in later sections. On the one hand, changes in the global political economy over the course of the twentieth century have impacted upon the perceived capacity of states to pursue welfare options. In a sense this is precisely why there is such a groundswell of support for the discussion of global economic reform. In addition, however, those same structural shifts must be taken into account when assessing the nature and extent of social response. Simply put, a UK campaign for global reforms like the Tobin Tax must—by definition—work within the context of UK experiences of globalization (indeed, as the recent hits to the UK economy suggest, this context may now be turning in favour of the proposal). On the other hand, such changes necessarily impinge upon the range of opportunities open to any campaign organization. As the next section will argue, globalization attenuates the association between democracy and the state in such a way that democratic organization must be assessed in global context, that is, in terms of their capacity to engage a range of institutions and sites relevant to the discussion and practices of global governance.

Gamble (1994: xiv) argues that a clear trend of political and economic decline underpins many of the UK's experiences and orientations toward global politics: 'Two processes stand out—the absolute decline in the power and status of the imperial state, and the relative decline of the British economy with its longstanding failure to match the rates of expansion of its rivals'. To understand British experiences of globalization, we must therefore address the principle ways in which successive British governments have mediated the fact of post-imperial decline. Two policies stand out. The first, dealt with here, concerns the evolution of a special relationship with the United States. The second, dealt with both here and in the next section, is the move to (re-)create the City of London as the economic powerhouse of the United Kingdom.

The real linchpin of the British post-war consensus is the one least often discussed: the alliance ('special relationship') with the United States. It was the policy which all governments maintained and, although occasionally questioned, it never looked remotely like being overthrown or seriously challenged. Although both parties gained in various ways from the relationship, there were a number of strains. For instance, as American capitalism started to 'take off', the United States became more in favour of free markets, currency convertibility and open trade. Indeed, there was open

American hostility to the United Kingdom on some issues, especially the last vestiges of empire. In policy-economic terms the relationship should have been fairly mediated via the Bretton Woods System of fixed exchange rates and capital controls, allowing some degree of autonomy with respect to currency policy. In practice, though, it was not.

A range of structural factors served to mitigate against the kind of policy autonomy envisaged in the original Bretton Woods agreement, including a significant balance of payments imbalance and a concomitant demand for dollar reserves, an overvalued pound and low levels of investment in an increasingly weak productive base. These structural problems led to the first of what was to become many currency crises in the UK over the next thirty years, as the dollar became established as the more secure, attractive option, particularly in the context of a Europe suffering systemic balance of payments problems. Even the Bretton Woods attempts at embedding liberal internationalism in the global political economy could not forestall the decline of the British economy and a general sense that the United Kingdom is fighting to defend itself.

In the context of trade liberalization and the decline of manufacturing competitiveness, the financial sector in the United Kingdom has risen to a level of almost unquestionable preponderance, aided by significant deregulatory moves (Strange 1986; see also Helleiner 1994). Massive profits go unquestioned because of the belief that the overall net benefit to the economy is positive. Similarly, such profits remain relatively undertaxed by a treasury that sees fit to allow the existence of more than twenty tax havens in and around the UK shores themselves. In this sense the burden of taxation is shifting very quickly from capital to labour as a result of globalization. Moreover, the decision by Gordon Brown to privatize the Central Bank has largely depoliticized macro-economic policy in a way unthinkable under any previous Labour government.

This latter point ties in with a new development in the political economy of everyday life which might be termed the *financialization* of the UK populace.[6] From the 1980s onwards, individuals in the United Kingdom have been encouraged to place more and more of their lives into the financial realm. This is evident in most countries where the possession of a bank account has become a de facto aspect of citizenship. But in the United Kingdom, the trend has expanded to a situation of potential systemic risk. Many individuals own their house via the use of borrowed funds.[7] Similarly, in recent years, private debt has ratcheted up due to an emergent and largely unchecked obsession with credit card debt. And, finally, the failure of major companies to underwrite the pension funds of their workers has led most pension funds to actively enter global financial markets via hedge fund investments, the largest and least regulated investment sector of all (Langley 2004, 2006).

The preceding considerations portray the United Kingdom as a hard case of neoliberal globalization which—although absolutely contingent and mutable—must present critics of globalization with a number of problems. With such a hard market to sell a campaign for financial regulation, the UK campaign for a Tobin Tax is further hindered by a somewhat categorical block on its range of agenda options. UK charities are allowed to operate in a tax-free manner so long as they do not engage in political campaigning or show any form of political affiliation.[8] Given that the majority of the UK campaigns funding is drawn from the charity and developmental sector, this places a heavy burden on the potential subjects it can address.

TOWARD A GLOBAL DEMOCRATIC ANALYSIS OF THE UK CAMPAIGN

As the preceding section has shown, changes in the global political economy over the course of the twentieth century serve to structure the context of the UK campaign for a Tobin Tax. The experience of post-imperial decline, a shift toward a finance-oriented political economy and a set of legal constraints on the activities of charities mean that the likelihood of a large social democratic agenda for the political reform of globalization is less practicable, if not unthinkable. However, that said, this section will look at the flip side of the coin. Although globalization acts to constrain political and/or social campaigning on some levels, it also creates a host of opportunities for engagement at levels other than the state. Globalization attenuates the close association between democracy and the nation-state and prompts the need to think of social responses to globalization in a multilevel (as opposed to an exclusively state-centric) fashion. In this view, global civil society comes to act as a key agent for global democracy and should therefore be analysed in terms of specific criteria of global democracy outlined in subsequent sections.

Globalization is an often used and radically underspecified term. It has been variously ascribed the characteristics of economic liberalization, internationalization, universalization, Westernization and deterritorialization (Scholte 2005). Causal dynamics differ between perspectives, but they all include some notion of heightened economic, communicative and technological interconnection. In the 1990s, globalization for many governments appeared to become a normalizing discourse of power that conditioned policy responses to the perception, if not always the reality, of global market integration. But this hyper-globalist view overemphasized the ascendancy of the market and was too quick to write off the importance of the state both politically and economically. Much of the initially popular and populist debate around globalization centred on a rationalist-driven 'states versus markets' dichotomy. Such a seemingly zero-sum contest belied both a capacity of the state to secure a more gradual transformation in state–market relations, and potential for a positive-sum diffusion of power among non-state actors operating in multiple sites of authority in the global system.

A subtler rendition of the relationship between states and markets sees it as a perpetual process of reconstruction of the mechanisms for sustaining capitalist accumulation in an era of global structural change. From this standpoint, we can accept the augmented power of the structures of global finance and production while recognizing that there is still no substitute for the state as the repository of sovereignty and rule-making and as provider of national security. But it is a state that is in a process of adaptation. States have been joined by a host of non-state actors operating at multiple sites of authority, both public and private, in the global policy process. A diffusion of power and influence through international organizations like the International Monetary Fund (IMF), World Bank, the World Trade Organization (WTO), European Union and the Bank for International Settlements (BIS), as well as the growing salience of private and voluntary regulatory bodies, has also meant a complex expansion of the public sphere (Brassett and Higgott 2003).

Although contested, this expansion has led to growing political interconnectedness. Manifest in the vast and interlocking network of global regulation and sites of decision-making where policies of a global nature are made, an important dimension to capture is the growing sense of 'community' that appears to be developing beyond the confines of the state. Indeed, an important element of international political life has been the multiplication of global gatherings, such as the World Social Forum (WSF), that debate the validity of a multiple array of global principles and practices.

These changes hold important implications for how we think about democracy in a global context. As Scholte suggests, 'the state, being territorially grounded, cannot be sufficient by itself as an agent of democracy *vis-à-vis* global relations' (2001: 13). In this sense, democracy must be thought of today in a global perspective. If globalization acts to constrain political and/or social campaigning on some levels, at the same time it creates a host of opportunities for engagement at levels other than the state. Exclusively state-centric understandings and critiques of the UK campaign for the Tobin Tax are therefore unhelpful and, in terms of even day-to-day operations, unrealistic. Why study the impact at UK government level when the campaigners are all working in Mumbai? Developing this point, there is an increasingly pressing need to take account of the non-territorial sources of (political) identity and legitimacy that accompany this shift to multilevel (un)democratic governance, which transcend conventional territorialized notions of 'the people' to encompass substate and trans-state solidarities (Scholte 2001: 13–14).

On these terms, there is far more at stake in the analysis of global civil society than simply the success or failure of a particular campaign. Indeed, even a limited operation like the UK campaign for the Tobin Tax necessarily involves large and diverse audiences in a discussion of global financial governance that they would not otherwise partake in. Moreover, the very fact that these organizations are drawing attention toward the existence of

North–South inequality via an albeit moderate reform like the Tobin Tax is a signal that the agenda of global governance has shifted from one of mere technical or bureaucratic efficiency.

POSITIVE ASPECTS OF THE UK CAMPAIGN FOR GLOBAL DEMOCRACY

As the preceding analysis has argued, globalization should be understood as both a context and constitutive force in articulating the limits, as well as presenting possibilities for global civil society. Just as changes in the global political economy throughout the twentieth century have impacted upon the structural limitations of political debate in the United Kingdom, so such changes present a new arc of possibilities for activists within global civil society. Simply stated, the contours of democratic practice no longer end at the boundaries of the state. To speak of the UK campaign in a state-centric manner therefore misses the huge interdependence between campaigns and campaigners across the world. Moreover, as the following section attests, it understates the importance and impact of the UK campaign at multiple levels in the global polity.

The following appraisal follows the framework for analysing global civil society developed by Scholte (2001). A campaign might enhance global democracy via public education, providing voice to stakeholders, fuelling debate about global governance, increasing transparency and accountability within institutions of financial governance and promoting a sense of democratic legitimacy for global finance. Negatively, it may not pursue explicitly democratic aims, they may be poorly conceived, the institutions being lobbied may be ill-equipped for such engagements, civil society may be co-opted by certain interests, the civil society group may itself be unrepresentative or come from an overly narrow cultural base (for example, white, male, middle class) or a civil society group may be internally undemocratic.

Public Education

In broad terms the public education component of the UK campaign for the Tobin Tax is quite strong. The website is easily accessible and provides straightforward summaries of the debates surrounding the Tobin Tax and issues of North–South inequality. Moreover, the technical reports produced are organized with straightforward non-technical summaries at the start.

It can be argued that a lot of the education function is geared toward the sentimental aspects of global inequality (Brassett 2009): videos emphasize the helplessness of Southern people to the ravages of globalization in general and global finance in particular. Moreover, the UK campaigners are keen to spread the message of their campaign in large-scale public forums, such as the Make Poverty History (MPH) campaign, the World Social Forum and even the Glastonbury music festival.[9] In this sense, could it be suggested that the UK campaign acts to 'dumb down' the issues at stake in the discussion of the Tobin Tax? Certainly in comparison with Attac's programme of summer schools and public teach-ins, the UK campaign is geared toward a more sound-bite oriented approach (increasingly so following the shift to the 'Robin Hood Tax' framing).

But this view is limited on two counts. First, it ignores the structural contingencies faced by British NGOs discussed in the third section. And second, the nature of global campaigning means that events like the European (ESF) and World (WSF) social forums somewhat force the UK campaign to engage with broader and deeper ideas about the reform of globalization due to the context of open platforms and audience participation and critique. Thus, public education must be regarded as an interactive process.

Voice

The idea at the centre of the Tobin Tax campaign is to develop a generalized (social) democratic voice at the heart of global finance. Thus, in broad terms, the successful generation of publicity and policy-level engagement must be considered part of the story of the UK campaign. However, in more specific terms of achieving actual voice for disaffected or marginal individuals or groups, the UK campaign for a Tobin Tax scores less well. As previous sections have argued, the War on Want/Stamp Out Poverty agenda is effectively an elite-driven and elite-orientated development campaign. Although the plight of marginal actors in the developing world is a core consideration of the campaign—as exemplified by the prominence given to impoverished women who went into prostitution after the Asian financial crises (War on Want 2002a)—the 'voice' of such people is rarely included in campaign documents or elite level meetings, serving more as examples.

That said, the ambiguities of this question must be understood. The nature of global civil society discussion forums at the WSF, the ESF and indeed at internal campaign meetings is such that all interested parties are welcome, indeed, encouraged to take part in discussions.

Driving the Debate on Global Governance

The UK campaign has placed the issue of taxing financial markets onto the agenda of global governance in a number of ways. First, no matter how limited the outcomes, there has been a credible attempt to tie up the Tobin Tax with ongoing debates over innovative sources of financing for development. Although the UK campaign has usually been forced into the position of having its substance excluded from the debate, it has been an important mainstream critic of the credit based proposals adopted. Second, again with limited outcomes, the move to European-level lobbying has contributed toward existing debates that place social redistributive agendas onto the agenda of European-level governance currently geared toward monetarist supply-side organization (see European Central Bank [ECB] 2004). And third, with greater result, the UK campaign has contributed extensively to the discussion of global taxation within the European and World Social Forums.

Promoting Transparency and Accountability

The promotion of transparency and accountability in the regulatory frameworks of global finance has had, of course, a limited impact in general, and the results of the Tobin Tax campaign provide little exception. Benefits include the close association of the Tobin Tax with early discussions of reforming the global financial architecture, although these very quickly moved away from the kind of strong regulatory reforms that many advocated (see Porter 2005). Despite enduring structures and practices, piecemeal successes should be noted. The UK campaign—especially the Stamp Out Poverty variant—was intimately bound up with recent popular discussions about G8 reform. First, Make Poverty History brought forth a number of government statements on North–South Inequality and successfully broadened the constituency of interest for issues such as debt, fair trade and the kind of Official Development Assistance (ODA) that the Tobin Tax could support. Second, the European campaign forced the ECB to justify its position on taxing capital (ECB 2004).

Promoting Legitimacy

Again the actual results of the global campaign and the UK campaign, in particular, are limited. Although the GFA reform debates pushed transparency and accountability centre stage for a few years after the East Asian financial crises, this move is both limited and increasingly distanced from the UK campaign. That said, the UK campaign has been a vociferous lobbyer and critic of the British government. In policy meetings and numerous press articles it has promoted awareness of the limitations of free capital mobility, attempting to tie the effects of financial crises to the actions of Northern banks. It has closely monitored the debate over innovative sources of financing for development. And it was among those key civil society critics of eventual reforms arising from the G8 meetings in Gleneagles in 2005.

NEGATIVE ASPECTS OF THE UK CAMPAIGN FOR GLOBAL DEMOCRACY

As the preceding section argued, there is much to be drawn from the UK campaign that both supports and develops global justice/global democracy.

Successful communication of a straightforward message through media, social forums, financial organizations and (with less impact) policy circles must be read as a major plus for the task of democratizing global governance. Moreover, with specific reference to the question of building North–South solidarities on questions of inequality, the UK campaign has been prominent in World Social Forum meetings and has tied itself to a successful North–South coalition for air-ticket levies. However, despite these positives, the balance sheet of democratic engagement must be tallied. In this final section, a number of potential negative impacts of the UK campaign are addressed.

Anti-Democratic Aims

Straightforwardly, there is nothing within the UK campaign for the Tobin Tax which is uncivil, illegal or anti-democratic. However, the move to a 'Robin Hood Tax' campaign does potentially open spaces to redefine how democracy and legality are thought of and practiced. Invoking the 'democratic illegality' of the Robin Hood myth asks demanding questions about the prevailing legal structures of the GFA, which may themselves be thought of as anti-democratic in this context—the seeming virtue of Robin Hood's illegal interventions calls the dominant structures into question.

Coherence and Comprehensiveness of Agenda

As the preceding sections have argued, the UK campaign for the Tobin Tax is generally very coherent in terms of presenting clear objectives via a well-designed strategy. However, this coherence is arguably bought at the price of comprehensiveness. Concentrating on the minimal version of the Tobin Tax means that the revenue-raising function is emphasized at the expense of the market-calming function. Moreover, as Patomäki (2005) has emphatically argued, this is also at the expense of broader programmes to democratize global governance. On the model of the Tobin Tax outlined by him, there is potential to build a new global democratic organization that would be a step on the way to a more cosmopolitan future. This kind of comprehensive blueprint is downplayed, although perhaps not ruled out by the UK campaign.

Adequacy of Institutions Lobbied

For the most part, the answer to this question relies upon which institution is being lobbied. For instance, DFID has in general been very happy to take part in discussions about the Tobin Tax and has allowed its economists to attend meetings. However, the UK Treasury has been less willing to engage. And when the Belgian members of the European campaign requested the

ECB to respond to the Belgian government's decision to support the Tobin Tax, its response was couched in straightforwardly economic technical language (ECB 2004). The ECB was therefore poorly equipped to deal with the political and ethical dimensions of the proposal or with the nature of civil society engagement. For example, no allowances were made by the ECB for engaging with civil society actors, such as recognizing them as concerned stakeholders via invitations to respond.

Co-Option of the Campaign

Co-option in the strong sense is hard to define, let alone prove. However, as has been argued in previous sections and, indeed, as the UK campaigners themselves boast, the technical details of the campaign are strongly geared toward producing a 'mainstream proposal'. Although the ultimate of this proposal is not—by any means—the first best option for proponents of neoliberal globalization in positions of power, there is a sense in which such technical arguments reduce the scope for 'debate and . . . space for dissent' (Scholte 2001: 20). To that end, it is important that the UK campaign continues to partake in the multi-party campaigns and forums with the same willingness as in the past. In this way, broader ideas about global financial reform can remain on the reform agenda if and when it comes into contact with policymakers.

Representativeness of UK Campaign

The representativeness of the UK campaign for the Tobin Tax can be questioned largely because it is avowedly a campaign rather than mass member mobilization. In this sense, the British campaign has often suffered in comparison with organizations such as Attac. The larger mandate of Attac, the range of issues it discusses and the large-scale nature of its membership mean that it can more easily claim to be a representative actor. However, even within the limited mandate of the UK campaign for the Tobin Tax, there are number of moves that could be made to improve its representative character. For instance, there could be more effort made to allow supporters to direct the focus and concerns of the campaign.

Currently, the website provides information about how to take part in the existing activities (including via lobbing Members of Parliament [MPs] and uploading videos), how to receive updates and (in an improvement over the pre–Robin Hood Tax campaign and the Stamp Out Poverty websites) spaces to criticize and ask questions (a facility also available through the Facebook page, which has over 150,000 members). However, the involvement of non-organizers is restricted to a responsive dynamic where activities are restricted to following the guidance of the campaign or to making suggestions. Opportunities for more organizational involvement do not appear to be forthcoming. The representativeness could also be criticized for a potentially Northern bias via the fact that the website is only in English, which could inhibit the inclusion of supporters from non-English-speaking areas.

Internal Democracy of War on Want/Stamp Out Poverty

In formal terms the internal democracy of the UK campaign is well appointed. There are regular emails and newsletters that are sent out to members and interested parties. Moreover, there is an ongoing series of meetings open but not limited to members of the organizations within the European campaign and affiliate NGO sector. And, furthermore, the UK campaign organizes public meetings that showcase levels of progress and action. However, there are several issues relating to the financial burden of 'global civil society' and the cultural base of the campaign which inhibit thicker notions of democracy.

First, a common issue for any actor within global civil society is the cost of travel to attend meetings no matter how open they are in formal terms. In this sense, activists are in general dependent upon the financial backing of their host organization, which can sometimes be limited. And second, an avowed element of the UK campaign seeks to target elites in the development sector and, more problematically, elites in the financial markets. As a strategy, this is by all means worthy, but in its execution this has sometimes involved taking on overtly 'middle-class', 'university-educated', 'financially minded' men. At the very least, such a focus reduces the scope of relevant members in the employment of the campaign. At the worst, such strategies risk marginalizing grass-roots or more radical political organizations.

CONCLUSION

This chapter has addressed the UK campaign for the Tobin Tax in critical terms. Existing treatments stress the conformist nature of the War on Want/Stamp Out Poverty proposal and lament the low levels of popular mobilization, as compared to the French movement of Attac (Patomäki 2005). However, although sympathetic to such positions, the chapter made the case to set the UK campaign in the context of structural changes in the international political economy associated with globalization. In this way, a more nuanced and potentially productive analysis of the UK campaign can be developed that remains sensitive to both the limits and the possibilities presented.

In a national context increasingly defined through 'financialization', ambitious and feasible reformism, which includes a high, universal and democratically administered Tobin Tax, may be hard to 'think', let alone 'sell'. Moreover, a host of legal regulations have encouraged the growth of an apolitical, charity-oriented, NGO sector as the mainstay of the British discussion on issues of North–South inequality and possible developmental responses. Although this general situation is perhaps lamentable for privileging certain elites and/or for reducing many issues of North–South inequality to a set of technical and top-down reforms, it is perhaps unfair to single out one campaign—the UK campaign for the Tobin Tax—for bearing the hallmarks of its contingency.

In this context, it was argued that a straightforward dismissal of the UK campaign for the Tobin Tax is both unwise and liable to miss the potential (democratic) contributions of the campaign from a global perspective. Indeed, globalization is argued to blur the association between democracy and the nation-state to such an extent that the UK campaign for the Tobin Tax should be analysed in a multilevel fashion. Only in this sense can we gain a true measure of the campaign, which has indeed engaged on regional, global and cyber-spatial levels. For these reasons, it was argued that a global democratic analysis of the UK campaign for a Tobin Tax is both viable and should proceed, while considering a balance of positive and negative contributions to global democracy (Scholte 2001).

In terms of positive impacts, the UK campaign has done much to foster discussion of the Tobin Tax and important themes of North–South inequality in social forums, public meetings, via its website and through social networking resources such as Facebook and Twitter. Moreover, the reports that have been produced go a long way to interpreting the often arcane workings of global financial markets in an easily and broadly understandable way. This is a fundamental prerequisite for building the kind of global public spheres that might contest and democratize global finance. The UK campaign has directly contributed to the development of a European campaign on the Tobin Tax, which has set up an office in Brussels. This both fleshes out the discussion of global governance and encourages bodies like the European Union and the ECB to think about their accountability in broader terms than simply economic and bureaucratic efficiency.

In negative terms, the UK campaign has thus far tended to emphasize the explicitly cash-based and redistributive elements of the Tobin Tax proposal to the detriment of broader questions of democratizing global governance institutions. Although the campaign is well conceived and very well targeted—at the bodies and parties that can make a difference—it was argued that more could be done to generate a broader-based (in socially and ethical terms) representative agenda. The narrative of poor people in the South who need to be protected from aggressive speculators and given money by civilized Northerners is a fairly limited and sometimes constraining depiction of the issues at hand (Brassett 2009). Finally, although internal democratic communication is very frequent and procedurally open, it should be stressed that a common and general problem of global civil society persists: funding toward attending meetings is dependent upon the wealth of the organization to which you belong. Simply put, if your organization does not have the resources, it is much harder to attend the meetings in Brussels, Seoul or Mumbai.

NOTES

1. Aspects of this argument draw upon Brassett (2010).
2. See http://www.stampoutpoverty.org.
3. Interview with David Hillman, July 2003, War on Want offices, Clapham.
4. Comments by Avinash Persaud at the Stamp Out Poverty, Progress and Action meeting, 19 November 2005, Camden Town Hall.
5. See http://robinhoodtax.org.uk.
6. Dore (2002: 116–117) defines financialization as 'the increasing dominance of the finance industry in the sum total of economic activity, of financial controllers in the management of corporations, of financial assets among total assets, of marketised securities and particularly equities among financial assets, of the stock market as a market for corporate control in determining corporate strategies, and of fluctuations in the stock market as a determinant of business cycles'. Although this definition is useful, it ignores the way in which such material dominance has important social consequences by constituting financial citizens with a limited range of life options (Brassett and Tsingou 2011).
7. Indeed, the size and sensitivity of the mortgage sector in the United Kingdom is a major factor behind the UK's ambivalence over joining the euro.
8. Gift Aid allows individuals who are subject to UK income tax to complete a simple, short declaration that they are a UK taxpayer. Any cash donations that the taxpayer makes to the charity after making a declaration are treated as being made after deduction of income tax at the basic rate (22 per cent in 2006–2007), and the charity can reclaim the basic rate income tax paid on the gift. For a basic-rate taxpayer, this adds approximately 28 per cent to the value of any gift made under Gift Aid. Higher-rate taxpayers can claim income tax relief, above and beyond the amount claimed directly by the charities. The rate of the relief for higher rate taxpayers in 2006–2007 is usually 18 per cent, the difference between the basic rate (22 per cent) and the higher rate (40 per cent) of income tax, although recipients of savings income (taxed at 20 per cent and 40 per cent) and dividend income (taxed at 10 per cent and 32.5 per cent) can achieve higher rates of tax relief (20 per cent and 22.5 per cent, respectively).
9. See http://www.stampoutpoverty.org/?lid=9954.

BIBLIOGRAPHY

Brassett, James. (2009). 'A Pragmatic Approach to the Tobin Tax Campaign: The Politics of Sentimental Education', *European Journal of International Relations*, 15 (3): 447–476.

———. (2010). *Cosmopolitanism and Global Financial Reform: A Pragmatic Approach to the Tobin Tax*, London: RIPE/Routledge Studies in Global Political Economy.

Brassett, James, and Higgott, Richard. (2003). 'Building the Normative Dimension(S) of a Global Polity', *Review of International Studies*, 29:29–55.

Brassett, James, and Tsingou, Eleni. (2011). 'The Politics of Legitimate Global Governance', *Review of International Political Economy*, 18 (1): 1–16.

Dore, Ronald. (2002). 'Stock Market Capitalism and Its Diffusion', *New Political Economy*, 7 (1): 115–121.

Eichengreen, Barry. (1999) *Toward a New International Financial Architecture: A Practical Post-Asia Agenda*, Washington, DC: Institute for International Economics.

European Central Bank. (2004). *Opinion of the European Central Bank of 4 November 2004: At the Request of the Belgian Ministry of Finance on a Draft Law Introducing a Tax on Exchange Operations Involving Foreign Exchange, Banknotes and Currency* (CON/2004/34). https://www.ecb.europa.eu/ecb/legal/pdf/en_con_2004_34_f_sign.pdf (accessed 1 May 2011).

Gamble, Andrew. (1994). *Britain in Decline: Economic Policy, Political Strategy, and the British State*, Basingstoke: Palgrave Macmillan.

Helleiner, Eric. (1994). *States and the Re-Emergence of Global Finance*, Ithaca, NY: Cornell University Press.

Kapoor, Sony. (2003). *The Tobin Tax: Enhancing Financial Stability and Financing Development*, London: Tobin Tax Network.

Langley, Paul. (2004). 'In the Eye of the "Perfect Storm": The Final Salary Pension Crisis and Financialisation of Anglo-American Capitalism', *New Political Economy*, 9 (4): 539–558.

———. (2006). 'The Making of Investor Subjects in Anglo-American Pensions', *Environment and Planning D: Society and Space*, 24 (6): 919–934.

Patomäki, Heikki. (2001). *Democratising Globalization: The Leverage of the Tobin Tax*, London: Zed Books.

———. (2005). *Reactionary and Progressive Versions of the Tobin Tax: A Critique of Sony Kapoor's Draft Report 'The Currency Transaction Tax: Enhancing Financial Stability and Financing Development'*, in J. Penttinen, V.-P. Sorsa and M.Ylönen (eds), *More Taxes! Promoting Strategies for Global Taxation*, Helsinki: Attac Finland.

Porter, Tony. (2005). *Globalization and Finance*, Cambridge: Polity Press.

Scholte, Jan Aart. (2001). *Civil Society and Democracy in Global Governance*. CSGR Working Paper No. 65/01, Centre for the Study of Globalisation and Regionalisation, University of Warwick, Coventry.

———. (2005). *Globalization: A Critical Introduction*, 2nd ed., Basingstoke: Palgrave Macmillan.

Spahn, Paul Bernd. (1995). *International Financial Flows and Transactions Taxes: Survey and Options*. IMF Working Paper WP/95/60, IMF, Washington, DC.

Spratt, Stephen. (2005). *A Sterling Solution: Implementing a Stamp Duty on Sterling to Finance International Development*, London: Stamp Out Poverty and the Cooperative Bank.

Strange, Susan. (1986). *Casino Capitalism*, Oxford: Basil Blackwell.

Tobin, James. (1978). 'A Proposal for International Monetary Reform', *Eastern Economic Journal*, 4 (3–4): 153–159.

Ul Haq, Mahbub, Kaul, Inge, and Grunberg, Isabelle. (eds) (1996). *The Tobin Tax: Coping with Financial Volatility*, New York: Oxford University Press.

War on Want. (2002a). *Costing the Casino: A Survey of the Economic and Social Impact of Currency Crises on Developing Countries*, London: War on Want. http://www.waronwant.org/resources/publications?start=60 (accessed May 2011).

———. (2002b). *The Robin Hood Tax: Concrete Proposals for Fighting Global Poverty and Promoting Sustainable Development by Harnessing the Proceeds from a Currency Transactions Tax*, London: War on Want. http://www.waronwant.org/resources/publications?start=60 (accessed May 2011).

12 Campaign or 'Movement of Movements'?

Attac France and the Currency Transaction Tax

Edouard Morena

INTRODUCTION

Much has been written on the Association for the Taxation of Financial Transactions and Aid to Citizens (Attac) and its pivotal role in the emergence of the French *altermondialiste* (or 'alter-globalization') movement in the late 1990s. Particular scrutiny has been given to the study of Attac's role as both a civil society organization and a platform of convergence for various French social movement actors and organizations through a shared critique of neoliberal globalization. If we look at Attac's founding statutes, we notice that the organization's original purpose was to promote an international tax on currency transaction taxes (CTT)1 and financial capital movements in order to put 'sand in the wheels' of international finance. This chapter, through an examination of the Tobin Tax campaign in France and its impact on policy assessment and practice, attempts to explain why Attac rapidly became more than it had initially been intended to be. Through reference to research on political opportunity structures,2 it is argued that the CTT question in France is inseparable from Attac and that its appearance on the French political agenda was the product of a triple convergence between Attac, mainstream politics and public opinion, a junction whose point of convergence was neoliberal globalization.

The discussion proceeds in the following manner. In the first section, the rise of Attac is situated within the broader political, social and cultural context of the late 1990s in France. In the second section, a framework is presented through which to understand the dynamics of policy change and the key actors that shape policy discourses and outcomes. In order to show the relevance of this frame to our analysis, the third, fourth and fifth sections explore the respective roles of public opinion, Attac's internal organizational structure and the group's apparent shift away from single-issue advocacy. The final section examines how and why global taxation issues were taken up by mainstream political circles.

CONTEXTUALIZING THE CTT MOVEMENT

According to Bernard Cassen, the first president of Attac, Ignacio Ramonet's 1997 appeal in *Le Monde Diplomatique* for a CTT 'was launched like a bottle into the sea, without any idea of what the reaction might be' (Cassen 2003: 41). By the turn of the century, the tax proposal had been unanimously taken on by practically all of France's political leaders. Why did the CTT issue gain such traction within the public debate and French policy? In order to attempt to answer this question, we need to place the initiative within the broader French political and cultural contexts.

The CTT proposal's appeal came from the way in which it touched upon a set of broader societal concerns which had already been raised by the social movement: globalization, the changing nature of political activism and the role of the state. Although criticized, the state's legitimacy has never been fundamentally questioned in France.3 The issue of neoliberal globalization is far more recent. In a context of rapidly developing communications' technologies and greater perceived interconnectedness, social inequalities were rapidly associated to what was generally perceived as a new phenomenon. Although it was perceived as a source of opportunities, globalization was also interpreted as a potential threat to French culture, to national sovereignty and to the regulatory state. In such a context, by focusing on financial globalization—and not capitalism—and by reaffirming the importance of the regulatory state, the nascent alter-globalization movement was soon able to attract widespread public and political support. Through its symbolic strength and compatibility with both globalization and state issues, the CTT proposal brought together a diverse set of social movement actors rapidly giving birth to a new organization, Attac.

The dual nature of the CTT proposal's objectives—namely, to serve as a regulating mechanism to discourage financial speculation and to collect funds for development purposes—made it possible to federate a wide array of organizations. The regulatory facet attracted groups concerned with finding alternatives to neoliberalism, whereas the redistributive aspect was of particular interest to organizations that focused on development issues. If we look at the composition of Attac France at the time of our study, we notice that the majority of the member organizations were not development non-governmental organizations (NGOs) but trade unions, alternative media, feminist groups and so on, most of which have clearly political takes on the globalization issue.[4] Although, historically, French NGOs have tended to be politically active, their limited presence among the founding organizations is quite revealing. In other words, the French CTT campaign—centralized within Attac—was, from the outset, primarily motivated by a desire to combat financial globalization.

Other important factors that need to be considered in order to understand both the emergence of the alter-globalization movement and the widespread public support for Attac are the evolutions within French mainstream politics, and notably within the political left.[5] Growing public disillusionment toward mainstream politics turned social movements into natural havens for individuals seeking to *faire de la politique autrement* (do politics differently). The rapid growth of Attac and the subsequent broadening of its agenda are, to a large extent, the result of this capacity to attract politically conscious citizens that no longer believe in mainstream politics' ability to 'change lives'.

The late 1990s represented an unstable time for global capitalism. A series of economic crises had taken place, all related to global finance. At the time of Ramonet's call, a new dynamic was already under way within French militant circles, a dynamic that was conducive to broad-based social mobilization. The Maastricht Treaty referendum, 1995 national and the 1997 campaign against the Multilateral Agreement on Investment (MAI) all formed moments in which various strands of civil society could meet, define common adversaries and plan new campaigns. In this sense, Ignacio Ramonet's (1997) editorial in *Le Monde Diplomatique*—and his proposal to create an organization whose raison d'être would be the promotion of the Tobin Tax—represented a new opportunity for organizations and individuals to converge. In addition to the advantages that were mentioned in the preceding, the CTT offered the added asset of being a tangible proposal, in theory, to regulate the international financial system while simultaneously acting as a source of income for development projects. The third factor relates to the very nature of the call. The call was published in a newspaper whose authors and readers include militants, academics and radical intellectuals whose ability to analyse and theorize the globalization phenomenon would prove essential in order for the movement to converge and define common strategies and adversaries. In a country whose political elite and media attach great importance to intellectuals, the presence within Attac of an intellectual foundation proved to be an important asset for the campaign.

The context was ripe for the establishment of a coalition of various social movement groups, alternative newspapers and progressive intellectuals. As Lusson, member of the Association Internationale de Techniciens, Experts et Chercheurs (AITEC) and Attac, explains:

> Attac was set up by a group of individuals who, for the most part, had acknowledged the proximities between their analyses with regards to neoliberal globalization and the crisis of 'mainstream politics' and that had learned to work together as from the November 1995 mobilization, the movement of the unemployed of the Winter 1997–1998 and the 1997 mobilization against the MAI, without, until then, participating in a common and structured association. (2007: 118)

Thus a double dynamic took place. A broad coalition appeared as the most appropriate organizational structure to press for the CTT. Conversely, the CTT was in its very nature a consensual proposal capable of triggering the creation of such a coalition.

From an organizational perspective, the new framework (Ancelovici's 'Politics against Global Markets') that was emerging and that gave birth to such networks as Attac or the social forums represented opportunities for organizations 'to revive themselves, reach a wider audience and gain greater visibility, without losing their specificities or autonomy of action' (Agrikoliansky and Sommier 2005: 35). In the case of Attac, the encounter between a coherent group of intellectuals and experienced organizers provided 'selective incentives to different constituencies' (Ancelovici 2002: 439). Unions, for instance, could widen their support base and legitimacy by extending their reach to new social movements and associations. For civic associations, participating in Attac granted them access to tangible (facilities, means of communication) and intangible (organizing and legal skills, expertise, social and symbolic capital) resources (Ancelovici 2002: 439; 2004: 50). Finally, in the case of the rank and file, the incentives were primarily of a symbolic and moral nature. Attac represented 'an opportunity to express [one's] disenchantment with institutional politics while rebuilding a sense of belonging and collective identity' (Ancelovici 2002: 439). For Bernard Cassen, the issue of size was also important: 'for the small organizations, it was gratifying to appear with larger groups and have access to a new platform, but for those that "weighed" the most, that is the trade unions, it was an opportunity to have a [cercle de réflexion], a common ["centrale"] that produces expertise on financial globalization, its consequences and possible alternatives' (Cassen 2006).

COMPLEX INTERACTIONS

Ignacio Ramonet's proposal must be situated within a specific context and its success explained by a complex combination of dynamics. Our next task will be to analyse his article's wider consequences through an analysis of the French CTT campaign's evolution between 1998 and 2006. In order to do so, we will use a model developed by Marco Giugni, which, while drawing upon political opportunity structures, also integrates a new and essential factor: public opinion. In the following paragraphs, we examine the evolutions that took place within French mainstream politics, within Attac and within French public opinion. In the latter case, we draw upon the idea that social and political actors are influenced by 'perceptions of inequality', of which opinion polls serve as important tools of measurement. In the case of the evolutions of mainstream politics, we distinguish between two important phases. In the first, which was characterized by a series of financial crises, capitalism was seen to be at risk and the political elites acknowledged the need for new regulatory tools. In the second phase, the implementation of a tax represented a dual opportunity for France to both regain an international status as global superpower and find new innovative sources of funding in order to comply with its Millennium

Development Goal (MDG) engagements. Finally, in the case of Attac, we look at its organizational evolutions and how they have affected its capacity to effectively embody the French CTT movement.

Three key sets of actors emerge that are of relevance to our analysis. First, we distinguish the alter-globalization movement (including Attac) as a hybrid amalgamation of militants bound together by their suspicion towards party politics. Second, there are institutional political actors who participate in electoral campaigns and promote specific policies. This set of actors is characterized by a growing convergence between the mainstream left and right and growing divergences between the mainstream and the extremes. The third actor relates to public opinion. Between these three actors, we have identified two closely interrelated issues around which interactions occur: the issues of globalization and the state.

The interpretation of and importance given by the various sets of actors to issues (such as neoliberal globalization) shape political discourses and related public policies (Giugni 2004:14).

PUBLIC OPINION

If we follow Giugni's approach, public opinion plays an essential role for our understanding of the various mechanisms that give rise to public policy. Two issues relating to public opinion have to be analysed. On the one hand, there is the issue of the relationship between public opinion and both policymakers and social movement actors. As Giugni contends in an earlier article, 'while it seems obvious that protest activities raise the awareness of the population on certain political issues, changes in public opinion can also help movements to reach their goals by making decision-makers more responsive to their demands' (1998: 379–380). On the other hand, we must take into account the ways in which the tools used to measure public opinion generate certain perceptions of inequality and how these perceptions enhance our understanding of the evolutions of policy decisions related to the broader issue of inequality (of which neoliberal globalization is one possible expression). In this section, we will briefly analyse the evolutions in the interpretations of public opinion—through a study of different opinion polls that were produced in relation to the globalization question and the CTT proposal. Our aim is to highlight possible correlations between perceptions of globalization, the state and North–South inequalities, on the one hand, and the evolutions of the CTT proposal within the public agenda, on the other.

Although there have been a number of studies on the relationships between governmental decisions and political preferences (notably through the concepts of responsiveness and congruence), the literature on public opinion remains rather divided with regards to the modalities of interaction between the various components of public opinion (for example, social category, level of education, degree of information, political affinities) and their relations to policymakers. Although it is difficult to identify the factors that determine a government's sensitivity to public opinion, it is nevertheless clear that governments take public opinion into account. As Blanc, Loisel and Scherrer (2005: 119) rightly point out, 'the various opinion polls that are ordered, the media reports and surveillance of protest marches all express a desire for governments to constantly stay informed about the state of public opinion'. As we have seen, not only do governments and mainstream political actors refer to public opinion, but social actors do so as well. They declare themselves to be acting for the public good, regularly referring to public opinion as guiding their actions.

Despite their inherent limitations, public opinion is usually calculated through opinion polls. In the following paragraphs, we analyse a series of opinion polls/surveys that were conducted by five polling organizations over the period stretching from 1998 (creation of Attac) to 2006.6 Our research specifically focused on three types of surveys: surveys that were explicitly on the CTT proposal (Tobin Tax), surveys that mentioned the CTT or other international taxes and surveys that were on issues that, in my view, could be directly associated with the CTT proposal (globalization, the role of the state, inequalities).[7]

During the period of study, a significant number of surveys (at least twenty-five) directly or indirectly focused on the globalization question and related issues (role of the state, North–South inequalities). Two surveys specifically looked at the Tobin Tax proposal. In a survey conducted in September 2001, asking whether or not those interrogated were in favour of implementing the Tobin Tax in order to help poor countries, 71 per cent of those interviewed answered that they were.[8] In another survey centred on aid to poor countries (published on 12 October 2001), 58 per cent of those interviewed felt that France should fulfil its development aid engagements (20 per cent felt that it should actually increase its development aid contribution).[9] In an earlier survey entitled *The French and the Regulation of Capitalism* (July 2000), when asked which organizations they believed should set the 'rules of the economy', a staggering 69 per cent of the respondents answered that it should be state and government.[10] In the same survey, when asked which phenomena (up to three) they considered to be the most worrying, 40 per cent answered 'world hunger'.[11] Of particular interest to our research are not necessarily the results (which tend to confirm the ideas that we have already put forward) but their frequency of publication. The regularity with which these surveys were published indicates the centrality of the globalization issue during our period of study.

What emerges from this table is the important number of surveys conducted in 2001 (ten on issues related with globalization, the role of the state, North–South inequalities and so on, two of which were specifically on the Tobin Tax) when compared to the other years of our study. The quantity of surveys represents, in itself, an indicator of the importance of

Table 12.1 Opinion Polls on CTT-Related Issues

Year	*Number of Observed Surveys (of which Specifically on Tobin Tax)*	*Key 'Alter-Globalization' Events*
1998	0 (0)	
1999	2 (0)	Seattle
2000	3 (0)	Larzac 1
2001	10 (2)	1st FSM Porto Alegre, Genoa, 9/11, French National Assembly passes Tobin Tax amendment
2002	1 (0)	Presidential elections
2003	5 (0)	Larzac 2, Cancún
2004	2 (0)	
2005	4 (0)	
2006	2 (0)	

Source: Compiled by the author.

the globalization issue within French politics at the time. The fact that all of the surveys were financed by national medias tends to support this idea.[12]

The political response to the Genoa events (during the G8 summit on 20–22 July 2001), for instance, corroborates the idea that public opinion plays an important role in the policy-making process. Mass demonstrations, like surveys, often serve as indicators of public opinion. Over 150,000 people gathered in the Italian city to demonstrate against the G8 summit. The impressive number of protesters, combined with the intense media coverage of the Genoa events and public criticism of Italian police methods (notably after the death of one of the protesters), created conditions for the discussion of alternatives. Shortly after the Genoa events, Lionel Jospin, the French socialist prime minister at the time, proposed that the European Union take the initiative with regards to the implementation of a Tobin Tax. Shortly after that, on 13 September, Laurent Fabius, then Minister of Finance, met with a delegation of Attac representatives and declared that the tax was a 'generous idea'. The culminating point of this period was the adoption by the National Assembly of a Tobin Tax amendment to the 2002 finance law. This amendment established the Tobin Tax on condition that other European countries followed suit. Although the link is difficult to establish, it seems rather interesting to note the relationship between the sequences of events that took place between July and November 2001 and the publication, by a wide range of medias, of opinion polls that either directly looked at the Tobin Tax proposal or focused on issues relating to globalization, North–South inequalities and development aid.[13] The particularly important number of polls published during the year (and especially in the Genoa period) on these issues attests of a window of opportunity for Attac to effectively press for the Tobin Tax proposal.

Although the globalization issue was at the centre of French politics in 2001, its centrality was clearly affected by the 11 September terrorist attacks. During a seminar entitled 'La taxe Tobin, les taxes globales et la redistribution' (organized by Attac in Paris on 17 May 2002), Pierre Tartakowsky recognized that the 9/11 attacks had had a direct impact on the issue of North–South inequalities and the ways of funding development. As he explains, 'another logic, the logic of war, pushed these issues to the background' (Tartakowsky 2002). As he then explained, 'the September 11th events have not broken the movement's dynamic; however they have had an impact on its credibility as a source for global alternatives'. In the post-9/11 context, a new issue came to the fore: insecurity.[14] Attac's response to this changing situation directly takes into account the public opinion issue. For Tartakowsky (2002), proposals relating to the Tobin Tax had to be re-evaluated, 'not to sell them off, but to collectively make sure that they are still relevant to the challenges lying ahead, understandable to the public, sufficiently convincing and unifying to become truly central and to impose [themselves]'. As Pierre Tartakowsky explains, 'Attac is capable . . . of influencing the political agenda when its concerns are in line with those of public opinion. It's not the tail that wags the dog [and] Attac is the tail' (cited in Uggla 2004: 19). The changes that occurred both nationally (new focus on insecurity) and globally (post-9/11 context) and their impact on the general public undoubtedly contributed to marginalize the CTT issue. Whereas a single-issue group would continue to push for the CTT proposal, Attac as a 'movement of movements' evolved by integrating society's shifting desires. As we will see in the following pages, the characteristics of, and evolution within, Attac's membership base undoubtedly impacted on its strategic priorities. As Jacques Cossart, member of Attac's Scientific Council, pointed out, there are 'more ex-members of Attac than actual members and the membership base constantly renews itself', and new members 'do not necessarily have the same origins or ideas'.[15]

INTERNAL ORGANIZATION

In order to understand the rise of Attac as well as the internal transformations that affected it (in terms of issues and forms of activism), it is essential to examine its internal organizational structures. For strategic reasons, Bernard Cassen had originally chosen to bring together the organizations—and not the individuals—who had responded to Ramonet's appeal (Cassen 2003: 42). These organizations were represented by individuals who had often been engaged in a variety of struggles, encompassing multiple political tendencies. They had often previously worked together during past political and social struggles (Lusson 2007: 118). Membership levels rapidly grew and, by October 1998, there were over thirty-five hundred registered members. Individual memberships and the creation of hundreds of Local Committees (CL) significantly impacted on the evolution of the Tobin Tax proposal within Attac. As Bernard Cassen explains, 'many of [the CL] saw in Attac a substitute to leftist partisan and trade union militancy. They wanted to act, and not only on the Tobin Tax' (Cassen 2006). The CL by not explicitly figuring in Attac's statutes generated problems of internal democracy through two conflicting structural logics: one starting at the summit and the other at the base (Pleyers 2003: 151). The national entities—comprising the Bureau (president, vice-presidents, treasurer, national secretary) Administrative Council (CA), the Collège des Fondateurs (CF) and the Scientific Council (CS)—played a centralizing role that did not always reflect the priorities and struggles of the individual members and local committees.

At the Local Level

Ever since Attac's creation, local structures for the association were discussed and the creation of CLs was placed on the agenda. The idea was to regroup members of the founding organizations not only at the national level, but at the local level as well. Never were these groups intended to have their own legal status or elected representatives in the national entities. Originally, the CLs were also imagined at the regional level, but with the rapid growth of the organization, CLs were created freely without any form of geographic distribution. For Elise Cruzel, this means that 'despite the existence of a national charter [Charte des comités locaux], there does not exist *one* Attac association but as many Attacs as there are local committees' (Cruzel 2004: 138). The ease with which it was possible to create a local committee and their freedom of action with regards to the national chapter of the association drew interest from political parties, especially the Ligue Communiste Révolutionnaire (LCR). Indeed, the extensive public interest toward Attac and its desire to 'do politics differently' attracted a wide array of citizens representing potential recruits for openly political formations.

Although political parties were particularly interested in Attac's militant potential, Attac's members regularly expressed their desire to keep their distances from mainstream politics, even though, as Achim Pfeuty explains, most individuals within the local committees had past or present militant engagements in political organizations or movements (2007: 195–196). Through their horizontality and loose organizational structures, CLs represented new and open spaces for the development and exchange of ideas. This characteristic clearly differentiates them from the national entities, especially the Bureau, which was regularly criticized for its 'reformism'. As Christian Losson and Joël Quinio explain when talking about internal democracy within Attac, 'for the local committees, it is a real problem, which doubles itself with an insinuation: the latent reformism of the Bureau has trouble adjusting itself to the affirmed radicalism of the membership base' (2002: 136).

At the National Level

As we have previously indicated, Attac divides itself into four main components at the national level: the Administrative Council (CA), elected by the General Assembly; the Scientific Council (CS), which is designated by the CA and which regroups academics and intellectuals; the 'Collège des Fondateurs', which regroups the founders (organizations and individuals) and which has representatives in the CA; and finally the 'Bureau', which is composed of the association's president, vice-presidents, treasurer and secretary. Many of Attac's leaders were 'dissident political figures, acting on the fringes of the Left, who had been marginalized by mainstream organizations' and 'who discovered in Attac a channel for their political views and an alternative institutional platform' (Waters 2004: 859).[16] They were individuals with recognized political views (Trotskyites, socialists, ecologists, communists, libertarians, *souverainistes*, internationalists and so on), who, at times, had ties with political parties.[17] A number of the organization's leaders could be qualified as 'intellectuals', drawn from academic and media circles.

The relative complexity of Attac's organizational structure mirrors the heterogeneity of its membership base. As a direct result of a decade of growing social movement activity, Attac's organizational form reflected the emerging *altermondialist* movement. In order to explain Attac's success and the rapid growth of its membership base, Julien Lusson does not refer to the Tobin Tax proposal per se but to the fact that Attac represented a new form of organization and in the French political setting, 'the most advanced reconfiguration (in terms of structure and ideas) of the "political" since the collapse of the two blocs' (2007: 118–119). Whereas Ramonet's article called for the creation of an organization that would campaign for the implementation of a Tobin Tax, the ensuing organizational structure outdid its original mandate by 'doing politics differently' (*faire de la politique autrement*). A way of doing this was to offer a new space for debate to the individuals and organizations that had been excluded from or that no longer believed in institutional politics.

SHIFTING FOCUS

The contextual shift that occurred in the wake of 9/11 and the rapidity with which the Tobin Tax proposal was sidelined within Attac illustrates the organization's inclination to act as a 'movement of movements' rather than as a single issue pressure group dedicated to the implementation

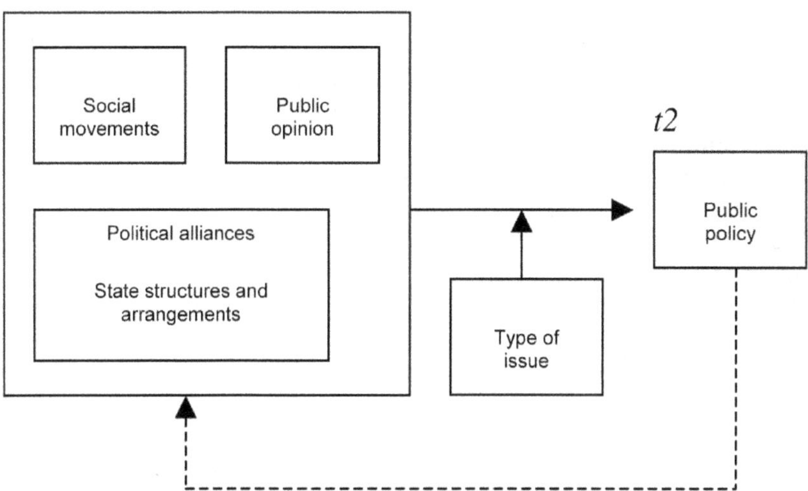

Figure 12.1 A simple model for the impact of social movements on public policy. Source: Giugni (2004: 14). Copyright permission granted by Rowman and Littlefield Publishers.

of the CTT. Despite an attempt to remobilize Attac's membership base and the general public through a campaign entitled 'Tobin tout de suite!' [Tobin now!], the September 2001 events stalled CTT-centred initiatives (Lignes d'Attac 2001). As we have previously noted when talking about public opinion, in the run-up to these tragic events, the Tobin Tax had been high on the French political agenda (2001 was the year in which the National Assembly passed a Tobin Tax amendment). During a CA meeting in 2002, Attac's leaders openly admitted that the Tobin Tax issue could not be pushed forward unless the organization took note of the perceived shifts within public opinion (Attac France 2002a). During an Attac seminar entitled 'The Tobin Tax, Global Taxes and Redistribution' (Paris, 17 May 2002), the Tobin Tax was no longer presented as the only possible solution to combating financial speculation and global poverty (Attac France 2002b). The CTT was presented as one of several possible global tax initiatives. Jacques Cossart, of the Scientific Council, described this evolution within his organization:

> We have greatly evolved on the Tobin Tax issue. Firstly, we no longer call it Tobin Tax. It is no longer concentrated on currency transactions but also on stock exchange operations. We have largely gone beyond Tobin because he only spoke of a single tax whereas we would like to broaden the debate to other types of taxes that draw enormous profits

> from globalization without giving anything in return and often contributing to the destruction of the planet. (Interview, 6 February 2007)

Although from a very early stage, there appears to have been a general consensus within Attac on the need to broaden the issue base beyond the Tobin Tax, it nevertheless retained a certain centrality within the organization. In the favourable pre-9/11 context, the CTT played a symbolic role, acting as a 'trademark' for Attac and the alter-globalization movement. The sudden political and media focus on insecurity—heightened by the run-up to the 2002 presidential elections—marked a symbolic break in the organization's determination to press for the Tobin Tax. The decision by Attac to open up the analysis to other forms of global taxation can be interpreted as an indicator that the Tobin Tax no longer played a pivotal role both within their organization and the wider political context. A key issue will be to evaluate whether the proposal served an instrumental purpose as a source of public visibility (for marginalized political activists), organizational unity (in a heterogeneous organization) or both. Attac's specificity lay in the fact that its declared objectives (those that are contained in Article 1 of the organization's statutes) have not always matched its actual activities and campaigns. This paradox arose in the run-up to Attac's 2002 General Assembly. One member, highlighting these inconsistencies, proposed a resolution modifying the statutes by giving them a broader interpretation that would be more consistent with Attac's actual engagements.[18] Although the CA rejected the proposal, the simple fact that it arose indicates that within Attac's membership base, the Tobin Tax question was no longer regarded as the organization's core area of focus.

The Issue of Time

Raphaël Wintrebert offers an interesting analysis of the process by which Attac went from being an organization that focused on financial speculation to one that was active on issues as varied as genetically modified organisms (GMOs) or nuclear energy (L'Humanité 2003). For Wintrebert, ever since its creation, Attac did not place itself in the short term nor in the long term but in the medium term. It sought to control its agenda by taking the time to analyse a given issue or situation before taking action. However, as Wintrebert suggests, this posture became increasingly difficult to hold. The organization's structure makes it particularly open to new proposals for action, and once it had begun to take on new topics that were not necessarily related to financial globalization, it became impossible to prevent new issues from being addressed. The result was a snowball effect that prevented the organization from 'taking the time to take its time' and controlling its agenda. Whereas this innovative structure was an essential reason for its extraordinarily rapid growth (in turn enabling it to lead and steer the public debate on the CTT proposal), it also led to an increase in the portfolio of issues covered often echoing the dominant, constantly shifting and highly mediatized political and societal debates. From being an *agenda setter*, Attac began responding to the public agenda. As a politician and ex-member of Attac put it, 'from an oecumenical movement of the Left, that organized the debate, they became stakeholders' (Gernelle 2005: 20).

A number of voices within the movement expressed their desire to halt this process of passive diversification by concentrating on certain key issues—not always including the CTT. As Jacques Nikonoff recalls, 'certain members [felt] that [the] organization should recentre itself on what they consider to be its "fundamentals" (the Tobin Tax and/or financial globalization). At the same time, others [wished], on the contrary, to see Attac contribute to the emergence of a new movement towards human emancipation, necessitating a global approach.'[19] The organization's leaders were finding it increasingly difficult to control their organization's agenda. From an organization able, through the Tobin Tax initiative, to set the agenda within the wider French political debate, Attac turned into an organization whose leading instances no longer even controlled (voluntarily or involuntarily) the agenda of the organization that they had been designated to lead.

As a means of responding to these growing difficulties, the CA launched in 2004 an internal consultation on 'the new dynamic for Attac'. The purpose of this initiative was to analyse the recent evolutions of neoliberal globalization and attempt 'to better specify [Attac's] medium and long term objectives' (Attac 2004c). This decision follows a long series of discussions (notably within the CA) in a difficult context for both the alter-globalization movement and Attac. These difficult times find

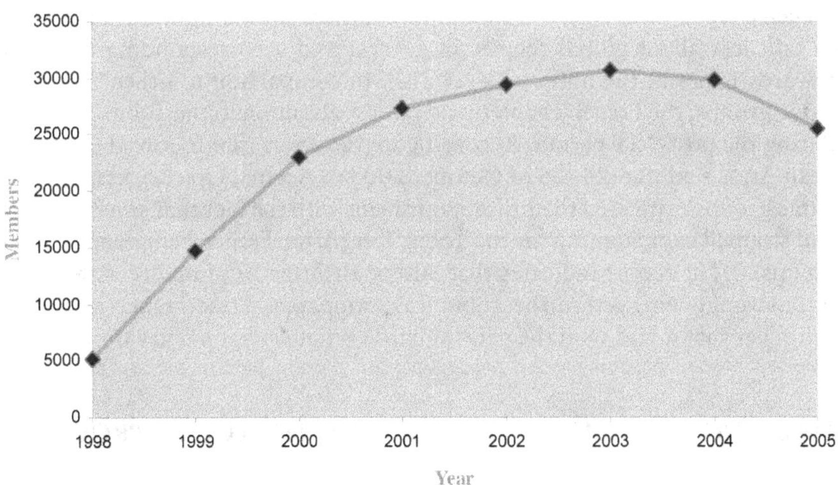

Figure 12.2 Evolution in Attac's members (1998–2005).

their expression in the evolution of Attac's membership base. From 2002 onwards the growth in membership started to slow down and by 2004 membership levels actually declined.

During a meeting in early 2003, there was an overall consensus within the CA on the fact that the visible slowing down in the number of new members 'probably had political origins relating to Attac's image and its role in society' (Attac France 2003b). They went on to ask themselves questions that directly relate to the Tobin Tax issue: 'by bogging ourselves down in technical debates (Tobin Tax, GATS [General Agreement on Trade in Services], for example), have we not gone from action oriented popular education to popular education full stop . . . ? Has this evolution not limited the core of our members to the middle classes, leaving behind those who suffer most from neoliberal globalization?' (Attac France 2003b).[20] The CA subsequently decided to focus on '[Attac's] rootedness within the working classes' (Attac France 2004a).

From the Global to the National

With—and not necessarily because of—this new desire to attract the working classes, a shift was observed in terms of the types of issues that were taken on. From a discourse that was openly concerned with financial globalization, Attac now focused on issues that were 'closer to home', such as employment, defence of public services and gender equality. In a 2004 comparative study of Attac in France and Sweden, Uggla (2004: 10) observes that the Tobin Tax—which, as Cassen explained, was a symbol of the struggle against financial globalization—had largely disappeared from the French organization's agenda. As he goes on to write, 'the dropping of the question of the Tobin Tax actually [reflected] a more general tendency within the French chapter of the organization. Indeed, there [was] a significant tendency to talk less about global themes in general and a corresponding tendency towards issues at the national level' (10). In comparison to other European Attac groups, the French chapter paid far less attention to the Tobin Tax issue during the post-9/11 period. According to the report that followed the European Attac seminar (24–26 of October 2003 in Aegina, Greece), a number of Attac groups expressed their disappointment with the fact that several Attacs had stopped campaigning for the Tobin Tax (Attac France being one of these groups).[21] The report indicates that, although Attac Belgium and Attac Italy were strongly engaged in the Tobin Tax campaign, Attac France expressed the belief that it had won the general battle on international taxation.

MAINSTREAM POLITICAL ACTORS AND THE POLICY PROCESS

Public opinion and organizational capacity are not the only factors explaining growing political interest in the CTT proposal. Although the Tobin Tax proposal was a useful response to increasing public unease toward globalization, it also served other political motives. Three such motives include: (a) the preservation of global capitalism; (b) the rehabilitation of France on the international political scene; and (c) the CTT as source of funding in view of French engagements with regards to development spending (notably those related to the MDGs).

In the wake of the various financial crises that took place in the late 1980s and 1990s, a number of political and economic personalities pronounced themselves in favour of greater regulation of the financial markets to save global capitalism (Barrillon 2001: 142–143). Jacques Chirac made this perfectly clear in his speech at the 2001 G8 Summit in Genoa. After declaring his continued faith in the principles of international free trade by stating, 'The development of trade is in its essence a creator of wealth and therefore, as long as this wealth is evenly distributed, a creator of well-being', Chirac stressed the need for democracies to play an active part in the regulation, civilization and humanization of globalization.[22] Besides using regulation as a means to 'simultaneously popularise the new legitimacy of the market and maintain the belief (necessary in France) in political state-led intervention' (Négrier 2000: 259), the notion of 'humanization' made good economic sense. Political and economic personalities that one would normally classify as free trade advocates (including people like Henry Kissinger in the United States or Alexandre Adler in France) expressed their support for greater regulation of the financial markets (Barrillon 2001: 142–148). For the G7 it was necessary to 'define the rules without which the world would be solely dependent on the financial market forces' (cited in Barrillon 2001: 143).

The pro-regulation discourse held a dual purpose for the French mainstream political class. On the one hand, it enabled policymakers to respond to growing public fears and uncertainties as to the effects of globalization on the French economy and culture. On the other, it represented an opportunity for France to regain a fading international aura and act as a countervailing force to what was increasingly perceived as U.S. hegemony in the governance of world affairs. Jacques Chirac was particularly attentive to the alter-globalization movement's demands and proposals (including the CTT) because they represented a way of reasserting France's desire to counter certain negative consequences of globalization—often associated with the standardization or 'Americanization' of culture (Gordon and Meunier 2002: 17).

By placing itself at the head of an international coalition of states in favour of a more humane globalization and greater North–South solidarity, France needed to set the example, particularly when it came to its international engagements relating to development aid. One such engagement was related to the MDGs.[23] Agreed upon in September 2000 by all of the world's countries and leading development institutions, the eight MDGs (ranging from halting the spread of HIV/AIDS to halving extreme poverty) were to be met by 2015. It soon became clear that the desired targets would not be met unless countries increased their efforts, notably with regards to their financial engagements. In late 2004, a French group of experts concluded that the official aid would have to double, increasing by about U.S.$50 billion a year, in order to achieve the Millennium Development Goals (Landau 2004: 10).

The context had therefore become particularly favourable to the emergence and discussion of new international regulatory and fundraising mechanisms. In order for France to 'reaffirm' its position as global leader in the fields of a more 'humane' globalization, multilateralism, the struggle against global poverty and the protection of cultural diversity, it needed to set the example by achieving the goals that had been unanimously set through the MDGs. In preparation for the Evian G8 summit (2003), meetings were planned between one of Chirac's diplomatic aids and representatives of civil society—including Attac—in order to discuss the summit's organization and the French proposals that were going to be made there. It was at this occasion that the various groups suggested the creation of a working group on international taxes.[24] Chirac's appointment, on 21 October 2003, of Jean-Pierre Landau, Inspector General of Finance, to chair a working group—the Landau Commission—whose mission was to 'reflect upon the feasibility of new international financial contributions to reduce poverty, to promote development and to finance global public goods such as the environment, public health and rare resources', was the materialization of this opportunity (Landau 2004:3). The working group consisted of fifteen predominantly French experts from academia, business, civil society, government and international organizations (Landau 2004:5). Attac was invited to participate in the group and Jacques Cossart, member of Attac's Scientific Council, was appointed as its representative. The group's focus was on international taxes—not just the CTT—as sources of funding primarily in view of the realization of the MDGs, but also as tools to raise funds for improved natural resource management. It was asked to submit its conclusions by the end of 2004. When we look at the official government documents, it would appear that the Landau Commission was set up primarily after noticing that the 2015 MDGs would not be reached through increases in development aid alone, and that development aid did not represent a sufficiently measurable or stable source of funding for development.[25]

What Cossart's participation in the Landau Commission indicates is that Attac's own perception of its political role appears to have changed over time. This was true from a very early stage if we compare Ramonet's (1997) article that called for a CTT, and the internal document entitled *Attac et le politique* (April 2000). As Danielle Tartakowsky explains, from an organization which was seen as a civic pressure group that 'could exert formidable pressure on governments to introduce [the] tax (Ramonet 1997), the 2000 document describes the organization as working in line with "traditional movements of popular education"' (2001: 652). Attac's self-description as an 'action-oriented movement of popular education' supports the idea that it did not see itself as a lobby, but as a constantly evolving source of social change. As Bernard Cassen (2003: 45) explains, 'our work is in the first instance—though not the last—educational'.

In the context of political and social unrest that characterized France in the late 1990s, Attac represented an opportunity for a new form of political organization that would provide much-needed space for the elaboration of alternatives to neoliberalism. Thus, Attac was not a single-issue pressure group; yet at the same time it was acknowledged as being the main promoter of a single issue: the Tobin Tax. From an issue that was at the top of the organization's agenda, external and internal factors led the CTT to progressively hold a secondary position. Other forms of global taxation were introduced into the discussion. Whereas the international and national political contexts were particularly favourable to the Tobin Tax in the period stretching from 1998 to 2001, the 9/11 events had an important impact on the 'alter-globalization' movement, in general, and the CTT campaign, in particular. Indeed, up to late 2001, within French political circles and public opinion, the issue of globalization was high on the agenda and there was a general desire to reaffirm the state's position in the face of what was perceived as a menace to both France's culture and social model. The series of financial crises also made international financial institutions (IFIs) and governments more open to regulatory measures that could preserve the international financial system. The vote by the French parliament of a Tobin Tax amendment to the 2002 Loi de Finance (voted in 2001) represented the high point of the French campaign. The Attac group at the National Assembly, primarily composed of Members of Parliament (MPs) from the Socialist Party, Green Party and Communist Party, exclusively campaigned for the vote of a Tobin Tax amendment. Although there was undoubtedly a tremendous amount of work on behalf of Attac's members to push for the implementation of the Tobin Tax, it is also fair to say that its success was the product of a favourable national context.

By early 2002, Attac refocused its work on national issues that were no longer necessarily related to financial globalization. In view of these contextual shifts, the Landau Commission's conclusions and proposals come as no surprise. We notice a significant departure away from Attac's initial demands: a very low tax rate on international financial transactions (lower than the 0.1 per cent originally proposed through the Tobin Tax); a tax on capital movements to or from countries that practise bank secrecy; a tax on the fuels used by air and sea transport; an airline ticket tax.[26] As one member of Attac wrote at the time, the Landau report 'follows only one logic: combating global poverty; the market regulation aspect and the fight against speculation is barred out [from the report].' For the member, the report even goes as far as mentioning 'the possible negative effects [of a high rate of tax]: disruption of the financial markets, reductions in transaction volumes (through the cost of the taxes), reduction in the market's liquidity, risks relating to double taxation, evasions, and outsourcing'.[27] At the workshop on International Taxation organized during the Paris Ministerial Conference on Innovative Development Financing (28 February–1 March 2006), the regulatory facet of the Tobin Tax was no longer present on the agenda.[28] As the workshop's programme explicitly explains: 'The name Tobin does not appear anywhere in either of the two documents (the French report and that of the six countries)' since 'the tax's sole purpose is to raise funds for development'. As the text goes on, 'the rate is very low, unlike that of the Tobin Tax, so as not to slow or disturb the markets and to maintain a broad taxable base'.

Two broad conclusions can be drawn. First of all, by 2004, Attac no longer sets the agenda on international taxation. Although it is clear that Attac launched a new dynamic with regards to international taxation,[29] the fact that the 'Landau' dynamic did not, even minutely, seek to 'disarm the markets' implies a dual shift: on the one hand, in Attac's capacity to advance its ideas and, on the other, in the CTT issue's centrality for the movement. When considering the transformations that have taken place within Attac, we are led to conclude that international taxation has become a by-product in an organization whose activities and campaigns reflected the shifting desires of its members and, in a context of decreasing memberships, those of the wider public that it hoped to attract.

The second conclusion is closely related to the first. The reasons that appear to motivate the Landau Commission and the 2005 Paris Conference reflect a reconfiguration of the French international taxation campaign as a direct result of its reappropriation by the French government. In addition to Jacques Cossart (Scientific Committee, Attac), the Commission was also composed of Henri Rouillé d'Orfeuil, the chairman of Coordination Sud (the largest French network of International Solidarity NGOs), and Kevin Watkins, research co-ordinator for Oxfam (another NGO). This opening up to new organizations indicates that Attac no longer personified the French taxation campaign and that the 'innovative fundraising mechanisms for development' facet had overrun the 'disarm the markets' aspect of the campaign.

CONCLUSION

2006 was an important year in Attac's short-lived history. It was during this period that an internal crisis broke out opposing the organization's *bureau*—led by Nikonoff and supported by Cassen—and a majority of the CA (notably, Susan George and François Dufour from Confédération paysanne). At the heart of this conflict were ongoing debates centred on what Attac's role should be within the French *mouvement social* and the relations it should entertain with mainstream politics.[30] Following the local committees' active participation in the 'NO campaign' for the 2005 referendum on the European Union Constitution, it looked as though Attac was set to play a durable role in French politics. Following our analysis, a number of important questions emerge relating to Attac's identity as a social movement group (Crettiez and Sommier 2006: 490–491). They unsurprisingly bring us back to the organization's origins and the question of its mission within the social movement sphere. Is it to generate within the general public a desire for a return to *politics* in its noble form? Or should Attac limit itself to acting as an apolitical lobby group whose sole function is to influence policymakers and push them to adopt a certain number of proposals (of which the Tobin Tax)?

As this chapter has shown, Attac was de facto the French CTT campaign at its creation. The evolution of the campaign is therefore closely linked to that of an organization whose uniqueness in terms of structure—as an amalgamation of individuals and organizations with sometimes conflicting views and strategic priorities—makes it more prone than 'traditional' lobbying organizations to contextual transformations. Public opinion, evolutions in mainstream politics, major international events and catastrophes, all create and adjust opportunities and ways in which Attac was able to influence the policy debate. Through our focus on one issue (the CTT proposal) which, by its very nature, symbolizes state intervention, reformist policies and the struggle against North–South inequalities, we can clearly see the links with two important types of external factors. On the one hand, permanent characteristics, such as the importance of the state, nationalism and the need to preserve French culture. On the other, a relatively new and highly mediatized issue: globalization. By looking at the evolutions of both the CTT issue within the organization (such as place on the agenda, type of tax to be promoted) and within Attac's political, social and international environment, correlations begin to appear. The events of 9/11, the 2002 French presidential elections in which there was a clear focus on national security and the subsequent evolutions in interpretations of public perceptions of the main preoccupations of the French public (notably through growing references to opinion polls by both social movement actors and mainstream politicians), all contributed to remoulding an organization whose horizontal nature made it far more malleable and capable of taking on new issues than other single-issue groups. As we have seen, this affected the level of importance and form of the CTT issue within Attac.

Attac, through the wide variety of organizations and individuals that compose it, is generally associated with the alter-globalization movement. Attac's structure is extremely open to change and to the integration of new campaigns. The campaigns and proposals that it develops are reformist in nature, and it has adopted a new vocabulary of neoliberalism, corporate globalization and regulation which breaks away from the traditional leftist discourse leading to a new interpretative framework.[31] By placing the blame on neoliberal globalization rather than capitalism, this framework has undoubtedly facilitated interactions with mainstream political parties (who have all, including the Socialist Party, taken on an openly pro-market stance). In a late 1990s context marked by intense public and media attention toward the globalization phenomenon, through its focus on issues such as the preservation of the centrality of the state and through the presence within its ranks of intellectuals and academics, Attac became an accessible, credible and respectable counterpart.

In this chapter, our main objective has been to show that the French CTT campaign, by being associated with one organization, in a first stage gained and in a second lost from this particularity. Indeed, the alter-globalization movement's popularity and Attac's central position within it contributed to push the CTT issue to the top of the public and political debate. However, in shifting external (international, national) and internal contexts, the CTT was gradually marginalized in a context of rapidly evolving priorities for Attac. This eventually weakened Attac's position as sole representative of the French CTT campaign, enabling other organizations (Coordination Sud and Oxfam) and even mainstream politicians (Chirac and Jospin) to take on the global taxation issue and, in the process, empty it of its critical elements (focusing only on the fundraising aspect).

NOTES

1. Also referred to as the Tobin Tax.
2. Much of the sociological research that has been carried out on social movements brings out the role of political opportunity structures. This field of research, which largely breaks with resource mobilization theory (which mainly focused on the resources that could be brought in by the movement itself), allows us to consider the opportunities that are opened up by the institutional system and the ideological dispositions of the political actors who are in power. For a detailed presentation of this research field, see McAdam, McCarthy and Zald (1996). In the course of this chapter, I will notably make reference to the work of Giugni (2004).
3. In this regard, it is interesting to note the relative marginality of the Anarchist movement in France and the existence of a strong *libertarian* movement. For a more in-depth analysis of this movement, one can refer to Dupuis-Déri (2005).
4. As was the case in the United Kingdom CTT counterpart, 'Stamp Out Poverty'.
5. This includes the Socialist Party (Parti Socialiste [PS]) and, to a certain extent, the Communist Party (Parti Communiste Français [PCF]).
6. The study was conducted by looking at the opinion polls of CSA, Ipsos, TNS Sofres, BVA and IFOP (online).
7. This study is not precise enough to reach definitive conclusions. However, tendencies have emerged.
8. http://www.csa-fr.com/dataset/data2001/opi20010912b.htm (Survey conducted on 11 and 12 September 2001 by CSA).

9. http://www.bva.fr/fr/archives/lacroix121001.html (Survey conducted on 28 and 29 September 2001 by BVA.)
10. Survey conducted on 7 July 2000 by TNS-SOFRES.
11. Survey conducted on 7 July 2000 by TNS-SOFRES.
12. France Info (national news radio); *L'Expansion* (news magazine); *Le Monde*, *L'Humanité*, *La Croix*, *Journal du Dimanche* (national newspapers); La Chaîne Info (LCI) (Private twenty-four-hour news television station).
13. From July 2001 to November 2001, my personal research found six opinion polls (all of which were ordered by the media)—July 2001: SOFRES/*Le Monde*: 'Les français et la mondialisation'; CSA/*L'Humanité*: 'Les français et la mondialisation'; September 2001: BVA/*L'Expansion*/LCI: 'Baromètre Taxe Tobin'; CSA/*La Croix*: 'Les français et la taxe Tobin'; October 2001: BVA/CCFD/*La Croix*: 'Aide aux pays pauvres'; November 2001: IPSOS/BFM/JDD: 'Mondialisation'.
14. Jacques Chirac placed it at the heart of his presidential campaign in a speech given at a rally in Garges-lès-Gonesse, 19 February 2002.
15. Interview with Jacques Cossart, 6 February 2007.
16. Waters notably sites Christophe Aguiton (expelled from the Confédération française démocratique du travail (CFDT), founder of SUD-PTT and AC!), Pierre Khalfa (expelled from the CFDT, representing the Groupe des Dix) and Annie Pourre (expelled from the Communist Party, founder of Droits devant!).
17. Cassen with the MDC (member of Chevènement's Ministerial cabinet), Christophe Aguiton (long-standing member of the LCR), Pierre Khalfa (links with the Green Party), Pierre Tartakowsky (member of the PCF until 1991 and representative of Communist-led trade union Union générale des ingénieurs, cadres et techniciens–Confédération générale du travail/UGICT-CGT), Jacques Nikonoff (member of PCF and party's national council until October 2001).
18. See Attac France (2002c). Article 1 of the statutes stipulates that the association's role is to: 'produce and communicate information, and promote and undertake various forms of actions to ultimately reconquer, through the citizens, the power that the financial sphere exercises on all aspects of the political, economic, social and cultural life of the world. One of these tools is the currency transaction tax (Tobin Tax)'.
19. See http://france.attac.org/a3491, Nikonoff, Jacques, 'Nouvelle dynamique pour Attac: Ebats et débats'.
20. These questions are in line with most of the conclusions drawn in the academic literature that looked at the social and cultural origins of alter-globalization activists through the study of social forums, countersummits and so on (see, for example, Agrikoliansky and Sommier 2005; Fillieule et al. 2004; Gobille 2005). Most of the research tends to underline the fact that the movement is generally composed of highly educated and often well-integrated individuals who are also frequently well acquainted with international affairs. Only a small minority of alter-globalization activists have working-class backgrounds.
21. See http://www.attac.de/ueber-attac/international/protokolle/2003_2 per cent20Report_october_2003_greece.rtf.
22. 'M. Chirac: "comprendre les manifestants"', in *Le Monde*, 22 july 2001.
23. See http://www.un.org/millenniumgoals.
24. See http://www.local.attac.org/13/aix/article.php3?id_article=457.
25. See http://www.diplomatie.gouv.fr/fr/actions-france_830/financements-innovants-du-developpement_14483/index.html.

26. See http://www.diplomatie.gouv.fr/fr/actions-france_830/financements-innovants-du-developpement_14483/index.html.
27. See http://www.local.attac.org/13/aix/article.php3?id_article=457.
28. *Workshop 3: Taxes on Financial Transactions.* The international conference, entitled 'Solidarity and Globalization: Innovative Financing for Development and against Pandemics', brought together more than one hundred countries, eighteen international organizations and over sixty NGOs. See http://www.diplomatie.gouv.fr/en/IMG/pdf/Workshop_3.pdf.
29. See Attac France (2006a). 'The President's proposal to implement an airline ticket tax places itself in line with these growing demands. It translates a growing popular demand. However it remains largely insufficient in view of the funding needs related to the struggle against Aids and it has strictly no regulatory impact on the markets.'
30. In a contribution entitled *For the Respect of Democracy within Attac*, Dessenne, Cassen and Nikonoff (2005) consider the consensus that had existed up to now to be over. They state that the alternative is now between, on the one hand, an independent organization (including from its founding organizations) capable of developing its own expressions, while at the same time serving as link to the different social movements, or, on the other, an organization that renounces having its own project and simply acts as a convergence point and relay for other active militant forces.
31. We have called this the 'Politics against Global Markets (PAGM)' framework, in reference to the work by Ancelovici (2002, 2004).

BIBLIOGRAPHY

Agrikoliansky, Éric, and Sommier, Isabelle. (eds) (2005). *Radiographie du Mouvement Altermondialiste—Le Second Forum Social Européen*, Paris: La Dispute.

Ancelovici, Marc. (2002). 'Organizing against Globalization: The Case of ATTAC in France', *Politics & Society*, 30 (3): 427–463.

———. (2004). 'Attac et le renouveau de l'antilibéralisme', *Raisons Politiques*, 16:45–59.

Attac France. (2002a). *2002—01—Conseil d'Administration du 12 Janvier*, 17 March. http://www.france.attac.org/archives/spip.php?article420 (accessed 7 May 20121).

———. (2002b). *03—Définition et Analyses des Taxes Globales*, 17 May. http://www.france.attac.org/archives/spip.php?article31 (accessed in 7 May 2012).

———. (2002c). *2002—08—Conseil d'Aministration du 22–23 Août*, 21 September. http://www.france.attac.org/archives/spip.php?article1079 (accessed 7 May 2012).

———. (2003a). *2003—04 Conseil d'Administration du 26 Avril*, 1 September. http://www.france.attac.org/archives/spip.php?article2145 (accessed 7 May 2012).

———. (2003b). *2003—05—Conseil d'Administration du 24 Mai*, 1 September. http://www.france.attac.org/spip.php?article2142 (accessed 7 May 2012).

———. (2004a). *2004—01—Conseil d'Administration des 30–31 Janvier et 1er Février*, 30 March. http://www.france.attac.org/spip.php?article2617 (accessed 7 May 2012).

———. (2004b). *2004—08—Conseil d'Administration du 24 Août*, 28 September. http://www.france.attac.org/archives/spip.php?article3571 (accessed 7 May 2012).

———. (2004c). 'Quelle nouvelle dynamique pour Attac?', 9 August. http://www.france.attac.org/archives/spip.php?page=discussion&id_forum=337&id_article=2250 (Accessed 7 May 2012)

———. (2006a). *1er Mars Colloque: Taxer les Billets d'Avion, pour Commencer?* 28 February. http://www.france.attac.org/spip.php?article5937 (accessed 7 May 2012).

———. (2006b). *Rapport Financier 2005*, 28 April. http://www.france.attac.org/archives/spip.php?article6201 (accessed 7 May 2012).

Barrillon, Michel. (2001). *Attac, Encore un Effort pour Réguler la Mondialisation!* Paris: Climats.

Blanc, Florent, Loisel, Sebastien, and Scherrer, Amandine. (2005). 'Politique étrangère et opinions publiques: Les stratégies gouvernementales d'influence et de contrôle de l'opinion publique à l'épreuve de son internationalisation', *Raisons Politiques*, 19:119–141.

Cassen, Bernard. (2003). 'On the Attack', *New Left Review*, 19:41–60.

———. (2006). 'Attac ou l' "exercice illegal" de la politique', *Politis*, 27 (July). http://bellaciao.org/fr/article.php3?id_article=31763 (accessed 7 May 2012).

Crettiez, Xavier, and Sommier, Isabelle. (2006). *La France Rebelle: Tous les Mouvements et Acteurs de la Contestation*, Paris: Editions Michalon.

Cruzel, Elise. (2004). 'Passer à l'ATTAC: Eléments pour l'analyse d'un engagement altermondialiste', *Politix*, 17 (68): 135–163.

Dessenne, Michèle, Cassen, Bernard, and Nikonoff, Jacques. (2005). *Pour Faire Respecter la Démocratie au Sein d'Attac*, 7 October. http://forumlo.cjb.net/index.php?showtopic=14483 (accessed 7 May 2012).

Dupuis-Déri, Francis. (2005). 'L'altermondialisme à l'ombre du drapeau noir: L'anarchie en heritage', in Eric Agrikoliansky, Olivier Fillieule and Nonna Mayer (eds), *L'Altermondialisme en France: La Longue Histoire d'une Nouvelle Cause*, Paris: Flammarion.

Fillieule, Olivier, Blanchard, Philippe, Agrikoliansky, Eric, Bandler, Marco, Passy, Florence, and Sommier, Isabelle. (2004). 'L'altermondialisme en réseaux. Trajectoires militantes, multipositionnalité et formes de l'engagement: Les participants du contre-sommet du G8 d'Evian', *Politix*, 17 (68): 13–48.

Gernelle, Etienne. (2005). 'Les appétits d'un ovni politique', *Le Point*, 18 August, No. 1718. http://www.lepoint.fr/archives/article.php/20876 (accessed May 2011).

Giugni, Marco. (1998). 'Was It Worth the Effort? The Outcomes and Consequences of Social Movements', *Annual Review of Sociology*, 24:371–393.

———. (2004). *Social Protest and Policy Change: Ecology, Antinuclear, and Peace Movements in Comparative Perspective*, Lanham, MD: Rowman and Littlefield.

Gobille, Boris. (2005). 'Les Altermondialistes: Des Activistes Transnationaux?' *Critique Internationale, Dossier 'Les altermondialismes'*, 27 (April): 131–144.

Gordon, Philip, and Meunier, Sophie. (2002). *Le Nouveau Défi Français: La France face à la Mondialisation*, Paris: Odile Jacob.

Landau, Jean-Pierre. (2004). *Les Nouvelles Contributions Financières Internationales*, Paris: La Documentation Française.

L'Humanité. (2003). 'Altermondialisation: L'enjeu pour Attac consiste à se donner du temps', entretien avec Raphaël Wintrebert, doctorant en sociologie à l'EHESS, 29 November..

Lignes d'Attac. (2001). 'Tobin tout de suite!', No. 9, 1 January. http://france.attac.org/spip.php?article1324 (accessed 7 May 2012).

Losson, Christian, and Quinio, Joel. (2002). *Génération Seattle: Les Rebelles de la Mondialisation*, Paris: Grasset.

Lusson, Julien. (2007) 'Un nouvel élan pour Attac', *Mouvements*, 49:116–123.

McAdam, Doug, McCarthy, John, and Zald, Mayer N. (1996). *Comparative Perspective on Social Movements, Political Opportunities, Mobilizing Structures, and Cultural Framings*, Cambridge: Cambridge University Press.

Négrier, Emmanuel. (2000). 'French Regulatory Path? State, Economy and Territory', *Tijdschrift voor Economische en Sociale Geografie*, 91 (3): 248–262.

Nikonoff, Jacques. (2004). 'Nouvelle dynamique pour Attac: ébats et débats', August. http://www.france.attac.org/archives/IMG/article_PDF/Nouvelle-dynamique-pour-Attac.pdf (accessed 1 May 2011).

Pfeuty, Achim. (2007). 'L'extrême gauche et le mouvement altermondialiste, l'extrême gauche dans le mouvement altermondialiste: Les réseaux militants dans ATTAC', in Dominique Reynié (ed), *L'Extrême Gauche, Moribonde ou Renaissante?* Paris: PUF.

Pleyers, Geoffrey. (2003). 'Le modèle français: 1995–2000', in Michel Wieviorka (ed), *Un Autre Monde . . . : Contestations, Dérives et Surprises dans l'Antimondialisation*, Paris: Balland.

Ramonet, Ignacio. (1997). 'Disarming the Markets', *Le Monde Diplomatique*, English edition, December. http://mondediplo.com/1997/12/leader (accessed 7 May 2012).

Tartakowsky, Danielle. (2001). 'Attac ou les échelles-temps du libéralisme', in Claire Andrieu, Gilles Le Béguec and Danielle Tartakowsky (eds), *Les Associations et Champ Politique*, Paris: Publications de la Sorbonne.

Tartakowsky, Pierre. (2002). *02—Introduction du Séminaire*, 17 May. http://www.france.attac.org/spip.php?article3 (accessed 7 May 2012).

Uggla, Fredrik. (2004). *A Movement of Popular Education Oriented towards Action? Attac in France and Sweden*. Paper prepared for the European Consortium for Political Research (ECPR) Joint Sessions, Uppsala, 18 April.

Waters, Sarah. (2004). 'Mobilising against Globalisation: Attac and the French Intellectuals', *West European Politics*, 27 (5): 854–874.

13 How Can Activism Make Change Happen?

Mario Pianta, Anne Ellersiek and Peter Utting

INTRODUCTION

Do civil society contestation and mobilization make a difference in terms of policy and institutional reform? What constellation of tactics and conditions is conducive to progressive changes in policy? This concluding chapter distils the main findings from the studies presented throughout the volume in terms of characteristics of mobilizations and political contexts, variations in demands and proposals and tactics, as well as policy and discursive impacts.

The analysis identifies key elements related to the global nature of the issues of contention, the institutional and historical context, power relations and political opportunities, as well as 'internal' dimensions of activist organization and networks, including issue framing and identities, access to resources, representation, legitimacy and alliance-building. These factors shaped the way demands for policy change were formulated, and thus the possibilities for success in affecting government decisions and the implementation of policies.

First, we summarize the main policy changes actually achieved by the mobilizations investigated in the preceding chapters. Second, we propose a synthetic overview of how activism can make change happen, identifying the key factors affecting outcomes and the main lessons emerging from this book. Third, a more detailed discussion of policy contexts and issues of contention is provided, with a comparative perspective across issue area, type of mobilization and country. Particular attention is given to a comparison of the cases of France and the United Kingdom in view of their differences in policy regimes and state-business-society relations. The chapter concludes with a reflection on the implications of the findings for activism in the contemporary context of global crises.

THE ACTIVISM–POLICY BALANCE SHEET

Building on the definition of the effects of activism provided in the introduction to this volume, the findings provide evidence of different impacts of global justice activism—at the national level as well as in their cross-border activities—in relation to:

1. The *framing of issues*, including the public understanding of global challenges.
2. The *building of consensus*, with the support of public opinion, as well as public participation in mobilizations and trust in activist agendas.
3. The *legitimation* and recognition of activists' role in such global issues; institutionalizing social dialogue with governments, international organizations and corporations; and other forms of participation in policy processes.
4. Specific *policy changes*, obtained in the life span of mobilizations, leading to government actions that were coherent with activist demands.
5. Longer-term *influences on policy-making*, including the setting of the policy agendas to be addressed by governments and decision-makers.

In this book we have mainly focused on the fourth type of outcome—the introduction of specific policy changes. The results of case studies point out four main types of policy and institutional reform or responses from governments and corporations:

- *The introduction of new legislation* inspired by activist demands, as in the cases of the introduction of the International Airline Ticket Tax initiated by the French government, of company reporting in the UK and of debt cancellation in Italy.
- *The stopping of policies* opposed by activists, as in the case of the Multilateral Agreement on Investment (MAI) and of the failure of the trade liberalization agenda at the Cancún WTO summit, slowing the pace of neoliberal reform.
- *Increased financing for development*, as in the case of recommitment (namely, at the Gleneagles G8 summit) of governments to the 0.7 per cent target for Official Development Aid as a percentage of GDP (although with frequent failures to deliver on such commitments[1]), as well as with funds coming from multinational corporations associated with corporate social responsibility (CSR) and public–private partnerships (PPPs).
- *Introduction of ethical considerations in the criteria for government policy*, particularly in the fields of trade and investment; cases include the withdrawal of support by the UK Export Credit Guarantee Agency as a response to the Sakhalin Island Project and increasing commitment of the UK government to promoting corporate social responsibility. Other well-known cases (not examined in this book) include initiatives to protect children's and labour rights in countries trading with Europe.

Conversely, in several cases no policy change emerged as a result of activism, as in most trade and international taxation mobilizations in Europe. Different reasons for failure have been identified.

First, failure may result from a lack of legitimation of activists. This emerges when justice issues are framed and campaigns organized by NGOs with limited representation and ineffective participation of subaltern groups that are victims of injustice. Northern NGOs have sometimes been accused of replicating the inadequacies of 'top-down' approaches typical of international institutions (Bendell 2006). Second, lack of success may be due to inappropriate strategies and inadequate resources, leading to activists' inability to 'stick with it' and achieve broad-based acceptance of their agendas (Smith 2007).

Third, whereas demands and proposals have often been initially developed as strong alternatives to existing policies, institutions and processes—ones that recognize the need for structural change—the positions eventually adopted by activists have frequently been watered down in the course of policy processes (such as from debt cancellation to debt reduction). Watering down is to be expected and can be part of a negotiated compromise that yields intended results. But it becomes more problematic when results are not achieved, and where dilution is associated with co-optation or giving up on structural change (Bebbington, Hickley and Mitlin 2008).

HOW CAN ACTIVISM MAKE CHANGE HAPPEN? LESSONS FROM THE EVIDENCE

The evidence of this book leads to five main results on the dynamics of activism on global issues in Europe and its impact on policies.

Global issues matter for national activism

Debt relief, trade policy, international taxation and corporate accountability—the fields of activism investigated in this book—are typical issues of contention associated to the global economy and development. A multilevel governance system exists, with decision-making power distributed in supranational organizations such as the WTO and the IMF, regional bodies such as the European Union, national governments and major business organizations, such as multinational corporations. National activism on such issues has emerged in parallel to the rise of cross-country links among mobilizations, resulting in common framing of issues and, sometimes, in common objectives, strategies and forms of action. The mobilizations examined in this book have been influenced by the presence of transnational networks such as *Jubilee 2000* on debt, *Our World Is Not for Sale* on trade, by links among national chapters of Attac on international taxation and by transnational experiences on corporate accountability. Activism in European countries has received an impulse to develop national campaigns from such cross-border links, but the ways the latter have evolved and defined their demands for policy change have much to do with national contexts.

National political cultures and policy regimes matter and differ across countries

Country case studies emphasize the specificities of each mobilization, their roots in national political cultures and their adaptation to a particular policy regime—aspects pointed out, among others by Giugni, Bandler and Eggert (2006). Common building blocks in terms of issue framing—such as the injustice of third world debt—and broad objectives (i.e. the need for debt relief) have been turned into in different national strategies, including calls for debt cancellation, for reduction and rescheduling and proposals of debt buy-back by civil society. This diversity across national mobilizations is the result of the long-term persistence of political identities, of the political opportunities and civic domains (Fowler and Biekart 2011) that existed and of the resources—political, organizational and financial—available for activists.

One evident result is the distinction between more 'radical' and more 'moderate' campaigns, with French and Italian mobilizations often taking a more radical political stance, and UK campaigns showing a closer interaction with government policy-making and business interests. Interestingly enough, it appears that more 'moderate' demands are not necessarily more successful in achieving policy change.

Another major distinction concerns the focus of activism. Mobilizations directed at political authority and changes in government policies were present in all countries. Efforts to change business behaviour were most evident in the UK. Experiences of self-organization of civil society, such as with fair trade groups linked to trade justice campaigns, were more common in Italy.

Activism for policy change is shaped by political opportunities, network links and strategies

In the cases examined in this book, specific demands for policy change emerge from the strategies of national mobilizations as a result of particular contingencies. The factors influencing such outcomes can be grouped into those 'external' to mobilizations, shaping political opportunities at the national and the transnational level, and those 'internal' to mobilizations, including the robustness of transnational networks supporting national activism, the strength of the national coalitions that are created, the effectiveness of political strategies and forms of action carried out by activists.

Important political opportunities that opened up at the *national* level include:

- Long-standing characteristics of national politics—for example, the contrasting attitudes on trade of French and UK states.
- The presence in power of a 'progressive' national governments, open to policy changes on global issues—for example, the interest of New Labour in the UK for a new development policy, and the opening on debt relief by the Italian centre-left government.
- The degree of access to policymakers—for example, the close links between development NGOs, politicians and ministry officials in the UK.
- The presence of elite business interests amenable to reform, as in the case of some corporate accountability initiatives in the UK.

Political opportunities at the *transnational* level were relevant when multilevel decision-making systems existed on specific cross-border issues. They included:

- The launch by intergovernmental organizations of policies that responded, even if inadequately, to activist demands, encouraging governments to take action. Examples included the IMF debt relief programme on Highly Indebted Poor Countries (HIPC), or the attention of some European institutions to proposals for a Tobin Tax.
- The possibility for activists to build tactical alliances on particular issues with like-minded governments in order to obtain policy change in supranational institutions. Examples include the veto posed by the French government in the case of the OECD talks on the MAI, and, the opposition to the trade liberalization agenda by a group of countries of the South at the WTO conference in Cancún.
- The presence of particular global events, attracting the attention of politicians and international public opinion, such as the G7/G8 summits or the Catholic Jubilee in the year 2000.

The main factors 'internal' to mobilizations include international networking and national strategies. The presence of *international* campaigns on the issues of debt, trade, international taxation and corporate accountability—such as Jubilee 2000 on debt—has provided national activism with important support and resources in terms of issue framing, understanding of highly complex and technical issues and the possibility to articulate policy demands in national contexts. Transnational networks contesting a particular global issue were able to open up an international debate, building shared frames (such as the view of debt, trade liberalization and corporate behaviour as unjust for third world countries). A strong network could lead to an intense international discussion among activists, building stronger and more common identities, leading to a common policy platform, especially when decision-making power was mainly located at the supranational level. Typical in this regard is the case of trade and the experience of *Our World*

Is Not for Sale. Weaker international networks on debt and international taxation were capable of framing the issues, but not of developing common policy demands that were shaped by national factors. At the other extreme, the weak international links of corporate accountability campaigns correspond to a more fragmented pattern of national activism. Similar findings are reported also in the comparison of several transnational campaigns by della Porta and Parks. (2012).

Conversely, at the *national* level, demands for policy change emerge as the result of national organizations or coalitions developing particular political strategies, leading to various forms of action. Domestic contexts are crucial for the possibility to build broad-based mobilizations. Activist strategies have to devise actions that reinforce identities and the urgency of the issue, building at the same time alliances with various actors so that mobilizations can be sustained over time. The policy changes that are demanded need to resonate with public opinion and engage political forces and decision-makers; actions are also needed to build their credibility and feasibility. The need to address such different objectives explains the wide range of actions—at the international, national and local levels—that were carried out in the mobilizations examined in this book, including street demonstrations and other protest actions, 'parallel summits' and alternative fora for presenting policy alternatives, media events, participation in consultative processes, lobbying of policymakers and so forth.

In sum, the ability of activism to advance demands for policy change appears to be shaped by the complex combination of external opportunities and internal capabilities, at both the international and national levels. Within these patterns, there may also be scope for the 'boomerang effect' (Keck and Sikkink 1998) whereby national mobilizations link up with transnational networks in order to obtain greater legitimacy and strength in national contestation.

Change includes short-term success and long-term influence on policy framing; change happens when strong, feasible demands find a political space and are supported by multiple actions at multiple levels

What, then, is the recipe for success of activism? First we need to identify more clearly what success is. The literature on the effects of social movements has pointed out that they may have a broad range of outcomes on state actions (including repression), political cultures, business practices, civil society, social behaviours and public opinion (see della Porta and Parks 2012; Giugni, McAdam and Tilly 1999). In terms of policy change—as pointed out in the previous section—our case studies show that two types of outcomes can be identified. First, success in the 'short term', that is, within the life span of a mobilization, with the introduction of a specific change in policy, such as legislation on debt relief or bringing a halt to a business practice demanded by corporate accountability campaigners. Second, mobilizations can influence policies in the longer term—even after they subsided—when the issue framing and policy proposals developed by activists becomes accepted by policymakers, political forces, business groups and communities of experts. The chapters of this book largely focused on the former effects; the latter require a longer historical perspective and the impact of mobilizations may be combined with a variety of other developments. Nevertheless, on the global issues of debt relief, trade policy, international taxation and corporate accountability we can find evidence of both types of effects. Short-term change did take place in a number of issue areas, with legislation on debt relief in Italy, new financing for development in France and the UK and increased attention to corporate responsibility in the UK. Longer-term change is still taking place with the rethinking of the trade liberalization agenda, growing support for a financial transaction tax and the evolution of business practices and international standards associated with corporate accountability.

In relation to policy changes achieved in the short term, what are the factors that led to the successes reported in the mobilizations we examined? On the basis of those considered in the preceding third point, it appears that policy change on a given issue is more likely to happen when:

- The issue at stake is framed as an important, urgent and feasible challenge, with a global relevance that resonates in national political cultures and public opinion, leading to a sustained mobilization.
- Political opportunities open up at both the international and national levels, with access to interested policymakers, when a strong transnational mobilization closely interacts with national activists.
- A broad coalition exists, with wide public opinion support and alliances with relevant institutional actors; when a variety of forms of action—protest, proposal of alternatives, lobbying, etc.—are used to advance all the preceding elements.
- The interaction of activists with policymakers, ministry officials and the community of experts facilitates the implementation of policy reforms.

Interestingly enough, it does not appear that more 'moderate' demands and greater access to policymakers necessarily leads to higher probability of policy change, as the UK experience shows.

When policy changes are introduced, their outcomes and implementation often fall short of activist demands

Disappointment is a frequent experience for activists, even after success is achieved. The cases examined in this book point out a systematic gap between the 'political' success of the announcement of a particular policy change and the outcomes that emerge from the actual implementation of novel policies. The diversity of effects at different points in the policy process has long been pointed out by the literature on the impacts of social movements (see Schumaker 1975). Several factors are important here.

First, the dynamics of negotiation typically involve a moderation of initial demands, as in the shift from requests for debt cancellation to accepting measures of debt reduction. Second, national policy-making on global issues is much less established and organized than government action on traditional, typically domestic issues. State institutions may have limited competences and resources for actual implementation, may need to go through learning processes and may operate in uncharted territory, and effective outcomes may fall short of expectations. Third, possibilities for policy reversals are high, when national governments (or key officials and experts) change, when international or business contexts become less favourable, when urgent domestic priorities may subtract resources from action on global issues. This happened with the implementation of debt relief legislation in Italy and the failure to follow through on a commitment to substantially increase development aid. Fourth, such 'watered down' results are partly a 'physiological' outcome of institutional action, associated with the structural gap between the issue-centred approach to policy advocated by activists and the process-based activities of policymakers and officials in state bureaucracies. This suggests that, in order to achieve effective change, activists need to continue their efforts even after the announcement of a change in policy, with close monitoring and lobbying for appropriate implementation of new actions. Fifth, business and political elites are 'hegemonic' in the Gramscian sense, and often accommodate elements of 'radical' agendas through discursive shifts and the piecemeal uptake of reforms, thereby controlling the process of reform on terms which do not pose a fundamental challenge to their interests and worldview.

Cycles of Mobilization on Particular Issues Are Part of an Evolving and Sustained Global Justice Activism

Case studies in this book have shown clear cycles of mobilizations on particular global issues, ending with different degrees of success. However, they also showed the strong persistence of political cultures and organizational links—at the national level as well as in increasing cross-border relationships—that connect one mobilization to another. Mobilizations for decolonization and anti-imperialism in the 1970s, for example, paved the way for the subsequent focus on development issues in the 1980s, laying the foundations for understanding the challenge of third world debt and trade injustice in the 1990s and 2000s.

Connections are visible not only over time, but also across issues. In fact, a major novelty of activism in the new millennium has been the rise of global movements—using transnational networks as 'backbones' (see Chapter 4)—supporting different waves of mobilization on specific themes and making links across different issues. As shown by a large literature (della Porta 2007; Pianta 2001a, 2001b) and by the decade-old experience of World Social Forums, global justice movements developed a common strategy of resistance to neoliberal globalization, and a vision of *globalization from below*, driven by cross-border civil society actions for economic justice, human and social rights, democracy and participation.

Set in this context, the case studies of this book can be seen as particular waves of activism that are part of an evolving and sustained global justice mobilization. The issues addressed—debt, trade, international taxation, corporate accountability—are all permanent themes of such long-term, cross-border activism. On most of them, the wave of neoliberal policies promoted by the 'Washington consensus' and by several EU governments appears to be subsiding. Third world debt is now less dramatic and the role of the IMF and rich countries as lenders has diminished. The drive to liberalize trade has lost some momentum, with the WTO unable to complete its 'Development Round'. The need for international taxation—as with the financial transaction tax, heir to the Tobin Tax—is increasingly accepted by the IMF and the EU. And initiatives associated with corporate accountability are more widespread.

Some major developments in economics and politics, such as the financial crash of 2008; the rising economic power of China, India, Brazil and other emerging countries; and the Obama administration in the United States, have clearly shaped the new policy landscape. But such changes can also be considered signs of the ability of mobilizations to influence policies in the longer term, even after the end of protest cycles. The framing of several global issues and some policy proposals developed by activists have become increasingly accepted by policymakers, political forces, corporations and communities of experts. Mobilizations for economic justice have anticipated a much wider understanding of the importance of global challenges and charted some of the paths to address them. Moving from the general findings summarized in the preceding, we now turn to national specificities and differences in policy regimes.

COMPARING POLICY REGIMES AND ISSUES OF MOBILIZATION

Policy regimes represent arenas of opportunity as well as constraints. The institutional context of policy regimes has long been recognized as a filter or mediator of activism, affecting the choice of strategies and capacity to bring about change (Hooghe 2008). Although the notion of transnationality and the universal nature of activist claims suggest a disengagement of justice activism from (national) policy regimes, the findings presented in previous chapters support the ongoing relevance of national contexts (Giugni, Bandler and Eggert 2006). This was seen clearly in relation to the issue of path dependence presented in Chapter 2, which partly originates from traditional relationships and functions associated with the state, business and civil society. Context related to the wider political culture is also key. Chapters dealing with movements and networks in France highlighted the extent to which certain positions and causes of French activist groups and organizations resonated with public opinion and 'French' anti-/alter-globalization sentiments and protest traditions. Survey data for 2003 presented in Tables 13.1, 13.2 and 13.3 show the somewhat more favourable public perspectives on global justice activism in France as compared to the United Kingdom and Italy.[2]

Table 13.1 Concerning Alter-Globalization Movements, Would You Say That They. . . . .?

	Raise points that deserve to be debated	*Raise my awareness of certain aspects of globalization*	*Propose concrete solutions to globalization*	*Succeed in influencing national political decision-makers*
France	88%	69%	47%	41%
UK	75%	68%	33%	37%
Italy	78%	62%	32%	30%

Table 13.2 Opinions Regarding Levels of Trust in Alter-Globalization Movements

	Absolutely trust	*Trust*	*No answer*	*Do not trust*	*Absolutely do not trust*
France	11%	51%	5%	45%	21%
UK	8%	41%	10%	49%	17%
Italy	8%	33%	3%	64%	28%

Table 13.3 Opinions on Levels of Influence of. . . . .

	Too much influence	*Just the right level of influence*	*Not enough influence*
International institutions	24%	32%	34%
European Union	21%	37%	34%
National governments	22%	32%	37%
Financial circles	59%	23%	37%
Multinational corporations	62%	21%	11%
Trade unions	15%	23%	55%
Anti-globalist movements	15%	25%	49%

As outlined in Chapter 1, within activist networks and movements power relations are complex and fluid, with elites and other interests simultaneously positioning and repositioning to gain or regain influence and control through diverse means and forums. Furthermore, political opportunity structures and activists' mobilizations are in a state of considerable flux, in contexts where the nature of governance has changed significantly in recent decades. The power and influence of activists must be seen not as a static unit or force of political power but relative, vis-à-vis other civil society actors and epistemic communities engaged in advocacy and lobbying and elite interests exercising power and influence.

Yet, the studies of this volume demonstrate that it would be too simplistic to view the manifold experiences of activism as being determined by either particular political regimes or corresponding activist traditions and forms of mobilizations alone. On the one hand, it is demonstrated—for example, by the mobilizations targeting the WTO summits in Cancún and Doha (Chapter 5)—that justice activism can successfully open up political opportunities through scale-shift, through which activists can capitalize via strategic alliances and other means, when their capabilities to explore and shape these opportunities and constraints define the very capacity to exert effective agency. On the other hand, equally strong concerns have been raised about the 'internal' difficulties that activists face in overcoming tradition-bound and new obstacles, engaging effectively in policy processes and reflecting critically on issues of elite domination, inequality and conflicting interests and agendas. The cases presented in the preceding chapters show that such capabilities and the strategies activists employ differ considerably across mobilizations. They may involve specific campaigns as well as broader-based alliances and networks, and they may display different degrees of organization, resourcefulness, durability, representativeness and strategic-orientation, amongst other factors, which all play a role in contributing to the success or failure of the collective actions.

The findings demonstrate the complexity of interactions at the policy–activism interface. Such interactions cannot be understood solely with reference to the political opportunities and constraints that activists encounter, or to the actions, agendas and capacities of activists to explore them. At issue is how specific initiatives interact with other actors and institutions under different social models, policy regimes and activist traditions. The cross-case analysis conducted for this concluding chapter provides insights into these interactions that shape the activist–policy nexus.

Justice-related discourse and policy are closely intertwined with 'global' paradigms and historical, often colonially imprinted, legacies and institutional trajectories. Such contexts result in certain configurations of power and other relationships among the state, business and activists that yield different degrees of leeway for activist agendas. A comparative analysis of the experience of activism in France, the UK and Italy reveals the variety of traditions and power configurations that characterize policy contexts and activist strategies. Differences in activist experiences and the activist–policy nexus across countries emerged clearly in the two contrasting cases of France and the UK, with regard to the four issue areas of debt, trade, international taxation and corporate accountability.

Debt

Policies and concrete governmental and intergovernmental action to reduce the debt burden of heavily indebted poor countries took hold after the turn of the millennium. In the case of France and the UK, there was a marked increase in debt relief from around 2003 (see Figure 13.1). In the UK, the issue of debt (re-)gained popularity in the 1990s under Labour and the leadership of both Tony Blair and, particularly, Gordon Brown, who strongly supported the Make Poverty History (MPH) campaign (Brown 2010).

Unlike the Jubilee 2000 coalition, however, which had succeeded in putting debt relief on the British government's agenda, the net impact of its successor, the MPH campaign, was less clear. Despite the strong public attention and support of the British government that MPH generated, Chapter 6 describes how—over the years and stages of the policy process associated with the debt issue (see Figure 13.1)—the approach to debt relief was considerably diluted. Initial demands that had centred on immediate and full cancelation of unpayable and unjust debt eventually gave way to debt relief as part of a wider approach to poverty reduction. Chapter 7 in contrast, describes how in France, the comparably more radical demands for total debt cancellation by *Plate-forme Dette et*

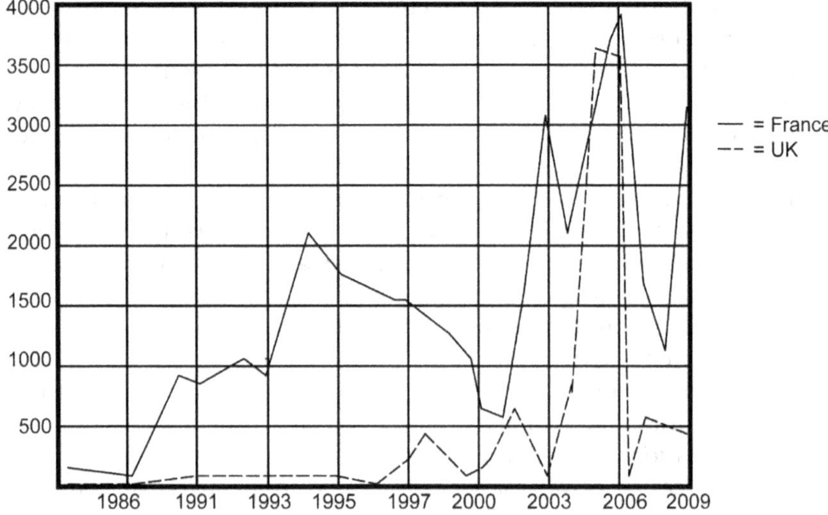

Figure 13.1 Debt relief: UK and France (1985–2010).

Développement (the successor initiative of the French branch of Jubilee 2000, 'Ça suffit comme ça') resonated with the 'alter-globalization' sentiment of the French public and other left-wing organizations (see Table 13.4). Both initiatives however, were deemed to be 'too radical' by many government officials, because they explicitly make a connection between contemporary North–South inequalities and the French colonial heritage, which was reflected in the slogan 'Debt, apartheid, colonies, enough!' Ultimately, the Platform failed to mobilize French public and governmental support to an extent that was sufficient to produce the change in policy that would have matched their demands.

Moreover both, the British and the French movements failed in successfully linking their efforts. The French '2005: plus d'excuses!' campaign distanced itself from the UK agenda, with French activists insisting on their demands for total debt cancellation, the inclusion of a reference to historical domination and the creation of a body of international law which would oversee the paying back of existing loans and all future debt-related multilateral and bilateral negotiations (see Table 13.4). Unlike Italy, where activists succeeded in pushing for a debt cancellation law (Chapter 8), in France and the UK, activist demands related to debt were not translated into binding policies. Instead, the concrete initiatives of the French and UK governments—related to an international airline tax to finance development and increased levels of ODA, respectively—have been driven to a

Table 13.4 Key Activists' Demands on Debt

France	*UK*
The immediate and full cancellation of debts of very poor countries and substantial cancellation of debt of middle income developing countries	Immediate and full cancellation of unpayable and unjust debts
The establishment of a Parliamentary Commission to inquire into and make transparent, the process by which developing countries have become over-indebted	The end of harmful conditions attached to debt
The organization of an international conference, under UN co-ordination, to formulate international law on debt	Relief through an increase of aid (beyond what has already been pledged as such)
	An open, fair and comprehensive long-term framework for insolvency
	Measures to avoid a repeat of the debt crisis and ensure transparency and accountability

considerable extent by the governments themselves and international *real-politik*. Consequently, the message conveyed by both governments, was more one of charity rather than justice, with the powerful leaders of the world seen to be helping the unfortunate rather than correcting their own countries' involvement in global trade and financial injustice.

Trade Policy

Different trade justice agendas have been pursued by French and British activists, each largely in line with those of their governments (Chapters 5, 7 and 8). The demands and positions of certain French government institutions and activists converged along protectionist and antiliberal lines, with a substantial agreement that trade policies lacked responsiveness to the issue of policy space for developing countries to protect and regulate their domestic—in particular agricultural—markets. Apart from divergent policy goals related to Non-Agricultural Market Access (NOMA), the position of British activists, represented, for example, by the British branch of the Trade Justice Movement (TJM), War on Want, Action Aid International, Oxfam International, the World Development Movement and Christian Aid, bears significant similarities with the position of the British government, calling for the end of (agricultural) subsidies and more policy space for developing countries.

Despite convergence around national agendas, key differences emerge with regard to degrees and types of interaction among different actors and in relation to policy impacts. In France, NGO agricultural specialists carried significant weight in consultative processes, and there was a high level of permeability between NGOs and government personnel in French trade policy-making. Despite a similar degree of access to policymakers enjoyed by British activists, Chapter 6 points to scant evidence that the government produced policy that took into account activists' demands when they diverged from the government's own stance. Apart from the 'Aid for Trade' initiative, no other aspect of British activists' trade policy agenda was incorporated in the government's G8 Gleneagles brief.

The agreements reached by governments and activists in each country had varying impacts on trade policy transnationally. Chapter 5 explains how, through strategic alliances and significant prior agenda building, activists were instrumental in temporarily derailing the conventional WTO trade liberalization agenda. At the Cancún conference there emerged a new assertiveness on the part of developing countries, manifested in the prominent role taken by the 'Group of 90' in collaboration with activists. At the following Ministerial Conferences in Hong Kong and Geneva, however, the unity of the South collapsed and Southern delegations went into negotiations of 'individual deals' with Northern countries, partly reflecting broader geo-political shifts associated with the rise of the BRICS.[3]

Whereas activists and national governments in France and the UK could find much common ground, these national agendas found little echo at the EU level, where authority for trade negotiation was centred (DG Trade). Before the G8 summit in Gleneagles in 2005, the UK asked to shift the agenda from negotiations on competition and investment to a transition period for tariff cuts, safeguards and alternatives to trade 'reciprocity'. The Committee of the French Parliament on the EU published an equally critical report on EU-ACP[4] trade policy agreements in 2006.[5] Although activists in both countries embraced these reports to the EU, political opportunities were missed, when activists, like their governments, failed in conciliating their agendas in a way that would have facilitated stronger joint action at the EU level. One can assume that by harmonizing and jointly targeting the EU, influence would have been stronger. The Director General for Trade acknowledged that 'celebrities and NGOs' had caused the EC to change its view on trade with the ACP in the face of persistent disagreement on the issue of agriculture;[6] however, this 'change' did not result in any substantial modification of policy.

International Taxation

Quite different activist positions on the issue of international taxation emerged in France and the UK. Chapter 12 outlines how in France, the majority of members of the 'Association for the Taxation of Financial Transactions and Aid to Citizens' (Attac), which included trade unions, alternative media, 'sans' movements and feminist groups, took on the issue of finding alternatives to neoliberalism, by initially emphasizing the 'regulative' aspect of global taxation (see Table 13.5) . Until 2001 the international and national policy contexts were favourable to this 'regulative' notion of the Tobin Tax proposal. In the following years greater attention was focused on using international taxation for funding development. Moreover, domestic developments and stagnating membership, led Attac to shift its attention to issues 'closer to home', such as employment, defence of public services and gender equality.

In the UK, networks of development NGOs were the main drivers behind international tax reform initiatives. British activists were primarily concerned with questions about financing for development (see Table 13.5). As such, Chapter 11 posits that the UK campaign fell within the 'moderate' spectrum of activist proposals for international taxation. In a number of policy briefs, British activists, notably War on Want, funded experts to produce detailed studies of how revenues could be leveraged for development and to fight poverty. The generation of these proposals, however, proceeded in conformity with official agendas, producing ideas that would be acceptable to both the New Labour government's position and the transnational business community. Such moderation may partially be explained by the strongly finance-oriented British economy and a set of

Table 13.5 Evolution of Key Activists' Demands on International Taxation

France	*UK*
1998 Calls for a very low tax rate on international financial transactions (lower than the 0.1 per cent originally proposed by the Tobin Tax).	2002 Calls for a universal Tobin Tax at 0.1 per cent and a new body under the aegis of the UN to formulate policy on the tax, to oversee compliance and to decide how to spend the revenue (e.g. War on Want).
2002 Calls for a tax on the capital movements to or from countries that practice bank secrecy.	2003 Calls for a Currency Transaction Tax to raise revenue for development (Stamp out Poverty campaign).
2004 Calls for a contribution on the fuels used by air and sea transport and a tax on airline tickets.	2005 Calls for a unilateral 'Stamp Duty' on the Pound Sterling at 0.005 per cent aimed at raising revenues to contribute towards the UK's commitment to the Millennium Development Goals (MDGs) (Stamp Out Poverty campaign).

legal constraints on the political activities of charities, which constrained the possibility of crafting a more encompassing agenda for the regulation of financial globalization. In contrast, in France a wide public debate framed around the threat of globalization favoured a convergence between Attac, mainstream politics and public opinion over the need to regulate global markets. Eventually, the positions of activists in both countries however, converged around an agenda of 'innovative sources of financing for development', which sidestepped the question of regulation. This position closely resembled that of the more moderate British view, rather than the initially more radical French position.

Corporate Accountability

In Chapter 2, account is given of the development of British and French state–market relations from colonial times. In France, close ties between the state and French corporations persisted long after decolonization, being anchored in a system of cooperation in dealings with the former colonies and characterized by tolerance of malpractice of French firms abroad, particularly in the oil industry. This analysis shows the limits of corporate accountability in France that result from such an institutionalist setting, key features of which were central government *dirigisme* and comparably low levels of involvement of French civil society. This was due to a long history of corporatist dialogue and public expectations and demands for social well-being directed at public authorities rather than at private firms.

In contrast, in the UK contemporary corporate social responsibility is rooted in a contractualist model of the firm and closer interaction with civil society actors. The UK case, analysed in Chapter 6, demonstrates how corporate accountability initiatives manifested themselves largely through voluntarism and self-regulation, influenced by a tradition of campaigning and 'naming and shaming' by activists that served as means to exert pressure on firms. Activist–policy interactions related to corporate accountability mainly involve well-supported NGOs, in collaboration with certain government agencies such as DFID, and involve 'private regulation' and partnerships between business and civil society. The UK activist networks referred to in Chapters 3 and 6—the Corporate Responsibility (CORE) Coalition, the Sakhalin Island Network (SIN) and the Publish What You Pay (PWYP) campaign—thus adopted a legalistic approach to activism targeting the legislative process and British commitments under international agreements, alongside the use of legislation associated with redress that was already in place.

Chapters 3 and 6 point out that British activism has been criticized for being dominated by a few large NGOs and for being too narrowly focused on particular issues and campaigns, rather than developing comprehensive alternative proposals to the neoliberal paradigm. In fact, compared to French activists, some British NGOs are more broadly involved in policy processes and enjoy stronger financial support from the government and (some) businesses. Hence, whereas the British collaborative governance approach seems to facilitate activist participation in mainstream consultative and policy processes, at the same time this approach causes rifts within the activist community. Chapter 6 demonstrates how British NGOs with very close relationships to policymakers and business are hesitant to embrace more radical agendas because they fear that they might alienate their more conservative supporter base and jeopardize their 'insider' status and reputation with policymakers and business allies. These relations thus often turn out to be 'too close for comfort' and detached from grass-root agendas.

This approach contrasts with that in France where tactics of targeting individual firms, or collaborative engagement of NGOs and firms, are still comparably rare. A strong presence of trade unions instead is a hallmark of the French activist tradition, as evidenced in the number of so-called international framework agreements signed by global union federations and French transnational corporations. The state remains the main target of collaboration between French NGOs and trade unions to push for more socially responsible business practice, for example, through the development of standards related to financial responsibility. Given the association of France with the so-called stakeholder model of capitalism, one might expect French corporations to be more proactive in relation to corporate accountability. Yet, there seems to be a double standard, whereby French firms at home need to comply with binding law that is advanced through legislation, while abroad, French corporations continue to benefit from near immunity (Capron 2009).

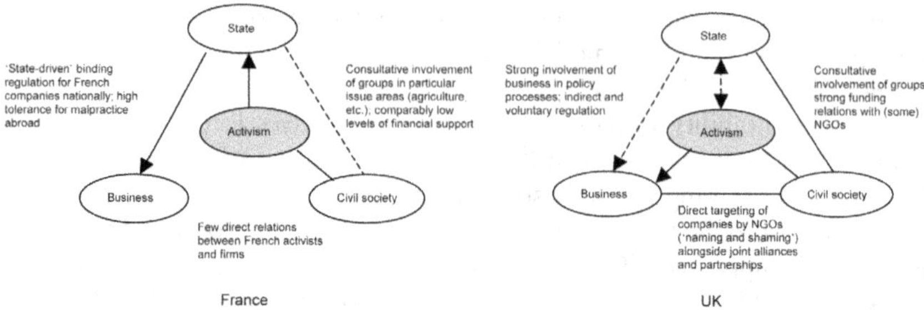

Figure 13.2 State-business-civil society relations in France and the UK.

From these different institutional trajectories and modes of interaction between different actors related to funding and the policy process, it is possible to identify schematically distinct configurations of state–business and civil society relationships and corresponding policy regimes (see Figure 13.2). Such configurations point to (a) quite different levels of interaction and convergence of agendas between civil society and business (relatively weak in France; stronger in the UK); (b) activism that targets the state in France and 'collaborates' with the state in the UK; (c) activism that targets and engages business in the UK, and far less so in France; (d) and in relation to state–business relations, a more *dirigiste* French state.

COMPARING STRATEGIES FOR CHANGE

The ability to mobilize effectively on issues of contestation depends on the capacities of activists to overcome limitations deriving from differences in traditions and policy regimes and to exert agency. This requires that conflicting interests and agendas among activists themselves be addressed. National and transnational networks and alliances between a broad range of diverse activist groups are a key mechanism to pool and generate resources and effectively employ them in the policy process. Recognizing and adequately addressing 'internal' impediments in the organization of collective action is particularly relevant for justice activists who denounce the democratic deficit in decision-making in institutionalized policy processes and stress the need for their radical reform.

Resources for Action

From various cases it is clear that the pooling of resources is one of the key motivations for activists to collaborate. Benefits were obtained from the exchange of resources between diverse groups, ranging from material ones, such as the financing of campaigns, to symbolic resources, such as legitimacy, information, member support and contacts with the media and policy actors. In addition, joint action served as a basis for the (co-)creation of new 'collective' resources, e.g. new approaches to and proposals for change.[7] In Chapter 5, Silva identifies such processes of knowledge creation and the emergence of a densely connected 'epistemic community' as one of the main reasons for 'success' in Cancún. In contrast, in Chapter 6, Bendell and Ellersiek identify resource *pooling* and *exchange* (in particular of material for campaigns) as the primary mode of resource management with much less attention given to processes of co-creation of alternative agendas. When some network members did think outside of their 'institutional box', this was largely the result of 'learning-by-doing'. This proved to be a challenge especially for the established groups, who had to leave 'their comfort zone in the NGO community'.[8] The limits of this approach are particularly evident with regard to the highly complex issue area of trade policy (Chapters 5, 6, 7 and 8). Here, the development of alternatives requires knowledge and competencies that go far beyond what can be brought to the network by any individual group alone. And activists need to delve into and jointly develop comprehensive proposals for change to resist the tendency to readily identify with existing ideas.[9] In summary, two limitations to such processes of resource creation and mobilization became apparent. The first concerns the limited capacities and willingness of groups to allocate adequate levels of resources, when those groups felt caught between two stools: their own individual organizational needs and the resource demand of the network. This occurred even in networks with well-resourced members. The second limitation relates to resource scarcity. This prevented the networks from implementing and sustaining an effective co-ordination mechanism (board structures, learning and evaluation tools, etc.). This is important for creating the structural preconditions that enable processes of resource co-creation and for preventing unilateral actions by some organizations to dominate the networks' agenda and action (Chapters 3, 6 and 8).

The Representative Function of Activism

One of the key resources of justice activism, its discursive legitimacy, builds upon the legitimate representation of the interests of others, who are not directly involved in the policy processes (Biekart 2008) but are disadvantaged by aspects of neoliberal globalization which they cannot control. Such aspects include, for example, inequitable terms of aid and trade and the burdens of debt and economic malpractices by corporations. Regardless of whether mobilizations target supranational powers or national policy-making related to 'global' issues, activists claim to represent not only their direct supporters but also millions of people without a 'voice'. The British Make Poverty History coalition, for example, discussed in Chapters 1 and 6, not only brought together over five hundred groups and organizations, but more generally spoke on behalf of 'the world's poor'. Laying claim to a representational function, however, presents major challenges for activists. With the exception of some unions, none of the groups or networks has a wide membership base. In such contexts, NGOs are vulnerable to criticism about promoting their own self-interest, rather those of the victims of injustice. A concern raised in the analysis of the 'success of Cancún' in Chapter 5, for example, was the instrumentalization of Southern government delegates for Northern activist goals.

A major problem relates to imbalances in the participation to international networks by Northern and Southern actors. Despite the global implications of the contested policies, Southern organizations and groups are often heavily under-represented. Even when they are involved, the representation of their interests in network-level decision-making is often in doubt. This occurs particularly in contexts where networks lack the organizational structures that enable reciprocal control, mutual learning and joint decision-making (della Porta 2007). Mechanisms to ensure the involvement and control of members over the ways their interests in network-level decision-making are represented were generally absent or ineffective in most of the cases examined in this volume. Although almost all the mobilizations examined in Chapters 3 and 8 were co-ordinated via boards and regular meetings of thematic sub-groups, at the same time concerns were voiced that resource scarcity prevented networks from establishing rigorous procedures to assure balanced representation in network-level decision-making.

Strategies of Engagement

To be effective, collective activism requires the development of both a common identity—the 'us' opposed to the 'other'—and the self-understanding of being part of something bigger than the efforts of single actors or groups acting alone. Building a shared identity emerged as crucial for diverse groups to cohere in networks and coalitions and for the effective communication of claims in the policy process. Favourable conditions for strategy building, such as a widely shared dissent and expert analysis—as occurred in the case of the initial CTT proposal in France (see Chapter 12)—may be the exception rather than the rule.

The study of the four activist networks in the UK in Chapters 3 and 6 found that when confronted with less favourable conditions, activists focused on identifying less disputable goals and more moderate strategies. These reflected the objectives of (powerful) core members, focusing on easier policy targets. Gerbaudo and Pianta (Chapter 8) describe how discrepancies arose about unnecessarily doubling efforts within the Italian debt movement. The Catholic Church founded its own initiative parallel to those of the secular groups to facilitate pastoral action on debt in order to avoid taking a 'too radical' political stance. Saunders and Papadimitriou (Chapter 9) point out how Jubilee 2000 members Oxfam and Christian Aid (for example) distanced themselves from the more radical street parties at the end of the 1990s when charity laws had only recently been relaxed. Frequently, the transformation of agendas and actions towards the more moderate view broadened political opportunities, allowing, for example, alliances with other groups and policy actors, while at the same time, considerably limiting representation and the range of potential policy proposals and responses.

The building and operation of networks, moreover, can be problematic. Whilst recognizing the added value of acting as a network, large organizations—typically, NGOs—may make little effort within networks for developing a common understanding of deeper policy issues. In the case of UK mobilizations, statements by British civil servants and businesses suggest that the message communicated came across as that of individual NGOs, rather than that of the network (Chapter 3 and 6). In a similar vein, membership and participation in European and global networks is often limited to advisory bodies, composed of national and regional representatives. Co-ordination efforts, in the sense of linking national efforts of activists to a broader justice movement tend to occur *en route*, in an ad hoc manner—in particular during major mobilizations for global events—rather than taking place in a more structured manner.

Monitoring Change

The potential and limits of activism also relate to the fact that processes of policy reform—including design, implementation and review of the required changes—can become extremely protracted, whereas the public attention span and related mobilizing efforts are fairly limited and not well suited to long-term engagement in policy and institutional change. This can affect not only the potential for new policy and institutional reforms, but also implementation and follow-through. Momentum may be lost due to multiple reasons, for example, when policy work through campaigns is relatively short-lived, which in turn may be related to the short attention span of the media and its narrow focus on specific events such as the WTO Ministerial Conferences and G7/8/20 summits. Or activist pressures may subside when partial gains have been achieved, such as in the cases of the UK Companies Act, the Extractive Industries Transparency Initiative (EITI) or the International Airline Ticket Tax. When adopted, such reforms potentially lock in gains and make it difficult for governments and businesses to backtrack. However, activist pressures may dissipate once agreement is reached or a law has been passed.

Yet, as seen in several of the cases in this volume, when activist proposals are internalized in policy and law, they are often diluted and deviate considerably from original demands. The French International Airline Ticket Tax (Chapter 12), for example, bypassed the core demand of the Tobin Tax proposal for regulating financial markets and became a 'financing for development' initiative that leaves financial markets unchecked. Similarly, whereas the Publish What

You Pay campaign had called for 'harder' legal reforms, the resulting EITI was a softer voluntary initiative. Many of the adopted policies and reforms lack the binding character envisaged by activists. Accommodated by 'voluntarism' and 'private regulation', policy reform often requires continuous attention and action to promote and monitor the uptake and application of voluntary standards. This can also occur when demands result in the adoption of 'binding' law. The annual adjustments in levels of ODA and commitments to debt relief, such as the debt cancellation law in Italy (Chapter 8) are such examples. Most national networks, however, were established in an ad hoc campaign-centred manner and tended to remain independent and were transitory. Continuous policy work would require a transformation in network structures to facilitate long-term commitment to complex justice-related issues.

THE EVOLUTION OF GLOBAL JUSTICE ACTIVISM

In the preceding we argued that, in spite of their limited time span, the mobilizations for global justice investigated in this book can be viewed as part of a longer evolution of global justice activism. In recent years, each of the issues examined has had a different trajectory in terms of mainstream practices, activist responses and policy changes.

The urgency of the issue of Third World debt has declined, and private lenders in global financial markets (rather than government lenders) have become key players. Mobilization at the global level has stopped, and only in countries affected by financial crises—most recently in Europe rather than in the South—foreign debt has emerged as an issue of contention.

The neoliberal trade agenda has failed to progress in the recent WTO Ministerial meetings, due to persisting differences between the United States, the EU, emerging powers of the South and poorer countries. Some of the criticism voiced by activists concerning the illusionary gains from trade liberalization has now become more widely accepted. Moreover, the global economic slowdown after the 2008 crisis has reduced export flows, and the prominence of trade as a policy issue.

Conversely, the financial crisis of 2008 has led to much greater attention to the potential of international taxation for reducing financial speculation and instability. The proposal for a Tobin Tax on currency trade has been turned into the project of a financial transaction tax—covering all financial deals—that is now supported by the EU, and even the IMF considers the tax to be feasible. The arguments activists developed in the 1990s have now become mainstream and are issues of continuing mobilization in global and European summits.[10] However, actual policy change may still be far away. The G20 Finance Ministers' meeting in June 2010 in Busan, South Korea, failed to reach agreement on a FTT. In 2011 Germany and France relaunched the idea in the context of the European crisis, and in September that year a concrete proposal was put forward by the European Commission. More governments and supranational institutions seem to be in favour of embracing mechanisms that stabilize financial markets and generate additional budgetary funds in times of severe constraints. However, activists' demands and proposals may easily become diluted again in any implementation of such a measure. Nevertheless, the current financial crisis and the considerable ground work undertaken by groups like Attac have put Financial Transaction Tax high on the agenda of policy change.

Corporate accountability has also become more widely accepted by the business and policy communities in recent years, in spite of modest activist campaigns. In the UK, civil society organizations, networks and 'experts' have influenced international policy processes, playing a significant role, for example, in the 2010 revisions to the OECD Guidelines for Multinational Enterprises, in the consultative processes associated with the UN 'Protect, Respect and Remedy' Framework for Business and Human Rights approved in 2011 and in the adoption of the ISO Guidance Standard on Organizational Social Responsibility.

Regardless of the precise trajectory of activism[11], ongoing repudiation of the neoliberal doctrine and the recent multifaceted crises and contradictions of capitalism—food, energy, finance and climate, as well as precarious employment and polarizing inequalities in and between countries—make the issues and demands formulated by justice activists ever more pertinent.

In Europe, opposition to neoliberal globalization has increasingly been taken up by national and grass-roots mobilizations, reflecting geo- and national political differences in the social and economic effects of the crisis (della Porta 2007). Paradoxically, shared grievances generated by economic globalization, which previously mobilized justice activists across borders, are presently expressed to a much stronger degree through local and 'sectoral' lenses and arenas. The current tendency is to focus on specific issue areas (for example, austerity measures, pensions, university fees, precarization of work and life) that mobilize specific groups, such as workers, public sector employees, students and youth. Although the systemic and global aspects of these developments are seen clearly by many groups and across the globe, efforts to coalesce become a challenge as activism disperses in this way (Tarrow 2005). The global protest of 15 October 2011, against the social effects of the economic crisis, inspired by the 'indignados' of Madrid and Athens, and by the 'Occupy Wall Street' movement, may open the way to new global mobilizations. According to the organizers,[12] on that day there were actions in 950 cities of eighty countries. The power of finance capital, the extreme wealth of the richest '1 per cent' of the population, austerity policies and the 'lack of future' of the young generation were common themes of the protest that may well evolve into a new wave of global activism.

New proposals for change continue to emerge and open up new spaces for mobilization and policy reform. Whereas the most overt (and visible in the media) expressions of mobilization, such as mass protests, wane periodically, global justice activism appears to be able to transmit values and visions over time and across countries, and to sustain repeated waves of mobilization, exerting more institutional influence.

The studies in this volume demonstrate that significant progress has been made by activists in understanding the multifaceted issues at the root of global injustice, developing and advancing comprehensive responses for achieving policy change. As spaces re-emerge for global justice campaigns, activists will have to confront, however, the challenges identified in this volume. In particular, they need to build and sustain mobilizations that connect multiple grass-roots and single-issue struggles and, at the same time, build a broader perspective for change that links different themes and leads to comprehensive alternatives.[13] Addressing such challenges is crucial if justice activism is to live up to its own claims and promises of change.

NOTES

1. For an assessment of compliance with commitments made by governments at Gleneagles, see Oxfam (2010).
2. Survey data adapted from Flash Eurobarometer (2003). Answers for Table 13.3 are based on EU 15 averages.
3. Brazil, Russia, India, China and South Africa.
4. The African, Caribbean and Pacific Group of States.
5. In particular from the debate about the Economic Partnership Agreements (EPAs) between the EU and the ACP countries.
6. With reference to MPH, see http://www.newstatesman.com/200505300004.
7. See also Bazán et al. (2008); Sikkink (2005).
8. This and the following quotes are taken from the interviews conducted for the case studies.
9. See also Bebbington, Hickley and Mitlin (2008).
10. At the International Peoples Conference that was held parallel to the G20 summit in Seoul, South Korea, in November 2010, the financial speculation tax was again high on the agenda. Before the conference, justice activists developed and communicated a global civil society statement in support of a financial speculation tax that was endorsed by 183 organizations from forty-two countries from the global North and South. The proposal, to be pushed at subsequent G20 preparatory and summit meetings, was to place a small levy on each trade of stocks, derivatives, currency and other financial instruments.
11. For different perspectives on the trajectory of activism, see Pianta (2001b).
12. See http://www.guardian.co.uk/world/blog/2011/oct/15/occupy-wall-street-times-square.
13. This clearly emerged in the Assembly of Social Movements that came together during the 8th World Social Forum in Belém, Amazonia (Bonfond 2010).

BIBLIOGRAPHY

Bazán, C., Cuellar, N., Gómez, I., Illsey, C., López, A., Monterroso, I., Pardo, J., Rocha, J.L., Torres, P., and Bebbington, A. (2008). 'Producing Knowledge, Generating Alternatives?' in A.J. Bebbington, S. Hickey and D.C. Mitlin (eds), *Can NGOs Make a Difference? The Challenge of Development Alternatives*, London: Zed Books.

Bebbington, A., Hickley, S., and Mitlin, D. (2008). 'Introduction', in A.J. Bebbington, S. Hickey, D.C. Mitlin (eds), *Can NGOs Make a Difference? The Challenge of Development Alternatives*, London: Zed Books.

Bendell, Jem. (2006). *Debating NGO Accountability*, United Nations Non-government Liason Service Development Dossier, UN-NGLS, Geneva.

Biekart, Kees. (2008). 'Measuring Civil Society Strength: How and for Whom?' *Development and Change*, 39 (6): 1171–1180.

Bonfond, O. (2010). *Assembly of Social Movements Meets in Dakar.* http://www.internationalviewpoint.org/spip.php?article1961 (accessed 20 December 2010).

Brown, G. (2010). *Beyond the Crash: Overcoming the First Crisis of Globalization*, New York: Free Press.

Capron, M. (2009). *De la Françafrique à la responsabilité sociale des entreprises: Les dynamiques entre les firmes, l'Etat et les mouvements sociaux en France.* Programme on Markets, Business and Regulation, Paper No. 6, UNRISD, Geneva.

della Porta, D. (ed) (2007). *The Global Justice Movements. A Cross-National and Transnational Perspective*, Boulder, CO: Paradigm.

della Porta D. and Parks, L.. (2012). 'Contentious EU politics: A comparative analysis of protest campaigns', in Kauppi, N. (ed.), *A Political Sociology of Transnational Europe*, Colchester: ECPR Press (forthcoming).

Flash Eurobarometer (2003). Realised by EOS Gallup Europe upon the request of the European Commission, 151 b. http://ec.europa.eu/public_opinion/flash/FL151bGlobalisationREPORT.pdf

Giugni, Marco, McAdam, Doug, and Tilly, Charles. (1999). *How Social Movements Matter*, Minneapolis: University of Minnesota Press.

Giugni, Marco, Bandler, M., and Eggert, N. (2006). *The Global Justice Movement: How Far Does the Classic Social Movement Agenda Go in Explaining Transnational Contention?* Programme Paper No. 24, UNRISD, Geneva.

Fowler, Alan, and Biekart, K. (2011). *Civic Driven Change: A Narrative to Bring Politics Back into Civil Society Discourse.* ISS Working Paper No. 529, International Institute of Social Studies, The Hague.

Hooghe, M. (2008). 'The Political Opportunity Structure for Civil Society Organizations in a Multilevel Context: The European Union,' in W.A. Maloney and J.W. van Deth (eds), *Civil Society and Governance in Europe: From National to International Linkages*, Northampton, MA: Edward Elgar Publishing.

Keck, Margaret, and Sikkink, Kathryn. (1998.) *Activists beyond Borders*, Ithaca, NY: Cornell University Press.

Oxfam. (2010). *Gleneagles, Five Years Later.* Oxfam Media Briefing 24 June. http://www.oxfam.org/sites/www.oxfam.org/files/gleneagles-5–years-later-oxfam-media-briefing-24jun2010.pdf (accessed 8 August 2011).

Pianta, M. (2001a). *Globalizzazione dal basso. Economia mondiale e movimenti sociali*, Roma: ManifestoLibri.

———. (2001b). 'Parallel Summits of Global Civil Society,' in H. Anheier, M. Glasius and M. Kaldor (eds), *Global Civil Society 2001*, Oxford: Oxford University Press.

Schumaker, P.D. (1975). 'Policy Responsiveness to Protest-Group Demands', *Journal of Politics*, 37 (2): 488–521.

Sikkink, K. (2005). 'Patterns of Dynamic Multi-Level Governance and Insider-Outsider Coalition', in D. Della Porta and S. Tarrow (eds), *Transnational Protest and Global Activism*, Lanham, MD: Rowan and Littlefield.

Smith, J. (2007). *Social Movements for Global Democracy: Themes in Global Social Change*, Baltimore, MD: Johns Hopkins University Press.

Tarrow, S. (2005). *The New Transnational Activism*, Cambridge: Cambridge University Press.

Index

Note: Page numbers ending in "f" refer to figures. Page numbers ending in "t" refer to tables.

For Product Safety Concerns and Information please contact our EU representative GPSR@taylorandfrancis.com
Taylor & Francis Verlag GmbH, Kaufingerstraße 24, 80331 München, Germany

www.ingramcontent.com/pod-product-compliance
Lightning Source LLC
Chambersburg PA
CBHW070549270326
41926CB00013B/2249

* 9 7 8 1 1 3 8 9 2 0 5 6 9 *